Discourse In and Through the Media

Discourse In and Through the Media:

Recontextualizing and Reconceptualizing Expert Discourse

Edited by

Marina Bondi, Silvia Cacchiani and Davide Mazzi

Cambridge Scholars Publishing

Discourse In and Through the Media:
Recontextualizing and Reconceptualizing Expert Discourse

Edited by Marina Bondi, Silvia Cacchiani and Davide Mazzi

This book first published 2015

Cambridge Scholars Publishing

Lady Stephenson Library, Newcastle upon Tyne, NE6 2PA, UK

British Library Cataloguing in Publication Data
A catalogue record for this book is available from the British Library

ISBN (10): 1-4438-8254-2
ISBN (13): 978-1-4438-8254-5

TABLE OF CONTENTS

PREFACE

MARINA BONDI
UNIVERSITY OF MODENA AND REGGIO EMILIA, ITALY

There are always many people behind a book, many more than are listed in the table of contents or the references. This book is no exception. It is indeed one of the results of collaboration with a network of universities in Italy and abroad working on corpus approaches to language variation in a discourse perspective: the CLAVIER (Corpus and Language Variation in English research) centre. The centre and all its members have provided stimuli and encouragement for new explorations. The present volume is an interesting addition to previous investigations of specialized discourse, and academic discourse in particular. The focus this time is on the processes of reconceptualizing and recontextualizing expert discourse in and through the media.

If it is true that there are now a very large number of books devoted to media discourse, yet there are still relatively few projects on the role of the media in the dissemination of expert knowledge: What processes are at play in the communication of knowledge? How is expert knowledge presented to the non-expert audience? How far do the media actually "mediate" between different worlds of knowledge? How is the relevance of expert knowledge made clear to a wider audience? These are some of the questions that the volume tackles.

The nature of the media, inevitably addressing an audience that goes well beyond the limits of the closed community of experts, suggests that we pay attention to the different social practices originating from different settings of knowledge circulation and ultimately to the process of recontextualization that the media operate on the discourse of knowledge by illuminating its social meaning. As I have argued elsewhere, the process can be seen as one of bridging across discourse communities with different background knowledge and different purposes. The process creates a "third space" requiring specific communication strategies, whether in forms of mediated or unmediated communication of expert knowledge. Reconceptualization will first of all involve replacing a conceptual representation with one that is more suited to the intended addressee: simplification, explicitation, reformulation, comparison, metaphor and simile may all be involved. The process of recontextualization, on the other hand, is aimed not only at making specialist knowledge available to the wider public as such, but also at making it relevant or interesting for the non-specialist reader, by highlighting the novelty and value of the area investigated, its relevance to the everyday life of readers/listeners, or to their communities and identities.

It is almost inevitable, when addressing media discourse, to consider the role of technology. In discourse studies, the notion of literacy has long been extended to the new media, drawing attention not only to the inevitable semiotic complexities of multimodal communication, but also to the impact of new technologies on written communication in terms of interactivity and hypertextuality. Early studies on web discourse focused on the impact of the medium on the text. It is now the time to look more closely into how the extended participatory framework of the web increases the range of interactive patterns and discursive identities construed in each text, thus influencing both language choice and communicative practices.

The complexity of the object requires a multiplicity of perspectives. The dominant methodological standpoints in the volume combine corpus and discourse analysis, usually favouring integrated approaches. The fields of application are also multiple, ranging from scholarly communication, to corporate and institutional discourse. A great many of the papers explore specific genres or communicative situations: attention is drawn to different types of interaction. The readers may thus not be able to find a unitary approach to the topic, but what they will find is a clear representation of the range of problems and issues that characterize the field of enquiry. For this clarity and this variety the editors are most grateful to all the contributors.

DISCOURSE IN AND THROUGH THE MEDIA: RECONTEXTUALIZING AND RECONCEPTUALIZING EXPERT DISCOURSE

MARINA BONDI, SILVIA CACCHIANI AND DAVIDE MAZZI
UNIVERSITY OF MODENA AND REGGIO EMILIA, ITALY

1. Introduction

This book stems from the 2013 CLAVIER Conference held in Modena in November 2013 and includes a selection of the papers presented on that occasion. As the title suggests, the aim of the conference was to stimulate the debate on a variety of aspects related to the representation of specialized discourse in and through the media, e.g. voice and point of view, argumentative practices, knowledge construction, multimodality, re-contextualization and re-conceptualization of knowledge, and peer-to-peer communication within genres aimed at knowledge dissemination and popularization. The conference was therefore intended to encourage cross-generic and cross-disciplinary investigations, in an attempt to advocate integrated approaches to the study of media discourse with a view to both theoretical background and practical applications.

Recontextualizing and reconceptualizing expert discourse has become increasingly important in modern society. Yet although *Knowledge Dissemination* (*KD*) is now receiving increasing attention, the discursive strategies and the pragmatics of KD in and through the media have yet to receive serious consideration. Knowledge dissemination can be seen as a form of 'asymmetric' communication between experts and lay-people, or 'mediation' of knowledge and intercultural and 'inter-discourse communication' (Scollon & Scollon 1995) between members of different cultures, discourse communities and communities of practice. This amounts to re-contextualization (Calsamiglia & Van Dijk 2004) and inclusion of types of 'intralinguistic' translations, whereby simplification, explicitation, reformulation (Mauranen 2006), reconceptualization of terms in the subject field 'translate' exclusive expertise into 'comprehensible' knowledge, suitable to the background of the addressee. In this connection, knowledge dissemination (Engberg 2014: *knowledge mediation*) is seen as a three-fold intra-linguistic and cross-cultural process that combines *representation*, *construction* and *communication* of knowledge intended for specific addressees (Kastberg 2010; Ditlevsen 2011).

This chapter is structured as follows. Section 2 concentrates on recontextualization and popularization across genres and knowledge domains. Section 3 gives an overview of the chapters included in this volume, thus addressing the tensions embedded in internal and external scholarly communication, KD in corporate communication and from institutions to lay audience, and audience empowerment in traditional and new media.

2. Recontextualizing expert discourse

In the field of language studies, *recontextualization* broadly denotes a process by which some part of discourse is extracted from one communicative context and conveyed into another. In comparison with the notion of *contextualization* inherent in dynamic interactions within situated language use (Gumperz 1992), recontextualization involves changes in meaning as parts of discourses or genres shift from one context to another. Linell (1998:155) notes that recontextualization "involves transformations of meanings or meaning potentials in ways that are usually quite complex". In particular, in the context of recontextualization processes, elements of discourse tend to undergo transformation through simplification or condensation, but also by refocusing, expansion, and elaboration. A prime example is the corporate annual report that typically unfolds from the original financial statement to the financial press release issued to media sources, and eventually the final product published on the Internet. Throughout such a genre chain, meaning is alternately condensed (in the numerical data contained in the financial statement), elaborated (in the integrated verbal message of the press release) and expanded (in the management narrative and images incorporated into the complete report).

Recontextualization may be observed to emerge at various discourse levels. It is intratextual when it occurs in the same text; intertextual, when it links up with other texts in specific contexts; or interdiscursive, when it entails the combination and cross-fertilization among different genres, discourses or activity types. Furthermore, various aspects of discourse can be recontextualized to take on new meanings, including both linguistic expressions and knowledge or values in a broader sense. A classic instance of the recontextualization of knowledge can be noted in the relocation from the scholarly genres used by specialized disciplinary discourse communities, to popularized forms of discourse envisaging the lay world as their intended audience. In that regard, Gotti (2014) defines popularized discourse as the transformation of expert knowledge for consumption by non-specialists, in terms of both information-giving and argumentative as well as promotional reasons. Health discourse is thus referred to as a case in point, in which factual information about novel treatments and therapies from the scientific research community is adapted and disseminated to the lay public. Interestingly, this may take the form of news reports, documentaries and promotional campaigns that aim to inform the public no less than they intend to affect beliefs, behaviors, policy and decision-making. The pivotal role of the media in the recontextualization process has been highlighted by Calsamiglia and Van Dijk (2004), who deal with the semantic devices used in the Spanish daily press to report scientific findings on the sequencing of the human genome. Such items as definition, description and metaphor are discussed as widespread tools through which the press stresses the social dimension of knowledge – e.g. by expatiating on the scientists involved and the conflicts, along with the real-world applications of findings – instead of delving into the specific scientific content of the news. As Calsamiglia and Van Dijk (2004) themselves argue, rather than acting as second-hand, passive mediators of scientific knowledge, the media occupy a prominent role in the creation of common knowledge and perceptions about science. It is noteworthy that this may overlap with the inclusion of views and information that do not necessarily stem from scientifically accredited sources.

This fundamental aspect has been associated with a number of implications in the study of the argumentative practices of epidemiological investigations. In her works on forms of fallacious reasoning in both the AIDS and the BSE inquiries, Cummings (2004, 2005, 2009) focuses on the consequences of the extensive deployment of analogical reasoning and argument from ignorance in media accounts to the general public. In positive terms, the parallel between hepatitis B and AIDS in early perceptions and thinking about AIDS is shown by Cummings (2004) to have brought about far-reaching effects, in that it led to epidemic effective guidelines for the prevention of HIV infection – e.g. the recommendation to avoid sharing body fluids. In more critical terms, on the other hand, the use of argument from ignorance as the mainstay of ministerial pronouncements about the alleged lack of risk of BSE to human health is considered by Cummings (2005, 2009) to be symptomatic of the vested interests at stake in the crisis management. Thus, the oft-repeated standpoint that there was no evidence that BSE in cattle would cause Creutzfeldt-Jacob Disease is investigated by Cummings (2005:123) as a strategy of politicians and commercial parties "to distort the interpretation of science […] for the purpose of justifying policy decisions and informing the public of the risk, respectively". In that light, the study of fallacious reasoning becomes a significant contribution to the public understanding of science.

As was pointed out above, recontextualization has served as an eclectic analytical framework in the study of discourse processes in the most diverse domains of specialized communication. As far as political discourse is concerned, recent research illustrates how naturally-occurring discourse from daily politics collected by means of ethnographic research was recontextualized in a markedly heterogeneous communicative context, i.e. the fictionalized politics of a popular television series (Wodak 2011). In that regard, the complex mundane rituals of politics as they appear in official discourse are the object of an interesting process of simplification for lay viewers, along the lines of a well-known polarization between the good and the bad, as it were. Without going to such extremes, however, the different facets of good and bad and, more generally, the various dimensions of evaluation, play a significant role in scholarly dissemination in the news, knowledge dissemination from institutions and corporate websites, and audience empowerment in and through traditional, new and social media.

Recontextualization has been investigated in the broad area of business discourse. In Thomas (2003), for instance, the framework of recontextualization is implemented to illustrate the way management discourse changes as it moves through different spheres of activity, whether it be the academia, consultancy or practice. With specific reference to the notions of *competitive advantage* and *competitive strategy*, discourse is thus analyzed in its shifts from theoretical models among academics, to promotional instruments among consultants, and finally to strategic objectives among practitioners. In corporate communication, Catenaccio (2006a) focuses on the specificity of the information in press releases issued by Enron as of the accounting scandal of 2001, in comparison to that from the subsequent coverage of the issue in the financial press. As a result of a process of recontexualization, information contained in the press releases was carefully filtered into financial news sources, so that the original meanings were rendered in more distinctively evaluative terms.

Moreover, current research emphasises the importance of communicating expert knowledge to the general public, especially in the medico-scientific field. Rather than viewing this as a simple act of simplification, recontextualization is all the more used in these contexts to unveil the strategies through which knowledge is transformed as it moves from the expert context to the lay one. A common line of research has been to question how scientific discoveries with the potential to affect everyday life are reported in the media (e.g. Catenaccio 2006b; Taylor 2010).

The reporting and representation of scientific research in the popular and non-specialist media are currently seen as raising serious issues.[1] For example, in studying the reporting of research into inherited breast cancer, Henderson and Kitzinger (1999) show that the process of translating knowledge from one media format or outlet to another has strong implications for both the quantity and the nature of representation. They highlight the dilemma faced by both media and researcher: 'soft' reporting, e.g. focusing on individual human-interest stories, has the advantage of engaging public interest and increasing the accessibility of the information more than fact-based 'hard' reporting; on the other hand, the 'soft' reports run the risk of masking scientific information behind an emotive story. Similarly, Allan et al. (2010) throw light on the consequences of the competition between different claims-makers during the crucial pre-market phase of nanotechnology development. They stress the need for accuracy, and for avoidance of both over-positive and over-negative representation, which might raise unjustified expectations or incite public resistance to desirable developments.

One implication of this kind of study is that research into expert-lay discourse has a value beyond simply identifying how information transmission takes place. Becoming aware of communication strategies can be seen as a complex process that may contribute to an aware and informed citizenship: Horning (2011), for example, argues that sensitizing people to how language is used to produce and reproduce knowledge across contexts may ultimately assist them with the development of meta-cognitive awareness of text structure, context and language as well as skills in analysis, synthesis, evaluation and application in line with the standards of a trained readership.

There is growing interest in the use of new technologies and the role of new and social media, such as the Internet (Cline & Haynes 2010; Murphy 2010; Garzone 2012), blogs (Luzón 2013; Riboni 2014), wikis (Kuteeva

---

[1] Source: *Novel neurotechnologies: intervening in the brain*. Report issued by the Nuffield Council on Bioethics, June 2013 (http://www.nuffieldbioethics.org/neurotechnology).

2011; Leuf & Cunningham 2001) and phone apps (Pandey et al. 2013), for building and sharing information and opinions between heterogeneous discourse communities, some but not all of it relating to health matters. Some researchers have focused specifically on the discourse of medical self-help websites, considering issues such as degree of empathy or the role of Affect (Cline 2002; Hojat et al. 2002; Scott 2011; Pounds 2012) for trust generation and health consumer empowerment.

In terms of comparisons between languages, the issue of the non-equivalence of knowledge in the translation process has been studied and discussed. In the law, for instance, Engberg (2010) shows that legal drafters from different countries often work with concepts that are not fully stable entities. Instead, concepts are subject to 'tuning' by relevant legal experts, and are an issue of debate within the parent discourse community. This insight is relevant to conceptualizing the task of translators or legal drafters, because it highlights their role in creating rather than transmitting concepts.

A growing body of research exists that is relevant to such diverse issues. Some of it, however, focuses on accuracy and comprehensiveness of content, rather than on the linguistic analysis of communication strategies. Where language is the focus, studies tend to be small-scale. Given that communication and social interactions are increasingly taking place through Information and Communication Technology, careful investigation is needed into the dynamics of knowledge transmission and opinion formation in emergent and planned groups and social networks. While this is first and foremost the job of (computational) social science, a strong motivation for this volume is the scarcity of research into the fine-grained linguistic, textual and argumentative mechanisms behind the reformulation of knowledge within lay settings in and through the media.

3. Overview of Chapters

The volume concentrates on the need for providing new insights into the multiple facets of recontextualization. For ease of exposition, the chapters are organized around four points along the cline from scholarly communication through expert-to-lay communication to knowledge transmission from knowledgeable non-experts to lay audience or other knowledgeable non-experts. Section I (Chapters 1 and 2) addresses scholarly communication in digital media and multimodal environments. Section II (Chapters 3 to 5) lays emphasis on the dissemination of scholarly knowledge. Third, knowledge transmission and opinion formation in institutional and corporate interactions with lay audience are the object of Sections III and IV (Chapters 6 to 10). Section V (Chapters 11 to 13) then concludes the discussion on recontextualization by focusing on audience empowerment via the active participation to the process of knowledge construction.

Since recontextualization is ubiquitous in knowledge transmission and opinion formation, the volume offers insights into a vast array of genres, knowledge domains, environments, media and discourse configurations. The analyses presented in the individual chapters address the motivations and mechanisms behind the recontextualization and reconceptualization of expert discourse.

Section I opens with a chapter by CORNELIUS PUSCHMANN – *A digital mob in the ivory tower? Context collapse in scholarly communication online*. The chapter concentrates on the effects of digital media on important dimensions of scholarly communication, both internal (scholarly discourse) and external (science communication). Importantly, formal scholarly communication comprises a number of well-established, peer-reviewed formats (monographs, publications in high-impact journals, proceedings in the sciences, etc.) that legitimize and certify scholarly value. On the other hand, digitization (Borgman 2007) has impacted on the dissemination, curation and preservation of publications, whose promotion can combine traditional and novel means (e.g. circulating copies and tweeting about one's research).

Turning to external communication, professional communicators (i.e. science journalists) have traditionally been in charge of mediating scholarly knowledge and simplifying scientific facts for a passive recipient, the lay audience. Scholarly blogs, however, are now creating new reader-writer interactions; they present scientists to both scholars (for relationship management) and broader publics, and they may engage the latter and enlist their support for the specific scientific endeavor (Bucchi 1996; Colson 2011). Engaging the interested public via digital and social media also reflects a push towards the democratization of science (Wilkins 2008), from open access (circulation of information on results) to more participatory or open science.

Context collapse is inherent to social media: internal communication among peers gives way to external, often informal, online communication, with larger publics that might put scholarly research under scrutiny. This overlay blurs the line between science on the one hand, and the general public on the other. One consequence of this trend is that reconceptualization shifts from a traditional view of popularization as 'educating the public' to dissemination in informal communication as well as new regimes of evaluation with a part in legitimating scientific research (e.g. next to citation indexes and journal impact, downloads, Facebook likes, Mendeley saves, Twitter re-tweets, or other indicators championed by the altmetrics movement).

But informal and external communication do not in fact substitute for well-established forms of internal communication. In general, as we have seen, peer-reviewing is the key to scholarly legitimation. Given the current transition to digital publishing, however, preservation and permanence of paper formats in online platforms is no less important. Another crucial issue is how the capabilities and affordances of the digital media change communication dynamics and information flows for traditional genres that undergo remediation (Bolter & Gruniz 2002) and resemiotization (Iedema 2003) from print to screen pages. In this connection, the chapter by JAN ENGBERG and CARMEN DANIELA MAIER – *Exploring the hypermodal communication of academic knowledge beyond generic structures* – concentrates on Elsevier's *Article of the Future* project (Zudilova-Seinstra 2013). The project suggests possible avenues for revolutionizing the dissemination/communication of academic knowledge by devising prototypes for research articles in online formats that integrate standard generic structure with hypermodal resources (Lemke 2002). Specifically, prototype pages would comprise: (i) in the middle pane, the equivalent of a pdf, with Research Highlights for promotional purposes and the established generic structure of traditional RA; (ii) in the left pane, clickable headlines and visuals from the main content area; (iii) in the right pane, task or content-specific additional features and information (from keywords through interactive versions of the figures to information about the author(s)).

While opening to new communication dynamics, multiple information flows and individualized trajectories, the Article of the Future prototypical format poses new challenges to the scholarly community. Even if not accepted in full, the format requires a specific *multiliteracy* on the part of writers and readers. Based on the publisher's template, it invites *multilevel knowledge building processes* such as elaboration, extension and enhancement through multimodal interaction, and knowledge expansion and enhancement based on dynamic hypertextual interaction enabling inclusion of core or peripheral knowledge. Hypermodality is thus expected to create a special type of knowledge dissemination asymmetry, between scholars that master the new knowledge building processes and scholars that might lag behind and refrain from embracing hypermodal communication beyond the traditional research article structure.

Section II in the volume reflects on more traditional formats based on more standard conceptualizations of scholarly dissemination, reconceptualization and popularization. In Chapter 3 – *Talking Science: Science in the news on BBC Radio* – SUSAN HUNSTON presents a pilot study based on 18 interviews with scientists on the BBC radio programme *Today*, covering a range of scientific issues (e.g. health, the environment, and space exploration). In line with the organizational structure of scientific journalism, in real time interviews interviewee-interviewer interactions instantiate the traditional role configuration of expert and layperson, while in prepared stories the informed science correspondent interprets and mediates knowledge for the lay-audience, including competing voices in the broadcasts (e.g. 'mainstream' and 'maverick' science).

In this connection, the chapter explores the interpersonal strategies used by scientists 'selling' themselves and their work to the general public. Successful strategies enlist the listener (tax-payer) to the research being presented. They comprise recourse to: evidentials and status markers; the downplaying of uncertainty of results and emphasis on features such as novelty of results or value of the research (in terms of reliability of the methodology adopted, ability to achieve goals, usefulness, and practical applications), positive evaluation of procedure or results, departure from the type of depersonalization that characterizes professional writing, and expression of Affect. These strategies are also used to balance confidence and caution when discussing hypothetical results or making unwarranted claims.

Besides interpersonal strategies, recontextualization involves intra-linguistic translation, or *reconceptualization* of exclusive expertise into comprehensible knowledge that is suitable to the specific background of the intended addressees (cf. Section 1). In Knowledge Dissemination and popularization, a conceptual representation (R1) – and its linguistic expression – is thus replaced with another one (R2) that is felt by the expert (scholar or professional mediator) to be more in line with the world of his/her intended addressees – semi-experts or the lay-audience. Reformulation (Mauranen 2006) might serve this purpose in that it signals an equivalence between two terms or two propositions (R2 is thus regarded as another way of naming R1). Other options here are comparison, metaphor and simile, which involve non-equivalent experiences: metaphors "create similarities rather than reflecting them"; literal comparisons are 'intra-domain' and assess "what two entities share"; similes, or figurative comparisons are 'inter-domain' in that they "compare things that are normally felt to be incomparable" (Israel et al. 2004:124). In Chapter 4 – *Comparison as a mode of re-conceptualization in popularization: Focus on expressions of similarity* – ELSA PIC and

GRÉGORY FURMANIAK further add into the equation inclusion of homogeneous comparands (either 'expert' or 'non-expert') in intra-domain literal comparison, and the comparison of comparands that belong to different speech communities ('expert' and 'non-expert') in heterogeneous literal comparison as well as in figurative inter-domain figurative comparison. Based on a quantitative and qualitative analysis of research articles (RAs) from peer-reviewed journals and a comparable corpus of relatively high-brow popularized articles (PAs), the authors thus investigate expressions of similarity and comparison (*similar* and equivalents; *like* in its uses as preposition, conjunction and adjectives) in expert discourse and expert mediation. Interestingly, the data shows that expressions of comparison are frequent across RAs and PAs. However, they show different distributions: adjectives are mostly found in intra-domain comparison within RAs, where they are used for metadiscursive and descriptive purposes, and as cohesive devices; inversely, *like* is used in heterogeneous comparisons and inter-domain figurative comparison within PAs for the type of reconceptualization that is distinctive of knowledge mediation.

STEFANIA MACI's chapter – *"The data supports the provocative view that…": Evaluation in medical academic posters* – concludes the section on scholarly dissemination with an exploration into the types, uses and distribution of evaluative *that*-clauses across the IMRD structure of academic posters from epidemiology conferences and journals. Though little studied in EAP and somewhat neglected in the soft sciences, posters have rapidly become a major knowledge dissemination genre in the hard sciences and in medicine in particular: posters effectively show research and research outcomes at conferences, and can further contribute to follow-up discussion when uploaded to the conference website or published in journals. While *that*-clauses are not found in the Methods section and authorial (self-)reference is a feature of the Introduction – which aims at establishing scientific credibility – Results and Discussion move steadily towards data reference for laboratory work and experimental practice, where visuals that are a fundamental part of the co-text efficiently summarize facts and findings. It is therefore easy to see how posters give voice to data that speaks for themselves, Drawing on Hyland and Tse's (2005) categorization of evaluative *that*-clauses in academic genres, the chapter thus demonstrates how expressions of epistemic stance that denote maximum certainty and objectivity are a key to constructing scientific reliability in relation to facts. Also fundamental are verbal evaluative expressions that describe research acts like *demonstrate*, *show*, *indicate*, or mental processes like *suppose*, *assume* or *hypothesis*.

Sections III and IV of the volume are devoted to varied types of interdiscursive recontextualization (Linell 1998), where the media (and the digital media in particular) involve communication of knowledge (Ditlevsen 2011) to the lay audience, from institutions and corporate websites. In Chapter 6, ALISON DUGUID concentrates on *Public apologies and media evaluations* using selected search words to investigate uptakes of public apologies (complete apologies, partial apologies and refusals to apologize) in a corpus of UK broadsheets newspaper texts, a corpus of White House briefings and data gathered from a TV news corpus. The data shows that press representation of politicians' media apologies proceeds through the expression of the journalist's explicit opinion: the journalist expresses evaluation (mainly negative evaluation) along parameters such as quantity, timeliness, sincerity and spontaneity, and the 'humiliation factor', whereby apologies are seen as cues to the politician's inability to achieve a goal rather than as a beneficial attempt to redress a wrong. Rather than simply reporting events, recontextualizing meaning in press uptakes of public apologies is therefore a matter of providing an authoritative interpretation of events and thus shaping the reader's opinions.

ILARIA MOSCHINI's chapter – *Facebook.com/WhiteHouse: A multimodal analysis of the social media recontextualization of the institutional encoder* – concentrates on another type of recontextualization of institutional communication. One of the central ideas of this contribution is that the White House's facebook profile illustrates the case of recontextualization of top-down institutional discourse into a peer-to-peer social network semiotically mapped onto a combination of the yearbook model onto diary blogs. Importantly, the chapter combines insights from Lakoff's (2002) Conceptual Metaphor Theory on moral politics and society with work on multimodal metaphor (Forceville 2006) and hypertextual narratives (Thibault 2012), to show how visual and written information interact on the page to conceptualize Obama as a Nurturant Parent.

The sequencing of Chapters 6 to 8 reflects a gradual shift from traditional media and traditional genres to generification, multimodality and hypertextuality in the Web 2.0. In Chapter 8 – *Digital vividness: Reporting aviation disasters online* – CARMEN SANCHO GUINDA addresses the place of vividness in the online aircraft-accident dockets issued by the U.S. National Transportation Safety Board. The contribution argues for seeing NTSB dockets as currently evolving into 'catastropops' - in her words, a popularized blend of visual journalism, technical detail and storytelling. Evidence for this comes from the quantitative and qualitative analysis of an electronic corpus of fatal probable-cause accident dockets published online between 2005 and 2012. Since prevention is the overall purpose of this lay-genre, popularization and instruction come with the disclosure of information about accident circumstances and actors' behaviours that is at the same time intelligible and transparent, accessible and memorable, so as to be retained at the personal, cognitive and habit-based levels. We therefore see effective recourse, among others, to verbal and audiovisual vividness in multiple representations: whereas abstracts and short technical reports with term description come with testimonies characterized by 'cinematic' style, audiovisuals such as weather animations, flight paths and 3-D reconstructions further transduct (Kress 2010) information for immediacy and intimacy.

While also laying emphasis on interdiscursive recontextualizaton, the chapters in Section IV share a common interest in corporate communication, corporate identity and corporate image in Web 2.0 environments. In the first chapter – *Social media in corporate communication: Focus on text and discourse* – GIULIANA ELENA GARZONE provides an extensive discussion of the linguistic make-up and patterns of corporate communication in social media by corroborating a linguistic analysis of data from the PepsiCo website (http://pepsico.com/) with insights from experts based at one of the most important Italian social communication agencies.

A comparison of topic-centric image blogs, collaboration-oriented Facebook pages and affordances, and twits/re-twits in the relatively more dialogically-oriented Twitter environment, shows increasing degrees of fragmentation and shortening of the text contributed by the posts of, in a row, blogs, Facebook and Twitter. As a consequence, the classical view of textuality is seen to apply to blogs, and, although shorter, Facebook posts are still cohesive to some extent. Conversely, twits constitute an extremely fragmented and deconstructed pattern of communication, where speech acts and units of conceptual meaning occur in isolation, and cohesion as connectedness at the level of signantia gives way to cohesion as achieved by means of hyperlinks and hashtags. In line with an overall tendency in the development of Computer-Mediated-Communication and social media, deconstruction, fragmentation and reduction of the (meta-)discursive resources traditionally available to the text proceed on a par with dialogization and engagement.

As regards the contents presented, the aim of corporate communication in the social media is threefold: the company engages with customers for promotional purposes, to build a sense of community, and, importantly, to leverage on values, interests and activities. When, however, social media only achieve limited interaction with the customer, what is then needed for effective communication is a general rethinking of the major dimensions involved: from content selection, discursive strategies and language choices, through the use of visuals and other semiotic resources, to an appropriate timing of updates.

Another study with implications for marketing and brand management is *From corporate communication to consumer blogs: Analyzing recontextualization of brand identity in fashion*. Here, BELINDA CRAWFORD CAMICIOTTOLI concentrates on the shift from expert professional communication in the webpages of three international fashion houses based in Italy to social communication among lay fashion bloggers that construct themselves as highly informative and opinionated commentators within the fashion discourse community. More particularly, the qualitative and quantitative analysis of adjectives in corporate websites shows that they are used to encode and promote the desired brand personality along the lines of dimensions such as sincerity, excitement, sophistication, competence and ruggedness (cf. Aaker 1997). The purpose, of course, is to establish brand associations and create unique brand images in the mind of consumers. This is where evaluative adjectives in topic-centred consumer blogs come in handy as evidence for the interdiscursive recontextalization of brand identity from the expert producer's to the lay consumer's perspective: whereas the comparison of adjectives in the website datasets and in the corresponding blogs dataset suggests a high degree of alignment between company-defined and consumer-perceived brand identity, recontextualization in fashion blogs proceeds though the expansion and elaboration of company-defined meanings into new meanings with different or added facets.

Clearly, this constructs bloggers as 'empowered' knowledgeable commentators. Chapter 10 thus provides a transition to Section V, which concludes the volume with three case studies on audience empowerment and active participation to the process of knowledge construction on the part of knowledgeable non-experts. Construction and communication of lay theories are the object of Chapter 11 – *"I'm not an expert": Lay knowledge, its construction and dissemination in personal weblogs*. Here, PETER SCHILDHAUER focuses on home-page and posts of personal blogs that are used either to share knowledge and experience with peers or give advice based on the blogger's everyday personal experience.

The author thus brings home the following points. Intended lay-audience and fellow authors are clearly selected by relying on topical headings and other topical signals, meta-comments on the relevance of the contents to the readership and speech act indicators such as *A warning*. The purpose of communication is twofold – to explain simple and complex theories and also instruct, in line with the basic human need to understand the world and share knowledge with one's peers. Knowledge construction proceeds through two subsequent steps: an initial narrative is followed by concluding reflections drawn on an individual or general level, with underlying IF-THEN relations, a shift across moves from past to present tenses, and markers of evidentiality such as *find* and *realize* in the conclusions.

The next chapter, by JUDITH TURNBULL, takes a patient-centered approach to health communication and health information (Balint 1969) to concentrate on *Knowledge dissemination online: The case of health information*. As is clear, Web 2.0 has significantly changed the health communication environment. While the varied linguistic and cultural background of lay patients is still an open issue, the increasing accessibility to health information is now leading towards peer-to-peer healthcare and more participatory medicine, with patients increasingly conceptualized as unique and active health consumers and, importantly, as having a right – and a social responsibility – to empowerment, that is, to make informed decisions about their health and health care.

In this context, the paper concentrates on diabetes, a life-long condition, and compares and contrasts knowledge dissemination in the webpages of three websites: *Patient.co.uk*, managed by doctors, *diabetes.org.uk*, run by a registered charity with healthcare professionals, volunteers and diabetics among its members; *diabetes.co.uk*, a community website with information provided by expert professionals, volunteers, diabetics, their relatives and friends. Given the successful integration into a hypermodal environment of styles and genres, and of multiple voices and perspectives on the varied facets of the condition, *diabetes.co.uk* qualifies as the most situationally adequate of all three sites. Where expert knowledge is mediated to lay-diabetics, we can expect extensive recourse to omission of biomedical detail, simplification and explicitation/explanation of specialized terminology, e.g. via specific visual and/or written metaphors and analogy across domains. But there are other points to be made: first, the voices and perspectives of professionals and of individual patients are juxtaposed in a hypermodal environment, e.g. static information on the webpage is complemented by popularizing videos starring professionals, and by videos where patients recount their own success stories. Second, it is worth pointing out that among the genres and modes in the site, the online discussion forum run by diabetics clearly shifts the focus from factual knowledge to experientially-derived knowledge: asking for advice, giving advice and sharing experiences are all key to foster learning and promote health literacy.

What this means for a reflection on Knowledge Dissemination is that one is no longer certain about who the expert exactly is: along with professionals, long-time diabetics are at the core of the community emerging around this life-long condition. In this respect, Wikipedia might illustrate an even more vexed case, as demonstrated by MORANA LUKAČ and ROBERT GUTOUNIG – *From Usage Guides to Wikipedia: Re-contextualising the discourse on language use*. Starting from the assumption that since the eighteenth century usage guides have been the traditional sources on language use for the 'linguistically insecure', the authors compare the entries on selected usage items on Wikipedia and in the *HUGE database* (http://huge.ullet.net/), a database of usage guides and usage problems developed at Leiden University Centre for Linguistics. The data suggests that Wikipedia entries on usage items are more visited and more heavily and collaboratively edited than the average Wikipedia article. But surely this is all the more so when the editors are language experts or have more real-life expertise in language-related fields. Wikipedia entries include significantly more references to other sources and linguistic terminology than usage guides; they refrain from adopting the more narrative and personalized style of usage guides, and provide objective descriptions rather than prescriptive or proscriptive rules. The qualitative analysis of the Talk pages gives us the right interpretation of these findings: crowd sourcing and collaboration of many contributors and compliance with Wikipedia principles (e.g. the principle of Verifiability), balanced discussions on Talk pages and regular edits, enable Wikipedia entries on language use to largely reflect critical, up-to-date information that relies on actual usage and linguistics rather than on single authorities.

4. Conclusions

The main point of this chapter has been to consider and discuss research on the recontextualization and reconceptualization of knowledge in and through the media. The volume is intended to encourage cross-generic and cross-disciplinary investigations, in an attempt to advocate integrated approaches to the study of media discourse with a view to both theoretical background and practical applications. Secondly, it aims to foster debate on a variety of aspects related to the representation of specialized discourse in and through the media, e.g. voice and point of view, argumentative practices, knowledge construction, multimodality, recontextualization and re-conceptualization of knowledge (hence, knowledge transmission), opinion formation and peer-to-peer communication within web genres aimed at knowledge dissemination and popularization in and through traditional, digital and social media.

Taken together, the contributions to the volume provide extensive exemplification of the type of research that is currently conducted on these issues. The variety of the questions posed and the wide array of methods used in the chapters are therefore intended to make a substantial contribution to sharpen existing knowledge and further the ongoing debate among scholars in the field.

References

Aacker, Jennifer L. 1997. Dimensions of brand personality. *Journal of Marketing Research* 34. August. 347-356.

Allan, Stuart, Alison Anderson & Alan Petersen. 2010. Framing risk: Nanotechnologies in the news. *Journal of Risk Research* 13. 1. 29-44.

Balint, Enid. 1969. The possibilities of patient-centred medicine. *Journal of the Royal College of General Practitioners* 17. 269-276.

Bolter, David & Richard Grusin. 2002. *Remediation: Understanding New Media*. Cambridge, MA: The MIT Press.

Borgman, Christine L. 2007. *Scholarship in the Digital Age: Information, Infrastructure, and the Internet*. Cambridge, MA: The MIT Press.

Bucchi, Massimiliano. 1996. When scientists turn to the public: Alternative routes in science communication. *Public Understanding of Science* 5. 375-394.

Calsamiglia, Helena & Van Dijk, Teun A. 2004. Popularization discourse and knowledge about the genome. *Discourse and Society* 15. 4. 369-389.

Catenaccio, Paola. 2006a. Looking beyond Today's headlines: The Enron crisis from press releases to media coverage. In Marina Bondi & Julia Bamford (eds.), *Managing Interaction in Professional Discourse: Intercultural and Interdiscoursal Perspectives*. Rome: Officina Edizioni. 159-172.

—. 2006b. The SARS crisis coverage in the British Medical Journal and New Scientist. In Maurizio Gotti & Davide S. Giannoni (eds.), *New Trends in Specialised Discourse Analysis*. Bern: Peter Lang. 279-301.

Cline, Rebecca J. W. & K. M. Haynes. 2001. Consumer health information seeking on the Internet: The state of the art. *Health Education Research* 16. 6. 671-692.

Cline, Rebecca J. W. 2002. Everyday interpersonal communication and health. In Teresa Thompson, Alicia Dorsey, Katherine Miller & Roxanne L. Parrot (eds.), *Handbook of Health Communication*. Mahwah, NJ: Lawrence Erlbaum. 285-313.

Colson, Vinciane. 2011. Science blogs as competing channels for the dissemination of science news. *Journalism* 12. 7. 889-902.

Cummings, Louise. 2004. Analogical reasoning as a tool of Epidemiological investigation. *Argumentation* 18. 427-444.

—. 2005. Giving science a bad name: Politically and commercially motivated fallacies in BSE inquiry. *Argumentation* 19. 123-143.

—. 2009. Emerging Infectious diseases: Coping with uncertainty. *Argumentation* 23. 171-188.

Ditlevsen, Marianne G. 2011. Towards a methodological framework for knowledge communication. In Margrethe Petersen & Jan Engberg (eds.), *Current Issues in Specialized Communication.* Bern: Peter Lang. 187-208.

Engberg, Jan. 2010. Knowledge construction and legal discourse: The interdependence of perspective and visibility of characteristics. *Journal of Pragmatics* 42. 48-63.

Forceville, Charles. 2006. Non-verbal and multimodal metaphor in a cognitivist framework: Agendas for research. In Gitte Kristiansen, Michel Achard, René Dirven & Francisco J. Ruiz de Mendoza Ibañez (eds.), *Cognitive Linguistics: Current Applications and Future Perspectives.* Berlin/New York: Mouton de Gruyter. 379-402.

Garzone, Giuliana. 2012. Blogging science for popularization. Paper presented at LINKD 2012 - *Language(s) in Knowledge Dissemination*, Modena, 11-13 October 2012.

Gotti, Maurizio. 2014. Reformulation and recontextualization in popularization discourse. *Ibérica* 27. 15-34.

Gumperz, John J. 1992. Contextualization and understanding. In Alessandro Duranti & Charles Goodwin (eds.), *Rethinking Context: Language as An Interactive Phenomenon.* Cambridge: Cambridge University Press. 229-252.

Henderson, Lesley & Jenny Kitzinger. 1999. The human drama of genetics: 'Hard' and 'soft' media representations of inherited breast cancer. *Sociology of Health and Illness* 21. 5. 560-578.

Hojat, Mohammadreza, Joseph S. Gonnella, Thomas J. Nasca, Salvatore Mangione, Jon Veloksi & Michael Magee. 2002. The Jefferson Scale of Physician Empathy: Further psychometric data and differences by gender and specialty at item level. *Academic Medicine* 77. 58-60.

Horning, Alice S. 2011. Where to put the manicules: A theory of expert reading. *Across the Disciplines* 8. 2. http://wac.colostate.edu/atd/articles/horning2011/index.cfm.

Hyland, Ken & Polly Tse. 2005. Hooking the reader: A corpus study of evaluative *that* in abstracts. *English for Specific Purposes* 24. 123-139.

Iedema, Rick. 2003. Multimodality, resemiotization: Extending the analysis of discourse as multi-semiotic practice. *Visual Communication* 2. 1. 29-57.

Israel, M., J.R. Harding & V. Tobin 2004. On Simile. In Michel Achard & Suzanne Kemmer (eds.), *Language, Culture and Mind.* Stanford: C.S.L.I. Publications. 123-135.

Kastberg, Peter. 2010. Knowledge communication. Formative ideas and research impetus. *Pragmatic Perspectives* 2. 1. 59-71.

Kress, Gunther. 2010. *Multimodality. A Social Semiotic Approach to Contemporary Communication.* London/New York. Routledge.

Kuteeva, Maria. 2011. Wikis and academic writing: Changing the writer-reader relationship. *English for Specific Purposes* 30. 44-57.

Lakoff, George. 2002 [1996]. *Moral Politics. How Liberals and Conservatives Think*. Chicago, IL: The University of Chicago Press.
Lemke, Jay L. 2002. Travels in hypermodality. *Visual Communication* 1. 3. 299-325.
Leuf, Bo & Ward Cunningham. 2001. *The Wiki Way: Quick Collaboration on the Web*. Boston: Addison-Wesley Longman.
Linell, Per. 1998. *Approaching Dialogue: Talk, Interaction and Contexts in Dialogical Perspectives*. Amsterdam/Philadelphia: John Benjamins.
Luzón, Maria J. 2013. Public communication of science in blogs: Recontextualizing scientific discourse for a diversified audience. *Written Communication*. Online first. doi: 10.1177/0741088313493610.
Mauranen, Anna. 2006. Speaking the discipline. Discourse and socialization in ELF and L1 English. In Ken Hyland & Marina Bondi (eds.), *Academic Discourse across Disciplines*. Bern: Peter Lang. 271-294.
Murphy, Glenn D. 2010. Using Web 2.0 tools to facilitate knowledge transfer in complex organisational environments: A primer. Paper presented at *ICOMS Asset Management Conference*, Adelaide, 21-25 June 2010.
Pandey, Ambarish, Sayeedul Hasan, Divyanshu Dubey & Srikant Sarangi. 2013. Smartphone apps as a source of cancer information: Changing trends in health information-seeking behavior. *Journal of Cancer Education* 28. 1. 128-143.
Pounds, Gabrina 2012. Enhancing empathic skills in clinical practice: A linguistic approach. *Journal of Work Organisation and Emotion* 5. 2. 114-131.
Riboni, Giorgia. 2014. Constructing (cyber-)space on Twitter: A study of place deixis in Tweets. In Julia Bamford, Franca Poppi & Davide Mazzi (eds.), *Space, Place and the Discursive Construction of Identity*. Bern: Peter Lang. 217-236.
Scollon, Ron & Suzanne W. Scollon. 1995. *Intercultural Communication: A Discourse Approach*. Oxford: Blackwell.
Scott, Helen. 2011. *Empathy in Healthcare Settings*. PhD Dissertation, Department of Psychology, Goldsmiths (University of London). http://eprints.gold.ac.uk/6704/1/PSY_thesis_Scott_2011.pdf.
Taylor, Charlotte. 2010. Science in the news: A diachronic perspective. *Corpora* 5. 2. 221-150.
Thibault, Paul J. 2012. Hypermedia selves and hypermodal stories: Narrativity, writing and normativity in personal blogs. In Mariavita Cambria, Cristina Arizzi & Francesca Coccetta (eds.), *Web Genres and Web Tools*. Como/Pavia: Ibis. 5-49.
Thomas, Pete. 2003. The recontextualization of management: A discourse-based approach to analysing the development of management thinking. *Journal of Management Studies* 40. 4. 775-801.
Wilkins, John S. 2008. The roles, reasons and restrictions of science blogs. *Trends in Ecology & Evolution* 23. 8. 411-413.
Wodak, Ruth. 2011. *The Discourse of Politics in Action. Politics as Usual*. Basingstoke: Palgrave Macmillan.

Zudilova-Seinstra, Elena. 2013. Designing the *Article of the Future*. http://www.elsevier.com/connect/designing-the-article-of-the-future. Accessed 30-01-2015.

SECTION I:

NEW MEDIA AND NEW MULTIMODAL ENVIRONMENTS FOR KNOWLEDGE DISSEMINATION

A DIGITAL MOB IN THE IVORY TOWER? CONTEXT COLLAPSE IN SCHOLARLY COMMUNICATION ONLINE

CORNELIUS PUSCHMANN
HUMBOLDT UNIVERSITY, BERLIN

Abstract: What are the effects of digital media on scholarly communication, both internal and external, and how do scholars react to the problem of context collapse, the situation that arises when internal communication among peers is suddenly put under public scrutiny? We approach this question by reviewing and contrasting the different functions of scholarly publishing and science communication for the academic community through a series of cases, and then discussing the relative reluctance of scholars to engage with new social media channels, such as blogs and Twitter, before this background. We close by describing different definitions of scholarly impact, and the role of novel approaches to evaluation that involve not just the academic community, but a wide variety of stakeholders.

1. Introduction

Around the 30th of June 2014 an intense debate erupted on the Internet about a psychological experiment conducted by three researchers at Facebook, the University of California, and Cornell University. The scientists aimed to test the hypothesis that emotions are contagious, that is, that happiness and sadness can spread from one person to the next by exposure. This phenomenon was previously known from laboratory settings, but it had never been studied in a computer-mediated setting and on a large sample of subjects before. In the experiment, conducted in early 2012, close to 700,000 Facebook users were randomly selected and their News Feed was adjusted to filter out specific posts with positive and negative emotion words, posts that the users would normally have been exposed to. Subsequently the emotional content of the subjects' posts in the following period was studied. The study found that users exposed to less negative emotive content would also post fewer negative status updates, and that those exposed to fewer positive emotions would in turn post fewer negative status updates, though the observed effect size was small. No content was added to the News Feed of any users, and the percentage of posts filtered out in this fashion from the News Feed was very small.

The results of the study were published in *Proceedings of the National Academy of Sciences* (PNAS), a very reputable journal, as an open access article (Kramer, Guillory & Hancock 2014). Ironically, the openness of the article and the fact that it was digitally available may have considerably spurred the furor that erupted a month after the publication of the original article, when the piece was picked up first by *The Atlantic*, *Forbes*, *Venture Beat*, *The Independent*, *The New York Times*, *The Wall Street Journal* and *The Financial Times*, and then by a number of scholars and privacy activists. The British parliament considered an official inquiry to investigate whether users rights had been breached in the course of the study. The first author, Adam Kramer, published a response via Facebook in which he noted that it had not been the aim of the study to cause anxiety among users and surmised that the company had made numerous improvements since the experiment had been first conducted (Kramer 2014). Facebook's chief operating officer, Sheryl Sandberg, remarked in a statement to *The Wall Street Journal* that the study "had been poorly communicated" (Krishna 2014).

The controversy surrounding the study touched a wide range of issues, from research ethics to privacy to the representation of scientific research in the media. Scientific controversies followed by mediated disputes are hardly new (cf. Nerlich & Halliday 2007; Saguy & Almeling 2008). Yet, one aspect of the research was largely overlooked in the debate following its publication, namely that it reached a very large and heterogeneous audience by being published in an open access publication, and that this apparently contributed to its controversial reception, which, in turn, was in part a result of the configuration of the discourse: scientists (i) with access to a huge trove of user data, (ii) reporting on analyzing that data, (iii) influencing the behavior of their test subjects without their knowledge, and (iv) doing so in the privileged environment of an academic journal. It is ironic that the very fact that this research was openly published led to a significant backlash, yet it also demonstrated the tensions embedded in the exclusivity of academic discourse.

2. Scholarly Discourse and Science Communication: Convergence and Diversification

Let us approach these tensions by examining the relationship of scholarly communication and the Internet. The great proliferation of digital technology in Western countries in the past two decades has dramatically altered access to information, making it significantly cheaper, faster, and more varied, with far-reaching implications for science and scholarship (Borgman 2007). High hopes exist with regards to the ability of new technologies to improve science, and yet not all of these have been fulfilled so far. One reason for this is the opposition between what is technologically possible and what furthers or conflicts with the vested interests of established actors in the ecosystem of scholarly communication.

The differentiation of *internal communication* (scholarly discourse) and *external communication* (science communication) has been blurred considerably in recent years, both by societal forces pressing for more transparency in publicly funded research and by the advent of digital media. Scandals involving the falsification of research results and unethical practices in science are unlikely to have strengthened the public's faith in science. Perhaps even more importantly, an increasing democratization of information and knowledge more generally has spurred the demand for constant interaction of science with other societal actors. How science is assessed by government, the media, the business world, and NGOs, plays an increasingly important role, both in forms of direct assessment and evaluation, but also in the competition for societal recognition and acceptance. Public outrage over research that is considered unethical or unnecessary arguably has a growing impact, and scientists must work to gain and sustain the public's trust. Enlisting public support is a key objective in approaches such as crowd science and virtual citizen science, which also aim to change not only scholarly communication, but the fashion in which research itself is conducted.

Science communication and scholarly discourse historically play very different roles. While science is inconceivable without scholarly discourse, science communication is a relatively recent invention, born out of the need to legitimize big science projects in the postwar period of the 20th century. In the following we will discuss science communication in the mass media and how it has been impacted by the shift towards digital communication.

Furthermore, we focus on the role of social media for new regimes of evaluating scientific impact, and that these new regimes are set to serve as important indices of scientific legitimacy in the future. We argue that social media has an important role to play in the future because it enables the seamless evaluation of all forms of scholarly output by a diverse community of stakeholders, and that the need to engage such a community is the plausible outcome of a democratization of knowledge, a configuration of conspiring technological and social change that Christine

Borgman refers to as a "co-evolution of technology and behavior" (2008:4).We begin by discussing the increasing codependence of science and media from a perpetrated ideal state of scientific independence to one of growing reliance of science on public legitimization through the media. We furthermore focus on the legitimatory role of social media in particular, its popularity adding to the pressure to "open" science up, a trend that historically reaches back much further. Finally, we examine alternative regimes of evaluating scientific impact, so-called *altmetrics*, which offer new ways of evaluating how scholarly output is received. We argue that, in the long run, scholarly communication is likely to follow certain broader trends initiated by shifts in the configuration of genres and actors, to both *diversify* and *consolidate* its form. We discuss the evolution of digital scholarly communication and its impact on three levels, namely:

(1) the distinction between formal and informal communication;
(2) the distinction between front stage and back stage in knowledge production;
(3) the distinction between different forms of impact (allocated by experts vs. allocated by the broader public).

We furthermore identify aspects of scholarly communication that are functionally stable and contrast them with aspects which are subject to change and diversification.

3. The Digital Evolution of Scholarly Communication

While initially a novel and exotic phenomenon, Computer-Mediated Communication between individuals has since its inception become a thoroughly mundane mode of communication, fully integrated with both face-to-face communication and the mass media (Baron 2008). We live in increasingly mediatized environments, in which communication through an array of digital devices which are constantly connected to the Internet is the norm (Deuze 2012). While there are significant discrepancies in its distributions, the spread of digital media is no longer restricted to Western countries, but is firmly established in emerging economies and has achieved a critical size even in poorer countries (International Telecommunications Union 2014). Roughly one third of the world's population have some degree of access to the Internet, and growth with regards to general access, but also with respect to usage intensity, is robust.

It has been widely argued that the Internet facilitates open debate among equals, reducing the technical and organizational barriers that otherwise inhibit the open flow of knowledge and ideas (Shirky 2008). Among other areas, this also extends to science, and accordingly arguments have been made for the increased integration of social media into the established modes of academic discourse, with the aim of reshaping expert communication in order to make it more open and pluralistic (Weinberger 2012). It is not purely due to technological innovation that this situation arises: there is also a political focus on achieving "a democratization of science" (Wilkins 2008:411) through more open dissemination of scholarly research. From demanding access to scholarly research results (*open access*) to opening the entire research process to public scrutiny (*open science*), the notion that science should be a more participatory endeavor is taking hold, though it remains to be seen whether this is merely a short-term fad or a more sustained development. This push for more democratization is not restricted to publishing, but seeks to encompass all stages of the research process. Open science aims to make research increasingly transparent under the banner of public stakeholdership in science. Rather than merely making the fruits of scholarly research available to the public, citizens are increasingly regarded as active stakeholders in the scientific process.

This pressure is accompanied by both a diversification and magnification with regards to the role of the media for science. Whereas mass media has an important role as an intermediary in the dissemination of scientific concepts and popularization of scientific fields, the role of social media is more complex, as it serves to blur the boundary between different, previously seemingly neatly divided modes of scholarly discourse and between different, previously clearly delineated stakeholder roles.

4. Formal and Informal Functions of Scholarly Discourse

Academic research is founded on communication. Meadows (1998) points out the defining role of early journals not just for the dissemination of scholarly knowledge, but for the constitution of science as such, pointing its historical origins. Scholarly communication can at the onset be defined as being associated both with a particular goal and with a specific professional community (Borgman & Furner 2005). Beyond both of these areas, the exchange of information and the transmission of knowledge obviously also take place in a variety of settings and among numerous actors.

Borgman (2007) differentiates between three core functions of scholarly communication: (i) *legitimization*, (ii) *dissemination*, and (iii) *access*, *preservation* and *curation*. The second and third aspects have been profoundly impacted by digitization. Research is disseminated more rapidly through digital publishing than was previously the case, and has the potential of reaching broader audiences, both scholarly and public. A combination of well-established, traditional and novel means are used to promote publications, such as disseminating review copies, but also tweeting about one's research (Bar-Ilan et al. 2012; Mahrt, Weller & Peters 2014). Digital archiving and curation has also sought to keep pace with technological developments, with an ever growing number of repositories and digital archives to insure the long-term availability of content. Measures such as the introduction of persistent identifiers (DOI for publications, ORCID for authors) have been taken to standardize access and make retrieving, saving and citing easier for authors. Legitimization is established in a number of ways: through publication in prestigious journals, by means of quantitative indicators such as the journal impact factor, and via citation numbers of articles. The latter have recently been joined by a large number of additional quantitative indicators in conjunction with the so-called *altmetrics* movement, which aims to assess impact coming from a number of sources, such as downloads, Facebook likes, Twitter retweets, Mendeley saves and other sources. Legitimization may well be the distinctive feature of scholarly communication. Borgman (2007:76) notes that "self-publishing is an oxymoron in the scholarly world" – dissemination of content without licensing through peer-review means nothing in terms of academic achievement. What is more, the combination of different strata of legitimization is crucial: publishers, libraries, and the media all have a role to play. As different forms of communication converge, with a greater variety of actors engaging with one another, "research in general and science in particular are less isolated from society" (Borgman 2007:83). Greater convergence of different academic fields and of applied and basic research are affected in this way, as are science and society more broadly.

For centuries the distinction between formal and informal scholarly communication was medially underpinned by the one being ephemeral, while the other was permanent. This is no longer an issue, as virtually all digital content can be considered permanent and the importance of other indicators of scientific quality has therefore been increased accordingly. The style and presentation of a scholarly work identify it as such, as does peer review, the most crucial component. The core criteria distinguishing scholarly communication from other kinds of discourse is that value judgments by third parties – reviewers, evaluators, advisors – are made to license knowledge as established, and accordingly much of the processes of licensing is central to scholarly communication in terms of the time, energy, and money allocated to it.

Formal scholarly communication is conducted in a variety of well-established formats, such as monographs, journal articles, book chapters in edited collections, and conference papers. While a range of genres and subgenres exist, there are also significant differences. Whereas papers in conference proceedings have little significance in the humanities, they are of high prestige in computer science, partly due to the field's long history of distributing publications electronically. In the life sciences, but also in the behavioral and social sciences, journal articles are the most prestigious form of publishing, though there are considerable differences with regards to the allocation of prestige. While some fields strongly follow quantitative measures such as Thompson Reuters journal impact factor, others allocate prestige more strongly through 'soft' factors, such as the reputation of the editors, the editorial board, or the publisher.

The formal characteristics of publications differ strongly from one field to another, in terms of style, length and integration of empirical data. Some fields are also considerably more uniform than others in terms of how they organize and present their research. The age of the respective formats also differ, with conference papers being a fairly recent innovation whereas scholarly monographs follow a long tradition. The tandem role of technology and the evolution of formats, driven by cultural change and the increasing professionalization of science, also becomes quite apparent in this context. In addition to differences in fields and their adoption of new technology notwithstanding, scholarly texts have changed with their mode of distribution, from monographs which were delivered in long form for economic reasons to conference papers which have become more prevalent as proceedings can be delivered electronically.

The previous two decades have seen a considerable market concentration in academic publishing, and it seems very likely that this trend will continue. While differences in this area too are significant, technological shifts towards digital publishing mean that smaller private publishers and university presses are under great pressure to remain competitive. While the number of academic publications overall continues to grow, large corporate actors are controlling ever larger market shares (Jinha 2010). These companies are also able to publish digital content in the appropriate quality through their publication platforms, making them much more likely to persevere in the future than smaller competitors who may not survive the transition to a fully digital scholarly ecosystem

(Houghton 2010). The technological changes have by now long reached all publishers, whether in the sciences or the humanities. Both journals and monographs are by now published digitally, with many areas already fully or significantly reliant on digital texts for all aspects of scholarly knowledge exchange. It is clear that in these contexts, rather than having any material aspect, the terms ‘book’ and ‘journal’ are simply metaphors, but this does not impede their salience. Scholarly communication seems set to become fully digital in the course of the next few years, both as a result of policy initiatives, economic pressure, and usage practices that facilitate this change. This development is a notable contrast to (for example) literary publishing, where the dynamics are quite different, and readers are considerably less utilitarian in their expectations.

5. The Lasting Importance of Peer Review

The cornerstone of scholarly communication is peer review. It is hard to overstate its universal importance, and easy to underrate it in relation to technological or economic aspects of academic publishing. As we will argue in the course of this chapter, scholarship has proven to be very adaptable when it comes to certain aspects of scholarly communication, but resistant to change in others. Peer review is one such point where we observe a large degree of stability in practices, even though there have been calls to innovate peer review through alternative or variant procedures (van Rooyen et al. 1999). Peer review plays such as crucial role in formal scholarly communication because it licenses the quality of the research and certifies it as scientific content. This is crucial for the accumulation of scholarly credit, on which junior academics rely in order to achieve tenure and promotion. As competition in science continues to grow, so does the pressure to collect as many tokens of scholarly quality as possible. The more competitive a field is, the more likely it is that only those junior researchers with a strong and unwavering focus on certified forms of knowledge dissemination in the shape of formal publications will succeed, while competitors will fall behind (Merton 1968).

While the economics and the technology underpinning scholarly publication have changed dramatically in the course of the last decades, this is not the case with regards to the scholarly value system, which has remained stable. The core aim of researchers is to acquire status and build a reputation, to which the production of certified knowledge makes a major contribution. The certification process, as described above, is under discussion in respect to its potential for optimization, but the underlying idea that knowledge must be certified by other (more senior) researchers is alive and well. The accumulation of social capital in the scholarly community is the key prerequisite for tenure and promotion, and carries further secondary rewards, such as funding and public visibility. Scholars compete for scarce resources when they apply for grants or professorships, and in this process the certification of quality by peers is crucial. The pressure to acquire a high level of certification is greatest where the competition is strongest and where the value attached to standardized forms of certification is most significant, such as in the hard sciences, with well-established large scale journals and high impact factors. This situation of sustained competition affects the way in which scientists communicate, because it forces them to plan communication strategically and regard its product as their capital. Creating a publishing record becomes paramount, particularly to junior scholars.

A central role in the context of accruing social capital is that of *invisible colleges* (Crane 1969), that is, communities of scholars that work together, cite one another and progress together in terms of career development, without being formally affiliated, part of the same institution, or geographically proximate to each other. The existence of invisible colleges in particular contributes to the importance of informal digital communication, as it seems likely that communication patterns in email, Twitter, and other channels will reveal invisible colleges to a degree.

Informal scholarly communication has traditionally played a considerably less noticeable role than formal communication. Preprints have been circulated since the beginning of the system of journal publishing, and the importance of personal correspondence was established long before this system was put into place, and before credit and reward became paramount as a result of the professionalization of science. This professionalization went hand in hand with the formalization of its genres, an observation that we will return to later. The rise of digital communication has made informal genres of scholarly discourse much more visible than was previously the case. Mailing lists, message boards, scholarly blogging and social media all play an increasingly important role in informal scholarly discourse, but this role is so far unrelated to the certification of knowledge that translates into scholarly credit which we have described. Informal communication is hard to evaluate because it does not serve the licensing function of formal scholarly communication as it generally lacks peer review. This hardly diminishes its role, as the result of several surveys shows (see below). Scholars regardless of age and discipline strongly rely on different tools for informal scholarly communication, be it email to discuss research with colleagues, mailing lists to exchange news regarding job vacancies, conference calls and research projects, or blogs to publicize their research or share ideas. Mediated informal scholarly communication plays an important role and can be assumed to have increased significantly, considering the wide array of channels that can be used to conduct it (cf. Barjak 2006; Gruzd, Staves & Wilk 2012; Levine, Boehm & Christensen 2013; Lupton 2014). This is unlikely to have impinged on face-to-face interaction, rather it seems likely that scholars simply communicate more in general, and more visibly. But while the significance of informal scholarly communication to scholars is undiminished, it does not yet play any formal role in acquiring status, at least not one that would be easily observable. While scholars doubtlessly benefit from connecting to peers and sharing information, these benefits are less immediate than those derived from social capital gained through formal publishing. It is still a requirement for researchers to publish formally – their informal communication is merely a valuable extra that has added benefits for them.

Informal scholarly communication in social media arguably plays a role in addition to formal publishing, but it shows absolutely no tendencies to displace publishing in scholarly journals, monographs or conference papers (Bader, Fritz & Gloning 2012; Levine, Boehm & Christensen 2013; Pscheida, Albrecht, Herbst, Minet & Köhler 2013). Whereas informal discourse has a role to disseminate, discuss, reference and curate the output of scholarship, it does not infringe on that primary output, but merely frames it. The fact that informal scholarly communication is increasingly recorded and sometimes also public (as is the case with blogs and Twitter) opens it up as a resource for the study of scholarly communication more broadly (Mortensen & Walker 2002; Mauranen 2013).

6. Front Stage and Back Stage in Academia

Both formal and informal scholarly communication have become much more publicly visible than was previously the case, with far-reaching consequences. As scholarly communication is conducted digitally and increasingly also open access, the work of scientists is increasingly publically scrutinized, to the extent that it also draws more attention from the media and the general public (Borgman 2007; Evans & Reimer 2009). Previously research results could be assumed to be read first and foremost by other scientists, though it has been shown that much published research is never read by anyone at all apart from its author and the reviewer.

The push for more openness has significant implications for the *front stage/back stage* distinction that characterizes science. Sociologists of science argue that belonging to a particular epistemic culture is constituted by specific codes, practices and beliefs that form the basis of the scientific community (Knorr-Cetina 1999). But membership is inherently exclusionary: only by barring others from joining the club can the club be upheld. This poses problems when the codes which index group membership are exchanged under a degree of public scrutiny, at least to the extent that it is less clear who has access to what is being exchanged and what potential exists for misrepresentation. The case cited at the beginning of this chapter attests to this problem of *context collapse* (Marwick & Boyd 2010). In the case of the Facebook study, a published article was scrutinized first by the press and then by bloggers, activists and scholars. But since the article was online, many responses, both in the press and by bloggers, did not merely discuss the study abstractly, but linked directly to the source. The author, Adam Kramer, wrote a response on his Facebook page that he later referred to as an official response. What this and similar examples underpin is the loss of a definitive separation between audiences and discussants. The availability of the research results enables a much broader scrutiny than would have been the case under different circumstances.

7. Science, the Media, and the Public

In a classic essay on the sociology of science, Robert K. Merton (1973) notes how the relationship of science and society has shifted multiple times in its development from the 17th to the 20^{th}century. He recalls how the entrenchment of modern science from the early struggles of the natural philosophers to attain legitimacy eventually led to the post-war scientist to regard himself "as independent of society" and to see science as "a self-validating enterprise which was in society but not of it" (Merton 1973:268). Arguably the relationship of science with the broader public has changed significantly in Western societies in recent decades as a result of social change. The "frontal assault on the autonomy of science"(1973:268) that Merton described in the 1970s has given way to much more pragmatic regimes of science policy. This viewpoint that sees science *in* society, rather than distinct from it, is captured by the concept of the triple helix of science, government and industry (Etzkowitz & Leydesdorff 2000). Science is hardly seen as independent of society anymore by most sociologists of science, but rather as both constitutive to and a product of the post-industrial knowledge society.

Shifts in science policy and the ascendency of the mass media have both had a combined influence on this development. Weingart (1998) thoroughly criticizes the traditional dichotomous view of science and the general public, in which the mass media acts as intermediate between the two. As he points out, in such a view science possesses an implicit monopoly on factual knowledge, while the public relies only on meager common sense. In this view the media acts as science's "translator and propagandist" (Weingart 1998:870), seeking to win the public's support. The relationship is one of extreme asymmetry: science establishes facts and disseminates them to the public, with journalists taking on the role of mediators. Media and science are alike, Weingart points out, in that media creates its own reality and actively sets an agenda. He further argues that while interaction between science and the public is nothing new "[n]ovelty is in the form and intensity which emanates from a closer connection between science and its social environment as well as the new role of the media in observing this connection" (1998:872).

In descriptions of science and the public as sociotechnical systems, both are frequently treated as discrete and opposed forces, with scientists seen as rational and informed by logic, and the public as irrational, emotional and inherently unpredictable (Cook, Pieri & Robbins 2004). Cook et al. provide a detailed study of how the public is characterized by scientists in a series of interviews with academics and find that it is both regarded as passive, fearful, incapable of grasping risk, and as in need of education. Not only is there an inherent rift between experts and laypersons in such a model, there is also a power imbalance between the two parties: whereas scientists articulate demands towards the public and are disappointed if they are not met, the public lacks understanding of complex scientific issues and must be educated (Jacoby & Gonzales 1991). In practice, however, the perception of the actual situation is markedly at odds with this characterization. Science and the public are both much more diversified and fuzzy than their neat rhetorical separation would make us believe, and their relationship has a much less hierarchical character than in the bygone era of big science. Scholars in the twenty-first century are engaged in a constant competition not only for the acceptance and endorsement of their colleagues in peer review, grant applications, and tenure proceedings, but they also struggle for public recognition in the mass media and, increasingly, in digital media.

Meanwhile, the relationship between science and journalism is frequently characterized as being strained by tensions as a result of the asymmetry in power and authority. Dornan (1990:48) accuses the media of "prescriptive agitations" and Colson (2011:892) refers to "a kind of contempt displayed by scientists towards the media", while scientists are seen as arrogant by journalists. This differs from the situation inside science, due to its hierarchical organization. As Leah Lievrouw (1990:9) points out, "scientists as a subculture share very similar values about their work and can persuade one another of the value of their research based on a reasonably consistent set of standards and conventions". At the same time, science journalism has historically played an important role in reinforcing the authority of science as pristine, pure and at once superior to and outside of popular culture (cf. Fürsich & Lester 1996, who speak of a paradox situation). Lievrouw (1990) equates informal communication with face to face communication, highlighting the medial distinction between the two that prevailed up the 1990s. It is helpful to distinguish different aspects of scholarly communication and different stages in its evolution. It is also helpful to differentiate between micro and macro level communication (discourse among individual scholars vs. systemic change), and between a procedural view (often taken by science studies and the studies of the sociology of knowledge) and a view focused on the products of scholarly discourse (often taken in information science and bibliometrics).

Lievrouw (1990) further describes scholarly communication as a three-stage process in which knowledge is first *conceptualized*, then *documented*, and finally *popularized*. Mass media plays an important part in the third step of this process, but is traditionally excluded from the first two. The conceptualization of new knowledge occurs informally in hallway conversation and laboratory meetings, in notes and through email. The second stage, documentation, is concerned with bringing knowledge into a form that allows presentation. Finally, in the third stage scientific research is popularized. That is, communicated to a broader public. Importantly, the process of popularizing in research is in essence a process of assimilation in which compatible material is integrated into an already established theme. One example here is that of cold fusion research in the United States, an issue that received much attention because of its compatibility with public concerns. Hot fusion was regarded as dangerous and dirty, while cold fusion promised to be cheaper, safer and more efficient, and to offer the same advantages as traditional energy sources. Popularization is not merely a random effort. Rather, it is necessary to enlist support in the form of funding (which enables future research) public interest (which, among other things, helps to recruit junior researchers), political support (which can result in boost in attention and prestige), and other gains which cannot be obtained through internal communication. Work in the sociology of science has pointed to this interdependence of scientific communities and the role of consensus to establish scientific findings as facts, to be presented to the public.

8. From Dissemination to (More) Participation?

The relation of science and the media has been impacted considerably by the advent of social media, which enables a much broader participation in the scholarly process than is the case in traditional broadcasting or print formats. What Weingart (1998) calls the *science-media-coupling* in the 1990s could have been circumvented by a complex interdependence of science with a variety of actors who communicate through digital media and conduct what in political communication is referred to as a *permanent campaign* (Larsson 2014), an environment in which political actors are constantly vying for attention. While the mass media discussed by Lievrouw (1990) and Weingart (1998) is a social system of actors, digital media rather presents an infrastructure for communication and interaction that connects both established actors and systems of actors, and lends a stage to new ones. The technical infrastructure represents a powerful enabler of both old and new actors which facilitates a diversification of participants.

Weingart (1998) uses the term *medialization* to describe the media's impact on science. A similar set of effects can be applied to the impact of digital media on science, which partly overlaps with the characteristics of broadcast media and partly differs, as a result of the technicity of digital media. In online platforms, the individual is arguably the most salient category of representation. Self-representation permeates all levels of social media use. In science, countless indicators exist to measure and represent the impact of a scholar in a growing number of services and platforms.

Bucchi (1996) describes innovative forces in science communication beyond the canonical dissemination and mediation approach. In the classical model, scientific facts are mediated by professional communicators (usually journalists) to a lay audience. Not only are all three parties distinct from one another, they also have different capabilities and are assigned different roles: while the scientific content emanates from science, it is considered too complex and difficult for laypersons to assess. In the prominent metaphorical use, mediators must translate complex scientific knowledge to the public, necessarily 'dumbing down' the scientific facts. Both scientists and journalists play an active role, while the public remains a passive recipient. As Bucchi critically notes, the blame for 'miscommunication' is usually assigned to journalists for misrepresenting and to the public for misunderstanding scientific research, whereas scientists themselves are relatively unscrutinized. He aptly points out that rather than just concerning how scientists enter the media, there is increasing incursion of the public into science. In the same vein, Colson (2011) presents the result of a study on the relationship of science journalism and science blogging that highlights the tensions that arise as a result of a technological shift. Her study reveals that science journalists are skeptical of academics who blog, and that academics in turn see blogging as a way of circumventing the mass media – a step that is seen as an opportunity by Hermida (2010:80), who argues that "science journalism must continue to evolve and must now look beyond the print model and its inherent limitations". Shanahan (2011) describes scholarly blogs as "boundary layers" that create new writer-reader interactions. In contrast to traditional science journalism, the distance between writer and reader is greatly reduced in blogging. Whereas the science journalist takes on the role of translator or guide, science bloggers are forced to more directly interact with audiences. They are motivated by engaging in discussion and participating in debates about the topics they raise in their blogs (Puschmann & Mahrt 2012; Shema, Bar-Ilan & Thelwall 2012).

It is worth pointing out that enlisting the public is by no means a novel phenomenon in scholarly communication. Bucchi (1996) describes the kind of constitutive boundary work that takes place to constitutionalize new fields to the public at large. Examples from the 19th century, a period in which modern science had to establish its authority, illustrate how actively engaging laypersons played a considerable role in the motives of scientists such as Helmholtz. Whereas 19th century mediatization ultimately aimed to disseminate results to the public so as to enlist its support for scientific endeavors, proponents of open science see social media as an instrument for the co-production of knowledge. This dynamic challenges the traditional role configuration of expert and layperson, posing potential threats to the organizational structure of science.

9. Adoption of Social Media in Science

In spite of many calls for more integration of social media into science to fill the demand of making science "more open", reactions have been mixed. The internet arguably plays an increasingly important role in how academics present themselves both to peers and to broader publics. The convergence of all forms of digital technology and their proliferation into all spheres of life has spurred this development. Over time, the attitude towards social media in science has become more integrative, for example

Priem, Piwowar and Hemminger (2012:2) contend that “these tools do not create new types of scholarly practice so much as they facilitate existing practice”. In a similar vein, Colson (2011:890) cites biochemist and blogger Daniel Brown: “science bloggers run the gamut of career levels, from lay people with a strong interest in science to teachers, graduate students, postdocs, and an increasing number of principal investigators”.

Borgman and Furner (2005:4) describe the process of scholarly communication as becoming ever-more integrated: “The cycle of scholarly activities is blending into a continuous, looping flow, as people discuss, write, share, and seek information through networked information systems.” They list the countless devices that can be used to access and disseminate digital information, and the numerous formats and data types they support. These formats are in turn increasingly dynamic in being available for constant updating and editing, rather than remaining static. The authors highlight the particular role of bibliometrics for the ongoing assessment of science in the context of growing integration and an increasingly utilitarian view of academia. This applies particularly to the social life of scholarly publications (Brown & Duguid 1995, in Borgman & Furner 2005). Anderson (1997:27) highlights the role of communication technology for science, finding that scholars who communicate more are also more productive. As a result of the increased mobility and connectivity brought about by the Internet, she goes on to argue that “the potential for greater inclusiveness in the invisible college brought about by scholars’ use of computer mediated communication necessitates a global examination of the behaviors and attitudes of scholars regarding CMC”, also noting that particularly informal communication is a strong predictor of membership in an invisible college.

Barjak (2006) finds similar results pointing to the relation of productivity and use of digital technology in informal scholarly discourse. Views diverge on whether the digitization of scholarly discourse changes science and scholarship as such, or whether it only affects work practices, rather than affording more fundamental epistemological changes as well. Interestingly, publication activity correlates positively with all forms of Internet usage. In Barjak’s words, “the more productive scientists are, the more they use the Internet for all the investigated purposes (social communication, information retrieval and dissemination)” (2006:1363).

Following up on these results, Lupton (2014) conducted a study among an international and interdisciplinary sample of 711 academics about their use of social media. This enabled her to gain insights into the strategic ways in which some scholars use social media and the benefits they have experienced for their academic work. According to Lupton, benefits included connecting and establishing networks not only with peers, but also with stakeholder groups outside of universities, promoting openness and sharing of information, publicizing and development of research, and giving and receiving support. On the other hand, Lupton also found that while the majority of the respondents were very positive about using social media, they also expressed a range of concerns. These included issues of privacy and the blurring of boundaries between personal and professional use, the risk of jeopardizing their career through injudicious use of social media, lack of credibility, the quality of the content they posted, time pressures, social media use becoming an obligation, becoming a target of attack, too much self-promotion by others, possible plagiarism of their ideas, and the commercialization of content and copyright issues. These findings exemplify the pressure of outside forces on academia as a result of the diversification of relevant science policy actors. They also point to the versatility of social media for purposes going far beyond knowledge dissemination per se. Seeing social media through the lens of knowledge dissemination misses the point that they increasingly play a role for informal networking and relationship management among many academics.

In a similar vein, Bell (2012) explores the use of science blogs for the dissemination of scholarly knowledge, focusing in particular on how science bloggers regard their own role and the relation to their audience. Drawing on Brake's (2007) research on how bloggers conceptualize their audiences, she notes the long history of criticism towards science in his approach to communication, which systematically excludes the public. Importantly, Bell notes how the values of social media – interactivity and openness – clash with values associated with the scientific career path. She also points out that bloggers form cliques online in ways very similar to the invisible colleges recognized by Crane (1969). Additionally, many of the motives of scholarly bloggers that she notes fit with those described by Kjellberg in her study of early scholarly bloggers (2009).

Blogs as a form of personal publishing highlight the diversification of channels available to present and discuss scholarly knowledge (Kirkup 2010; Kjellberg 2009). As emphasized by Amsen's (2008) small interview study with five scholarly bloggers, blogs are used widely by individuals at the intersection of science and science communication. The bloggers she interviews argue that blogs are value to present ideas, for debate, to connect to others and to present both their field and science more broadly. However, there is a distinct tendency to associate blogging with the popularization of science, rather than with presenting original ideas. One blogger states that he doesn't want to risk getting scooped (Amsen

2008:10) and there are risks associated with disclosing potential confidential information. At the same time, she refers to blogs as "a playpen for new ideas" (p. 13), in line with the findings in other studies.

Bell (2012) finds similar motivations in her interview study of bloggers in neuroscience and psychology. Her respondents note the freedom of expression that their blog afforded them, allowing them both to publish things not fitting neatly into formal publishing regimes but also personalizing their communication to reflect their interests and viewpoints more broadly, rather than sticking to a particular subject matter in science. She also notes a tension between bloggers oriented more towards science and those identifying more closely with journalism (Bell 2012:259). The resulting conflict is one that points to the diversification of roles that follows a diversification of tools and information sources.

To summarize, the adoption of social media in academia has, in those places where it has succeeded, relied on a combination of curiosity and enjoyment of experimentation, on the belief that reaching broader audiences will have career benefits, and on the view that new forms of scholarly communication have long-term potential. However, there has been very little pressure to integrate social media into scholarly workflows and, accordingly, adoption has been limited. A key issue is the allocation of time: secondary communicative activities outside formal scholarly communication are conducted on top of established practices, posing challenges to the time budget.

10. Public Evaluation and "Flavors" of Impact

Scholarly communication has been widely studied from an outcome perspective as a proxy for the impact of science. *Bibliometrics*, a subfield of information science, is concerned with studying citation behavior and with utilizing citations as an indicator of different types of scholarly behavior. Using citation data, the productivity of individual researchers and their relative influence can be studied, the interaction between fields and nationalities can be scrutinized, as can the evolution of an area of research over time and (more broadly) the trajectory of science as a whole (Evans 2008).

Several forces converge when it comes to assessing the impact of scholarly communication, namely (i) the availability of more scholarly content in both digital and open form, (ii) the availability of social media tools that can be used to both disseminate the content further and record some sort of interaction, and (iii) a push for more openness and public scrutiny of science by society in general. The evaluation via publication indicators is not restricted to individuals, but also extends to departments, universities and countries which are compared to determine scientific performance on a European and global scale. As Borgman and Furner (2005) point out: a major problem of link analysis is that it is not necessarily clear what the predicate denotes, i.e. in what context a given author cites a particular work. These issues are magnified studying indicators such as tweets, likes, shares, etc., for which both the reader community and the context of link creation remain largely opaque.

A core contention associated with the development described above is that it may lead to a unilateral focus on the impact of publications (and ultimately authors) over other forms of licensing quality (e.g. through the reputation of journals or institutions, availability of content), while diversifying this measure away from citations to other, faster measures (downloads, clicks, etc.). The possible risk associated with this is that popularity (public impact) in the broadest sense could trump quality (scientific impact). Whereas impact in any form was previously cumbersome and difficult to measure by comparison, this is increasingly simplified by various tools. It seems plausible that the speed and ease with which social media can serve to associate reference from individuals to scholarly works will advance the significance of social media instruments to point to scholarly works. While citations are still the gold standard, other forms of impact assessment are likely to gain relevance simply by being readily available. There is also reason to believe that while increased metrification will probably lead to more transparency, it may also result in more control. The style in which Priem, Pimowar and Hemminger (2012:1) describe *altmetrics* betrays a degree of mistrust in current scholarly practices, as made immediately clear by their claim that altmetrics will contribute to "exposing and fixing scholarly processes once hidden and ephemeral".

The abovementioned studies have to date largely focused on the usage perspective of scholars, namely the adoption of and attitudes towards social media. Increasingly, the potential of social media for the evaluation of scientific impact also plays a relevant role. Impact assessments are important for the assignment of funding and in the tenure process, thus significantly influencing career development. But seeing the impact of science through the lens of traditional impact metrics comes with a number of limitations. To quote Priem et al. (2012) again, "citations measure impact only on that minority of an article's audience with the means and inclination to cite it in the literature, leaving out clinicians, the general public, and even most scientists". Given the increasing pressure to improve the return on investment in science form the public perspective, wide dissemination and impact of research seems crucial. Whereas previously a unilateral definition of impact as either a high impact factor of the publication or silent agreement among experts regarding the high prestige of a particular journal or press, was sufficient, it seems likely that this will shift towards more holistic measures of impact, as tools to provide such measures are more widely used by scholars.

Priem et al.'s (2012:13) main point is that different social media measurements of impact fall into four discreet clusters or *flavors* of impact, which identify separate audiences and usage practices and vary depending on how and by whom the research is used: work that is cited; work that is saved and shared; popular hits; and expert picks. Important dimensions in the context of impact measurement are the availability of measures and the democratization of how to "make" impact. Whereas previously only slow citation measures would leave any kind of visible dent, now many more indicators are available. Some of these, such as the statistics reported by Mendeley (saves to a bibliography) or SSRN (downloads) are arguably closer to citations in terms of signaling engagement, while others (e.g. abstract views, likes on Facebook, tweets mentioning the source) are perhaps less of a signal of engagement.

The diversification of these impact measures is important because it does not constitute a singular effect on how the output of a stable process will be presented. Rather, it is likely to result in a feedback to the practice itself, and this effect goes hand in hand with institutional changes that have shaped scholarly communication in past years, namely the need for greater measurable impact in the context of scientific evaluation, which influences the allocation of funding, the awarding of tenure, and the success of promotion processes.

11. Conclusions

In this chapter we have argued that the form and function of scholarly communications is defined by the individual needs of stakeholders, the organizational and cultural shaping of science as a community of practice and of the specific disciplines that comprise scholarship, and, finally, by changes in technology. These changes conspire to create a new type of medial setting in which scientists can address a range of stakeholders, rather than having to choose between clearly defined audiences. At the same time, the need to communicate in rigorously defined forms in traditional scholarly communication remains unchanged as a result of how scholarship is licensed by peers. But increasingly in addition to these genres, a wide variety of other formats are also used to promote research and reach out to further audiences. This also creates challenges for academics who are faced with the anger of context collapse.

We believe that in the long term, this will lead to more convergence between formal and informal communication, and between formats that target specific audiences. We furthermore believe that the emphasis of communication will shift from popularization to dissemination and evaluation, generating legitimacy for scientific research, rather than 'educating the public'. Such a shift marks a long-term departure from a neat conceptual separation between science and the public at large, a shift driven both by robust societal forces and technological innovation.

References

Amsen, Eva. 2008. Who benefits from science blogging? *Hypothesis* 4. 2. 10-14. doi: 10.5779/hypothesis.v4i2.56.

Anderson, Cary M. 1997. Computer-mediated communication, the invisible college and visiting scholars: An exploratory study. *Journal of Computing in Higher Education* 9. 1. 27-48.

Bader, Anita, Gerd Fritz & Thomas Gloning. 2012. *Digitale Wissenschaftskommunikation 2010-2011 : Eine Online-Befragung*. Gießen: Gießener Elektronische Bibliothek.

Bar-Ilan, Judit, Stefanie Haustein, Isabella Peters, Jason Priem, Hadas Shema &Jens Terliesner. 2012. Beyond citations: Scholars' visibility on the social web. In Éric Archambault, Yves Gingras & Vincent Larivière (eds.), *Proceedings of 17th International Conference on Science and Technology Indicators*. Vol. 52900. Montréal: Science-Metrix and OST. 98-109.

Barjak, Franz. 2006. The role of the Internet in informal scholarly communication. *Journal of the American Society for Information Science and Technology* 57. 10. 1350-1367. doi: 10.1002/asi.20454.

Baron, Naomi. S. 2008. *Always On: Language in an Online and Mobile World.* Oxford/New York: Oxford University Press.

Bell, Alice. 2012. 'Science Blogs is a high school clique, Nature Network is a private club': Imagining the communities of online science. *Canadian Journal of Media Studies* 10. 240-265. http://cjms.fims.uwo.ca/issues/special/Bell.pdf.

Borgman, Chrstine L. 2007. *Scholarship in the Digital Age: Information, Infrastructure, and the Internet*. Cambridge, MA: MIT Press.

Borgman, Christine L. & Jonathan Furner. 2005. Scholarly communication and bibliometrics. *Annual Review of Information Science and Technology* 36. 1. 2-72. doi: 10.1002/aris.1440360102.

Brake, David. 2007. Personal webloggers and their audiences: Who do they think they are talking to? In Marika Lüders, Lin Prøitz & Terje Rasmussen (eds.), *Personal Media: Life between Screens*. Oslo: Gyldendal. 141-163.

Bucchi, M. 1996. When scientists turn to the public: Alternative routes in science communication. *Public Understanding of Science* 5. 375-394. doi: 10.1088/0963-6625/5/4/005.

Colson, Vinciane. 2011. Science blogs as competing channels for the dissemination of science news. *Journalism* 12. 7. 889-902. doi: 10.1177/1464884911412834

Cook, Guy, Elisa Pieri & Peter T. Robbins. 2004. 'The scientists think and the public feels': Expert perceptions of the discourse of GM food. *Discourse & Society* 15. 4. 433-449. doi: 10.1177/0957926504043708.

Crane, Diana. 1969. Social structure in a group of scientists: A test of the 'invisible college' hypothesis. *American Sociological Review* 34. 3. 335-352.

Deuze, Mark. 2012. *Media Life*. Cambridge: Polity Press.

Dornan, Christopher. 1990. Some problems in conceptualizing the issue of 'science in the media'. *Critical Studies in Mass Communication* 7. 48–71.

Etzkowitz, Henry & Loet Leydesdorff. 2000. The dynamics of innovation: From National Systems and 'Mode 2' to a Triple Helix of university-industry-government relations. *Research Policy* 29. 2. 109-123. doi: 10.1016/S0048-7333(99)00055-4.

Fürsich, Elfriede & Elizabeth P. Lester. 1996. Science journalism under scrutiny: A textual analysis of 'science times'. *Critical Studies in Mass Communication* 13. 24-43.

Gruzd, Anatoliy, Kathleen Staves & Amanda Wilk. 2012. Connected scholars: Examining the role of social media in research practices of faculty using the UTAUT model. *Computers in Human Behavior* 28. 6. 2340-2350. doi: 10.1016/j.chb.2012.07.004.

Hermida, Alfred. 2010. Revitalizing science journalism for a digital age. In Donald Kennedy & Geneva Overholser (eds.), *Science and the Media*. Cambridge, MA: American Academy of Arts and Sciences. 80-87

Houghton, John W. 2010. Alternative publishing models: Exploring costs and benefits. In Cornelius Puschmann & Dieter Stein (eds.), *Towards Open Access Scholarship. Selected Papers from the Berlin 6 Open Access Conference*. Düsseldorf: Düsseldorf University Press. 27-40.

International Telecommunication Union. 2014. *ICT Statistics. Measuring the Information Society*. http://www.itu.int/en/ITU-D/Statistics/Pages/publications/mis2014.aspx.

Jacoby, Sally & Patrick Gonzales. 1991. The constitution of expert-novice in scientific discourse. *Issues in Applied Linguistics* 2. 2. 149-181.

Jinha, Arif E. 2010. Article 50 million: An estimate of the number of scholarly articles in existence. *Learned Publishing* 23. 3. 258-263. doi: 10.1087/20100308.

Kirkup, Gill. 2010. Academic blogging: Academic practice and academic identity. *London Review of Education* 8. 1. 75-84. doi: 10.1080/14748460903557803.

Kjellberg, Sara. 2009. Scholarly blogging practice as situated genre: An analytical framework based on genre theory. *Information Research* 14. 3. 1-17. http://www.informationr.net/ir/14-3/paper410.html.

Knorr-Cetina, Karin. 1999. *Epistemic Cultures*. Boston, MA: Harvard University Press.

Kramer, Adam. D. I. 2014. Facebook message. https://www.facebook.com/akramer/posts/10152987150867796.

Kramer, Adam. D. I., Jamie E. Guillory & Jeffrey T. Hancock. 2014. Experimental evidence of massive-scale emotional contagion through social networks. *Proceedings of the National Academy of Sciences* 111. 24. 8788-8790. doi: 10.1073/pnas.1320040111.

Krishna, R. Jai. 2014. Sandberg: Facebook study was "poorly communicated'. *The Wall Street Journal*. http://blogs.wsj.com/digits/2014/07/02/facebooks-sandberg-apologizes-for-news-feed-experiment/?mod=LS1.

Larsson, Anders O. 2014. Online, all the time? A quantitative assessment of the permanent campaign on Facebook. *New Media & Society*. doi: 10.1177/1461444814538798.

Levine, Kenneth, Reid Boehm &Rob Christensen. 2013. *Trust and Authority in Scholarly Communications in the Light of the Digital Transition. Final Report.* Knoxville, TN: University of Tennessee & CIBER Research Ltd. http://ciber-research.eu/download/20140115-Trust_Final_Report.pdf.

Lievrouw, Leah. A. 1990. Communication and the social representation of scientific knowledge. *Critical Studies in Mass Communication* 7. 1. 1-10.

Lupton, D. 2014. *'Feeling Better Connected': Academics' Use of Social Media*. Canberra: News & Media Research Centre, University of Canberra. http://www.canberra.edu.au/faculties/arts-design/attachments/pdf/n-and-mrc/Feeling-Better-Connected-report-final.pdf.

Mahrt, Merja, Katrin Weller &Isabella Peters. 2014. Twitter in scholarly communication. In Katrin Weller, Axel Bruns, Jean Burgess, Merja Mahrt & Cornelius Puschmann (eds.), *Twitter and Society*. New York: Peter Lang. 399-410.

Marwick, Alice & Danah Boyd. 2010. I tweet honestly, I tweet passionately: Twitter users, context collapse, and the imagined audience. *New Media & Society*13. 1. 114-133. doi: 10.1177/1461444810365313.

Mauranen, Anna. 2013. Hybridism, edutainment, and doubt: Science blogging finding its feet. *Nordic Journal of English Studies*12. 1. 7-36.

Meadows, Arthur J. 1998. *Communicating Research*. San Diego, CA: Academic Press.

Merton, Robert K. 1968. The Matthew effect in science. *Science (New York, N.Y.)* 159. 3810. 56-63. doi: 10.1126/science.159.3810.56.

Mortensen, Torill & Jill Walker. 2002. Blogging thoughts: Personal publication as an online research tool. In A. Morrison (ed.), *Researching ICTs in Context*. Oslo: InterMedia. 249-279.

Nerlich, Brigitte & Christopher Halliday. 2007. Avian flu: The creation of expectations in the interplay between science and the media. *Sociology of Health & Illness* 29. 1. 46-65. doi: 10.1111/j.1467-9566.2007.00517.x.

Priem, Jason, Heather A. Piwowar & Bradley M. Hemminger. 2012. *Altmetrics in the Wild: Using Social Media to Explore Scholarly Impact* (Digital Libraries). http://arxiv.org/abs/1203.4745.

Pscheida, Daniela, Steffen Albrecht, Sabrina Herbst, Claudia Minet, & Thomas Köhler. 2013. *Nutzung von Social Media und onlinebasierten Anwendungen in der Wissenschaft*. Dresden. Science 2.0-Survey 2013 Datenreport. http://nbn-resolving.de/urn:nbn:de:bsz:14-qucosa-132962.

Puschmann, Cornelius & Merja Mahrt. 2012. Scholarly blogging: A new form of publishing or science journalism 2.0? In Alexander Tokar, Michael Beurskens, Susanne Keuneke, Merja Mahrt, Isabella Peters, Cornelius Puschmann, Timo van Treek, K. Weller (eds.), *Science and the Internet*. Düsseldorf: Düsseldorf University Press. 171-181.

Saguy, Abigail C. & Rene Almeling. 2008. Fat in the fire? Science, the news media, and the 'obesity epidemic'. *Sociological Forum* 23. 1. 53-83. doi: 10.1111/j.1573-7861.2007.00046.x.

Shanahan, Marie-Claire. 2011. Science blogs as boundary layers: Creating and understanding new writer and reader interactions through science blogging. *Journalism* 12. 7. 903-919. doi: 10.1177/1464884911412844.

Shema, Hadas, Judith Bar-Ilan & Mike Thelwall. 2012. Research blogs and the discussion of scholarly information. *PloS One* 7. 5. e35869. doi: 10.1371/journal.pone.0035869.

Shirky, Clay. 2008. *Here Comes Everybody: The Power of Organizing Without Organizations*. New York: Penguin.

Trench, B. 2012. Science blogs – glimpses behind the scenes. In Simone Rödder, Martina Franzen & Peter Weingart (eds.), The Sciences' Media Connection – Public Communication and its Repercussions. *Sociology of the Sciences Yearbook 28*. Dordrecht: Springer Netherlands. 273-289. doi: 10.1007/978-94-007-2085-5.

van Rooyen, Susan, Fiona Godlee, Stephen Evans, Nick Black & Richard Smith. 1999. Effect of open peer review on quality of reviews and on reviewers' recommendations: A randomised trial. *BMJ* 318. 7175. 23-27. doi: 10.1136/bmj.318.7175.23.

Weinberger, David. 2012. *Too Big to Know: Rethinking Knowledge Now That the Facts Aren't the Facts, Experts Are Everywhere, and the Smartest Person in the Room*. New York, NY: Basic Books.

Weingart, Peter. 1998. Science and the media. *Research Policy* 27. 8. 869-879. doi: 10.1016/S0048-7333(98)00096-1.

Wilkins, John S. 2008. The roles, reasons and restrictions of science blogs. *Trends in Ecology & Evolution* 23. 8. 411-413. doi: 10.1016/j.tree.2008.05.004.

EXPLORING THE HYPERMODAL COMMUNICATION OF ACADEMIC KNOWLEDGE BEYOND GENERIC STRUCTURES

JAN ENGBERG
AND CARMEN DANIELA MAIER
AARHUS UNIVERSITY, DENMARK

Abstract: The present study belongs to an extensive project in which we investigate knowledge issues appearing in academic research articles, academic visual essays and academic video essays. The data of our analysis comprises prototype research articles in 7 scientific disciplines and is collected from the homepage of Article of the Future project. This project is an ongoing initiative aiming to revolutionize the traditional format of the research article. In this chapter we focus on the analysis of one of the prototype articles. In order to deal with and reflect upon the implications related to knowledge dissemination of the new multi-resources flows proposed in the prototype article, we adopt a multimodal approach in our analysis. We address the semiotic modes' interaction and combination in order to identify the roles of the semiotic interplay in creating and multiplying meaning at various levels of the generic organization in the hypermodal context. This study aims to extend the focus on 'asymmetric' communication between experts and lay-people, and addresses asymmetries that can appear between experts due to the new requirements for disseminating academic knowledge. The findings of this research work can contribute to a better understanding of the strategies required today and in the future for disseminating academic knowledge across several semiotic modes and media in research genres.

1. Introduction

In this chapter we explore the new hypermodal communication means that are made available for the academic communities on the website of *Elsevier* publishing house. As part of our extended research work focused on academic knowledge communication (Maier & Engber 2013, 2014, in press), "we investigate attempts at realizing the traditional purposes, but under the changed situational conditions of accessibility of more modes, due to the changes in technologically based affordances of the present media" (Maier & Engberg, in press). In the present chapter, we have chosen to focus upon one article (Langus & Nespor 2010) from the publishing house Elsevier's *Article of the Future* project (cf. description of the project below). This shall enable us to demonstrate in some detail the type of analysis we consider appropriate in order to assess the dimensions central for describing the changes with relevance for the knowledge communication process. The aim of the chapter is thus mainly to offer an analytical approach and not to solve a concrete problem.

One of the central assumptions in our work with these new formats of academic knowledge communication and one of the reasons for investigating the format in detail are that there is a literacy issue connected to the introduction of the formats. New formats create new requirements among text producers to master them in order to convey the intended knowledge, among other things because publishers and editors urge authors to comply with new guidelines. And they create new ways of conveying and building knowledge. In order to have access to the knowledge conveyed this way, readers need relevant insights into the new formats as elements of knowledge building processes. We see analyses of the type presented here as ways of explicating the consequences for knowledge building of introducing the new formats. Consequently, we see this chapter and our project as a contribution to creating the basis of acquiring new literacies among researchers.

In their seminal article, Goody and Watt (1963) investigate the differences between non-literate and literate societies and the impact of widespread literacy for the members of the society. Their focus is upon the importance of literacy for the development of a society. They list the following three consequences of literacy for handing on cultural heritage from one generation to the next:

> First, the society passes on its material plant, including the natural resources available to its members. Secondly, it transmits standardised ways of acting. These customary ways of behaving are only partly communicated by verbal means; […] But the most significant elements of any human culture are undoubtedly channelled through words and reside in the particular range of meanings and attitudes which members of any society attach to their verbal symbols. These elements include not only what we habitually think of as customary behaviour but also such items as ideas of space and time, generalised goals and aspirations, in short the *weltanschauung* of every social group. (Goody & Watt 1963:305)

We consider the elements of the new formats as equivalents to the verbal symbols in the quote, i.e. as meaning carriers for which 'readers' need special expertise to be able to understand them according to the intentions of the authors. In previous work (cf. Maier & Engberg 2014), we have investigated some of the advantages of traditional and of more visually oriented presentation of academic knowledge, respectively. There is in any case a question of literacy understood as mastering the presentation format involved here in knowledge building processes. For the advantage of a literate system is dependent on how widespread the knowledge of the system is. Goody and Watt (1963:314) mention as an example that the introduction of written systems of communication in the Egyptian, Mesopotamian and Chinese cultures was limited to "a literate elite of religious, administrative and commercial experts". Participation of citizens outside the group was limited, and thus the advantages of a literate society were limited. In connection with the impact of modern technology, Pauwels (2006:23) highlights the role of a visually literate scientist along the same lines as suggested above:

> Modern technology offers many complex ways of generating images, but few users have a clear understanding of all the steps involved. To counter this "black box syndrome", it is clear that scientists need to keep track of new media technologies to the extent that they offer new ways of looking and (not) knowing.

In the context of this chapter, we replace the *visual literacy* label with *multiliteracy*, spanning multimodal as well as multimedia literacies, when we discuss the complex set of requirements that we are facing today because we need to take into consideration both multimodal and multimedia literacies:

> Multi*modal* literacy can be described as the way in which the audience constructs meaning across the different modes through which content is disseminated. Multi*media* literacy – in contrast – implies the capability of interpreting and creating meaning which is distributed through several media (Maier et al. 2007:456)

The chapter attempts to exemplify how the hypermodal analysis of one of the prototype articles appearing on the above mentioned publishing house' website (*Article of The Future* project, http://www.articleofthe future.com/) can provide relevant insights about the knowledge building processes that can take place when accessing such articles. We hope that achieving such insights may help us all avoid a situation in which distribution of scientific insights is dependent upon a small elite of specialists in the newly introduced formats. In order for the reader of this chapter to have a general understanding of the format of the text analysed here, in Figure 1 we present a screenshot of the beginning of the article that we have chosen for the demonstration of our analysis (Langus & Nespor 2010):

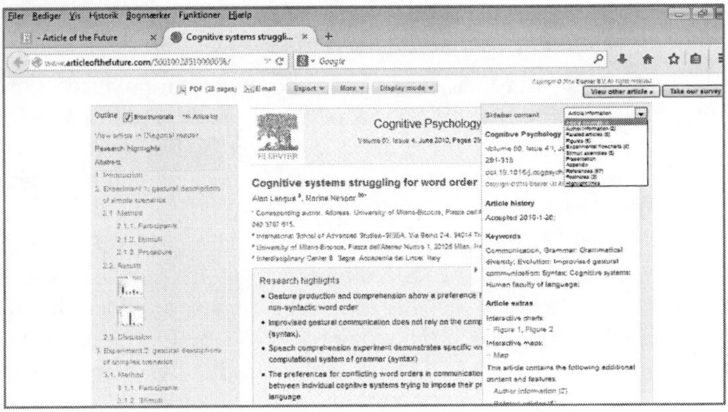

Fig. 1: Screenshot of the article's webpage

As in all articles from the Article of the Future project, the basic layout consists of three basic elements (cf. Zudilova-Seinstra 2013):

- A main content area in the middle, containing the actual article and thus carrying the main burden of the knowledge communication effort of the text. On the webpage, there is also a link to a pdf version of the article. This has a layout similar to the printed version of the journal. In the main content area, the layout has been varied a little, among other things accommodating the research highlights of the article, which are not contained in the pdf version.
- A left pane aimed at enhancing navigation by the reader. It contains the section headlines as clickable links, together with the figures of the article.
- A right pane carrying information supplemental to what is conveyed in the central part. To this belong, among other things, the keywords of the article, information about the authors and some interactive versions of the figures.
- We can thus see that the new format takes advantage of the hypertextual affordances of presenting the article on the screen. For the time being, this superficial description will suffice. In later sections, we will present a systematic analysis.

2. Theoretical Perspectives

2.1 Hypermodality and Knowledge Communication – A System of Analysis

We have started our analytical work with two main premises. Obviously, the first one is that any exploration of these prototype articles should be based on understanding them as *hypermodal texts* because they are designed by exploiting the "conflation of multimodality and hypertextuality" (Lemke 2002:301). These articles are multimodal because they combine several semiotic modes from written text, through still and moving images, to speech and sound. Simultaneously, a network of several types of hyperlinks is at play across the three panes provided by the web environment in which the articles appear. By labelling them in this way, namely hypermodal texts, we can explain how the communication of academic knowledge takes place through processes of *resemiotization* (Iedema 2003) and *remediation* (Bolter & Gruzin 2002).

The second premise, which is closely related to understanding the articles as hypermodal texts, is that, "the distinction between communicatively presenting research in the traditional print format or in a screen format is central" (Maier & Engberg, in press) for the analysis of these articles. Therefore, we have concentrated on the affordances of the screen format that differentiate these prototype articles from the traditional ones (which can, of course, be multimodal too). The fundamental multimodal affordances that are simultaneously offered by the screen format are *multimediality* and *hypertextuality*. The co-presence of several media and hyperlinks is a dynamic means of embedding various generic structures and items of information that can be accessed according to the specific trajectory chosen by the individual user. In this way, the multiliterate user can choose to access various types of knowledge in the most adequate format. Certainly, "the knowledge building processes" (Maier & Engberg, in press) are first of all influenced both by the author's communicative purposes and by the template designed by the professional media experts of the publishing house. But the users can ultimately reconfigure and refine their knowledge building experience in multiple ways due to these affordances. Snyder also states clearly that hypertext "blurs the boundaries between readers and writers" (Snyder 2006:127). While highlighting that "the significance of links in a hypertextual environment is often underestimated", when Burbules examines various hyperlinks from a rhetorical perspective, he also finds that: "selecting and following any particular line of association between distinct textual points involves an interpretation of the nature of the association that link implies" (Burbules 2006:104). Such interpretations may vary from user to user and may also differ from what the author intends to communicate in the article to a higher degree than in the case of traditional research articles.

We adopt Bateman's (2007) general analytical distinction according to which there are two broad categories of features that have to be taken into consideration when approaching "multimodal artefacts": "features concerned with the properties inherent in the document being analysed, and features describing aspects of the conditions of production/consumption of the document" (2007:155).The first category is represented in our analysis by the verbal text of the article and the multimodal relations provided by the static layout features as these are inherent properties of the prototype article. The second category is represented in our analysis by the screen affordances with the dynamic hyperlinking network that has influenced both the production of the article and can also influence the "consumption" of it in various ways.

We have chosen to focus on *multileveled knowledge building processes*, namely knowledge building processes appearing on three levels. At a first level, knowledge building processes are made possible due to the semantic and structural affordances of the verbal text. The strategies to communicate academic knowledge employed at this level are beyond the scope of this chapter. They have been approached many times before from various theoretical perspectives (cf., e.g., Hyland 2009).

At the next two levels, the multimodal relations provided by the static layout features and by the dynamic hyperlinking network represent the fundamental means through which *multileveled knowledge building processes* can potentially take place according to the user's choices:

- At a second level, the static layout features facilitate the appearance of multimodal knowledge building processes.
- At the third level, the hyperlinks facilitate dynamically the appearance of other multimodal knowledge building processes that might include or transform those established statically at the layout level.

While the layout features constituting the second level establish *obligatory relations* between the semiotic modes, in the sense that when reading the text, the reader has no other choice than accepting those relations embedded in the multimodal layout, the hyperlinking network constituting the third level establishes *optional* ones as it gives the user the chance to choose particular trajectories of hypertextual activities. The optionality of those relations influences most of the knowledge building processes and ultimately the understanding of the whole article.

In order to explain the obligatory relations provided by the static layout features,we have employed a categorization of multimodal interactions based on Martinec and Salway (2005), van Leeuwen (2005) and Unsworth (2006):

Tab. 1: Overview of the main categories of multimodal interactions (Maier 2014:126)

KNOWLEDGE BUILDING PROCESSES THROUGH MULTIMODAL INTERACTION (knowledge building inside the document through static layout features)	Concurrence	Elaboration(between text and image)	Specification
			Explanation
		Elaboration (between images)	Similarity
			Overview
			Detail
	Complementarity	Extension	Augmentation
			Contrast
	Connection	Enhancement	Temporal
			Spatial
			Causal

Tab. 2: Knowledge building processes through hypertextual interactivity (Maier & Engberg, in press)

KNOWLEDGE BUILDING PROCESSES THROUGH HYPERTEXTUAL INTERACTIVITY (knowledge building through user's dynamic navigation options)	Knowledge expansion	Core knowledge	Central topics (according to the title of the article's title and abstract)
		Peripheral knowledge	Necessary and presupposed (= part of researchers' background expertise)
			Supplementary (= information items relevant for further reading and research)
	Knowledge enhancement	New domain-specific knowledge	
		Repeated knowledge	
		Other types of new knowledge (usually appearing in other (non-academic) genres)	

For analysing the hypertextual interaction, we draw upon a descriptive system developed in Maier and Engberg (to appear) on the basis of the concept of knowledge building as presented in Scardamalia and Bereiter (2006). The system works with two basic dimensions of description, *knowledge expansion* and *knowledge enhancement* (Table 2). The first dimension concerns the breadth of the knowledge to be built on the basis of the hypertextual interaction (core vs. peripheral knowledge), whereas the second dimension concerns the depth of knowledge, ranging from domain-specific knowledge over repetition to the introduction of knowledge usually appearing in other genres.

These two sets of descriptive systems will be applied in the analyses below.

2.2 Genre

As far as genre is concerned, we depart from characterizing these hypermodal texts as belonging to a staged genre although the rather rigid template imposed by the publishing house might have persuaded us to do so. However, as Thibault highlights:

> The notion of a staged generic structure puts the emphasis on a hierarchical structure that is relatively homogeneous and internally consistent. […] By contrast, hypertext tends towards loosely coupled coalitions of resources that function cooperatively. (Thibault 2012:13)

Thibault's comment is, of course, correct in a general sense. However, the genre of which we investigate an example here is different in the way that it is an attempt to improve researchers' work with research articles online, but without shying researchers away from the journals. In a post on Elsevier's own website one of the people behind the project states that a long process of interviews, group discussions and observations preceded the prototypes presented as part of the project. A central result of these surveys was that reading research articles was mainly done via PDFs, i.e. a print format distributed via the internet: "Our findings clearly indicated that there is a definite need for discipline-specific improvements, but also that scientists plainly love their traditional PDF format." (Zudilova-Seinstra 2013). As a consequence, although the texts of the investigated genre are presented in an online medium and although the idea behind the project is to adjust the scientific article better to this online medium and to take advantage of the affordances of on-screen reading, still the developers have opted for a format that is not in accordance with the characteristics stated by Thibault above:

> Therefore, our starting point in the Article of the Future design was to introduce the discipline-specific content enrichments that only the online format could provide *on top of* the advantages of a PDF reading experience. In this way we would ensure that the new article format would be used and appreciated, and users would not flee to the basic PDF format for basic readability reasons. (Zudilova-Seinstra 2013)

From the point of view of the characteristics of the genre of the investigated text this implicates a certain trend towards hybridity. In order to convince possible skeptical readers the developers have limited the scope of development. This is a good example of the fact that generic evolution is influenced by many different factors. In her work on the development of new genres of corporate reporting (corporate responsibility reports and green advertisements), Garzone (2014:10) distinguishes between influencing factors originating from within the professional discourse communities themselves, on the one hand, and factors stemming from evolutions in society at large, so-called exogenous factors, on the other hand. In the case of the evolution of corporate reporting genres, the exogenous factors play the leading part, as the new types of reporting emerge due to requirements from the society to which the companies belong. In the case of the *Article of the Future* project, the picture is more mixed. The stated goal of the project is "to offer new content and tools that would help researchers in their specific scientific needs" (Zudilova-Seinstra 2013). But at the same time, the surveys cited above showed that many researchers were totally satisfied with the existing PDF format. So the push towards the development represented in articles of the type analyzed here hardly comes from within the discourse community underlying the scientific research article. The push probably comes from two sides:

- From a development in technological possibilities enabling new formats that are explored in many other parts of society and makes traditional presentation formats appear old-fashioned (Maier & Engberg 2014:113).
- From the publisher's intent to create more valuable products in order to enhance the publisher's position in the market and offer services that may distinguish them from their competitors.

An evolution driven mainly by exogenous factors would also be possible here. But the characteristics described in the quote by Zudilova-Seinstra above suggest that the publishers see the scientific journal article as a genre inherently belonging to the discourse community, which therefore has to be driven mainly by endogenous factors. The publishers may suggest changes, but they rely on acceptance from the researchers. The analysis may also give us information on the distribution of power between these two types of factors.

3. Presentation of an Example Analysis

3.1 Main Questions, Basic Description

The analysis of prototype articles of the type investigated here should start with exploring the ways in which hypermodality (cf. above) can influence academic knowledge communication. Our main questions are:

- How does the hypermodal communication of academic knowledge take place?
- What kinds of knowledge building processes are made possible through the text inherent multimodal interactions (level two) and the screen inherent hypertextual interactivity (level three)?

As already stated, we have chosen one of the prototype articles, *Cognitive systems struggling for word order* (Langus & Nespor 2010), in order to exemplify our analytical work, and we have analyzed the article focusing on the multileveled knowledge building processes.

The middle pane which presents the core article includes the following structural sections: *Research Highlights*, *Abstract*, *Introduction*, three sections presenting experiments, *General Discussion*, *Acknowledgements*, *Appendices* and *References*. Each of the experiment sections has the same structure, namely *Method*, *Results* and *Discussion*, while the method part is divided in *Participants*, *Stimuli* and *Procedure*. So, apart from *Research highlights*, we can encounter all the structural sections that might also appear in any traditional research article. *Research Highlights* could also in principle appear in the printed version of a research article, but Elsevier has chosen not to do so:

> Highlights are a short collection of bullet points that convey the core findings and provide readers with a quick textual overview of the article. […] Highlights will be displayed in online search result lists, the contents list and in the online article, but will not (yet) appear in the article PDF file or print. (http://www.elsevier.com/journal-authors/highlights)

As the Research Highlights section does not contain clickable links, so the choice to only implement the section in the online version is not based on a wish to offer hypertextual interactivity as a possibility to the user. It may be based on browsing formats inherent to the online medium: search engines like Google may easier find the articles if central research points are repeated in the text. So the section is there to present to the user the advantages or reading the article. The communicative function of the section is thus probably promotional in nature. In conclusion, the multimodal relations made available in all these sections do not remove this article from the established genre of the traditional research articles either.

This is rather the case with the left and the right panes of the article. In the left pane intended for navigation, the content is verbally displayed with hyperlinks for each section and subsection of the core article. The figures appearing in the core article are inserted here, too, in a smaller sized version, and they are hyperlinked to the bigger sized versions from the middle pane. In the right pane, "task or content specific" (*Article of The Future* project homepage, 2014) additional features and information are embedded and hyperlinked: link to the journal, article history, key words, and links to author information, related articles, figures, experimental flowcharts, stimuli examples, presentation, appendix, references, footnotes and highlight links. Consequently, we find here elements that may also be found in the traditional research articles, but presented in different modes due to the different medium. They are thus examples of the consequences of the remediation process. As we will see below, the remediation of the communicative event actually also creates possibilities of conveying new knowledge.

3.2 Multileveled Knowledge Building Processes – Level Two

As already mentioned, we do not address in this chapter the processes of knowledge building facilitated at the first level by the semantic and structural affordances of the verbal text, but we start at the second level, namely with the categories of multimodal interactions that are established between the semiotic modes and which are provided by the static layout features in the three panes of the article. The number of obligatory relations provided by the static layout features is limited and their characteristics are – not surprisingly – similar to those that can be found in traditional research articles.

In the middle pane, there are several types of images that enter in various relations with the accompanying texts. The first and biggest image accompanies the *Research Highlights* part and displays a white human profile on a light blue background with the superimposed black and white photos of three persons taken from a bird eye view; they have typed words and some geometrical figures at their feet. In front of the profile, the smaller versions of the five figures appearing later in the article are also displayed. Due to the fact that, clearly, this is a metaphorical image, it enters in a complementary relation of augmentative extension with the accompanying text. Usually such metaphorical images which seem borrowed from an advertising context (as both the title and the communicative purpose of this section seem to be, cf. above) are not part of the multimodal structure of traditional research articles, where the emphasis on precision and objectivity is a stringent requirement. The inclusion of this multimodal relation thus underlines the special character of the section. We agree with Lemke (2002), who states that:

> When we combine text and images, each specific imagetext (Mitchell, 1994) is now one possible selection from the universe of all possible imagetexts, and that universe is the multiplicative product of the set of all possible linguistic texts and the set of all possible images. Accordingly, the specificity and precision which is possible with an imagetext is vastly greater than what is possible with text alone or with image alone. (Lemke 2002:303)

However, in the case of the combination of this section, *Research Highlights*, and its accompanying metaphorical image, the acquired "specificity and precision" are not improving the communication of academic knowledge but, instead, advertising it, so the created meanings do not serve the traditional communicative purposes of a research article.

The middle pane contains a single interactive map which enters in a relation of elaborative concurrence with the accompanying text, as the text makes it more specific. The same relation characterizes all the middle pane's figures (be they interactive charts or not) and the accompanying texts.

The right pane contains a wider variety of both still and moving images, but these can be viewed only when accessed by hyperlinking to the webpages embedded in this pane. For example, on the *Author Information* page, the coloured close-ups of the article's authors are displayed with captions containing their names. These images enter in relations of *elaborative concurrence* with their captions as the images make the captions more specific. The five images existing in the middle pane are repeated in this pane, on the *Figures* page, each of them entering in a relation of *elaborative concurrence* with the accompanying caption. From the four *Experimental Flowcharts* pages, hyperlinks give access to several layers of other embedded pages. The still images and the videos existing on these pages enter in complementary relations of *augmentative extension* with the accompanying captions as the images add further information to the text. The sets of 32 vignettes from the same pages enter in relations of *elaborative concurrence* with each other due to their similarity. The eight complex frames into which the 32 simple vignettes are randomly embedded enter into a relation of *elaborative concurrence of overview* with the respective vignettes. The dominant multimodal relation at this level of analysis is thus the elaborative concurrence, in which text and image(s) together convey more specific knowledge than they would if they were not connected to each other. This relation is inherent in the traditional research article too, realized typically in the relation between figures and captions. At a prominent place, at the beginning of the article, we find, however, a different multimodal relation, which also indicates the boosting of the normally more hidden function of research articles to promote the researchers and their ideas and results. Here, the multimodal relation supports the promotional function of a research article, whereas the most frequent relation rather supports the information function.

3.3 Multileveled Knowledge Building Processes – Level Three

At the third level, we have analysed a series of hyperlinks that, due to their dynamic character, facilitate the appearance of new knowledge building processes. Focus is thus here not upon the interaction relations between the multimodal elements, but upon knowledge expansion and knowledge enhancement through hyperlinking interactivity. Hyperlinking interactivity is made available to the user in several ways: inside the article as presented in the middle pane (to other multimodal and multimedial items of information belonging to the respective article), outside the article (to other related articles (in various formats), and across panes. However, in the following analysis we will not use this classification as a guiding principle for structuring the text. Instead, the text will be structured in order to present examples of different knowledge building processes.

Along the dimension of *knowledge expansion*, the main distinction is between the knowledge built by the user belonging to the core knowledge of the article or being peripheral. The hyperlinks from the left pane give only access to the sections, subsections and figures from the middle pane. Therefore, the knowledge built by the hypertextual interactivity of a user in this pane is *core knowledge*. However, from the references section, through hyperlinks to the full documents of the articles that are cited in it, the access to *new supplementary knowledge* is also facilitated. In this way, "the whole research process that exists at the root of the prototype article is made more transparent when users can read the cited articles if they are interested in doing that" (Maier & Engberg, in press). This supplementary knowledge may be accessed through hypertextual interaction from all three panes. A user engaged in this hypertextual interactivity that gives access to related articles may gain a lot of *supplementary knowledge* through knowledge building processes of knowledge expansion. Although it could ease further research work, this hypertextual interactivity may also dilute the impact of the article because the knowledge expansion could take the user to peripheral areas of the domain-specific knowledge that the article is focused on. It is thus an example of supplementary knowledge being useful, but also endangering for the process of accessing the core knowledge. The traditional research article carries this same potential problem, but it is our claim that the ease of accessing supplementary knowledge via hypertextual interactivity strengthens the problem.

In the right pane, hyperlinks also give access to the authors' homepages and email addresses, *Facebook* personal pages and *LinkedIn* profiles from the *Author Information* page. Certainly, authors' homepage addresses and email addresses are also made available to the readers of traditional research articles; but access to *Facebook* personal pages and *LinkedIn* profiles are definitely new. The knowledge to be built is supplementary and does not belong to the core knowledge from the research article. Furthermore, instant access to this kind of information might delay or even hinder the (quality of the) knowledge building processes that are supposed to be experienced by an academic user in contact with the article, but it might also facilitate future collaborations with the respective author at a higher speed. This is another example that supplementary knowledge may be useful, but also potentially counterproductive, to the central knowledge building process.

Concerning the dimension of *knowledge enhancement*, the last-mentioned example of knowledge that can be built through access to the social media networks might also belong to class of *other types of new knowledge*: It is hardly part of the core academic knowledge that the authors are members of different organizations on *LinkedIn*. However, the knowledge may be academically relevant as part of processes of finding relevant partners for research projects and funding application.

We also find an example of directly relevant enhanced knowledge in the right pane. The experiments' pages include the embedded pages of four experiments: gestural descriptions of simple scenarios, gestural descriptions of complex scenarios, gesture comprehension and speech comprehension. Each of the experiment pages permit access to experimental flowcharts and sample stimuli consisting of a series of still images, audioclips and video clips. For example, one experiment reported in the article consists in observing the order of the elements, when participants make gestural descriptions of simple scenarios presented to them in the form of a still picture (Fig. 2). Their performance has been videotaped, and examples are presented and accessible from the right pane. We claim that the knowledge built through access to these experiment pages is *new domain-specific knowledge* because the core knowledge is enhanced through multimodal and multimedial details that are necessary both for the understanding of the article and for further research work.

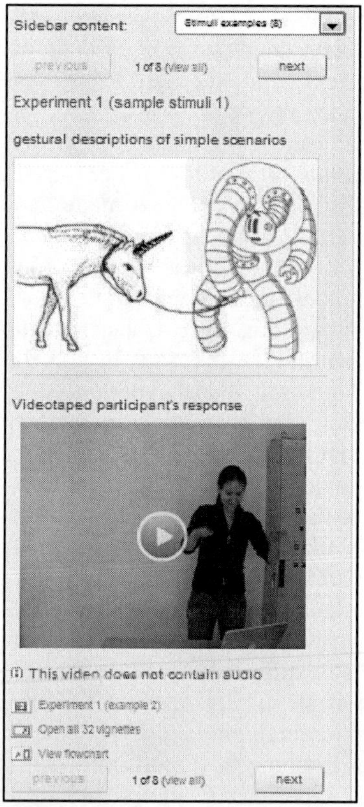

Fig.2: Screenshot of the right pane

Finally, as we mentioned previously in this section, the same texts and images can be accessed from various places in all the three panes and thus give rise to the building of *repeated knowledge*. In the example of the links in the References section to full versions of other articles outside the article itself, the texts may be accessed in the same format; in this case no new knowledge building processes appear; the same knowledge is just replicated. The knowledge enhancement that can be attained through the user's interactivity with the text might affect or even hinder the understanding of the article as it has been intended by the author. However, when in other prototype articles the hyperlinks make available the same texts, but in other formats (for example, in the PowerPoint format for direct use in the class room) which can imply processes of resemiotization, the very purpose of the communicated knowledge is affected as "the primary purpose of the prototype articles, i.e., to build and present new domain-specific knowledge, is accompanied by a secondary new purpose, namely an instructive one" (Maier & Engberg, in press).

6. Conclusions

Two questions should be addressed in connection with our concluding remarks on the presented analysis: the efficiency of the hypermodality inherent in the new format for publishing research articles, and the question of the power relations between researcher and publishers over the development of the genre. Concerning the first question, we have shown that hypermodality may be helpful as well as potentially detrimental to the basic purposes of the genre. Of course the prototype character of the *Article of the Future* texts means that they will as a tendency apply more technological means than absolutely necessary, which also may support our result of finding instances of supplementary and repeated knowledge possibly leading to counterproductive knowledge building processes. But there is no reason to be generally sceptical towards applying the possibilities offered by multimodal and multimedial communication the context of publishing academic research. We have shown that there are many opportunities to enhance knowledge building via these tools.

However, in order to approach the second question, an important point is the relation of power between the different players influencing the development of the genre. As we discussed in the introduction, the new format requires a specific literacy, and this creates an interesting situation to be investigated in future work. The project to which the article analysed here belongs is a case in point. As stated above, the push towards developing the new format comes from the publisher, and the project is carried by software developers and designers (Zudilova-Seinstra 2013). These players have a specific kind of expertise (on the presentation side rather than the generation side of the research article) and may as part of the power struggle claim a place for this knowledge and expertise. Researchers have a different expertise and a different kind of interest, i.e., in the generation side of research results. Expressed in abbreviated form, researchers will be centrally interested in the construction of the core knowledge, whereas publishers will (also) have an important interest in the peripheral knowledge, in order to widen the possible audience of the outlet. However, in the context of this upcoming struggle it should not be forgotten that researchers are by no means disempowered in this connection: researchers are the users (and thus customers) for the products offered by the publishing houses, and it is unlikely that a scholarly journal may exist without the acceptance of the scholars. We are thus heading for an interesting struggle for the power over formats for academic publishing in the following years, which it will be interesting to follow, also analytically.

References

Bateman, John A. 2008. *Multimodality and Genre: A Foundation for the Systematic Analysis of Multimodal Documents*. London: Palgrave Macmillan.

—. 2009. Discourse across semiotic modes. In Jan Renkema (ed.), *Discourse, of course: An overview of research in discourse studies*. Amsterdam/ Philadelphia: John Benjamins. 55-66.

Bateman, John A., Judith Delin & Renate Henschel. 2007. Mapping the multimodal genres of traditional and electronic newspapers. In Terry D. Royce & Wendy L. Bowcher (eds.), *New Directions in the Analysis of Multimodal Discourse*. Mahwah, NJ: Lawrence Erlbaum. 147-173.

Bolter, David & Richard Grusin. 2002. *Remediation: Understanding New Media*. Cambridge, MA: The MIT Press.

Burbules, Nicholas C. 2006. Rhetorics of the Web: Hyperreading and critical literacy. In Ilana Snyder (ed.), *Page to Screen: Taking Literacy into the Electronic Era*. London/New York: Routledge. 102-123.

Garzone, Giuliana. 2014. Evolutions in societal values and discoursive practices: Their impact on genre change. In Giuliana Garzone & Cornelia Ilie (eds.), *Genres and Genre Theory in Transition: Specialized Discourses across Media and Modes*. Boca Raton, FL: Brown Walker. 39-63.

Hyland, Ken. 2009. *Academic Discourse. English in a Global Context*. London: Continuum.

Iedema, Rick. 2003. Multimodality, resemiotization: extending the analysis of discourse as multi-semiotic practice. *Visual Communication* 2. 1. 29-57.

Langus, Allan & Marina Nespor. 2010. Cognitive systems struggling for word order. *Cognitive Psychology* 60. 4. 291-318. http://www.articleofthefuture.com/S0010028510000058/.

Lemke, Jay L. 2002. Travels in hypermodality. *Visual Communication* 1. 3. 299-325.

Maier, Carmen Daniela, Constance Kampf & Peter Kastberg. 2007. Multimodal analysis: An integrative approach for scientific visualizing on the Web. *Technical Writing and Communication* 37. 4. 453-479.

Maier, Carmen Daniela & Jan Engberg. 2013. Tendencies in the multimodal evolution of narrator's types and roles in research genres. In Maurizio Gotti &

Carmen Sancho Guinda (eds.), *Narratives in Academic and Professional Genres*. Bern: Peter Lang. 149-175.

—. 2014. Tendencies of multimodal gradations in academic genres network. In Jan Engberg, Carmen Daniela Maier & Ole Togeby (eds.), *Genre: Encounters between Literature, Knowledge and Developing Communicative Conventions*. Tübingen: Narr. 113-147.

—. In press. Challenges in the new multimodal environment of research genres: What future do Articles of the Future promise us?. In Natasha Artemeva (ed.), *Trends and Traditions in Genre Studies*. Canada: Inkshed Publications.

Martinec, Radan & Andrew Salway. 2005. A System of Text-image Relations in New (and Old) Media. *Visual Communication* 4. 3. 337-371.

Mitchell, William J. T. 1994. *Picture Theory: Essays on Verbal and Visual Representation*. Chicago, MA: University of Chicago Press.

Pauwels, Luc. 2006. A Theoretical framework for assessing visual representational practices in knowledge building and science communication. In Luc Pauwels (ed.), *Visual Cultures of Science. Rethinking Representational Practices in Knowledge Building and Science Communication*. Hanover, NH: Darthmouth College Press. 1-26.

Scardamalia, Marlene & Carl Bereiter. 2006. Knowledge building: Theory, pedagogy, and technology. In Robert Keith Sawyer (ed.), *Cambridge Handbook of the Learning Sciences*. New York: Cambridge University Press, 97-118.

Thibault, Paul. 2013. Hypermedia Selves and Hypermodal Stories: Narrativity, writing, and normativity in personal blogs. In Mariavita Cambria, Christina Arizzi & Francesca Cocetta (eds.), *Web Genres and Web Tools. With Contributions from The Living Knowledge Project*. Pavia: Ibis. 7-49.

Unsworth, Len. 2006. Towards a metalanguage for multiliteracies education: Describing the meaning making resources of language-image interaction. *English Teaching: Language and Critique* 5. 1. 55-76.

Van Leeuwen, Theo. 2005. *Introducing Social Semiotics*. London/New York: Routledge.

Zudilova-Seinstra, E. 2013. Designing the Article of the Future. http://www.elsevier.com/connect/designing-the-article-of-the-future Accessed 22-08-2014.

SECTION II:

DISSEMINATING SCHOLARLY KNOWLEDGE

Talking Science: Science in the News on BBC Radio

Susan Hunston
University of Birmingham

Abstract: Scientists talking on a BBC radio daily news programme face a number of challenges. They need to present their research so as to persuade the public of its value, and balance a concern with newsworthiness with a need for professional caution. The news programme as a whole is faced with a requirement to present a balanced view of controversial issues while prioritizing science over non-science. This paper examines the strategies used in 18 broadcasts, covering a range of scientific issues including health, the environment, and space exploration. In the most successful broadcasts, scientists manipulate the concept of status, to stress their role as interpreters of evidence. They also stress both the novelty and usefulness of their work, and add an affective dimension by indicating that research is interesting or exciting. The paper examines in detail some instances of balancing caution and confidence, as well as the challenges faced by programme makers in attempting to include competing voices in the broadcasts.

1. Introduction

This paper presents a pilot study designed to explore the interpersonal strategies used by scientists presenting their work to the general public in radio interviews. The study is based on 18 interviews with scientists on the BBC radio programme *Today*. It asks three main questions about the interviewees:

- What strategies do scientists use to persuade the public of the value of their research?
- How do the scientists balance the need for persuasion with the need for judicious caution?
- Can 'more successful' and 'less successful' interviewees be identified?

The paper also looks at the role of the interviewer as co-constructor of the representation of research. It examines instances, including one from a television news broadcast, where competing views are presented and considers the consequences of the programme-makers' concerns with balanced reporting.

2. Background to the Study

Tab. 1: Texts used in the study

SEGMENT	TOPIC OF THE SEGMENT	TYPE	DATE OF BROADCAST
A	*Discovery of the Higgs Boson particle*	RTI	4 July 2012
B	*FMRI scanners*	PS	3 Sept 2012
C	*Success in implanting frozen embryos*	RTI	4 Sept 2012
D	*FMRI: Neuroscience and psychiatry*	PS	5 Sept 2012
E	*FMRI: Connectomes*	PS	8 Sept 2012
F	*Galaxy zoo*	RTI	11 Sept 2012
G	*Stress and heart disease*	RTI	14 Sept 2012
H	*Exploration of Mars*	RTI	28 Sept 2012
J	*Polar ice caps*	RTI	15 Oct 2012
K	*Pesticides causing bee death*	RTI	22 Oct 2012
L	*Genes and discordant identical twins*	PS	23 Oct 2012
M	*Explorations of Mercury*	RTI	1 Dec 2012
N	*Interview with Paul Nurse*	RTI	27 Dec 2012
P	*Using biometrics to identify criminal behavior*	RTI	3 Jan 2013
R	*Link between spirituality and mental health*	RTI	3 Jan 2013
S	*Exploration of Mars*	RTI	4 Jan 2013
T	*Patients delay in visiting doctor*	RTI	30 Jan 2013
V	*Formation of stars*	RTI	19 April 2013

The texts used in this study are transcriptions of short reports of scientific research that have been broadcast as part of the BBC radio programme *Today*. This flagship news program is broadcast live daily from 6am to 9am (http://www.bbc.co.uk/programmes/b006qj9z).[1] It consists mainly of news, sports and weather reports and short segments about current affairs: world events, national politics, major crime incidents etc. Segments typically last between 3 and 6 minutes each. Once or twice a week, approximately, the programme includes research-based segments, focusing on health issues (especially research into cancer or heart disease),

[1] In the examples used in this paper, the interviewers are all male, though *Today* interviewers are not exclusively male.

environmental issues (such as evidence of reduction in the polar ice cap, or concerns about bee population failure), or major science projects such as the Large Hadron Collider or the Mars Rover experiments. Table 1 lists the segments studied, in date order. The letter codes will be used in this paper to identify the individual segments.

This paper distinguishes two types of *Today* science segment. For convenience these are referred to below as the *real time interview* (*RTI* in Table 1) and the *prepared story* (*PS* in Table 1). In the real time interview, one of the *Today* presenters interviews a scientist, or occasionally two. The presenter plays the role of intelligent but largely ignorant 'person in the street'. As evidence of this, example 1 is a presenter contribution from a real time interview:

(1) The thing that really makes *your* head hurt if *you*'re an ordinary person and not one of *you lot* is the idea that *you* can look at something that was happening thirteen billion years ago. (V)

The interviewer in this example draws on two uses of *you*: general *you* (the ordinary person) and specific plural *you* (the scientists). In so doing he contrasts the non-expert whose 'head hurts' when faced with extraordinary ideas, with whom he himself identifies, and the expert who is comfortable with such ideas. The apparent rudeness of the phrase *you lot* is mitigated by the acknowledgement that the scientists understand things that ordinary people are incapable of understanding.

In the prepared story, a *Today* journalist, usually the Science Correspondent, presents a series of pre-recorded interviews juxtaposed to form a coherent story. The Correspondent plays the role of informed interpreter of information: he is as likely to make statements as to ask questions. Example 2 is a contribution from the Science Correspondent in a segment about identical twins whose physical differences in adulthood are a source of information about gene switching mechanisms. The correspondent's persona is of fellow-scientist rather than member of the general public:

(2) The mechanism responsible for this built in unpredictability is epigenetic switching, the layer of chemical instructions that overwrites the genetic code, dictating how and when individual genes are switched on or off... (L)

The difference between the roles played by the interviewers is important. In the real time interviews there is no continuity between the viewpoint of the interviewer and that of the interviewee. In example 3 the interviewer sets up a research goal which is not that of the interviewee and which the interviewee later disputes (example 29 below). In example 4 the interviewer challenges the ethical basis of the research, which the interviewee then defends.

(3) That is the next step isn't it you're going to have to try to find some way of working out whether there are micro-organisms there… (H)
(4) What a lot of people listening to this will think is very ingenious but potentially hugely dangerous. (P)

Research into these texts therefore has to draw a distinction between what the *interviewer* says and what the *interviewee* says. In the prepared stories, there is no obvious discontinuity, which means that the researcher can and should treat the interviewer's utterances as constituting part of the scientists' own discourse. On the other hand, the interviewer can be observed to make stronger claims, or claims in stronger terms, than the interviewees do, and there is no evidence as to whether or not the interviewees endorse this. For example, in the identical twins segment (L), all the claims about the medical potential of the research are made by the interviewer. Example 5, spoken by the interviewer, illustrates this.

(5) It's a finding that offers both a new way to diagnose breast cancer and a novel direction for future drug development that aims to turn down the dimmer switch on overactive gene expression. (L)

In segment D, criticisms of psychoanalysis expressed by the interviewees are summarized by the interviewer in a more extreme statement than that used by any of the interviewees: *Freud is bunk*.

All the segments in this paper were broadcast in 2012 and 2013. They were accessed via the *Today* website archive and transcribed by the author.

3. Evidence and Ideology: Marking Status

The attribution of knowledge claims to a source, general or specific, has been studied under a number of headings, including evidentiality, engagement, or the *marking of epistemic status* (e.g. Chafe 1986; Myers 1992; Martin & White 2005; Hunston 2011).

Verbs such as *find*, *hypothesize*, *conclude*, nouns such as *discovery*, *argument*, *evidence*, adverbs such as *clearly*, *possibly*, and adjectives such as *clear*, *possible*, are all resources for negotiating the evidence base of a proposition and the likely reader response to it. The evidence base can be unspecified (*It is clear that*), or specified as a person (*Darwin hypothesized that*) or as a research entity (*The results demonstrate that*). Specifying a person both acknowledges authorship of a claim and contributes to a view of research which highlights the interpretative role of the researcher. Specifying a research entity tends to occlude that interpretative role. The grammatical resources of English make it possible to express complex interactions of propositions in a brief space. Example 6 comes from a popular science text written by an academic biologist.

> (6) However, in the last fifty years, abundant *evidence* from molecular biology has amply *confirmed* Darwin's *suspicions* making it dramatically *clear* that all living organisms on this planet – from humans to hydrangeas, from mollusks to microbes – are descended from a single organism. (Pallen 2009:64)

In this example, the underlined proposition (*all living organisms ... are descended from a single organism*) co-occurs with *making it clear*; this phrase attributes the knowledge claim to an unspecified group and also marks it as having a status paraphrasable as 'this is known'. The proposition is also marked as having previously been only 'thought' (by Darwin) by the noun *suspicions*. The transition from 'thought' to 'known' has come about by the gathering of unspecified 'knowns': *evidence*. The effect of the evidence in producing something 'known' is indicated by the verb *confirmed*. The example illustrates a common finding in science writing: propositions with the lower status of 'thought' are often ascribed to people (e.g. *Darwin's suspicions*) whereas propositions with the higher status of 'known' are ascribed to non-human entities (e.g. *evidence has confirmed*).

The occlusion of the personal or subjective in describing the movement towards knowledge is essential to the construction of a particular ideology of science and is a feature of some of the most mundane words in scientific discourse, such as *show*. In example 7, a nominalized proposition (paraphrasable in full form as 'the fossils are affiliated to some existing animal group') is marked as 'known' (*show*) and attributed to a non-human entity (*Cambrian fossils*). Example 8 is a paraphrase of example 7 that makes clearer the role of the scientist in interpreting data and so constructing knowledge:

> (7) ...even bizarre *Cambrian fossils*, when scrutinized in detail, often *show* affiliations to some existing animal group. (Pallen 2009:161)
>
> (8) When scientists look at Cambrian fossils, they conclude that the fossilized creatures are affiliated to some existing animal group. (Invented)

Attributing a proposition to a non-human entity and thus eliding the interpretative role of the researcher(s) is an important strategy in professional scientific discourse, as it marks the proposition as independent truth, not contingent upon human input, and thus raises the status of the proposition. On the other hand, it does also elide the role of the researcher as expert, who uses his/her skill and knowledge to draw conclusions. For the scientist speaking to (or writing for) other experts, the 'independent truth' effect is more important than the 'expert researcher' one, so formulations similar to (7) are preferred to those similar to (8). As we shall see below, researchers speaking to the general public may make different choices.

As an illustration, consider two examples that describe findings derived from the Mars rover vehicle, Curiosity (segments H and S). In segment H, the speaker attributes to human researchers a proposition marked as a something *found* (example 9), but more frequently attributes to them what is speculation rather than what is known (examples 10, 11).

(9) …we've *found* something scientists have been after… (H)
(10) …scientists were *wondering* if water flowed on Mars (H)
(11) …we sort of *imagine* that what we've got here… (H)

Other knowledge in this segment is attributed to non-human entities, *rocks* (example 12) and *evidence* (example 13).

(12) …rocks provide confirmation of that (H)
(13) …there was clearly evidence for very vigorous flows (H)

In contrast to this, the speaker in the later segment S uses *we* and *scientists* with verbs (*discover*, *realize*, *figure out*) that mark the status of the following statements as 'known' (examples 14-17).

(14) …we've *discovered* our first habitable environment… (S)
(15) …we've *realized* we've landed right on top of an ancient stream bed… (S)
(16) …we've *figured out* all our instruments work fine… (S)
(17) ...we've had scientists…*figure out* where the one site on Mars is… (S)

Conversely, all but one of the propositions marked as 'known' are attributed to scientists. The exception is example 18, where the (nominalized) proposition is attributed to *a site*, but the construction '*tell* someone *about* something' allows for the introduction of the human researchers as *us*.

(18) ...*a site* that would *tell us* about the habitability... (S)

This might be compared to example 12 above, where the possibility to introduce the researchers into a dialogue with the evidence ('the rocks provide us with confirmation...') is not taken up.

In short, the speakers in segment H and segment S present essentially the same information as 'known', but whereas speaker H makes choices more usual in professional scientific discourse (humans speculate, nature shows), speaker S makes rather different choices (humans find out, nature shows humans). Attributing 'known' propositions to researchers in segment S conveys success and confidence. In segment H, attributing 'known' propositions to non-human entities, and speculations to the researchers, arguably gives a less positive impression of the research.

Attribution of knowledge claims can be used to good effect in situations of conflict between researchers. In segment D, for example, a distinction is drawn between the 'real science' of neuroscience and the 'pseudoscience' of psychoanalysis. Example 19 shows how status markers are used in the argument. Status markers are in italics and are discussed below.

(19) *What we've found* is that the unconscious mind is not really th- worked the way Freud Jung and people in the twentieth century *believed*... They they would *extrapolate* and form *ideas and theories* based on talking to their patients. The unconscious is not hidden from us for emotional or motivational reasons as Freud *thought*... (D)

In this example, the knowledge attributed to Freud and Jung is downgraded in status terms, using markers of low factuality: *believed*, *extrapolate*, *thought*; *ideas*, *theories*. By contrast, the knowledge attributed to the speaker and colleagues is given the higher status marker *found*. As in the examples above, the speaker chooses to attribute this knowledge to human researchers (*what we've found is that...*) rather than to their research as a non-human entity (e.g. 'what our research has indicated is that...').

The same set of segments (B, D, and E) illustrate another feature of evidentiality: the high level of reliability attributed to visual evidence. Interviewees in these three segments all refer to the value of the FMRI scanners in providing visual evidence, using the verbs *see*, *look* and *watch* (examples 20-24), thus attributing knowledge to visual evidence.

(20) Functional magnetic resonance imaging or FMRI has allowed scientists ... to *see* what's happening... (B)

(21) ...these non-invasive techniques that allow us to actually *look* inside the human central nervous system... (B)

(22) Functional Magnetic Resonance Imaging allows researchers to *see* what's happening… (D)
(23) Suddenly scientists could *look* into the brain and *watch* it at work… (D)
(24) …by looking with higher resolution we'll actually be able to *see* something visibly wrong in the brain… (E)

Attributing knowledge and marking epistemic status, then, is one way that a positive representation of research can be made. Through judicious use of language resources linked to status, researchers not only assess the propositions they express as 'known' but also tell a research story in which the role of the researcher as 'see-er' and as 'thinker' is crucial to the success of the enterprise.

4. The Value of Research: Novelty and Usefulness

For the scientist contributing to the *Today* programme, it is not sufficient that the reported research should be successful in terms of making discoveries. The speakers also argue for the value of the research in terms of its novelty and its practical applications.

A large part of the newsworthiness of scientific research lies in its application to 'real world' problems. Table 2 shows a short example from each segment (where the segment contains such examples) that illustrates evaluation addressing the *utility* criterion. Of the 18 segments, 13 include assertions that the research reported has applications outside the immediate academic environment. In some cases (e.g. segment D) the evaluation is very overt, and this occurs where the utility value of the research has been questioned in the past. In the segments relating to environmental issues (J, K, W) the importance is taken for granted rather than asserted. The segments dealing with space exploration are less likely to claim utility. In segment S, however, the speaker does relate the exploration of Mars to a kind of utility: meeting the human need for exploration. In segments B and L, the evaluation is made by the interviewer rather than by an interviewee. Special attention might be drawn to two of the segments where the utility of the research is questioned rather than asserted by the interviewee. The speaker in N challenges the notion that she is 'finding a cure for cancer' and replaces this with a prediction that treatments of limited effectiveness will be found for some cancers. In segment R the interviewer proposes a practical application of research into the correlation between 'non-religious spirituality' and poor mental health ('tell people suffering from poor mental health not to be spiritual'), but the interviewee rejects this.

Tab. 2: The *usefulness* of research: examples

SEGMENT	EXAMPLE
A	None
B	IR: Similarly rapid advances in our understanding of the genetics and basic chemistry of the brain have raised the prospect of genuine breakthroughs across a range of previously intractable neurological disorders including Alzheimer's and Parkinson's
C	these findings are very reassuring for cryopreservation programs and very reassuring for women who have got frozen embryo transfer
D	all mental illnesses are brain disorders that warrant proper investigation of a biological nature including scanning and that it will be of use of clinical utility in the near future
E	So by looking with higher resolution we'll actually be able to see something visibly wrong in the brain of people with er disorders like schizophrenia or autism
F	None
G	what we've found is people who reported high job strain that's high levels of job demands coupled with low job control were at increased risk for the development of a heart attack
H	None
J	if that continues you know that holds the prospect that we might see an ice free Arctic only during the summer in the peak of the Arctic summer for perhaps even only one day
K	they're important pollinators of both agricultural crops and wild plants so we rely on them er not only to pollinate … the crops for foods that we eat but also to maintain the … diversity of flora in the landscape that we enjoy
L	IR: The first of a series of papers from Professor Specter's team looking at epigenetic switching in breast cancer has identified one particular gene, DOK7, that when stuck in the on position appears to increase an individual's risk of developing the disease.
M	None
N	In my lifetime I believe there will be a progression in the treatment at least so maybe not a cure but the treatments of cancer will improve definitely to a point where there will be certain types of cancer that we might be able to treat to a sufficient stage that somebody could live with
P	we were working with the metropolitan police and we had to match a bag snatcher on two different days and we could come up with a matching procedure which was sufficient … for the court's purposes
R	IR: But I mean are you seriously saying to people don't think of yourself as spiritual and you'll [laughs] you'll be better… IE: That's the utilitarian implication of what does this research mean in terms of people's health but- No I don't think you can think like that.
S	People across the world not just in the in the US here er we have astronauts and we have human space explorers because we want to be out there exploring ourselves. It's the reason we climb mountains and sail across oceans and et cetera. And so I think we're going to go- send human beings to Mars and it will not just be for science it will be for human exploration
T	we need to research further what what might be causing people to worry about wasting the doctor's time
V	None

Novelty value greatly enhances the newsworthiness of research. Table 3 gives examples of evaluations of the reported research as new. Eleven of the 18 segments include evaluative language of this kind. Apart from segment S, where the novelty is expressed in the word *first*, the speakers contrast what was known before (e.g. *we were always worried in past* [sic]; *we used to think that…*) with what is known now. The novelty of the research also enhances its importance, and some of the segments include evaluative expressions of heightened intensity: *a series of major breakthroughs* (segment B); *has caused a revolution in our understanding* (segment D); *defies all expectations of what our current theories would predict* (segment V).

Tab. 3: The *novelty* of research: examples

SEGMENT	EXAMPLE
A	We know something about the universe that we didn't yesterday
B	I think we're really on the cusp of a series of major breakthroughs in our understanding of the brain.
C	very reassuring for women who have got frozen embryo transfer and pregnancies as a result of them because we were always worried in past that what freezing is going to do to embryo and the resulting baby
D	Scientists were suddenly able to connect the behaviour with processes in the brain and that- that's caused a revolution in our understanding of the unconscious mind.
E	IR: You'll all have heard of the genome and if you're up to date with cutting edge concepts in science you'll have heard of the epigenome. Well there's another -ome coming around for you to impress your friends with, it's the connectome – the network of all the pathways that link the neurones in your brain.
F	None
G	the old view that stress at work is simply to do with having too much to do has really been refined by this notion of how much discretion and control you have over how the work is done
H	None
J	we know that the area of the ice has been going down for about thirty years but what's new is we're now actually able to measure the thickness
K	None
L	We used to think that biology and genetics was pretty simple. You had DNA which really composed of genes and genes made proteins which ran your body. But we know it's not that simple.
M	None
N	None
P	IR: You want to catch a criminal in the old days well you'd use fingerprints perhaps an identity parade if the miscreant had shown his face and well that was really about it. Now of course there's DNA we can also scan faces even eyes but we are on the cusp of going much further.
R	None
S	we've already discovered our first habitable environment

T	None
V	we've seen this this galaxy with the Herschel Space Observatory … that defies all expectations of what our current theories would- would predict

Two of the segments (B and P) use the phrase *on the cusp of* (examples 25 and 26).

(25) …we're really *on the cusp of* a series of major understandings… (B)
(26) …we are *on the cusp of* going much further (P)

Technically this downgrades the importance of the findings, in the sense that the important breakthrough is imminent but has not taken place yet. Pragmatically, though, it implies that an important discovery is imminent and certain.

5. The Value of Research: Doing Good Research

It has been demonstrated that in scientific research articles, where objectivity is valued over subjective response to the evidence, one way that an evaluation of the work undertaken can be implied rather than stated is by asserting that a *goal of the research has been achieved.* In the *Today* segments, also, research is given positive value by stating that it has achieved its stated goals. Table 4 gives some examples. Of the 18 segments, 13 express an evaluation of this kind. Some simply state a research goal and a finding (e.g. segment K: *to see how exposure might affect... we found that*). Others are more emphatic about the goal (e.g. segment H: *something that many scientists have been after for quite a long time now*) or about the equipment necessary to produce a result (e.g. segment B: *these non-invasive techniques that allow us to actually look inside the human central nervous system*, or segment V: *the Herschel Space Observatory is a great way of finding these galaxies*). It might be noticed that in many cases the assertion that a goal is achieved is linked with an indication of Affect (see below).

Tab. 4: Research *achieves its goals*: examples

SEGMENT	EXAMPLE
A	The Higgs is the last piece of the standard model and it's great that we've completed that
B	what's been particularly fantastic in the past ten to fifteen years has been the arrival of these non-invasive techniques that allow us to actually look inside the human central nervous system
C	None
D	Until fairly recently neuroscience has not really been delivering very clear messages about human behaviour about the human mind but we're getting very close to that at least some people would say we are.
E	None
F	another thing humans are good at are finding the really unusual galaxies and each of those can tell us something fundamental about what happens
G	None
H	What we've found is something that er many scientists that study Mars have been after for quite a long time now
J	we're now actually able to measure the thickness from which we can get the volume which actually gives you the total amount of ice in the Arctic not just how much area is covered.
K	my colleague Richard Gill and I were looking at it to see how exposure to realistic levels of two pesticides might affect bumble bees and we found that the two pesticides affected bees in rather different ways and exposure to both at once had more severe effects on the colonies
L	None
M	None
N	So I've taken these pictures on the microscope I've stained the outer layer of the cells so I can see the outside of it so I can get an accurate measure of this population of cells and exactly how many microns they are in length.
P	and if you measure them carefully enough you can absolutely tell even if someone's completely covered their face and every other part of their body if you get a shot of their ear you can tell who they are
R	that's a really important issue. And we have some forthcoming research that tried to tackle this question by following people over a long period.
S	so using these orbiters we've mapped the planet in detail and we've actually had several hundred scientists work for better part of five years to figure out where the one site on Mars is that we would send this rover to both understand the habitability of ancient Mars
T	IR: it happens to such an extent indeed that researchers think it helps explain why we are less likely to survive cancer than people in so many other countries
V	the Herschel Space Observatory is a great way of finding er these galaxies so that the team using it are searching for all sorts of distant galaxies

One difficulty for the researchers is that the interviewers (in real-time interviews) may have their own idea about what the goals of the research should be. In segment H, for example, the interviewer uses his questions to establish hypothetical goals for the research: discovering whether life existed and might still exist on Mars (examples 27 and 28).

(27) … are you going to find out do you think now how long ago that water was on the surface and really crucially whether any of the life that it might have supported might still be there in some form… (H)
(28) That is the next step isn't it you're going to have to try to find some way of working out whether the- there are micro-organisms there or or or past micro-organisms and and bringing us that kind of that crucial evidence that's missing (H)

The interviewee explains that these goals cannot be met for the foreseeable future:

(29) … we don't really have the ability to do life detection… (H)
(30) … hopefully some day we'll be able to answer your question… (H)

In allowing the interviewer to set the agenda in this way, the interviewee runs the risk of making the research appear ineffective, even though its own goals have indeed been met.

For goals to be met, and for outcomes to be reliable, the research procedure has to be robust. For the most part, the segments give little detail about the *research methodology* used, but 13 of the 18 segments do evaluate their methodology positively, often in tandem with stating that the methodology successfully achieves the research goals (see table 5 for examples).

Tab. 5: Comments on *research methods*: examples

SEGMENT	EXAMPLE
A	None
B	the arrival of these non-invasive techniques that allow us to actually look inside the human central nervous system
C	we collated the data from eleven studies so the number got quite large up to thirty seven thousand pregnancies the ideal scenario was- would- that we would do a randomized control trial comparing fresh embryos with frozen embryos we kind of have to settle for this kind of study which is trawling the literature and making associations between previous published studies
D	Suddenly scientists could look into the brain and watch it at work
E	by looking with higher resolution we'll actually be able to see something visibly wrong in the brain of people with er disorders like schizophrenia or autism, brain diseases like Alzheimer's and so on
F	you go to Galaxy Zoo dot org and there're a couple of simple questions so we say things like can you see any spiral arms in this galaxy can you see whether the galaxy has a bulge in its centre

G	None
H	with the Rover is just driving along we've found the kind of rocks that that really finally er provide confirmation of that
J	as far as the CryoSat measurements go we've been able to er validate our measurements using both two sets of aircraft a European Space Agency aircraft and NASA aircraft and also some moorings in the ocean underneath the ice which measure how thick it is so we know that CryoSat is probably making measurements accurate to about ten centimetres in thickness which is good enough to say what our decline in volume is
K	None
L	None
M	None
N	So I've taken these pictures on the microscope I've stained the outer layer of the cells so I can see the outside of it so I can get an accurate measure of this population of cells and exactly how many microns they are in length
P	we could come up with a matching procedure which was sufficient and er for the for the court's purposes
R	this was a national survey in this country
S	It's one of the reasons we have deployed orbiters around Mars for several years before attempting to land with our you know kind of you our eggs in one basket in this billion dollar Rover in one location and so using these orbiters we've mapped the planet in detail and we've actually had several hundred scientists work for better part of five years to figure out where the one site on Mars is that we would send this rover
T	None
V	we've seen this this galaxy with the Herschel Space Observatory and then other other ground based observatories

Segment C goes furthest in evaluating a methodology both positively and negatively, with the meta data study being judged against a hypothetical randomized trial. Segment N is unusual in that it goes into a great deal of detail about the importance of carrying out large numbers of (rather tedious) measurements in order to make reliable statements. In the other segments, a recurring theme is the value of equipment (FMRI scanners in B, D and E; telescopes in J and V; the Mars rover in H and S) and the value of being able to 'see' as opposed to 'deduce' something (as noted above).

6. The Value of Research: The Affective Dimension

An obvious distinguishing feature of the radio segments discussed here is the overtness of the evaluation used. In addition to the examples discussed above, there are instances where overt expressions of *Affect* are used. For the most part, speakers express themselves *excited* by discoveries (example 31), or *interested* by questions (example 32), or *concerned* by possible outcomes (example 35). In the FMRI segments they describe the brain patterns they are seeing as *beautiful* (example34).

(31) We are extremely excited it's a momentous day for science (A)
(32) … there's a number of interesting questions that this paper kind of throws out (L)
(33) The most exciting thing is really… (S)
(34) these layers inside the hippocampus really beautifully here it has this beautiful the swirls of the hippocampus (B)
(35) these are things we should be that we should be concerned about (K)

7. Finding a Balance: Confidence and Caution

Research into the reporting of science in news media has identified the competing priorities of the journalists and scientists (Hansen 1994; Highfield 2000). It is suggested that scientists must grapple with the difficulty of achieving a balance between "topicality, sensation and relevance to readers" on the one hand and "the canonical scientific values of caution, qualification and precision" on the other (Jones 2012:970). Some researchers argue that the demand from news channels to stress the important and the exciting tends to lead to scientific 'hype'. The complaint of hype is well-known in the scientific community and in December 2012 was the subject of an interview on the *Today* programme with Nobel prize-winner and President of the Royal Society Paul Nurse (Segment N; see Table 1). Nurse argued that the demand of the media for big stories and emotionally engaging interviewees leads to a misrepresentation both of the process of research and of the significance of results.

Scientists on the *Today* programme, then, are challenged to *balance confidence in their work with caution about asserting claims* that might be premature. In this section I look at three illustrations of how speakers negotiate this difficult ground, using a variety of strategies.

The first illustration comes from segment E. This is the final of three prepared segments about the potential of FMRI scanning. Segment E is about work on connectomes, defined as *the network of all the pathways that link the neurones in your brain*. This work is described as being beyond current resources and highly speculative, as explained in example 36.

(36) Mapping that complexity even in a mouse brain is proving to be a colossal computational challenge … It would take a hundred thousand person years for someone to do for a cubic millimeter of

> brain tissue… The complete map of the human connectome then remains a distant long-term goal… (E)

What is interesting is that because this raises unanswerable questions it is comparable to example 29 and 30 above, from segment H. However, whereas examples 29 and 30 might be interpreted by listeners as indicating a lack of success, example 36 is contextualized in a way that suggests a greater degree of optimism. It is immediately followed by example 37:

> (37) But the hope is we won't have to complete the picture to begin to pick up useful insights into how information thoughts and memories are encoded in the brain or what might be going wrong as individuals begin to develop degenerative diseases or psychological conditions like schizophrenia and autism (E)

The strategy used by this speaker is to embed the more challenging nature of their work in the context of its usefulness in tackling real-world problems. What is unknown is subordinated to the fact that it has a high social value.

Subordination of one kind of information to another is found in the second illustration, from segment S. Example 38 is an extended extract from the interview.

> (38) *The most exciting thing* is really that *we've already discovered* our first *habitable environment*. You know this is *the mission is all about* is *figuring out if* the environments in the past were such that that they *could support microbial life*. And the fact that we've realized that we've landed right on top of an- of an ancient stream bed where *water was flowing you know ankle deep or knee deep at some point in the past* is *is pretty exciting*. (S)

What is interesting about this example is that, as similar segments explain, the Mars rover is not designed to establish whether life ever existed on Mars. The aim of the project is to find evidence of conditions that could have supported life, not to investigate whether they ever did so. Example 29 above expressed this negatively. In example 38, however, the position is expressed positively. The fact that life is only potential, and of a low level, is placed in a subordinate position, modifying nouns (*habitable environment; microbial life*) and verbs (*could support*) and these in turn are subordinated to markers of high epistemic status: *we've already discovered…; figuring out if…*, and to evaluations of affect and of importance: *the most exciting thing is...; the mission is all about…; …is pretty exciting*. Thus, although limitations on the research are expressed, the grammatical structures used ensure that the overriding impression is one of success and importance.

Perhaps most striking of all in example 38 is the clause *water was flowing ankle deep or knee deep at some point in the past*. From the figurative *ankle deep or knee deep* it could be inferred that the water was experienced by a living entity possessing limbs, something that the Curiosity discoveries certainly do not indicate. Without actually exaggerating claims or violating professional caution, the interviewee nonetheless offers the listener the possibility of building a more detailed picture of life on Mars than the research fully justifies.

I shall discuss the final illustration in this section in a little more detail. Segment C comprises real time interviews with two interviewees on the topic of in vitro fertilization. The first interviewee has carried out a meta-data study, covering 37,000 pregnancies altogether, that demonstrates that embryos implanted after being frozen for a period of time are not more likely to suffer medical problems before or immediately after birth than are embryos that have been implanted without having been frozen. The second interviewee is asked to comment on the study. The second interviewee's contribution is discussed here.

The interviewee is cautious in his comments, as demonstrated in examples 39 to 41. The study is not ideal and we have to *settle for* it (39); the reassurance it offers is incomplete (40); it leaves essential questions unanswered (41).

(39) …the ideal scenario was- would- that we would do a randomized control trial comparing fresh embryos with frozen embryos. That would be quite a mammoth undertaking … so we kind of have to *settle for* this kind of study… (C)

(40) …it provides us with *an element of reassurance*… (C)

(41) …the long term health of these babies is *still in question* and *what this study does is it shows* that during the pregnancy and around the time of the delivery *everything looks great*. (C)

Looking more closely at example 41, however, demonstrates how the element of uncertainty (*still in question*) is counter-balanced by the emphatic nature of the pseudo-cleft construction (*what this study does is it shows…*) and by the positive evaluation *everything looks great*.

Another example of counter-balance is co-constructed by the interviewer and interviewee. As shown in example 42, a question about the level of certainty to be attached to the research is answered with a positive reply token (*yeah*) followed by the positive evaluation *provides*.

This balances and is balanced by the more cautious *element of reassurance*.

(42) IR: But does it tell us anything for certain do you think. IE: Yeah I think it *provides* us *with an element of reassurance…* (L)

Finally, the interviewee stresses the novelty and potential agenda-changing nature of the research, whilst at the same time indicating that there are missing elements to it. What is missing is expressed in terms of *interesting questions* (Affect) and the need to reconsider previously-held assumptions (*perhaps we've been looking at this in the wrong way … which we don't yet fully understand*) (novelty) (example 43).

(43) Yeah there's a number of *interesting questions* that this paper kind of throws out. The first is there could be subtle differences between the women um having the fresh and frozen cycles. … And *perhaps we've been looking at this in the wrong way...* maybe the selection and freezing of which embryos to freeze and which survive the thawing process imposes another level of selection *which we don't yet fully understand.* (L)

In sum, this speaker expresses a considerable level of caution and uncertainty, but does so in the context of expressing confidence where it is warranted and stressing the novelty and potential of the research. I would argue that he manages to convince that the research is of value and successful without exaggerating its claims.

8. Finding a Balance: Managing Conflicting Voices

A second common theme in research about science in the news is the role of *editorial 'balance'* in giving undue influence to 'maverick' or 'pseudo-scientific' voices and allowing them equal weight with mainstream scientific views (Tanner 2004; Sumptner & Garner 2007; Taylor 2010). This is a complaint made by Paul Nurse (see above, segment N), who argues that the BBC's legal obligation to present 'balanced' accounts has led programme-makers into giving equal air time to 'maverick' pseudo-science as to genuine science. Where the public gives greater credence to the maverick point of view there can be negative consequences, for example in the area of public health.

To investigate how balance is managed discoursally I look at two examples. The first comprises two segments concerning the decline in the bee population. Segment K is a *Today* real time interview; for the second I turned to a prepared story presented on BBC World News television (dubbed here segment W). Segment K presents only one view: that experiments show that when two unnamed pesticides are used in combination they exacerbate bee mortality. The research is evaluated as important, because a healthy bee population is important (example 44). There is an affective dimension, but related to worry and concern rather than to excitement (example 45). Finally, the status accorded to the research is carefully modulated. High epistemic status is indicated by *we found that…* and *our research is showing* (example 46), but the researcher concedes that other contributing factors to bee death should be considered as well (example 47).

(44) a serious threat to the survival of the bumble bee… they are essential pollinators… they're important pollinators of both agricultural crops and wild plants… [the pesticides] are actually having serious effects on both individual behaviour and colony performance. (K)

(45) I think these are things we should be that we should be concerned about. (K)

(46) *we found that* the two pesticides affected bees in rather different ways and exposure to both at once had more severe effects on the colonies… I think *our research is showing* that even at relatively low levels sort of *realistic concentrations bees might be exposed to in the wild* are actually having significant effects on both individual behaviour and colony performance. (K)

(47) these pesticides are one stress that the bees are facing and there's a lot of stress on bee colonies at the moment… habitat changes are important, nutrition might be important new diseases that are coming in also important but this is one element. (K)

The research is not challenged in the interview; nothing is made, for example, of the fact that the research was carried out in a laboratory rather than under field conditions, though this is referred to obliquely in example 46: *realistic concentrations bees might be exposed to in the wild.*

Subsequent to this news item, a group of pesticides known as neonicotinoids have become the subject of a European Union ban (http://www.bbc.co.uk/news/world-europe-22335520). There is both support for and opposition to this ban within the UK, and segment W reports this debate. It consists of brief statements from four individuals, linked by an unseen interviewer. On the side of the ban, and against the use of neonicotinoids, there is an organic bee-keeper and a representative of the Soil Association. Opposing the ban, and supporting the use of neonicotinoids, there are representatives of the Food and Environment Research Agency (the only researcher appearing in the segment) and of the National Farmers Union. Speaking informally, either side – the 'environmental activists' or the 'narrow-minded famers' – could be the mavericks. I shall argue, however, that the segment itself construes the pro-neonicotinoid-use side as mainstream science and the anti-neonicotinoid-use side as maverick science, surprisingly in the light of segment K, and that, even more surprisingly, the maverick side is presented more favourably.

The arguments in the segment might be summarized as follows. The bee-keeper and the Soil Association representative, against the pesticides, argue that: bee populations are declining; bee death is a serious problem because of the importance of bees to pollination; there is evidence that neonicotinoids are contributing to this decline. The representatives of the Food and Environment Research Agency and of the National Farmers Union, in favour of the pesticides, argue that: because there are a number of factors that contribute to bee population decline, changing only one factor is not helpful; there is insufficient evidence that neonicotinoids are a major factor in bee deaths; neonicotinoids are useful to farmers, and banning them will have negative consequences.

The interviewer achieves neutrality, in Greatbatch's (1992) terms, by using the same kinds of markers of epistemic status for each side. Reporting the Soil Association he ascribes a statement to 'belief '(*believe*):

(48) some *believe* the pesticides called neonicotinoids are making matters worse (W)

He uses similar language (*belief*) in reporting the Food and Environment Research Agency:

(49) *here* at the food and environment research agency near York they say the issues are far more complex… the *belief here* is that far more research is needed (W)

Where higher status is construed, it is again done for each side equally. Example 50, anti-neonicotinoid and using the status marker *show*, is balanced by example 51 reporting contradictory research and using the status marker *found*.

(50) many of the scientists are *showing* erm that there's a huge problem in terms of the impact of neonicotinoids (W)
(51) They studied bumble bees and *found* no adverse effect (W)

Although the interviewer constructs neutrality, balance is not so evident when it comes to the interviewees. As examples 50 and 51 suggest, empirical research has been carried out on both sides, but the only scientist to speak for himself is from the Food and Environment Research Agency, on the pro-pesticide side (example 52). The Soil Association representative does not speak as a scientist but simply reports research carried out by others (example 53). Furthermore, the interviewer uses the deictic *here* (twice) in example (49), implying an alignment with that point of view that is not present when the other interviewees are introduced.

(52) It's the weather conditions that play the most important role, impact of pests and diseases, colony management (W)
(53) Really many of the scientists are showing erm that there's a huge problem in terms of the impact of neonicotinoids … (W)

Thus it appears that it is the pro-neonicotinoid-use side of the debate that is construed as mainstream science, the view that is to be believed. It is perhaps surprising, then, that one piece of information that supports the mainstream science argument is omitted while another is given little prominence, though both can be gleaned from other items on the BBC website.[2] The argument that without access to neonicotinoids farmers would fall back on (even) more harmful pesticides is not mentioned in the segment. The argument that the research discovering the harmful effects of neonicotinoids was carried out in the laboratory rather than in the field is referred to obliquely in a subordinate clause (*If … real world*) used by the National Farmers Union representative in example 54:

(54) *If we can't find those harmful effects in the real world* then we sure know that we will not be able to measure any benefits resulting from a ban on neonicotinoids (W)

The omission of these points would seem to weaken the mainstream science argument and thus favour the maverick argument. The structure of the segment also favours the mavericks. It begins and ends with pictures of bees and statements about how important bees are as pollinators and the fact that bee colonies are dying. The opening of the segment in particular is arguably emotive, as the beekeeper displays a hive containing dead bees. This argument – bees are both important and at risk –is not in itself evidence for or against the action of the neonicotinoids, but the structure of the segment suggests that the connection exists. The interviewer's final utterance, ending the segment, maintains neutrality technically but implies support for the maverick side (example 55).

---

[2]See, e.g., http://www.bbc.co.uk/news/science-environment-22339191 (accessed 13 August 2013).

(55) It's [Pollination by bees is] a huge help to the very farmers that those supporting a ban believe are worsening the plight of the honey bee. (W)

This somewhat convoluted statement might be paraphrased as: 'It is ironic that bees help farmers, but farmers are killing them by using neonicotinoids (some people say)'.

In short, the segment demonstrates a concern to avoid bias, but two factors nevertheless contribute to bias: parts of the mainstream science argument are omitted or downgraded; and the segment is structured in such a way as to stress emotively the dire consequences of bee population decline rather than to question the link between that decline and neonicotinoids. The conclusion, however, begs the question of the accuracy of casting the anti-neonicotinoid lobby in the role of 'maverick' and the pro-neonicotinoid lobby in the role of 'mainstream science'. As noted above, it is the segment itself that assigns these roles, creating a dichotomy between 'correct but unappealing' and 'unproven but emotionally appealing'. The risk is that both sides of the argument suffer: the one side because it is dull and emotionally unsatisfying; the other side because its science is unconvincing.

The second example is a rare instance of disciplinary conflict (segment D). In this prepared story, the discipline of Neuroscience is contrasted with traditional Psychology. The findings produced by FMRI scanners are evaluated positively as having a 'known' status, whereas earlier researchers such as Freud made statement that were more speculative (see the discussion of example 19 above). The FMRI procedures are also evaluated positively as constituting 'real science', using technology to make direct observations (see the discussion of examples 20-24 above), in opposition to the 'pseudo-science' of Freud and Jung. Example 56 illustrates both the contrast of status (*found* versus *believed*) and the negative evaluation of the psychoanalysts (*they weren't even scientists*).

(56) What we've *found* is that the unconscious mind is not really th- worked the way Freud Jung and people in the twentieth century *believed* who didn't have access to these new technologies and in fact *they weren't even scientists*.

In line with a commitment to balance, the psychoanalytical view is given a voice, from a professor of psychology, who adopts three strategies, each illustrated in example 57.

(57) *It's like looking at a painting* in terms of the chemical components of the paint… *It's an extreme materialist position.* It's one that says well *I can see the brain that's what really must be going on*. Feelings emotions thoughts ideas we can't see them therefore they're not real. And that leads to *a distortion of human experience* and also it affects the way we want to treat people. So instead of coming to understand them and to help them come to *a richer understanding of* their lives we would like to manipulate their brain.

One strategy is to label the opposing view negatively: *an extreme materialist position*; *a distortion of human experience*. Another is to contrast the value of 'seeing' (*I can see the brain that's what really must be going on*) with that of 'understanding' (*a richer understanding of their lives*) as alternative views, both of what is real, and of what is useful in helping people suffering emotional distress. This could be said to counter the neuroscientists' strategy of drawing on visual evidence as the most likely to convince. The third strategy is the use of analogy (*it's like looking at a painting…*), which places the debate within a more general context of the validity of both materialist and humanist perspectives on a single phenomenon.

As in the neonicotinoids segment (W), the interviewer achieves neutrality by citing views assigned to others:

(58) IR: And what this new evidence-based understanding of the unconscious mind tells us, Leonard Molodnov argues, is that there's no hidden meaning or emotional value attached to the subliminal processing that goes on in the brain…. Psychologists have rejected this narrow biologically determinist view

The last word, however, is given by the programme-makers to the neuroscience viewpoint:

(59) Even concepts like love and hate and fear and anger and friendship and loyalty we will get some kind of mechanistic description of those. After all if we don't then what other sort of explanation could there be.

9. Conclusion

Although this is only a preliminary and exploratory study, it is now possible to return to the questions raised at the beginning of this paper.

What strategies do scientists use to persuade the public of the value of their research? The paper has demonstrated the use of evidentials and status markers and has argued that these features are used not only to persuade the listener that the research has led to believable results, but to enhance the role of the researcher in achieving those results. It has also shown the establishment of a number of value parameters, notably *utility*, *novelty*, *achieving goals* and *reliable methodology*.

How do the scientists balance the need for persuasion with the need for judicious caution? A number of examples have been given. In many cases, a lack of research certainty is balanced by evaluations of other kinds, such as utility. In some cases it has been argued that the researchers have made more significant claims that are warranted, often by implication rather than by outright statement. Figurative expressions such as the fixed phrase *on the cusp of* and more creative figurative language such as *knee-deep* for hypothetical water are among the features used in these implications.

Can *more successful* and *less successful* interviewees be identified? It has been suggested that less successful interviewees stick more closely to the kind of language used in professional scientific writing, such as attributing knowledge claims to non-human entities. More successful interviewees lay claim to importance and novelty and downplay any uncertainty. In making this distinction, *success* has been interpreted subjectively as meaning something like 'likely to enthuse the listener (and tax-payer) about the research'.

What is the role of the interviewer and programme maker? These aspects have been mentioned in passing. In some of the segments, the interviewer suggests a goal or a significance for the research that the interviewee then has to contradict. Programme makers play a very significant role in choosing to present research either as non-controversial or as an argument. Where it is presented as an argument, an appearance of *balance* constructs *science versus maverick*. Some of the interviewers' contributions – for example, asking whether a consequence of research could be dangerous (example 4), or proposing an exaggerated research outcome that is bound to be rejected (see Table 2, segment R) – appears to be somewhat akin to 'teasing', and this is something to be followed up in future research.

Another avenue for future research is the construal of 'mainstream' and 'maverick' science by the programme-makers. From the little evidence presented here, it would seem that, especially in the area of environmental science, programme-makers find themselves in a position of both respecting scientific knowledge and yet not trusting the outcomes of scientific research. This is certainly something worth exploring further.

It will be noted that the work reported in this paper is somewhat different from many studies of the popularization of science. Unlike, say,

Calsamiglia and Lopez Ferrero (2003) or Sumptner and Garner (2007), for example, it does not focus on a specific news story. The research projects reported in the *Today* segments do not relate to major news stories with scientific implications. They most probably originate in research institute press releases, that is, they are initiated by the researcher rather than by the programme makers. Neither does the paper consider the process of translation, mediation or re-telling that is of primary consideration when professional discourse is contrasted with popularized discourse (see also Myers 2003). It has tended to focus on the speaker as a 'seller' of scientific research within a portion of the UK discourse community (that portion that regularly listens to *Today*) and has speculated on the success or otherwise of various speakers in convincing listeners of the value of research. The study is extremely small-scale, but raises questions that might be tested on a larger data-set in the future.

References

Bednarek, Monika. 2006. *Evaluation in Media Discourse: Analysis of a Newspaper Corpus*. London/New York: Continuum.

Bienvenido, León. 2008. Science related information in European television: A study of prime-time news. *Public Understanding of Science* 17. 443-460.

Calsamiglia, Helena & Lopez Ferreto C. 2003. Role and position of scientific voices: reported speech in the media. *Discourse Studies* 5. 147-173.

Chafe, Wallace. 1986. Evidentiality in English conversation and academic writing. In Wallace Chafe & Johanna Nichols (eds.), *Evidentiality: The Linguistic Coding of Epistemology*. Norwood: Ablex. 261-272.

Greatbatch, David. 1992. On the management of disagreement between new interviewers. In Paul Drew & John Heritage (eds.), *Talk at Work: Interaction in Institutional Settings*. Cambridge: Cambridge University Press. 268-301.

Hansen, Anders. 1994. Journalistic practices and science reporting in the British press. *Public Understanding of Science* 3. 111-134.

Highfield, Roger. 2000. Essays on science and society: Selling science to the public. *Science* 289. 59.

Hunston, Susan. 2011. *Corpus Approaches to Evaluation: Phraseology and Evaluative Language*. London: Routledge.

Jones, Allan. 2012. Mary Adams and the producer's role in early BBC science broadcasts. *Public Understanding of Science* 21. 968-983.

Labov, William. 1992. *Language in the Inner City*. Philadelphia: University of Pennsylvania Press.

Martin, James R. &Peter R. R. White. 2005. *The Language of Evaluation: Appraisal in English*. London: Palgrave.

Myers, Greg. 1992. 'In this paper we report…'. Speech acts and scientific facts. *Journal of Pragmatics* 17. 295-313.

—. 2003. Discourse studies of scientific popularization: questioning the boundaries. *Discourse Studies* 5. 265-279.

Pallen, Mark. 2009. *The Rough Guide to Evolution: Darwin's Big Idea that Changed the World*. London/New York: Rough Guides.

Tanner, Andrea H. 2004. Agenda building, source selection, and health news at local television stations. *Science Communication* 25. 350-363.

Sumptner, Randall S. & Johny. T. Garner. 2007. Telling the Columbia story: Source selection in news accounts of a shuttle accident. *Science Communication* 28. 455-475.

Taylor, Charlotte. 2010. Science in the news: A diachronic perspective. *Corpora* 5. 221-250.

COMPARISON AS A MODE OF RE-CONCEPTUALIZATION IN POPULARIZATION: FOCUS ON EXPRESSIONS OF SIMILARITY

ELSA PIC AND GRÉGORY FURMANIAK
UNIVERSITÉ SORBONNE NOUVELLE-PARIS 3, PRISMES EA4398, FRANCE

Abstract: This corpus-based study examines the use of several expressions of similarity (*like* and a set of adjectives such as *similar* or equivalent) in two scientific genres: research articles (RAs) and popular science articles (PAs). We show that, although PA writers need to re-conceptualize complex experiences into more accessible experiences for the benefit of the lay-reader, it would be an oversimplification to assume that they resort to comparative devices more often than RA writers. Expressions of comparison are as frequent in the two genres, but show different distributions. RAs use adjectives more than PAs, which make extensive use of grammatical markers.

This difference is accounted for through a syntactic and semantic analysis of expressions of similarity. Because of their properties, adjectives fit the communicative purposes of RAs better than those of PAs: they are almost exclusively used for intra-domain comparison, for descriptive and metadiscursive functions, and they can function as cohesive devices, the need for which is more acute in RAs, which are much longer texts. By contrast, *like* is more frequent in PAs because it has a wider array of functions. In particular, it encodes the two types of re-conceptualization (inter-domain comparison and heterogeneous comparison) that are expected in popularization.

1. Introduction

This paper is part of a research project that compares the linguistic properties of two scientific genres, research articles (RAs) and popular science articles (PAs), across disciplines. Here, we investigate the use of some markers of comparison. Being one of the linguistic strategies that permit re-conceptualization, comparison constitutes a major issue for this volume's topic.

Following Langacker (1987:431), we shall define *conceptualization* as the mental representation, reflected in language, of "a facet of either the real world [...] or a constructed world". The same experience (or situation) can be conceptualized – and therefore expressed – in many different ways depending on several factors (cf. Croft & Cruse 2004:46), including perspective and, most interestingly for our present purpose, "the shared knowledge, beliefs and attitudes of the interlocutors" (Croft & Cruse 2004:46) – which determines "what we choose to express in utterances and how we express it" (Croft & Cruse 2004:60).

Re-conceptualization can therefore be defined as a pragmatically-motivated process that involves replacing a conceptual representation (R1) – and its linguistic expression – with another one (R2) that is felt by the speaker to be more in line with his/her present communicative purposes.

In that respect, if the mediation of expert discourse aims at "transmitting knowledge from those knowing something to those knowing less" (Biezunski 1985:183, in Varttala 2001:179), we would expect this function to be partly achieved through the re-conceptualization of R1s specific to the community of experts into R2s that are part of the lay-audience's world.

However, because re-conceptualization can be achieved in several ways (reformulation, metaphor, simile, comparison, etc.), and a comprehensive analysis of all strategies would be well beyond the scope of this paper, we focus on one particular such tool, namely: comparison, and more precisely, *expressions of similarity*.[1]

Beside the more general issue of whether markers of comparison are used in the same way in RAs and PAs, the questions we wish to address in what follows are: Is the kind of re-conceptualization achieved through comparison specific to PAs? If not, is it used in the same way in RAs? Do all forms of comparison permit re-conceptualization? If not, what are their other communicative purposes? Are these other uses different in RAs and in PAs?

The outline of this paper will be as follows: we first provide a few definitions of comparison and related concepts and give an overview of the literature on comparison in discourse. We then present our corpus and our methodology. In Section 3, we give an overview of all the markers of

[1] For a detailed study of reformulation in our corpus, see Pic, Furmaniak & Hugou (2013).

comparison before moving on to a more detailed analysis of similarity adjectives (Section 4) and of the grammatical word *like* (Section 5).

2. The Notion of Comparison and its Use in Discourse

Before embarking on the investigation of forms of comparison within our corpus, it is necessary to define the notion of comparison and to distinguish it from other re-conceptualization processes: reformulation, metaphor and simile.

2.1 Basic Concepts: Comparison, Metaphor and Simile

First, *reformulation* stricto sensu is best understood as the – often explicit – signalling of equivalence between two terms or two propositions, the latter being considered as a re-conceptualization of the former (cf. Pennec 2006:33). For example, in (1), R2 (bold) is presented (by the marker *that is*) as referentially equivalent to R1 (italics).

(1) For instance, *the tiling problem*, that is, **whether a given bunch of shapes will tile a lane** belongs to a class of mathematical problems called nonrecursive. (Pm)[2]

To say that both formulations are semantically equivalent would be wrong, of course, since we consider that the truth-conditional contents of an expression do not exhaust its semantics. The point, however, is that they are two different ways of naming the same experience.

By contrast, metaphors, similes and comparisons can be described as involving non-equivalent experiences. R2 is never regarded as merely another way of naming R1. Rather, R1 and R2 are representations of experiences that are kept distinct, but which are judged sufficiently similar (or dissimilar) to be likened.

The relation between comparison, simile and metaphor has been hotly debated since at least Aristotle (cf. Rhetoric III, 4) and cannot be discussed in detail here. Let us just say that we first formally distinguish metaphor, on the one hand, and (literal) comparison and simile on the other hand, the latter being conveyed explicitly via a marker of comparison (cf., for instance, Morinet 1995:201). From a semantic perspective, we adhere to

[2] In the examples taken from our corpus, the first letter of the tag refers to the genre ('P' for PAs and 'R' for RAs), and the second to the discipline (where 'a' stands for astronomy, 'e' for economics, 'h' for history, 'm' for applied mathematics, and 'p' for philosophy).

Israel et al.'s (2004) view that comparison, simile and metaphors are distinct analogical processes. *Metaphors* "create similarities rather than reflecting them" (Israel et al. 2004:124). They do not necessarily reflect objective similarities between source and target domains. It is more a figure of thought than a figure of speech (which is confirmed by the fact that many conceptual domains are metaphorically structured – cf. e.g. Lakoff & Johnson 1980). In contrast, *literal comparison* consists in the "actual assessment of what two entities share" (Israel et al. 2004:124). It is "a mental act in which two or more entities, the comparands, are evaluated along some parameter" (Israel et al. 2004:125), the *tertium* (or standard of comparison). The *tertium* may be explicit (cf. *important* in (2)) or implicit, as in (3) – where the extent to which Mars and the Earth are alike is not specified.

(2) Such considerations indicate that control over time is at least as *important* as time itself. (Re)

(3) [T]he rovers have revealed that Mars was very much like our own Earth at one time in its ancient past. (Pa)

With comparisons, there is always a marker of comparison, but depending on its form, it may endow the comparison with a *Figure/Ground* structure, as in (2), where *time itself* is the Ground (also called Source or Landmark), that is, the entity relative to which *control over time* (the Figure/Target/Trajectory) is assessed with regard to their importance. In other cases, as in (4), the comparison has no such Figure/Ground structure, the comparands being on an equal footing, as it were.

(4) Here we see that the proportion of those with first births after 10 years of marriage is *similar* across education levels. (Re)

Like literal comparison, *simile* (or *figurative comparison*) is an explicit assessment of the comparands and it uses the same linguistic constructions (e.g. *is the equivalent of*, *(no) more … than*, *has the character of*, *think of X as a kind of*, *view X as …*). Unlike literal comparison, it compares "things normally felt to be incomparable" thereby suggesting "unexpected connections between source and target" (Israel et al. 2004:124). This is exemplified by (5).

(5) The two black holes are like chalk and cheese. (Pa)

Thus, a simile can be defined as an *inter-domain* comparison (i.e. the comparands belong to two different domains of experience) and necessarily has a Figure/Ground structure. By contrast, literal comparison is intra-domain, since, to paraphrase Israel et al. (2004), it compares entities that are felt to be comparable, as in (6).

(6) Like McCarthy, Sheen offered no proof for his assertion, yet stated it as fact. (Rh)

Intra-domain comparison can either have a Figure/Ground structure, as in (6) – where *McCarthy* is conceived as the Ground and *Sheen* as the Figure, or no such structure as in (7), which expresses a *set comparison*[3] and compares sequences at the same level.

(7) These sequences are *similar*, in that they correspond to the same sequence of genes, but not *identical*. (Pm)

Because inter-domain comparison is likely to be a feature of PAs by virtue of its capacity to re-conceptualize expert knowledge into representations familiar to the lay-audience, we would expect similes to be typical of PAs. However, there are no such implications for literal comparison. First, there is no obvious reason why comparisons with no Figure/Ground structures should be more typical of PAs (insofar as they are not used for re-conceptualization). Second, intra-domain comparison takes different forms and, thus, cannot be said to be attracted to one genre or to the other. Indeed, while intra-domain comparison always implies that both R1 and R2 represent experiences belonging to the same domain, a further distinction is needed between *homogeneous comparison* where both comparands are denoted by terms belonging to the same register or speech-community (either that of experts, which we shall call 'specialized terms', as in (8),[4] or that of non-experts, as in (9)), and *heterogeneous comparison*, where the comparands are designated by terms belonging to different speech communities (i.e. expert versus non-expert), as in (10).

---

[3] We have a set comparison because, in this context, the sentence receives a reciprocal interpretation: 'these sequences are similar to each other'. In another context, it could be understood as 'these sequences are similar to the one just mentioned', for which we would speak of term comparison. For a full discussion of *term comparison*, *set comparison* and *reciprocals*, see Huddleston and Pullum (2002:1137).

[4] For proper nouns, we made a – necessarily subjective – distinction between the names that seem to be used only within the speech-community of experts (e.g. Rorty or Hodgskin) and those that can be assumed to be known to the general public (e.g. Roosevelt or Socrates).

(8) Perhaps, once upon a time, *Miranda* had geysers just like *Enceladus* does today. (Pa)

(9) *The UK fishing industry*, of which Scottish fisheries are now the largest part, has, like *most other industries*, changed and developed hugely in the past half century. (Pe)

(10) The sorts of mathematical deductivist methods that economists use are, like all research methods, types of tools. (Re)

We may therefore expect examples such as (8) to be more frequent in RAs and the likes of (9) and (10) to be a feature of PAs – which does not preclude that both types can occur in both genres. What emerges from these definitions is that, even granting that re-conceptualization is characteristic of PAs, comparison appears in too various kinds – not all used for re-conceptualization – to allow for any safe prediction concerning its use in PAs and in RAs. Figure 1 shows the types of comparison we have discussed and their respective features (in italics). Only the types (A2) and (B) can be used for re-conceptualizing, thereby encoding the kinds of processes that can be expected in PAs, namely inter-domain comparison and heterogeneous intra-domain comparison.

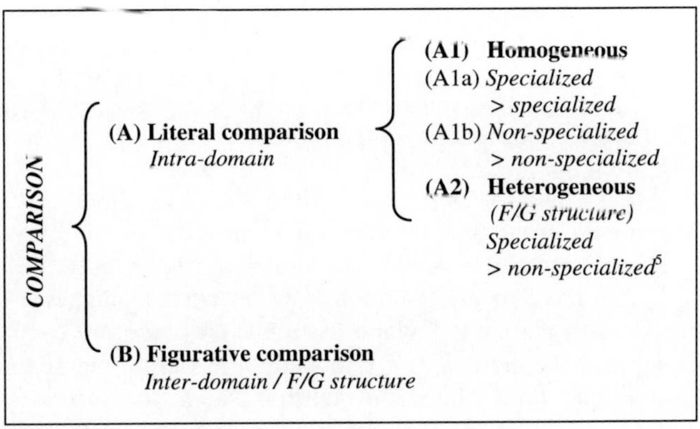

Fig. 1: Types of comparison

2.2 Comparison in Academic Discourse and in Popular Science

While the literature on metaphors in academic discourse is abundant, few scholars have examined the use of comparison (whether literal or

[5] Notice that *non-specialized > specialized* comparison is theoretically possible but pragmatically odd. No such examples were found.

figurative) in this kind of discourse. Yet, previous studies have highlighted some of the general rhetorical and discourse functions of comparison and Hyland (2010) has made a few insightful comments on the use of comparison in popular science.

First, Israel et al. have suggested that both literal and figurative comparisons "serve the basic rhetorical functions of *description and evaluation*" (2004:126). They attribute further functions to similes, which can have the effect of highlighting a theme in a *narrative*, conveying *irony*, injecting *humour*, or heightening the dramatic tension of a climactic scene.

Israel et al. (2004:133) also describe simile – but this is applicable to literal comparison as well – as "a figure of *description* and *elaboration*". In that respect, both literal and figurative comparisons can work as cohesive devices, since they "necessarily elaborate a previously mentioned referent or relation" (p. 133) and can be expanded. Both the descriptive and the cohesive functions of comparison are exemplified by (11), where *similar* provides a description of the spiral staircase that points back to – and can only be interpreted relative to – *a large spiral ramp*.

(11) One of Foster Partners' past projects provided a clue: the Reichstag in Berlin also contains a large hall, but in this case it is broken up by <u>a large spiral ramp</u>. The SMG created a model of a **similar** *spiral staircase* for the London City Hall and the company Arup Acoustics analysed the acoustics for this new model. (Pm)

To our knowledge, the only study that addresses – albeit briefly – the use of comparison in popular science is Hyland (2010). His hypothesis is that, since popularizations cannot assume a high degree of shared knowledge, they have to make connections to what readers are likely to know already. Comparisons, Hyland assumes, are therefore used to build upon that supposedly pre-existing knowledge, to define new concepts, to establish explicit links between entities and to offer on-the-fly clarifications. As for similes, they are used to relate complex processes to more familiar everyday events, as in (12):

(12) To get into the brain they must be shuttled across the bloodebrain barrier by specialized transport proteins. *Like passengers trying to board a crowded bus*, amino acids compete for rides on these transporters. Not only does tryptophan have paltry representation among the passengers; it also competes with five other amino acids for the same transporter. Aced out by other amino acids, tryptophan thereby has a tough time hitching a ride to the brain. (from Hyland 2010:120)

While given our above definition in terms of inter-domain re-conceptualization, it is easy to understand why simile would be a feature of popularization, we have seen that literal comparison involves entities belonging to the same domain. If it is more specific to PAs than to RAs, as Hyland's discussion would suggest, it needs to be confirmed empirically. The preceding sections lead to a number of hypotheses and questions concerning the use of comparison in PAs that call for a fine-grained data analysis, namely:

(i) Simile is expected to be a feature of PAs for the following reasons: (ia) By definition, it expresses inter-domain comparison, which seems to fit one of the communicative needs of popularisation, namely, to re-conceptualize expert knowledge into 'ordinary' world experience; (ib) It is a feature of the narrative and descriptive modes which, as shown in Pic and Furmaniak (2012), are typical of PAs; (ic) It is often humorous, which helps accomplish one of the purposes of PA-writers, namely to entertain the reader (cf. Kunzig 2006:130).

(ii) We expect the case of literal comparison to be more complex than assumed by Hyland as only one kind of literal comparison, the A2 type, is obviously compatible with the communicative purposes of PAs.

3. Corpus and Method

3.1 Corpus

To conduct our research, a one-million-word corpus of scientific writing in British English was compiled. It comprises five disciplines (History, Philosophy, Astronomy, Applied Mathematics, and Economics) and it is divided into two sub-corpora of comparable size:[6] a specialised section, which contains RAs taken from peer-reviewed journals, and a popularizing section with PAs mostly written by experts but intended for a wider audience (cf. Figure 2).

To limit sociolinguistic and diachronic variation, we only selected texts written between 2000 and 2012 by British authors who are experts in their

[6] The RA-subcorpus contains 525,703 words, while the PA-subcorpus contains 516,887 words. Because of this slight difference, all the results are normalized to 500,000 words.

fields. This guarantees that the linguistic variations observed between the two genres can be safely attributed to the intended audience-parameter.

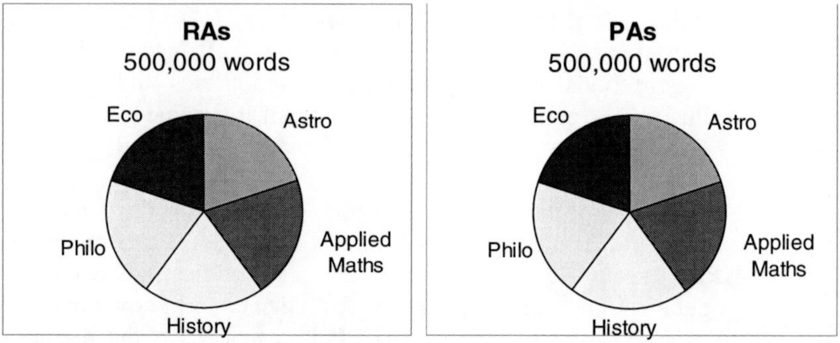

Fig. 2: Composition of the corpus

It was also important that PAs on the one hand and RAs on the other hand address comparable audiences across disciplines. The task was easy for RAs, which were all taken from peer-reviewed academic journals (e.g. *The Historical Journal*, *Cambridge Journal of Economics*, *Metaphilosophy*, etc.). For PAs, however, it was necessary to consult the editorial profile of the sources. The presence of search words such as *accessible*, *general public*, *entertaining*, etc. in the presentation of the magazine or in the 'Advice to authors' section was a condition for including the source in the corpus.[7] For example, *History Today* describes itself as "a unique cultural institution, bringing the best in historical writing and research to a wide audience"; *Astronomy Now* explicitly states

[7] More specifically, our corpus is comprised of RAs and PAs gathered from the following journals and magazines: *The Historian* (Wiley-Blackwell); *The Historical Journal* (Cambridge Journals); *History Today* (History Today Ltd.); *IMA Journal of Applied Mathematics* (Oxford Journals); *Journal of Logic & Analysis* (University of York); *Journal of the London Mathematical Society* (Oxford University Press); *Plus Maths Magazine* (Millennium Mathematics Project, Cambridge); *Analysis* (Oxford Journals); *European Journal of Philosophy* (Wiley-Blackwell); *Journal of Moral Philosophy* (Brill); *Metaphilosophy* (Wiley-Blackwell); *Minerva - An Internet Journal of Philosophy*; *Proceedings of the Aristotelian Society* (Wiley-Blackwell); *Think* (Cambridge Journals); *Cambridge Journal of Economics* (Cambridge Journals); *Economic Affairs* (Wiley); *World Economics* (Economic and Financial Publishing Ltd.); *Monthly Proceedings of the Royal Astronomical Society* (Wiley-Blackwell); *Astronomy Now Magazine* (Pole Star Publications Ltd.); *Popular Astronomy* (quarterly magazine of The Society for Popular Astronomy).

that “[it] falls into the kind of ‘popular science magazine’”. However, although the editors aim at reaching the widest audience possible, the fact that it is written by experts and published in thematic magazines whose readers are not totally unfamiliar with the topics being dealt with, makes the type of popularization we are concerned with relatively high-brow – what Bondi (2012) calls “expert mediation”.

3.2 Method

Laurence Anthony’s (2011) *AntConc* was used to extract all the forms expressing comparison in the corpus. The list of these forms was set up by consulting various dictionaries, thesauri and grammar books. This provided us with an overview – in purely quantitative terms – of which forms were used in each sub-corpus. Because it was not possible to offer a fine-grained analysis of all these forms, we decided to focus on a few expressions of similarity – similarity (or likeness) corresponding to one of the four types of comparative construction distinguished by Huddleston & Pullum (2002:1099), namely, the conjunction of the features “non-scalar” and “equality”. The expressions of similarity we chose to examine were the five most frequent adjectives in the corpus and the grammatical word *like*.

After excluding all the uses that did not express similarity (for example, occurrences of *like* as a verb), all the relevant examples were saved to an Excel spreadsheet with sufficient context and analysed according to a number of formal and semantic criteria (see Section 5.2). The data were then fed into the statistical software *Trideux*, which helped reveal phenomena and interpretations that a manual analysis could not have shown.

4. Markers of Comparison and of Similarity in the Corpus

A raw count of 45 lexical and grammatical forms expressing this notion (*as … as*, *so … as*, *like*, *as if*, *as though*, *similar to*, *analogous*, etc.) was conducted. Quantitatively, these markers appeared to be slightly more frequent in PAs than in RAs (4,216 vs 3,900 tokens) but the difference was not sufficient to support the hypothesis that comparison is a feature of popular science. The results also hide the fact that the two genres do not use the same markers: grammatical forms like *as (if/though)*, *as/so … as*, *(-like)*, *more … than*, *the most…*, etc. are preferred in PAs, while authors of RAs more often resort to adjectives of comparison such as *analogous*, *similar*, *equivalent*, *identical*, *comparable*, etc. This therefore called for a more detailed qualitative analysis, necessarily restricted to a smaller set of forms.

Table 1 features quantitative results limited to the twelve markers expressing similarity in the corpus. They confirm the general tendency. First, the quantitative difference between RAs and PAs is not significant. Secondly, as far as the distribution of lexical and grammatical markers of comparison is concerned, adjectives account for 40% of the similarity markers in RAs but only 18% in PAs, whereas grammatical forms make up 60% of the expressions of similarity in RAs against 82% in PAs.[8]

Tab. 1: Quantitative overview of comparative markers in the corpus (per 500,000 words)[9]

	RAs	**PAs**	**Total corpus**
(-)like	277	568	845
as (+3 wds)...as	282	340	622
similar	273	148	421
equivalent	76	31	107
as if	29	45	75
be like	28	23	51
comparable	25	15	40
identical	16	18	35
analogous	20	5	25
as though	1	9	10
reminiscent	5	4	9
not different	1	1	2
not unlike	0	1	1
Total adjectives	**416**	**223**	**639**
%	40%	18%	29%
Total grams	**617**	**985**	**1602**
%	60%	82%	71%
Total	**1033**	**1208**	**2241**

4.1 *Similar*, *Identical*, *Analogous*, *Equivalent*, *Comparable* and *Like*

To understand these differences, we now focus on two classes of markers expressing similarity: (i) *like*, employed as a preposition (e.g. *[they] act like blackbodies*), as a conjunction (e.g. *its magnetic dipole axis is aligned much like Earth is to the Sun*) and as a suffix (e.g. *star-like*

[8] The difference between RAs and PAs with respect to the respective frequency of grams and adjectives is highly significant: $X^2 = 129.9537$; df = 1; p = 0.

[9] The results have been normalized to 500,000 words.

point); and (ii) a group of five adjectives (*similar*, *identical*, *analogous*, *equivalent*, *comparable*).[10] Each marker was analysed according to the following set of formal and semantic criteria:[11]

(i) What grammatical class (preposition, conjunction, suffix, adjective) does the marker belong to?
(ii) What is the grammatical function (predicate, attribute, apposition, etc.) of the marker or the phrase it heads?
(iii) Is there an explicit *tertium* (or standard of comparison)?
(iv) What is the ontological class of the comparands? Following Lyons's (1977) and Paradis's (2005) ontologies, we distinguished between first-order entities (people, objects, etc.), second-order entities (events and states) and third-order entities (shells, such as *problem sentence*, *assumption frequency*, etc.).
(v) Is the comparison inter- or intra-domain?
(vi) Is the Ground-term – if any – a specialized term?
(vii) What communicative function (description, explanation, evaluation, exemplification, categorization, etc.) does the comparison accomplish?

Before starting, we must stress that not all the criteria considered proved useful and/or interpretable. In what follows, we therefore comment only on the results which we found worthy of interest.

5. Syntax and Functions of the Adjectives in the Corpus

Table 2 features the distribution of the five adjectives in the corpus and the type of comparison they encode.

[10] *Same* was not included, since it expresses identity rather than similarity. If two entities entertain a relation of similarity, they are kept distinct. If their relation is one of identity, it implies that they are two members of the same category or that what was assumed to be two different entities is in fact just one entity that took on different forms (e.g. *They are one and the same*).
[11] Note that some of these criteria (e.g. grammatical class) were not relevant for the adjectives at hand.

Tab. 2: Distribution and function of the five adjectives in RAs and PAs (per 500,000 words)

	RAs					PAs				
	Total	Intra-domain		Inter-domain		Total	Intra-domain		Inter-domain	
			%		%			%		%
similar	273	273	100	0	0	148	144	97	4	3
equivalent	76	75	99	0	0	31	26	84	0	0
analogous	20	17	86	0	0	5	5	100	0	0
identical	16	16	100	0	0	18	18	100	0	0
comparable	25	25	100	0	0	15	15	100	0	0
Total	410	406	99	0	0	218	209	96	4	2

As mentioned before, these adjectives are almost twice as numerous in RAs as in PAs, except for *identical*, whose overall frequency is marginal. But what is most striking is that they are almost exclusively used to express intra-domain comparison and that the comparison is always homogenous. This raises a number of questions that can only be answered by more thorough data analysis:

(i) Why are the adjectives used solely for intra-domain homogeneous comparison?

(ii) The fact that the adjectives specialize in intra-domain homogeneous comparison and are therefore not used as tools of re-conceptualization explains why they are *not* used more often in PAs than in RAs, but it does not explain why they are more widely used in RAs. This question calls for two further questions:

(iii) What functions and communicative purposes do the adjectives accomplish in RAs?

(iv) What functions do they fulfil in PAs (considering that their relatively low frequency must not make us forget that they are also used in PAs)?

5.1 Impact of the Syntactic Properties of Adjectives on their Functional Properties

The syntactic properties of the adjectives under investigation partly account for their specialization in intra-domain homogeneous comparison. The adjectival phrase (henceforward AP) can have one of the following four functions: attributive, as in (13), predicative, as in (14), appositive, as in (15), and noun complement, as in (16).

(13) Small firms across the globe face *similar* challenges. (Re)
(14) The cases are *similar* and so we deal only with the left tilt. (Rm)
(15) *Similar to the previous examples*, these sketches may be a tangle of sketch marks, diagram and callout lines. (Pa)
(16) We use a technique *similar to the one used by di Serego Alighieri et al. (2000).* (Ra)

Yet Table 3, which features the distribution of the grammatical functions of adjectives, shows that attributive and predicative APs (exemplified by (13) and (14)) are largely prominent in both genres, with the attributive function making up for more than 50% of all occurrences.

Tab. 3: Grammatical functions of the APs in the corpus (per 500,000 words)

	RAs				PAs			
	ATTR	**PRED**	**APP**	**NC**	**ATTR**	**PRED**	**APP**	**NC**
similar	181	66	6	21	98	29	10	12
equivalent	11	57	7	1	9	11	6	6
analogous	9	10	1	1	2	1	1	1
identical	10	7	0	0	9	9	0	1
comparable	11	9	1	4	10	4	0	2
Total	222	147	14	27	127	53	16	21
%	**54%**	**36%**	3%	6%	**58%**	**24%**	8%	10%

So what do examples like (13) and (14) suggest? They show that, irrespective of whether they are interpreted as set comparisons (that is, as 'challenges similar to one another' or 'the cases are similar to one another') or as term comparisons (namely, as 'challenges/cases similar to the ones just mentioned'), the comparands are denoted by the same noun (*challenges* in (13) and *case* in (14)). When saying *the cases are similar* or *we face similar challenges*, one necessarily compares a case to another case, a challenge to another challenge, and there is therefore no room in these formal structures for domain and register variation.

There is in fact one construction that enables the adjectives to express inter-domain – as in (17) – and (potentially)[12] heterogeneous comparison.

---

[12] 'Potentially' is added here to point out that, in principle, it would be possible to have instances like: *Imagine passengers trying to board a crowded bus. Well, amino acids are a bit similar.* [Constructed, based on (12)]. However, no such occurrences were found in the corpus.

(17) In three dimensions, stable and unstable points are not the only equilibrium points: you can also have saddle points. If your object is balanced on a saddle point, then the balancing act is unstable in infinitely many directions [...] and stable in exactly one direction – if you give it a slight push in that direction, it will come back to the equilibrium point. This is similar *to a marble balancing on the mid-point of a saddle.* (Pm)

In examples like (17), the adjective is post-modified by a prepositional phrase (PP), or *comparative complement* (cf. Huddleston & Pullum 2002:542), functioning as the Ground. Such a PP is compulsorily present in appositive and noun complement APs – as in (15) and (16), respectively – and it is necessarily absent from attributive APs. In predicative APs, it is either absent – in instances of set comparison – or optional – in instances of term comparison. In the latter case, if the comparative complement is not expressed, it is necessarily retrieved anaphorically.

Noun complements and appositives are relatively marginal in the corpus, but it is noteworthy that the large difference observed for RAs and PAs with attributives and predicatives (+94 and +95, respectively) is quasi-null as far as appositives and noun complements are concerned. Interestingly, these are the two grammatical functions which systematically require the explicit presence of a Ground, and thus allow comparison of entities different in nature, as in (17) above or (18).

(18) So the tiny chance p is equivalent to winning around 1,000,000 lotteries in a row. (Pm)

But overall, as we can see in Table 4, only about 30% of the adjectives are followed by a comparative complement, although it must be mentioned that *equivalent* and *analogous* stand apart from the others as they occur *with* a comparative complement in about 60% of the cases (cf. Section 4.3).

Tab. 4: Frequency of adjectives co-occurring with a comparative complement (per 500,000 words)

	RAs			PAs		
	Total	+PP		Total	+PP	
similar	273	63	23%	148	30	20%
equivalent	76	50	66%	31	20	66%
analogous	20	11	57%	5	3	60%
identical	16	4	24%	18	4	21%
comparable	25	7	27%	15	4	25%
Total	410	135	33%	218	61	28%

5.2 Communicative Purposes of Comparisons Expressed by the Adjectives

We have seen that with adjectives the comparison is always intra-domain (type A1) and that this is accounted for in about 70% of the cases by the fact that they are used without a comparative complement. This constitutes their most distinctive syntactic property, which, we shall see, is what distinguishes them most clearly from *like*. Because they specialize in that type of comparison, which does not involve re-conceptualization, it is easy to understand why they are not frequent in PAs. The question that might be asked however is why, even when there is a comparative complement, the comparison encoded by the adjectives is still intra-domain. This, we suggest, is related to the communicative functions accomplished by these adjectives. These features are listed in Table 5.

Tab. 5: Communicative functions of the adjectives in RAs and in PAs (per 500,000 words)

	RAs							PAs						
	TOTAL	DESCR.		EXPL.		META		TOTAL	DESCR.		EXPL.		META	
			%		%		%			%		%		%
similar	273	231	85	0	0	42	15	148	141	95	5	3	2	1
equivalent	76	75	99	0	0	1	1	31	26	84	5	1	0	0
analogous	20	15	76	2	10	3	14	5	4	80	0	0	1	20
identical	16	14	88	0	0	2	12	18	18	100	0	0	0	0
comparable	25	19	77	0	0	6	23	15	15	94	0	0	1	6
Total	410	355	87	2	1	53	13	218	204	94	10	4	4	2

First, it appears that the *explicative* function, which might have been expected in PAs, accounts for only 4% of the occurrences in this genre. This function, exemplified by (17) – repeated here as (19) – in fact concerns cases of re-conceptualization where the writer compares a complex phenomenon to a less complex one to help the lay-reader grasp it.

(19) This is **similar to** a marble balancing on the mid-point of a saddle. (Pm)

However, Table 5 shows that these comparative adjectives are overwhelmingly used for *descriptive* purposes. The comparison was classified as descriptive when the comparands were likened on account of shared objective characteristics, as in (20) and (21).

(20) Katherine has been described as the queen who came from nowhere, yet her pedigree was **similar** to that of Henry's other English queens and she was well educated. (Ph)
(21) [The] oxygen-isotope signature uncovered in samples returned by Apollo astronauts is **identical** to that found on our planet. (Pa)

If two entities share objective characteristics, they are likely to pertain to the same domain, which entails that the comparison will be intra-domain. The metadiscursive function featured in Table 5 is in fact a special case of description. The comparands are textual entities that are part of the author's or other researchers' texts. This is illustrated by examples (22-23).

(22) The interpretation is **analogous** to that of Figure 2. (Rm)
(23) So the positive D regime that is considered in this paper is **equivalent** to the negative D regime considered in Bushby (2006). (Ra)

Adjectives encoding this function are much more frequent in RAs than in PAs. There are two reasons for this. First, metadiscourse is known to be an all-pervasive feature of RAs (cf. e.g. Hyland 1998), which therefore contain frequent intra-textual and inter-textual references. Second, given that intra-textual reference serves both a guiding and a cohesive function and since RAs are, on average, three times as long as PAs, one might expect more markers of guidance and cohesion in RAs.[13]

In fact, this explanation in terms of cohesion might apply to all the adjectives regardless of their function and might account for their lower frequency in PAs. As we have seen, the adjectives are mostly used without a comparative complement. In such cases (when we have a term comparison), the Ground is retrieved anaphorically, making the adjective work as a cohesive device. Again, it is only to be expected that there should be more such occurrences in longer texts like RAs than in relatively short texts like PAs.

5.3 *Equivalent* and *Analogous*

Before moving on to the case of *like*, let us say a few words about *analogous* and *equivalent*. As we have seen, these are the two adjectives that stand apart because they are mainly used with a comparative complement. In fact, *analogous* is too rare in both RAs and PAs to draw

[13] On the link between cohesion and text length, see Neuner (1987).

any conclusion except that its higher frequency in RAs has probably to do with the formality of the genre. As for *equivalent*, the reason why it is often followed by a PP is, we believe, because it is used for description like the other adjectives, but for a description of a special kind. Indeed, it mainly occurs in the 'mathematically minded' disciplines (only 12 instances out of 112 were found in the philosophy and history sections of the corpus) where it expresses a relation of similarity between two quantified or quantifiable entities. This is exemplified by (24) and (25).

(24) Furthermore, Greece had under-recorded military expenditure to an extent **equivalent** to 0.7% of GDP in 2003. (Pe)

(25) The bifurcation condition is given by <formula>,[14] (3.8) which, as expected, is **equivalent** to the dispersion relation (2.8) for <formula>. (Rm)

The fact that *equivalent* is often used to provide a numerical description of the Figure therefore helps understand both why it is followed by a PP – which contains the numerical description – and why it is more frequent in RAs – whose authors are more prone to give quantified evidence to support their arguments.

6. Syntax and Functions of *Like* in the Corpus

As Figure 3 shows, *like* is almost twice as frequent in PAs (white) as in RAs (black).

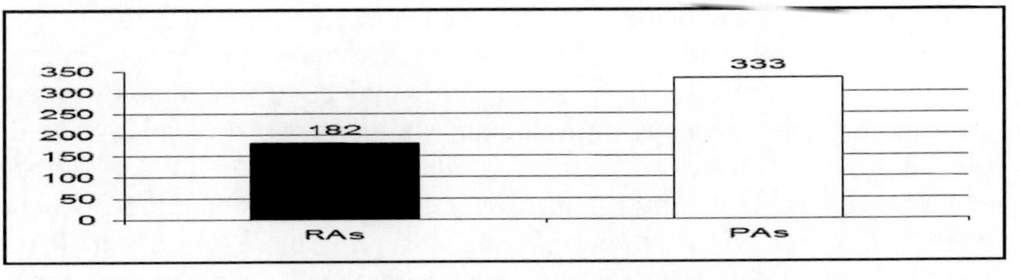

Fig. 3: Frequency of *like* in RAs and in PAs (per 500,000 words)

We suggest that this is because *like* can be used to encode all the different types of comparison described above, some of which fit both genres, while others are more in line with the communicative purposes of PAs than those of RAs.

[14] Mathematical formulae in the corpus were replaced with the <formula> tag.

6.1 Types of Comparison Encoded by *Like* in the Corpus

As expected, inter-domain comparison and heterogeneous intra-domain comparison are highly specific to PAs (see table 6).

Tab. 6: Grammatical categories of *like* and types of comparison expressed (per 500,000 words)

			RAs	PAs	DIFFERENCE (PA – RA)
INTRA-DOMAIN (A)	HOMOGENEOUS (A1)	Specialized > specialized	96	63	-33
		Non-specialized > non-specialized	37	122	+85
		TOTAL	133	185	+52
	HETEROGENOUS (A2)		23	49	+27
	TOTAL		156	234	+78
INTER-DOMAIN (B)			17	89	+72
Indeterminate			9	10	+1
Total			**182**	**333**	**+151**

It will be remembered that these types (A2 and B) are the two kinds of comparison that allow for the re-conceptualization of complex experiences and/or formulations into experiences and/or formulations accessible to the lay-reader; hence their higher frequency in PAs. In fact, the cumulated difference in frequency of these two uses between PAs and RAs (+72 for B and +27 for A2) partly accounts – quantitatively, at least – for the overall difference (+151) between the two genres. In other words, it is mainly because PAs make extensive use of the two types of comparison allowing for re-conceptualization that *like* is more frequent in PAs.

Two questions arise from this: (i) Why is *like* more apt to encode these two kinds of comparison?; (ii) What communicative functions do inter-domain and heterogeneous intra-domain comparisons serve in PAs (and, secondarily, in RAs)? A third point, however, requires further examination. Table 6 shows that if, overall, the A1 type is more frequent in PAs, the *specialized > specialized* sub-type is more specific to RAs, whereas the *non-specialized > non-specialized* sub-type is more characteristic of PAs. The third question that arises then is what communicative functions homogeneous comparison serves in RAs and in PAs and whether they are the same in the two genres.

6.2 Impact of the Formal Properties of *Like* on its Functions

The answer to the first question is quite straightforward. Unlike the adjectives, *like*, whatever its grammatical class (preposition, conjunction or suffix), necessarily marks a comparison with a Figure/Ground structure which, as we have seen, is a necessary – albeit not sufficient – condition for expressing inter-domain and heterogeneous intra-domain comparison. As with adjectives then, the syntactic properties of *like* have a direct impact on its semantic and pragmatic properties.

6.3 Communicative Functions of Comparisons Encoded by *Like*

Figure 4 shows the normalized frequency (per 500,000 words) of the different uses of *like* according to function, type of comparison and genre.

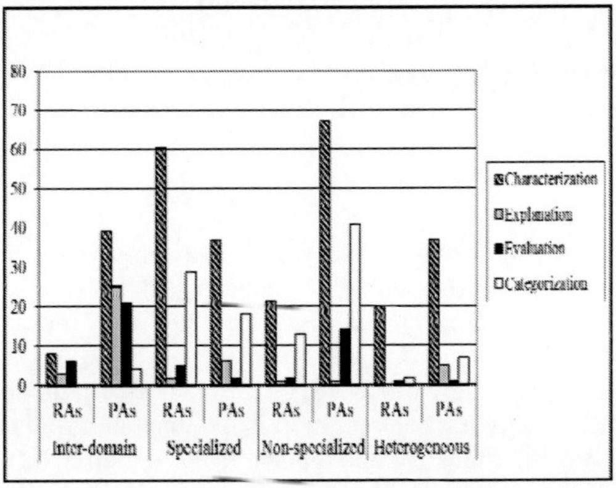

Fig. 4: Functions of *like* in RAs and PAs according to type of comparison (per 500,000 words)

Four main communicative functions have been identified for *like*. The defining criterion for each function was the communicative purpose of the process of comparison. Importantly, *like* is used to *characterize* the Figure, as in (26-27): the comparison contributes to the definition or (often physical) description of the Figure by pointing to objective characteristics it shares with the – assumedly familiar – Ground.

(26) Ascetic reasons are like exclusionary considerations in that they are reasons for not acting on other reasons. (Rp)

(27) Like the more famous Pinwheel M101, NGC 3814 is a face-on spiral galaxy with a classification of SAB, indicating it has a relatively large nucleus and tightly wound spiral arms. (Pa)

Second, *like explains* why the proposition expressed by the Figure is the case or how the entity or phenomenon denoted by the Figure works. Following Moirand (1999), we assume that an explanation answers either a *why* question or a *how-does-it-work* question. The comparison contributes to the explanation of the Figure by pointing to a similarity between the Figure and a Ground whose *raison d'être* or functioning is assumed to be known by the reader, or at least, easier to understand. Example (28) illustrates this.

(28) Each of the acute risks described above could be considered a lottery with a million tickets – if you expose yourself to a micromort it is like being given a ticket in this lottery, and if your number comes up then sadly it is the end of your life. (Pm)

Third, *like* can offer an **evaluative** judgement about the Figure, which can be qualitative (axiological, esthetical, etc.) or quantitative, by likening the Figure to a Ground which possesses the shared property to a remarkably high (or low) degree. This function is exemplified by (29-31).

(29) In Marylebone, for hours every day, for twenty years, labouring like a galley slave, and bound by typographical fetters, he pored over polyglots and teased out variora, distracted only by gardening and carpentry. (Rh)
(30) For lunar researchers like NASA's Dr Noah Petro, the torrent of data that LRO is beaming back to Earth is like manna from heaven. (Pa)
(31) She picked up the Cosmo magazine from her lap and froze for what seemed like ages. (Pm)

Finally, *like* is used to express a *categorizing* judgement. The comparison can be used to construct a subcategory of Xs such as 'the Xs that resemble Y', as in (32). The subcategory can also be built by means of exemplification, as in (33). In other cases, such as (34), the comparison expresses an approximate categorizing judgement, the phenomenon denoted by the Figure – in the form of an indeterminate pronoun like *something* – being described as belonging more or less to the category denoted by the Ground.

(32) Thinking that Gömböc-like shapes must appear somewhere in nature, Domokos turned his attention to tortoises. (Pm)
(33) Nevertheless, when it comes to internalist virtue epistemological theories like that offered by Zagzebski, the right question to ask is not whether there can be safe true beliefs which arise as a result of stable cognitive traits on the part of the agent but which do not arise out of the agent's good cognitive character. (Rp)

(34) Notice, however, that if Greco does end up appealing to sensitivity or something like it here, then this leaves his position open to precisely the same objection that I levelled against strong virtue epistemology above. (Rp)

6.3.1 *Like* in Inter-Domain Comparison (B)

Figure 4 shows that, with this type of comparison, *like* is more frequent in PAs whatever its function. Although they are not the most prominent functions, explication and evaluation are clearly specific to inter-domain comparison and to PAs. In examples like (28) above, the comparison is meant to explain exposure to a micromort by re-conceptualizing it into a more familiar kind of experience. Example (30) is an instance of inter-domain comparison with an evaluative function. Saying that the data is like manna from heaven is not a way of describing or explaining the data; it just amounts to saying that it is exceptional and extremely useful.

Now, Figure 4 shows that characterization is by far the most prominent function in inter-domain comparison and, in fact, in all types of comparison. A closer look at this function, however, reveals that it comes in different kinds according to the type of comparison and the genre. In type B comparison, thus, authors of PAs frequently use *like* for a special kind of characterization, namely physical description, as in (27). What is at stake here is helping the reader visualize the physical appearance of the Figure – which is confirmed by the frequent occurrence of the verb *look*, as in (35).

(35) Poisson is an odd looking thing, an ancient crater that has been overlain with a number of later impacts. It looks a little like a fish – the rarely seen deep sea blobfish (Psychrolutes marcidus) of Australia. (Pa)

6.3.2 *Like* in Intra-Domain Heterogeneous Comparison (A2)

With this type of comparison, which, we have argued, is also specific to PAs in that it allows for the re-conceptualization of complex experiences into experiences more familiar to the lay-audience, the dominant function is also characterization, despite a few occurrences of the explanation function. Again, the notion of characterization is probably too large to capture the specificities of each genre. Interestingly, in A2, RA-authors use a very special kind of characterization, which could be called epistemological. It is illustrated by (36).

(36) **Like Derrida, Rorty rejects the protocols of orthodox linguistic philosophy in favour of a conscious, even artful, play with stylistic possibilities.** [...] Bearing in mind the earlier tension between his claims for the literary and the poetic and the 'non-literariness' of his own procedures, together with *the apparent friction between his Derridean recognition of metaphysics' metaphoricity and the lack of metaphorical density in his own writing* (the fact, as highlighted earlier, that *Rorty's work is paraphrasable in a manner quite alien to the work of Derrida or Heidegger, or even Cavell*), Rorty's largely instrumental use of language seems at odds with his guiding emphasis on its 'non-inferential' or poetic capacities. (Rp)

Of course, the purpose here is still to characterize the Figure (Rorty), or metonymically, his theory. This is done, as usual, by starting with properties the Figure has in common with another entity (in bold), before moving on to the Figure's distinctive characteristics (italics). In epistemological contexts like (36), however, how an author or a theory stands in relation with another is in itself crucial and not a mere means to help the reader grasp the Figure's properties.

In PAs, characterization often takes the form of a physical description as in (37), or of a judgement of typicality, as in (38-40).

(37) According to his Meteorologica, some fixed stars also have tails like comets, and we have ourselves observed the fact. (Pa)

(38) Like any liquid, the jelly can be calm like the surface of an undisturbed lake, or it can ripple. (Pa)

(39) Akira took pleasure in origami when he was a child, and like most children, he gradually stopped as he grew older and found new things to occupy his time. (Pa)

(40) The Novo-Tikhvin Convent, like all others, ceased to exist as a legal entity. (Ph)

In examples like (38-40), the Figure is presented not only as similar to another entity but as similar to numerous other entities of the same kind, making it very typical and unremarkable.

6.3.3 *Like* in Intra-Domain Homogeneous *Non-Specialized > Non-Specialized* Comparison (A1b)

This type of comparison is also typical of PAs, where the most frequent functions are evaluation as in (41), categorization as in (42), and especially characterization as in (43).

(41) An infanticide case like no other occurred in 1651 and centred on an Oxfordshire maidservant. (Ph)

(42) The scale of evil that can be wrought by humans is truly shocking, and in situations like this it is hard to deny that some transpersonal forces may be at work. (Pp)

(43) Maybe we should take seriously the thought that religious belief, rather like my belief in Clarissa's love, is more like a passion, hope or way of seeing the world, rather than grounded in evidence – though that still leaves us with the unhappy reflection that some religious ways of seeing the world we must flee. (Pp)

Again, the kind of characterization we have in PAs differs from the one we find in RAs as it is often used as a means to provide a physical description of the Figure, as in (44).

(44) He's also developed a model which explains how asteroids, that aren't round like planets, but have sharp edges and flat areas, evolve their shapes […] (Pm)

The A1 type (whether it be A1a or A1b) is also the type of comparison where the categorization function is used the most. With A1b, it is mostly used in PAs, where the categorization is achieved through exemplification as in (45), or on the basis of a physical resemblance – often marked by *like* used as a suffix, as in (46).

(45) While it would be wrong to state categorically that such a tragedy could not occur within a system of private property rights in the cockle beds – where people come into contact with such powerful forces of nature, tragedies like this are always liable to happen – there is good reason to believe that a system of private property rights in the cockle beds would be superior to a system of state-regulated access. (Pe)

(46) What the intensity of the CIB does tell us is that, going back some 10-12 billion years, star formation was ten times more efficient than it is in the Milky Way today (the Milky Way produces at most the equivalent of ten Sun-like stars each year) to produce all that dust. (Pa)

6.3.4 *Like* in Intra-Domain Homogeneous *Specialized > Specialized* Comparison (A1a)

This is the only type of comparison where *like* is employed more frequently in RAs than in PAs, as can be seen in example (47).

(47) Just like with radiation pressure grains smaller than DSW or with <equation> would be removed from the system, where <equation>. (Ra)

Of course, examples like (47) are the exact – and expected – counterpart in RAs of examples like (43), which are particular to PAs, the difference lying only in the degree of specialization of the terms. In RAs, this type of comparison is mostly used for two purposes: characterization – especially of the epistemological kind, as in (48) – and categorization – especially to make approximate categorizing judgement, as in (49).

(48) Like De Marco, Blackman is confident that all asymmetric planetary nebulae are influenced by the presence of a binary companion. (Rp)

(49) The McDowellian and, I have argued, Heideggerian diagnosis offered here suggests that it is only if one first embraces something like the 'master thesis' that one comes to believe in a gap between rules and representations, on the one hand, and the world, on the other, a gap which a supplementary, nonrepresentational grasp or judgment would bridge. (Rp)

7. Conclusion

This paper shows that in order to study one particular linguistic phenomenon in one or several genres, it is necessary to carry out a detailed syntactic and semantic analysis of the forms under scrutiny. Otherwise, the risk is to make over-sweeping generalizations and simplifications such as "comparison allows for re-conceptualization, therefore it is a feature of popular science", which ignore the complexity – that is, the polyfunctionality – of linguistic forms. The data is complex and the analysis has to take this complexity into account.

More particularly, the study of several expressions of similarity in RAs and PAs suggests that comparison is sometimes used to re-conceptualize complex experiences into experiences more familiar to the lay-audience, making it a useful tool for writers of popularization. Yet, this is not the main use of comparison, which, in most cases, serves entirely different purposes (namely, characterization, explication, evaluation, categorization and metadiscourse). It is, however, this use that accounts for the different distributions between RAs and PAs of the markers under scrutiny. Writers of PAs seem to prefer a grammatical marker such as *like* because its syntactic properties make it easy to express re-conceptualization (through inter-domain or heterogeneous comparisons). By contrast, because of their syntax, the adjectives under study are more appropriate to express intra-domain comparison and functions (descriptive and metadiscursive), which fits the communicative purposes of the RA writer. Of course, these results need to be confirmed by the analysis of a larger set of comparative markers.

References

Anthony, Laurence. 2011. *AntConc 3.2.4w*. http://www.laurenceanthony.net/software/antconc/.

Aristotle. 1991. *Rhétorique*. Paris: Librairie générale française.

Biezunski Michel. 1985. Popularisation and scientific controversy: The case of the theory of relativity in France. In Terry Shinn & Richard Whitley (eds.), *Expository Science: Forms and Functions of Popularisation*. Dordrecht/Boston/Lancaster: D. Reidel Publishing Company. 183-194.

Bondi, Marina. 2012. Re-contextualizing knowledge. Past and present in popular history. Paper presented at the *4th International 360° Conference - Encompassing Knowledge Mediation*. Aarhus, Denmark, 10-12 May 2012.

Croft, William & D. Alan Cruse. 2004. *Cognitive Linguistics*. Cambridge: Cambridge University Press.

Huddleston, Rodney & Geoffrey K. Pullum. 2002. *The Cambridge Grammar of the English Language*. Cambridge: Cambridge University Press.

Hyland, Ken. 1998. Persuasion and context: The pragmatics of academic metadiscourse. *Journal of Pragmatics* 30. 437-455.

—. 2010. Constructing proximity: Relating to readers in popular and professional science. *Journal of English for Academic Purposes* 9. 116-127.

Israel, Michael, Jennifer R. Harding & Vera Tobin. 2004. On simile. In Michel Achard & Suzanne Kemmer (eds.), *Language, Culture, and Mind*. Stanford, CA: CSLI Publications. 123-135.

Kunzig, Robert. 2006. Gee whiz science writing. In Deborah Blum, Mary Knudson & Robin Marantz Henig (eds.), *A Field Guide to Science Writing*. 2nd ed. Oxford: Oxford University Press. 126-131.

Lakoff, George & Mark Johnson. 1980. *Metaphors We Live By*. Chicago, IL: The University of Chicago Press.

Langacker, Ronald W. 1987. *Foundations of Cognitive Grammar: Theoretical Prerequisites. Vol.1*. Stanford, CA: Stanford University Press.

Lyons, John. 1977. *Semantics. Vol. 2*. Cambridge: Cambridge University Press.

Moirand, Sophie. 1999. L'explication. In Jean-Claude Beacco (ed.), *L'astronomie dans les médias. Analyses linguistiques de discours de vulgarisation*. Paris: Presses de la Sorbonne Nouvelle. 141-167.

Morinet, Christiane. 1995. La comparaison en amont ou en aval de la métaphore. *Faits de langue* 5. 201-208.

Neuner, Jerome L. 1987. Cohesive ties and chains in good and poor freshman essays. *Research in the Teaching of English* 21. 92-105.

Paradis, Carita. 2005. Ontologies and construals in lexical semantics. *Axiomathes* 15. 541-573.

Pennec, Blandine. 2006. *La reformulation en anglais contemporain: indices linguistiques et constructions discursives*. Unpublished doctoral dissertation. Université Rennes 2.

Pic, Elsa & Gregory Furmaniak. 2012. Les modes de discours, interface entre texte et grammaire dans les langues de spécialité. *ASp* 62. 25-44.

Pic, Elsa, Gregory Furmaniak & Vincent Hugou. 2013. Etude comparative de quelques marqueurs de reformulation paraphrastique dans les articles de recherche et les articles de vulgarisation. *ASp* 63. 75-92.

Varttala, Teppo. 2001. *Hedging in Scientifically Oriented Discourse. Exploring Variation according to Discipline and Intended Audience*. Unpublished doctoral dissertation. University of Tampere. http://acta.uta.fi/pdf/951-44-5195-3.pdf. Accessed 13-07-2014.

“THESE DATA SUPPORT THE *PROVOCATIVE* VIEW THAT…”: EVALUATION IN MEDICAL ACADEMIC POSTERS

STEFANIA M. MACI
UNIVERSITY OF BERGAMO, ITALY

Abstract: In the hard sciences, posters have rapidly become a major format for scientific academic communication. For this reason, and in order to facilitate knowledge transfer and academic discussion, medical posters are uploaded on the Net. Due to space constraints, poster authors tend to ‘topicalize’ or thematize general and theoretical claims, rather than discuss them. One of the most powerful ways of thematizing attitudinal meanings and present an explicit statement of evaluation is by means of *that*-structures. This research will, therefore, investigate how evaluation is conveyed through *that*-structures. The study has been carried out using *Wordsmith Tools* and is based on the analysis of a corpus of 532 medical posters presented at international conferences and uploaded on the Web. In particular, the investigation tries not only to detect what type of verbs (whether cognitive, discursive or research ones) are exploited, but, above all, to understand why they are used across the Introduction-Methods-Results-Discussion sections of posters. Although such analysis certainly has some limitations, and needs to be triangulated, it may offer new insights into the genre of posters distributed via the Web.

1. Introduction

The poster is one of the genres used by the medical academic community to transfer its knowledge and findings. Poster sessions relating to the hard sciences made their first appearance as a conference genre in the U.S. at the *Biochemistry/Biophysics 1974 Meeting* (Maugh 1974) and, according to Matthew and Matthews (1996:97), they have since come to play a strategic role in scientific conferences. As explained by my informant, Dr. De Castro (Head of the Publishing Dept. of ISS, the Italian Health Institute), it is in the hard sciences that conference posters are mostly used and valued. They have an important function in scientific conferences and constitute a valid and interesting alternative to paper presentations, partly because it is recognised that medical knowledge can be absorbed more readily from poster sessions than from oral presentations (Whimster 1989). This now occurs to such an extent that, generally, a scientific board will either request that authors of papers present a poster instead of giving an oral presentation, or simply issue a *Call for Posters* – as with the *2011 International Conference on Meningitis and septicaemia in children and adults* held in London, 8–9 November 2011. In addition, lively post-conference discussions can continue as posters are usually uploaded to the Internet.

Most poster guidelines define a poster as a visual display of research key points, usually presented at medical conferences during poster sessions by the researcher him/herself or by one of the researchers if the poster is multi-authored. Indeed, as Dubois (1985a) claims, a poster is an alternative to the reading of a paper and can be a convenient way to publicly communicate research results at professional meetings. During such presentations, the presenter highlights key research points through an interaction with the audience.

As we can see from Figure 1 and Figure 2 below,[1] posters can vary in size, may contain tables and graphs, and may have an abstract but no references.

As we can see from the figures below, the main feature of posters is that their content is displayed as a 'visual unit' (MacIntosh-Murray 2007), contained within a single-view plane. In other words, what is described, explained and argued in several pages in a research article, must be expressed in few words and condensed into a very limited amount of space in a poster.

[1] I would like to thank Prof. Julie Zito (University of Maryland, Baltimore) for her permission to use and reproduce her poster (Figure 1) and Dr. David M. Svinarich, Director of Patient Care Research and SJHS Research and Development of Providence Hospital, Providence, U.S.A., for allowing me to reproduce one of the posters created by some 2010 Fellows and Residents and presented at medical conferences in 2010 (Figure 2).

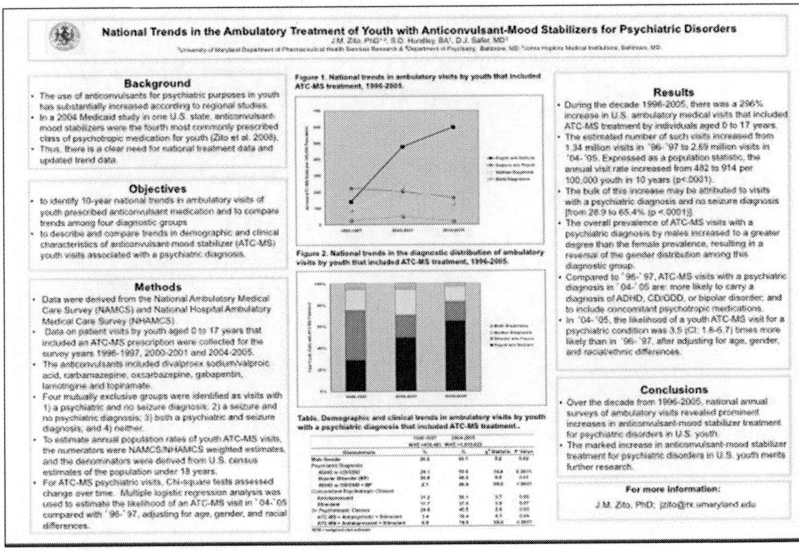

Fig. 1: Poster sample. Courtesy of Prof. Zito

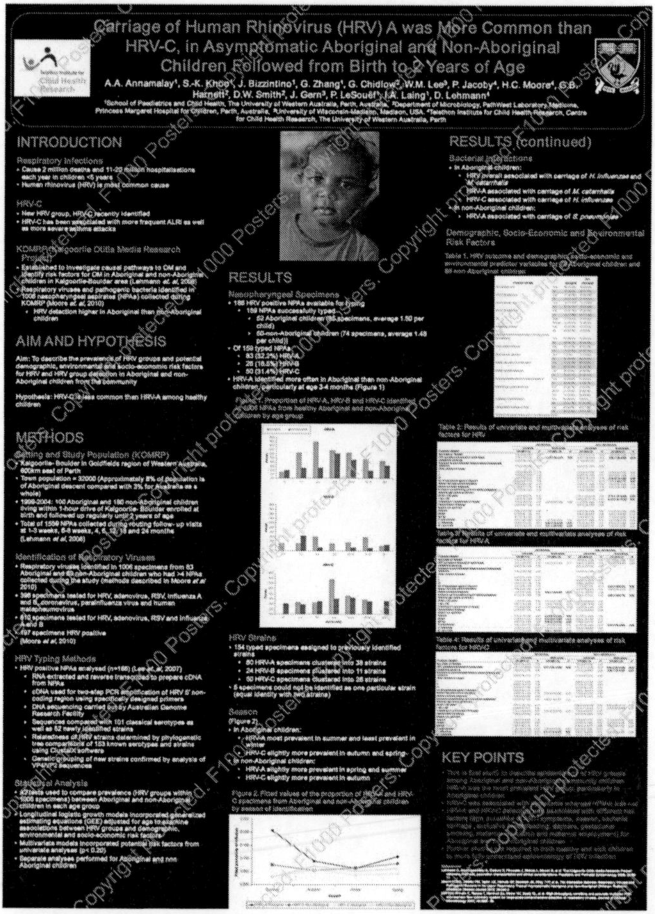

Fig. 2: Poster sample. Courtesy of F1000

1.1 Literature Review

As aptly pointed out by Hyland (2004, 2011), the way in which a researcher transfers his/her findings involves adopting a perspective as regards both the issue under investigation and the viewpoints of academic members on that issue. Yet arguments and writing tasks are valued differently by different disciplines.

Although posters can, ideally, be regarded as a genre in academic communication, similar to conference papers or journal articles (Hyland

1998), in certain disciplines posters are regarded as a "poor relation" to oral presentations (Swales & Feak 2000:81), or rather as a second-class research presentation tool for graduate students or novice researchers (Swales 2004:84). Despite recognizing the now widespread role posters play in the production of academic knowledge, MacIntosh-Murray (2007:367) indicates that professionals tend to assign lower prestige to a poster than to an oral presentation: the overall idea behind professionals' perception of posters is that a poster is presented because the paper is rejected. MacIntosh-Murray's (2007) investigation draws on studies by Dubois (1985a, 1985b), who first examined the genre features of posters[2]. More specifically, Dubois showed that medical posters in scientific communication have a popularization function and are exploited to attract the *invisible college*[3], made up of (medical) professional members working on a similar topics, and thus create potential networks amongst research teams. To the best of my knowledge, the most recent contributions in terms of multimodal analysis of academic posters are D'Angelo (2010, 2012) and Maci (2011, 2012).

Given the relevance of the genre to research within the scientific community and the lack of investigation from a linguistic viewpoint, I will now try to carry out an in-depth analysis of how scientific discourse is organized in medical posters.

2. Research Questions

Medical RAs are presented to readers in a highly codified structure that transcends national cultures (Dahl 2004:1822). Indeed, such a structure has a set of constraints that are set out in the *Uniform Requirements for the Manuscripts Submitted to Biomedical Journals*. Such *Requirements*, produced in 1978, are known as the *Vancouver Style*; they were published in 1991 in the *British Journal of Medicine* (*BJM*) by the *International Committee of Medical Journal Editors* (*ICMJE*), and the updated version (Apr 2010) is downloadable from http://www.icmje.org/.

---

[2] See, for instance, the poster-presentation guidelines for the 2012 National Cancer Research Institute (NCRI) conference at http://www.ncri.org.uk/ncriconference/abstract/presentation_guidelines.asp and for the 2012 Conference on Retrovirus and Opportunistic Infections (CROI) conference at http://retroconference.org/2012/abstracts/poster-presentation-guidelines.

[3] The concept of the *invisible college* has also been discussed in Kuhn (1962), Matthew & Matthews (2007) and Gross et al. (2002), who date its origins back to the seventeenth century.

In order to create a reader-friendly format, the poster author must have the writing skills to construct a recognizable and logic flow of information while attracting visual attention. This is indeed challenging, not only because the text must be highly condensed, but also because the poster is characterized by visual elements, which play an important role in displaying scientific information.

As claimed by MacIntosh-Murray (2007:351-352), successful academic communication via posters means combining written and oral modes, which makes the genre of posters a very complex one, since it comprises (i) academic *writing* combined with editorial constraints, and (ii) academic *discourse* mixed with informal interaction with an expected peer audience. The complexity is further increased by the fact that posters must be created in such a way as to stand alone and do the *talking* while *showing* medical research.

Medicine is an empirical science which exploits inductive reasoning, in that generalization and theoretical abstraction derive from specific observations of certain phenomena. Due to space/length constraints, claims are only lexicalized or 'topicalized', rather than discussed; therefore their relevance needs to be synoptically recognized. As Sala (forthcoming) claims, "this recognisability is obtained through adherence to accepted ways of conceptualizing and representing objects, processes and roles (Salager-Meyer 1990; Askehave & Swales 2000; Cross & Oppenheim, 2006; Dressen-Hammouda 2008), which are exploited as 'membershipping' features (Hyland 2007:66)". These are neither conventions nor the results of stylistic and generic crystallization Rather, they are ways of reflecting domain-specific epistemological peculiarities as to how knowledge and the process of knowledge-making are most effectively represented so as to persuade the reader of the associated poster's worth. Indeed, academic writers mould their texts not only in order to present their findings but also to evaluate them, while simultaneously creating solidarity with the reader. Such an evaluation is possible if authors adopt a position whose aim is to persuade their readers. As Hyland and Tse (2005:39-40) argue, "the linguistic resources used to achieve these interpersonal goals have been variously described under the headings of evaluation (Hunston & Thompson 2000), appraisal (Martin 2000), stance (Biber & Finegan 1989; Hyland 1999) and metadiscourse (Crismore 1989; Hyland 1998)". Evaluation is indeed amongst the main resources for meaning-making in text (Thompson & Hunston 2006). One of the most powerful ways to thematize attitudes or meanings and present an explicit statement of evaluation in academic discourse is by means of *that*-structures (Hyland & Tse 2005). Therefore, the research question posed here will be: how is evaluation 'thematized' as that-structures within the genre of posters?

My research will focus on evaluative sentences that introduce *that*-clauses, i.e. those complement clauses embedded in a superordinate one (the matrix clause) in order to complete its construction and project the writer's attitudes towards something (Hyland & Tse 2005:40): the superordinate or matrix sentence is the clause which contains both the evaluation and the source of evaluation (object or participant), while the *that*-clause projects the entity which is evaluated, as example (1) shows:

(1) We postulate that [MATRIX] this property leads to increased strand transfer by RT [PROJECTED CLAUSE] […] (P012)

To successfully obtain the reader's attention, the poster writer must demonstrate, via visuals and/or words, that s/he has something scientifically worth saying. If visuals represent facts, which speak for themselves (Maci 2011), texts express attitudinal meaning and evaluation.

3. Methodological Approach

As the first news item regarding medical posters was published in 1974 (Maugh 1974), I started my search from 1975 onwards via MEDLINE (http://www.medline.cos.com/*)* and PUBMED (http://www.ncbi.nlm.nih.gov/pubmed/*)*, the most authoritative online databases containing citations and abstracts taken from health and medical journals. Amongst all the medical journals available, I found that the journal which first began the publication of poster abstracts was the *American Journal of Epidemiology*. I therefore decided to concentrate on posters specializing in the epidemiological field. I then searched on the Internet for all available posters presented at congresses and published online by institutions and medical schools, as well as by online journals with an ISSN code and specializing in poster publication. I thus collected 532 posters (824,658 tokens; 27,669 types; STTR 31.35) written in English and presented at scientific conferences between 2001 and 2011 from the following websites:

(a) *Barts and The London NHS Trust*, http://www.ihse.qmul.ac.uk/cme/bscmeded/poster/index.html;
(b) The *2011 International Conference on Meningitis*, http://www.meningitis.org/posters;
(c) *International Conference on Retroviruses and Opportunistic Infections*, http://www.retroconference.org/;
(d) *Istituto Superiore di Sanità*, www.iss.it;

(e) *eposternet*, http://www.eposters.net/;
(f) *F1000*, http://f1000.com/posters.

A quantitative analysis was carried out with *WordSmith Tools 6.0* (Scott 2012) in order to detect *that*-clauses. It was decided to consider only cases which retained the complementizer *that*, despite the choice authors have to omit or retain *that* without changing the semantic value of the sentence, because "retention of *that* is overwhelming the norm in academic writing" (Hyland & Tse 2005:45).

The quantitative analysis was later followed by a qualitative interpretation of the findings of this research on the basis of a previous descriptive and quantitative analysis, since the former implied several subtle distinctions, which will be discussed later.

4. Results and Discussion

4.1 Overview: Classifying *Evaluative That*

To the best of my knowledge, the only scholars who have classified evaluative *that* clauses are Hyland (2005) and Hyland and Tse (2005), whose frameworks suggest grouping *that*-clauses into four main types:

1. The *evaluative entity*, which focuses on what the proposition following *that* refers to, and can indicate an interpretation of:
   - writer's claim(s);
   - content(s) of previous studies;
   - content(s) of research goals;
   - content(s) of research methods, models or theories that have been drawn on;

   What is evaluated is presented in the projected clause.
2. The *evaluative stance*, which refers to the author's attitude to the proposition in the *that*-clause, is typically realised by the controlling predicate and expresses:
   - attitudinal stance (i.e., the author's *affective* attitude towards the proposition);
   - epistemic stance (i.e., the author's *assessment* of the likely truth of the proposition).
3. The *source of evaluation.* Authors can choose to attribute the source of evaluation to either a human source (the author or other researchers) or an abstract source (data, methods, findings, results). The source can also be omitted. In this case, it represents a form of

authorial stance, in that it is a conscious decision not to accept responsibility for the interpretation of what follows.

4. The *evaluative expression*, which can be verbal or non-verbal. Verb forms can, in turn, be categorised according to the type of activity they refer to:
   - *research* acts, representing experimental activities (i.e., *demonstrate*, *show*);
   - *discourse* acts, focusing on the verbal expression of cognitive or research activities (i.e., *report*, *conclude*);
   - *cognitive* acts, considering the author's mental processes (i.e., *assume*, *believe*).

A summary of Hyland (2005) and Hyland and Tse (2005) is offered in Table 1 below: column one indicates the dimension according to which *that*-clauses can be classified, column two the corresponding subcategories, and column three gives examples through which aspect and categories can be better identified. The code found in round brackets, as in '(P011)', indicates poster ('P') and corresponding number ('011'), which refers to the chronological order of downloading. The examples in the third column are drawn from the corpus on which our investigation is based.

Tab. 1: Classification of sentences containing evaluative *that*

Aspect	Subcategory		Example
Evaluative entity	(a) Interpretation of the author's claim		*Our studies suggest* that HIV-1 enhances levels of cholesterol in the cell membrane […]. (P011)
	(b) Interpretation of previous studies		*Lee et al. have shown* that the combinatorial action of luminal CCR5 binding chemokine, CCL5, with CXCR […]. (P485)
	(c) Interpretation of the author's goals		*The hope is* that by including all important covariates, A4 plausibly holds […]. (P064)
	(d) Interpretation of methods, theories, models		*Current models hold* that one of these complexes, ESCRT-III, forms a membrane-associated lattice. (P289)
Evaluative stance	(a) Attitudinal	(i) affect	*It is noteworthy* that the effect of these mutants is mainly reproducible in these three cell lines […]. (P343)
		(ii) obligation	N.A.
	(b) Epistemic		[…] however, it seems likely that several mechanisms are at play. (P062)

Evaluative source	(a) Human – either to the author or other authors		We demonstrated that R5 gp120 […] (P485); Lee et al. have shown that the combinatorial action of […] (P485)
	(b) Abstract entity – inanimate source		The latter finding indicates that GPR15 could be used by […] (P484)
	(c) Concealed – unidentified source		It was recorded that sepsis was […] (P454)
Evaluative Expression	(a) Non-verbal	(i) Noun predicate	Our hypothesis is that […] (P343)
		(ii) Adjectival predicate	However, it seems likely that several mechanisms are at play. (P062)
	(b) Verbal	(i) Research act – actions in the real world	Conclusions: The findings described above demonstrate that HIV-1 can transduce […] (P009)
		(ii) Discourse act – linguistic activities	We postulate that this property leads to increased strand transfer by RT […] (P012)
		(iii) Cognitive act – mental processes	We believe that Vpr-induced nuclear […] (P006)

Clearly, the four categories overlap (cf. excerpt 2):

(2) *Our studies suggest that* HIV-1 enhances levels of cholesterol in the cell membrane […]. (P011).

This is an example of an author's claim (*our* studies), but also of a cognitive act (*suggest*) with an evaluative stance whose source is abstract.

In the following section I will try to apply such a framework to the evaluative *that*-clauses occurring in medical posters in order to see how they can be classified and how they are distributed across the IMRD pattern.

4.2 Frequency of *Evaluative That*

The concordance list of *that* indicates that 3,191 instances of *that* occurred. Only instances containing *that* as a complementizer were considered. This left us with 889 instances of *that* (18.3 TTR).

By applying Hyland's framework to my corpus, the frequency of evaluative *that*-clauses has the distribution indicated in Table 2. As can be

Tab. 2: Evaluative *that*-clauses in posters (from Hyland &Tse 2005)

ASPECT	SUBCATEGORY		ABSTRACT				BODY COPY				
			I	M	R	D	I	M	R	D	SUBTOTAL
(Interpretation of) Evaluative Entity	(a) Interpretation of the author's claim		32	1	27	33	73	2	49	80	297
	(b) Interpretation of previous studies		22	1	2	2	26	=	5	10	68
	(c) Interpretation of the author's goals		=	=	=	=	=	=	=	3	3
	(d) Interpretation of methods, theories, models		12	=	62	57	83	6	163	138	521
		subtotal	**66**	**2**	**91**	**92**	**182**	**8**	**217**	**231**	**889**
Evaluative Stance	(a) Attitudinal	(i) affect:	=	=	=	1	3	1	1	4	10
		(ii) obligation:	=	=	=	=	=	=	=	1	1
	(b) Epistemic		*66*	*2*	*91*	*91*	*179*	*7*	*216*	*226*	878
		subtotal	**66**	**2**	**91**	**92**	**182**	**8**	**217**	**231**	**889**
Evaluative Source	(a) Human- either to the author or other authors		32	1	17	5	52	2	42	45	196
	(b) Abstract entity – inanimate source		25	1	73	79	106	4	157	164	609
	(c) Concealed – unidentified source		9	=	1	8	24	2	18	22	84
		subtotal	**66**	**2**	**91**	**92**	**182**	**8**	**217**	**231**	**889**
Evaluative Expression	(a) Non-verbal	(i) noun predicate	6	2	2	9	26	=	8	44	97
		(ii) adjective predicate	2	=	1	3	7	1	6	2	22
	(b) Verbal	(i) Research act – actions in the real world	*24*	=	*65*	*44*	*87*	*2*	*121*	*83*	426
		(ii) Discourse act – linguistic activities	*13*	=	*16*	*28*	*31*	*3*	*61*	*76*	228
		(iii) Cognitive act – mental processes	*21*	=	*7*	*8*	*29*	*2*	*19*	*24*	110
		(iv) Relational acts	=	=	=	=	*2*	=	*2*	*2*	6
		subtotal	**66**	**2**	**91**	**92**	**182**	**8**	**217**	**231**	**889**

seen, there is a subcategory that does not occur in Hyland and Tse's framework, which is related to evaluative expressions (cf. bottom line of Table 2). There are indeed acts that Halliday and Matthiessen (2004:470-4) define as *relational*. *Relational* sentences are expressed by means of extraposed *that*-structures (Biber et al. 1999:675) such as *it seems that, the problem is that*. Though relatively rare, when used, they are most likely to occur in the expository prose register (news and academic prose), which often reports static information in an impersonal way. Here, the *that*-clause is not projected by a verbal or mental process with a conscious, evaluating agent, but is "ready packaged in projected form", allowing the writer to present a claim as an accredited fact (Hyland & Tse 2005:52).

For the purposes of this paper, I will discuss the most frequent trends, because these can reveal the epistemological tradition of the discipline.

4.3 Evaluative Entity: Focusing on Topic Interpretation

As said above, the *evaluative entity* can offer: (i) an interpretation of the writer's claim; (ii) the content of previous studies; (iii) the content of research goals; and (iv) the content of research methods, models or theories that have been drawn on. In other words, this category takes into consideration the interpretation of topics dealt with and projected in the clause introduced by complementizer *that*.

A summary of the findings characterising the corpus under investigation is given in Figure 3 below, where we can see what type of interpretation is offered (i.e. whether the author is interpreting his/her claims, goals, previous studies and/or models and theories) and in what section of the poster (i.e. whether they are in the *Introduction*, *Methods*, *Results* or *Discussion* sections):

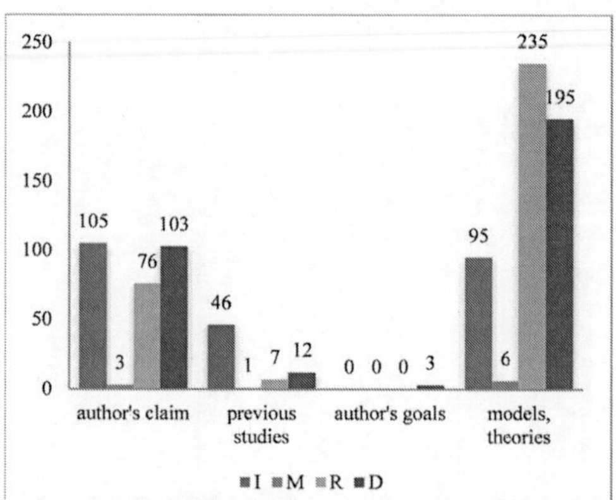

Fig. 3: Evaluative entity breakdown

From the evidence provided in Figure 3 we can say that the evaluative entity is expressed mainly in order to interpret the author's claims or put forward models/theories.

When authors' claims are interpreted by the evaluative entity, it comes as no surprise that the claims advanced by writers are introduced in the matrix clause, as this puts emphasis on the authors' credibility. When this occurs, it often, but not always, coincides with expressions containing the source of the evaluation with the evaluative function performed by the verbal expression, suggesting that the claim will be adequately demonstrated by the *paper* itself:

(3) *we* show that […] (P228)
(4) *we* demonstrate that […] (P227)
(5) *Our* results suggest that […] (P341)

These expressions normally occur in the *Introduction* section (105 hits), where the writer's primary role is that of establishing authority and credibility, while at the same time appealing to the reader.

They can also be found in the *Discussion* section (103 hits), where the collected data and results are discussed and interpreted. Here, however, before discussing findings authors tend to outline once again the purpose of their research and provide background information. As my previous studies suggest (Maci 2011), it is common practice within the medical community to summarize research aims in the *Discussion* section, because medics tend to scan a text and skip forward to the *Discussion* only if they find the poster of interest to them.

Generally, evaluated entities are highlighted by the poster author through the presentation of data, findings or supporting information in the matrix clause.

(6) This suggests that sequences from HIV sampled at different times […] (P004)
(7) CDC's estimate that 25% of PLWHA […] (P106)
(8) The 3-D models of CA show that […] (P406)

This occurs particularly in the *Results* and *Discussion* sections (235 and 195 hits respectively). Objectivity is the main issue here and indeed the text is supported by visuals, especially in the *Results* section: seeing the results expressed as graphs and percentages convinces the reader that an appropriate scientific procedure has been followed and that the protocol can be tried and tested in any laboratory under the same conditions as those linguistically described in the research.

4.4 Evaluative Stance: Focusing on the Author's Position about What is Said

The author's attitude to the proposition in the *that*-clause represents the *evaluative stance*, typically realised by the controlling predicate. The evaluative stance expresses either the attitudinal stance or the epistemic stance. When it is *attitudinal*, it indicates the author's *affective* attitude towards the proposition or the perceived *obligation* regarding what the author thinks should now be done. When the evaluative stance is *epistemic*, it indicates the author's "assessment of the likely truth or accuracy of the proposition" (Hyland & Tse 2005:46).

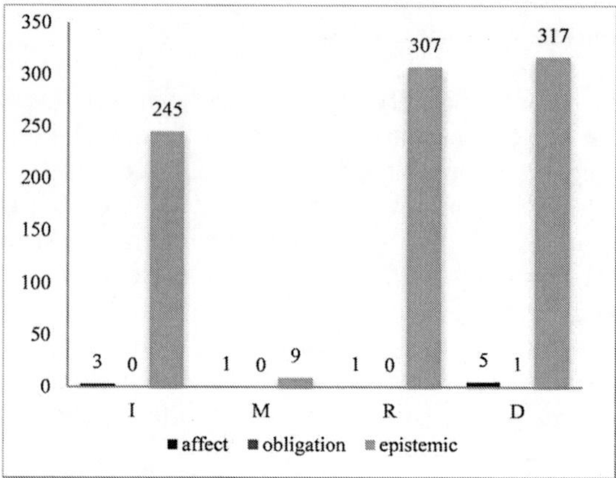

Fig. 4: Evaluative stance breakdown

As we can see from Figure 4, there is no obligation at all. The representation of the author's affective attitude towards the claim is represented sporadically throughout the IMRD pattern, with one particular example in P485 occurring in the *Methods* section and clearly anticipating the scientific position of the author as regards data analysis ("These data support the *provocative* view that [...]"), which is interestingly attributed to the *data* presented. Stance in my corpus is virtually expressed with an epistemic evaluative judgment (overall, 878 hits), by means of which the authors' assessment of the likelihood of the truth is represented:

(9) The biological arguments include [...] in vitro evidence that [...] (P228)

(10) Our results are consistent with the previous report that HIV-1 […] (P406)

Poster authors try to persuade the community that the claims put forward are legitimate and certain. This is implicitly supported by the widespread use of certain verbs, such as *show* (145 hits), *indicate* (112 hits) and *demonstrate* (81 hits), which belong to what Hyland (2005) defines as *research* act verbs, and with the rare presence of modal expressions. It is worth noting the fact that epistemicity, indicating the highest degree of certainty, is, linguistically speaking, minimal in the *Methods* section, probably because, here, scientific discourse follows a narrative pattern which offers the readership the opportunity to try out the scientific protocol with great precision.

4.5 Evaluative Source: Focusing on Who Evaluates

If we turn to the analysis of evaluative *that*-clauses in terms of the subject evaluating the proposition, we can see that this role can be assumed by human sources, abstract or inanimate entities and concealed sources. A summary of their distribution can be seen in Figure 5 below, from which the predominant use of the abstract source may immediately be detected.

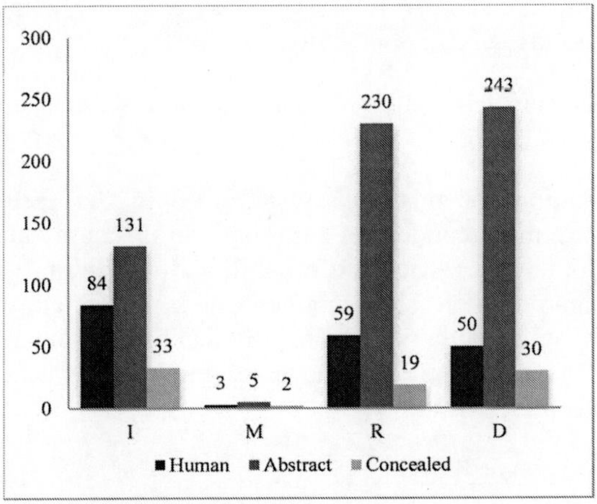

Fig. 5: Evaluative source breakdown

In the *Introduction* section, the source of evaluation can be human or abstract (84 and 131 occurrences, respectively), but there is a preference for the use of abstract sources:

(11) We demonstrated earlier that HIV vaccination of seronegative vaccines […] (P009)
(12) INTRODUCTION Current evidence suggests that HIV-1 and HIV-2 […] (P002)

Similarly, there is a recurrent exploitation of inanimate entities: the source of evaluation is assigned to the findings or the data in the *Results* (230 occurrences) and *Discussion* (243 hits) sections:

(13) Comparison of p11c+ T cells kinetics following SIVsmE660 infection suggests that these were very similar to […] (P064)
(14) Conclusion: These results suggest that dynactin is specifically required for the movement of endosomes associated (P341)
(15) Results: Our results demonstrate that GPR15 allows […] (P484)

This is purposefully employed. By shifting the reader's attention from the researcher to the research itself, the poster author strategically provides legitimacy for his/her claims.

The corpus presents very few occurrences of concealed sources (66 hits), which I would have expected considering that the suppression of agents in scientific discourse implies the removal of human agency and contributes to an increase in objectivity:

(16) Background: It is well established that on coretroviruses can […] (P009)

The explanation for this probably resides in the fact that posters represent an extremely condensed genre and so discourse must be direct, focusing on the author's scientific reliability. In addition, given the fact that most evaluative expressions convey epistemic certainty, there is no need to depersonalise authors' opinions: objectivity is obtained by means of attributing the source of evaluation to the results, which putatively speak for themselves.[4]

---

[4] Swales (2004) argues that data tends not to speak for themselves. Although this may be true, in those disciplines based on empiricism, as, for instance in medicine, this is not always the case. Furthermore, in the case of medical posters, where space constraints are extremely rigid and there is little space for argumentation and interpretation, the *Results* section is often 'visually' represented through tables and

4.6 Evaluative Expression: Focusing on How Things are Evaluated

As stated in Section 4.1 above, the importance of evaluation depends on how it is expressed, namely in non-verbal and verbal forms. Non-verbal forms based on nominal expressions (97 hits), such as those in excerpts (17) and (18) below, appear very rarely in my corpus:

(17) […] support the *hypothesis* that […] (P062)
(18) The biological arguments include […] in vitro *evidence* that […] (P228)

Even more infrequent are non-verbal forms based on adjectival structures, as in excerpt (19) below, of which only 22 occurrences were counted:

(19) However, it seems likely that several mechanisms are at play. (P062)

On the other hand, there is a preference for the use of verbal forms, in particular those expressing *research* and *discourse* acts, as shown in Figure 6 below. As Sala (forthcoming) explains, *research* acts are those formulations in which experimental activities are expressed. Discourse acts reveal the verbal expression of cognitive or research activities.

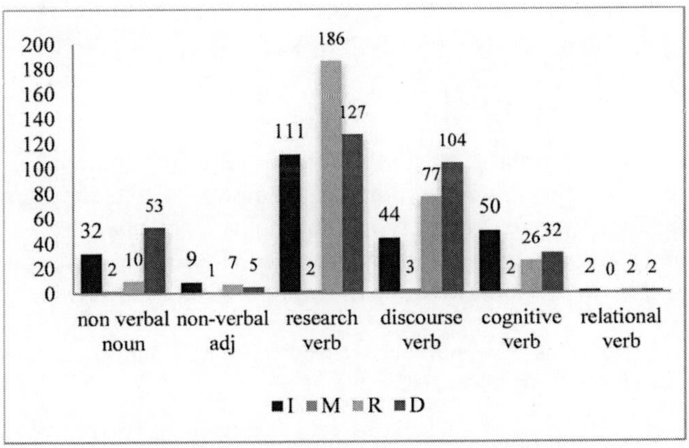

Fig. 6: Evaluative expression breakdown

graphs: here, results are literally depicted and never overtly reported or interpreted by the researcher's voice. See also Maci (2012, 2011).

Figure 6 above shows that there is great exploitation of *research* acts (426 hits, overall),which are used predominantly in the *Introduction, Discussion* and, in particular, *Results* sections (111, 127, and 186 hits, respectively):

(20) These results *demonstrate* that HDAC6 plays (P158)
(21) Figure 1 *shows* that (P227)
(22) We *demonstrate* that gp120 acts […] (P485)

The type of information conveyed here is evidential and concerned with finding reliability. By framing evaluation in research acts, the poster author implicitly signals that the claim is grounded in research practices, emphasising the importance of lab work and the value of experiment results, which is indeed supported by the fact that almost 46 per cent of *research* acts have an abstract entity source of evaluation.

There is also a trend revealing a preference for *discourse* acts (with 228 frequencies), particularly in the *Results* (77 hits) and the *Discussion* (104 occurrences) sections:

(23) This clinical observation *suggests* that […] (P254)
(24) Current models *hold* that […] (P289)

Cognitive acts (110 occurrences) are, on the contrary, less frequently used. When they are adopted, they are found mainly in the *Introduction* (50 hits) and *Discussion* (32 hits) sections:

(25) We *hypothesised* that […] (P158)

Their focus is on those mental processes requiring the construction of hypotheses and the interpretation of frameworks which significantly express the inductive reasoning typical of the hard sciences.

As far as *relational* verbs are concerned, these are verbs that report information in a very static way, as in example (26), below:

(26) […], it seems that brain-derived envelopes have higher fusogenicity than those from spleen. (P193)

Their frequency, however, is so minimal (6 hits in total), that they offer no meaningful insights for our analysis. A list of the types of verbal acts is offered in Table 3 below:

Tab. 3: List of verbal acts

RESEARCH ACTS (426 hits)	DISCOURSE ACTS (228 hits)
show (145), indicate (116), demonstrate (81), discover (6), find (41), reveal (31), identify (2), verify (2), evidence (1), signal (1)	suggest (179), report (16), note (12), confirm (9), describe (3), argue (2), anticipate (1), highlight (1), mean (1), point (1), propose (1), recommend (1), record (1)
COGNITIVE ACTS (110 hits)	RELATIONAL ACTS (6 hits)
hypothesize (39),o bserve (14), imply (5), know (5), predict (5), postulate (4), assume (3), believe (3), conclude (3), accept (2), establish (2), estimate (2), hope (2), expect (2), see (2), speculate (2), consider (1), ensure (1), exclude (1), hold (1), illustrate (1), notice (1), presume (1), prove (1), reason (1), recognize (1), reinforce (1), remain (1), support (1), surprise (1), worry (1)	be (4), seem (2)

Given the low occurrence of relational verbs, we will not take these into consideration in the following analysis. As we can see from Table 3, the number of verb types belonging to the *cognitive* act class exceeds that of other verb classes, but the frequency of verb types not belonging to the *cognitive* act class is superior to those belonging to it. Indeed, we can see that, within the *cognitive* act class, the only verb that occurs more than 30 times (corresponding to 5% of all verb occurrences) is *hypothesize* (39 hits, 5%); in the *research* act class, verbs occurring quite frequently are *demonstrate* (81 hits, 10.5%), *find* (41 hits, 5.32%), *indicate* (116 hits, 15%) and *show* (145 hits, 18.83%), while the *discourse* act class presents *suggest* (179 hits, 23.24%). Clearly, their distribution varies across the poster structure depending on (i) the evaluative entity and (ii) the evaluative source, as indicated in Table 4 below. The indication of the type of act found in medical posters, i.e. *cognitive*, *discourse* or *research* acts, is found in the first column. In the second, we see those verbs that have a frequency of at least 5% of occurrences in my corpus, i.e. the cognitive verb *hypothesize*, the discourse act *suggest*, and the research verbs *find*, *indicate*, *show* and *demonstrate.* In the third column, an indication of the source, *abstract* (A), *concealed* (C), or *human* (H) is given. All this has been cross-checked with both the *Introduction*, *Methods*, *Results*, and *Discussion* pattern (first row), and the evaluative entities (second row), thus offering an interpretation of: models and theories (IM), authors' claims/goals (IAC/G)and previous studies (IPS).

Tab. 4: Breakdown of verbal acts distribution across IMRD pattern, depending on evaluative entity and source

			Introduction			*Methods*			*Results*			*Discussion*		
			IM	IAC/G	IPS	IM	IAC/G	IPS	IM	IAC/G	IPS	IM	IAC/G	IPS
C	*Hypothesize*	H		**35**									2	
		C	2											
		A												
D	*Suggest*	H		4						5			**20**	1
		C	1									1		
		A	**22**		7				**46**			**72**		
R	*Find*	H		8						**21**			9	1
		C							1					
		A	1											
	Indicate	H	1	3						2		1	15	
		C	1											
		A	6		5				**51**			**31**		
	Show	H		**24**		1			1	8	2		**21**	4
		C												
		A	8		**19**	3			**40**			**14**		
	Demonstrate	H		**24**						2		2		
		C		2										
		A	9						**18**	5		7	12	

Legenda: C= Cognitive; D = Discourse; R= Research.

The results seem to indicate a precise pattern in the use of verbal acts. In the *Introduction*, whenever a *that*-structure offers an interpretation of the author's claims, and the source is human, there is a preference for exploitation of the cognitive verb *hypothesize* (35 hits). Under the same conditions, though appearing less frequently, the research verbs *show* (24 hits) or *demonstrate* (24 hits) may be used as alternatives. If, on the other hand, the *Introduction* section is giving way to an interpretation of methods and theories and the source is abstract, the verb normally employed is *suggest* (22 hits). The research act *show* (19 hits) can be utilized only if a *that*-structure is interpreting previous studies.

In the *Methods* section, *that*-structures are minimal and the only four found exploit the verb *show*, which is used in the interpretation of scientific models with an abstract source in three cases out of four.

All the verbs except the cognitive ones appear in the *Results* section. Interestingly, the interpretation of models is mainly conducted either by the use of the discourse verb *suggest* (46 hits) or the research verbs *indicate* (51 hits), *show* (40 hits) or *demonstrate* (18 hits) if the source is abstract or inanimate. In the case where a *that*-structure is interpreting the author's claims or goals and the source is human, then the verb used is *find* (21 hits).

The interpretation of models found in the *discussion* section is normally realized with the discursive act *suggest* (20 hits) with an abstract source of evaluation; less frequently the same interpretation is realized with the research verbs *indicate* (31 hits) and *show* (14 hits). *Show* (21 hits), on the other hand, seems to be preferred in the interpretation of the author's claims or goals when the source of evaluation is human. A summary of the results can be found in Table 5, below:

Tab. 5: Summary of verbal act distribution across the IMRD pattern

Introduction	*Methods*	*Results*	*Discussion*
Interpretation of claims • cognitive act: *hypothesize* • research acts: *show, demonstrate* • human source	=	Interpretation of model • discourse act: *suggest* • research acts: *demonstrate*; *indicate, show* • abstract source Interpretation of authors' claim • research act: *find* • human source	Interpretation of models • discourse act: *suggest* • research acts: *indicate, show* • abstract source Interpretation of authors' claims • research act: *show* • human source

The distribution of the verbal classes corresponds to the pragmatic purposes of the IMRD sections: in the *Introduction* the authors establish a niche where they can develop their own research space (Swales 1990). Therefore, finding human sources with cognitive or research verbs seems a quite obvious choice. Similarly, the *Results* section offers a description of the authors' findings as well as a preliminary interpretation of the data, hence the use of such verbs as *demonstrate*, *indicate* and *show* with an abstract source of evaluation, were the *data* is suggesting the results, rather than the author him/herself. Authors, in other words, are simply giving a voice to their findings. Indeed, they *find* data, while data *suggests*, *demonstrates*, *indicates* and *shows*. In the *Discussion* sections, authors simply *show* what they have found, and leave the responsibility for any interpretation of the scientific model to the data which *suggests*, *indicates* and *shows*.

5. Conclusions

This paper has sought to examine the way in which medical discourse is linguistically organized in medical posters, a genre highly-prized in the hard sciences in terms of the transfer of academic knowledge. This is largely due to the fact that, by being uploaded to the Internet, posters allow for follow-up discussion between members of the academic medical community. In particular, the aim of my research question has been to reveal if and to what extent evaluation is 'thematized' as *that*-structures.

Although the analysis carried out draws on Hyland and Tse's (2005) framework, it is experimental with a bottom-up structure. Indeed, the corpus used for my investigation has revealed some interesting behaviours, which differ somewhat from Hyland and Tse's (2005) model. Let us consider, for instance, the presence of *that*-structures formed by relational verbs such as *be* or *seem* and not detected by Hyland and Tse (2005).

As far as evaluation is concerned, the analysis of *that*-structures has shown the predominant use of epistemic expressions indicating that evaluative stance in all posters is realized as offering the highest degree of certainty and objectivity, regardless of the source of evaluation or evaluative entity. This seems to be closely related to the fact that argumentation is virtually absent in posters: there seems to be no need for persuasion when the facts speak for themselves. Indeed, the majority of *that*-expressions have an abstract source, indicating that the authors of the posters are merely giving a metadiscursive voice to the data, the real subjects (both grammatically and metaphorically) of the experiment under investigation. The verbal acts expressed in the matrix clause contribute to conveying such an illusion as they refer to the research procedure (*demonstrate*, *show*, *indicate*) and cognitive processes (*suppose*, *assume*, *hypothesize*) linked to the scientific mind at work. An indirect confirmation of this is provided by the fact that the only tentative form present in posters is the discourse act *suggest*.

In addition, we can see that evaluation is distributed differently across the IMRD pattern: in the *Introduction*, there is authorial (self-)reference, which is necessary to establish the credentials supporting scientific credibility and reliability. While in the *Methods* no *that*-structures appear at all, in the *Results* and *Discussion* sections we can see that there is a shift from authorial (self-)reference to data reference, thus giving way to descriptions of lab work and experimental practice which are supported by visual data and create the illusion that the facts speak for themselves. The authorial voice, therefore, is a mere instrumental tool to guide the reader metadiscursively towards a correct interpretation based on the 'facts' emerging from findings.

Such preliminary analysis undoubtedly has its limitations, and needs to be triangulated. Nevertheless, given the lack of applied linguistic research done on posters, my study may offer new insights into this neglected genre realized with a type of discourse aimed at constructing scientific reliability. It is hoped that the results will prove to be a valuable pedagogical resource in the future for the different academic communities represented in the corpus, as well as for EAP teachers.

References

Askehave, Inger & John Swales. 2000. Genre identification and communicative purpose: A problem and possible solution. *Applied Linguistics* 22. 195-212.

Biber, Douglas, Stig Johansson, Geoffrey Leech, Susan Conrad & Edward Finegan. 1999. *Longman Grammar of Spoken and Written English*. Harlow: Pearson Education.

Crismore, Avon. 1989. *Talking with Readers: Metadiscourse as Rhetorical Act*. New York: Peter Lang.

Cross, Cate & Charles Oppenheim. 2006. A genre analysis of scientific abstracts. *Journal of Documentation* 62. 4. 428-446.

D'Angelo, Larissa. 2012. Academic posters presentations. In Maurizio Gotti (ed.), *Academic Identity Traits*. Bern: Peter Lang. 263-281.

—. 2010. Creating a framework for the analysis of academic posters. *Language Studies Working Papers* 2. 38-50.

Dahl, Trine. 2004. Textual metadiscourse in research articles: A matter of national culture or of academic discipline? *Journal of Pragmatics* 36. 1807-1825.

Dressen-Hammouda, Dacia 2005. From novice to disciplinary expert: Disciplinary identity and genre mastery. *English for Specific Purposes* 27. 233-252.

Dubois, Betty. 1985a. Poster Sessions at biomedical meetings: Design and presentation. *The ESP Journal* 4. 37-48.

—. 1985b. Popularization at the highest level: Poster sessions at biomedical meetings. *International Journal of the Sociology of Language* 56. 67-84.

Gross, Alan, Joseph Harmon & Michael Reidy. 2002. *Communicating Science: The Scientific Article from the 17th century to the present.* Oxford: Oxford University Press.

Halliday, Michael A.K. & Charles Matthiessen. 2004. *An Introduction to Functional Grammar*. London: Edward Arnold.

Hunston, Susan & Geoff Thompson (eds.). 2000. *Evaluation in Text: Authorial Stance and the Construction of Discourse*. Oxford: Oxford University Press.

Hunston, Susan & Geoff Thompson. 2006. *System and Corpus*: *Exploring Connections*. London: Equinox.

Hyland, Ken. 1998. *Hedging in Scientific Research Articles*. Amsterdam/ Philadelphia: John Benjamins.
—. 2004. *Disciplinary Discourses: Social Interactions in Academic Writing*. London: Longman.
—. 2005a. *Metadiscourse*. London: Continuum.
—. 2007. *Disciplinary Discourses: Social Interactions in Academic Writing*. Ann Arbor, MI: University of Michigan Press.
— 2011. Disciplines and discourses: Social interactions in the construction of knowledge. In Doreen Starke-Meyerring, Anthony Paré, Natalia Artemeva, Miriam Horne & Larissa Yousoubova (eds.), *Writing in the Knowledge Society*. West Lafayette, IN: Parlor Press/The WAC Clearinghouse. 193-214.
Hyland, Ken & Polly Tse. 2005. Hooking the reader: A corpus study of evaluative *that* in abstracts. *English for Specific Purposes* 24. 123-139.
Kuhn, Thomas S. 1962. *The Structure of Scientific Revolutions*. Chicago, IL: University of Chicago Press.
Maci, Stefania.2011. Genre variation in medical discourse: The case of medical posters. In Srikant Sarangi, Vanda Polese & Giuditta Caliendo (eds.), *Genre(s) on the Move. Hybridization and Discourse Change in Specialized Communication*. Napoli, ESI: 169-190.
—. 2012. The genre of medical conference posters. In Maurizio Gotti (ed.), *Academic Identity Traits*. Bern: Peter Lang. 283-301.
MacIntosh-Murray, Anu. 2007. Poster Presentations as a genre in knowledge communication: A case study of forms, norms, and values. *Science Communication* 28. 3. 347-376.
Martin, James R.2000. Beyond exchange: Appraisal systems in English. In Susan Hunston & Geoff Thompson (eds.), *Evaluation in Text: Authorial Stance and the Construction of Discourse*. Oxford: Oxford University Press. 142-175.
Matthews, L. Diane 1990. The scientific poster: Guidelines for effective visual communication. *Technical Communication* 37. 3. 225-232.
Matthews, Janice & Robert Matthews. 2007. *Successful Scientific Writing*. Cambridge: Cambridge University Press.
Maugh, Thomas. 1974. Speaking of science: Poster Sessions: A new look at scientific meetings. *Science*. 184. 4144. 1361.
Sala, Michele. Forthcoming. Research article abstracts as domain-specific epistemological indicators. A corpus-based study. Paper presented at the *2012 CLAVIER Conference*, Modena, April 12-13, 2012.
Salanger-Meyer, Françoise. 1990. Discoursal flaws in medical English abstracts: A genre analysis per research- and text-type. *Text* 10. 4. 365-384
Scott, Mike. 2012. *WordSmith Tools Version 6*. Liverpool: Lexical Analysis Software.
Swales, John, M. 1990. *Genre Analysis. English in Academic and Research Settings*. Cambridge: Cambridge University Press.
—. 2004. *Research Genres. Explorations and Applications*. Cambridge: Cambridge University Press.
Swales, John M. & Christine B. Feak. 2000. *Academic Writing for Graduate Students: Essential Tasks and Skills: A Course for Nonnative Speakers of*

English (English for Specific Purposes). Ann Arbor, MI: University of Michigan Press.

Whimster, William. 1989. Wanted: Reader friendly posters. As much show business as science. *British Medical Journal* 298.6669. 274.

SECTION III:

KNOWLEDGE DISSEMINATION FROM INSTITUTIONS TO LAY AUDIENCE

PUBLIC APOLOGIES AND MEDIA EVALUATIONS

ALISON DUGUID
UNIVERSITY OF SIENA, ITALY

Abstract: This paper is concerned with the representation of public apologies in the media, the way the apologies are framed and evaluated, and the way in which the media act as judge of quality and quantity norms in the case of this public act, explicitly attempting to influence the way in which an utterance should be understood and how public apologies should be interpreted. Using a series of corpora from written and spoken sources, namely, the SiBol corpus comprising c.300,000,000 words of UK broadsheet newspaper texts, a corpus of White House briefings (c.1,500,000 words), a TV news corpus (c. 600,000 words) and an ad-hoc search-word-generated corpus of tabloid newspapers in their online form with *apology* as the search term (c. 194,000 tokens). Using the *Corpus-Assisted Discourse Studies* (*CADS*) methodology a number of preferred patterns of representation were found which evaluate public apologies, mostly negatively, through a number of parameters: timeliness, sincerity, spontaneity, and what might be called the humiliation factor.

1. Apologies

The *apology* can be defined for our purposes as an own-face-threatening act involving an explicit expression or acknowledgement of responsibility and regret. It is possible to apologise using a range of strategies and linguistic forms. Public apologies are mediated by the press and are subject to public evaluations, that is to say we are made aware of them through a mediated channel and at a time that they are usually being evaluated in some way. The *Centre for Conflict Resolution*[1] claims that a sincere apology is a powerful tool to bring peace, stop arguments and restore broken relationships. However they also warn that "bad apologies

[1] Established in 1968, The *Centre for Conflict Resolution* (*CCR*: http://www.ccr.org.za/index.php/about) is an independent, non-profit organization that focuses on promoting constructive, creative and co-operative approaches to the resolution of conflict, primarily through its policy-centered research, training programs, and capacity-building efforts.

can strain relationships and cause bitterness to remain." During recent decades, an abundance of apologies made by public actors has led to claims that we are living in the age of apology.

High profile public apologies receive significant coverage in both old and new media, and reactions to and evaluations of the perceived quality of the apology are broadcast and printed in a variety of mainstream media as well as receiving much attention in new media. Public apologies are performed with a third party audience of press and public; we rarely have access to them without the refracting lens of the media, so the main focus of the paper is on how such public apologies are treated and evaluated in the media; in particular we examine the lexical items *apology*, *sorry*, *regret* and related phraseologies and the patterns used to evaluate the apologies.

Politicians are self-conscious about how they interface with the news media and this self-consciousness has reinforced interest in reactions and evaluations. There have been many historical apologies (for the Irish potato famine, for the slave trade) and studies and discussion of their value. There have been a number of apologies by UK politicians recently: David Cameron after the Bloody Sunday report, and Nick Clegg on tuition fee rises, Maria Miller's apology to Parliament, Lord Rennard's apology to his colleagues; all met with extended coverage and evaluations in both new and mainstream media.

In politics and in the reporting of politics, language is constantly being reworked and adapted from other speech events: reports, opinions, announcements, reactions, discussions, and what have been called *news performatives*, part of the political process but also part of the communication of that process to the public. Fishman (1980:99) noted "Journalists love performative documents because they are the hardest facts they can get their hands on;" and Bell (1991:207) stated "Journalists love the performatives of politics where something happens through someone saying it. The fusion of word and act is ideal for news-reporting. No other facts have to be verified. The only fact is that somebody said something." The *public apology* is a particularly resonant performative. Speech events can of course be reported in a variety of ways: distancing or endorsement, stance signals, signals of interactional resistance, time frames and values can all be varied to fit a particular political or journalistic purpose. This paper hopes to show how this is actually done.

2. Apology Studies

There are many non-academic sources of judgments about apologies (see for example http://sorrywatch.com, a web site dedicated to public apologies) and institutions such as Debretts (http:// www.debretts.com/), which is interested in etiquette, and these devote space to establishing what makes a proper apology.[2] In the academic study of this speech act many earlier linguistic studies are based on the analysis of forms elicited as a response to simulated situations focusing on informal contexts, where interpersonal relationships are foregrounded, and do not use naturally occurring data; most deal with an analysis of speaker intuitions about relatively informal private apology situations where issues of politeness are at stake (Blum-Kulka & Olshtain 1984; Meier 1998; Lakoff 2001; Kampf 2009, 2011) and taxonomies have been drawn up of the components. Aijmer (1996) asserts that a key condition is that apologisers take responsibility and regret committing the offending act.

Apologies came under scrutiny in pragmatics in terms of *felicity conditions*, the conditions necessary for the acts to be performed legitimately or felicitously. Fraser (1981) considered that the apologiser has to both admit responsibility for committing the offending act and to express regret for the offence caused. Owen (1983) included the emotional element of sincerity. A statement of responsibility shows that the transgressor is aware that social norms have been broken, and so will be able to avoid committing such a transgression in the future. It also indicates that the event should not be attributed to the disposition of the offender - that it was not the 'true self' who committed the offence.

Among more recent studies, in particular one concerned with high profile public apologies of bankers involved in the 2008 banking crisis, Hargie et al. (2010:723) usefully summarise the necessary elements of an apology as being:

- An explicit *illocutionary force indicating device* (IFID); that is, a *statement of apology* ('I'm sorry'; 'I apologize for that')
- A *statement accepting responsibility* ('It was entirely my fault')
- A *denial of intent* ('I never meant to upset you')
- A *direct request to be pardoned* ('Please forgive me')
- An *explanation* ('I wasn't paying attention')

---

[2] "A *sincere apology* should always be offered when your actions have had a negative impact on other people. Even if you do not fully understand why someone is so upset, respect their feelings, and accept that your actions are the root of the problem." (http://www.debretts.com/british-etiquette/.../apologising).

- A *self-rebuke* ('I am such an idiot')
- An *expression of remorse* ('I feel terrible about this')
- An *offer of reparation* ('I will replace it for you')
- A *promise of future forbearance* ('This will not happen again')

Often bad apologies are evaluated as lacking particular elements from this list. Hargie et al. (2010:723) claim that the bad apologies of the CEOs lacked the two key defining features of apology: "admissions of blameworthiness and regret for an undesirable event."

More recent literature on the phenomenon of *political* apologies includes Harris et al. (2006) who used a discourse analysis approach, selecting data from a few high profile political apologies, and considered the reactions to them as well as the forms they took. They analysed the political apology as a speech event in pragmatic terms and identified the salient characteristics of different types of political apology. Harris et al. see an apology in terms of face and consider it as an own-face-threatening-act (Goffman 1971), involving *corrective face work*, that is to say attempts to restore face after it has been lost. In particular they underlined how one of its characteristics is the *highly mediated nature* of the event, thus differentiating the political from the informal and interpersonal apology.

The above cited Hargie et al. (2010) is another example of discursive analysis, but in the field of business studies: they analysed the public testimony of four banking CEOs to the Banking Crisis Inquiry of the Treasury Committee of the UK House of Commons in 2009. The high profile nature of the case included the fact that many felt the bankers had not taken responsibility so their aim was to explore how they attributed responsibility and blame through the medium of their public apologies. In their conclusions they characterized the bankers' discourse as an example of apology avoidance. This was reflected in much media and public commentary which centered on the seeming reluctance of the bankers to apologize (and hence accept responsibility) for their part in the banking crisis.

The present case study employs a different approach: a *Corpus-Assisted Discourse Studies* or *CADS* (Partington 2004; Partington et al. 2013) approach to media evaluations of the public apology. For our purposes we can define a corpus as a finite-sized, non-random collection of naturally occurring language, in computer readable form. It is non-random in that it is intended to be representative of a language, genre or text type and compiled for an intended functional purpose. Corpus research permits the observation of regularities over a large number of texts from which certain preferences can emerge as repeated regularities (Stubbs 1996; Partington 1998; Tognini Bonelli 2001; Sinclair 2004;

Baker 2005; Scott & Tribble 2006). The studies mostly use the software *WordSmith Tools 5.0* (Scott 2012 [1998]).

What a corpus analysis can do best is to uncover recurrent lexical patterns and the more subtle and pervasive meanings, in terms of distribution across contexts. By combining the automated statistical analyses of corpus linguistics with more traditional close reading text analysis, CADS is able to compare and contrast sets of language. With the use of concordances which bring together a series of fragments of text displaced from their original sequence and by aligning them vertically, one after the other, and ordering them in a variety of ways, to make repetition visible and countable, patterns emerge to the surface. The software also produces lists of collocations. A collocate is an "item that appears with greater than random probability in its (textual) context" (Hoey 1991:7), calculated by measures of statistical significance. Collocates, sorted into homogeneous groups, can make potential recurrent patterns visible; by then classifying collocates into semantic groupings we can identify recurrent semantic preferences and patterns and in particular recurrent evaluative patterns.

This study is a further contribution to a number of corpus-based studies dealing with aspects of pragmatics (McEnery et al. 2002; Partington 2003, 2006; Culpeper 2008; Jucker et al. 2009; Archer & Culpeper 2009; Taylor 2009, 2011), some employing the theoretical framework of (im)politeness in combination with corpus linguistics.

Other corpus studies have highlighted the role of the press: Jeffries (2006), investigating the speech act of apology, focused in particular on news commentators' views of Blair's apology for the Iraq war. Ancarno (2011) has more recently investigated press representations of public apologies, pointing out that most people access public apologies almost exclusively through the media. She examined press uptakes of (i.e. reactions to) public apologies in British and French newspapers with the aim of exploring the conditions of success, or felicity, of public apologies, as represented in the two different media cultures. She proposes a model accounting for the overt conditions of success assigned to public apology speech acts, using the media representations of what successful apologies are construed to be. Kampf (2011) also analysed uptake and the reasons for the interest taken by journalists in their extensive coverage, highlighting the active role played by the press at each stage of what she terms 'social dramas of apology' in Israeli public discourse. She illustrates ways in which journalists can be seen to actively generate, intensify and pacify social dramas of apology.

3. Methodology

In the present study, the term *apology* is used to refer both to complete apologies, partial apologies and refusals to apologise interchangeably, apologies being understood to be any apologetic speech act or act of contrition treated as an instance of apology in the press. Our research question is thus how such public apologies are treated and evaluated in the media. A second strand seeks to discover, by examining frequency data for institutional discourse in the form of public apologies and their representation in the press, how such representations and uptakes can be seen to re-contextualise and re-conceptualise the discourse of public figures. For the study, a number of previously compiled corpora were interrogated, namely, the *SiBol* corpus - comprising c. 300,000,000 words of UK broadsheet newspaper texts -, to shed light on how one particular discourse type represents the public apology; in order to have access to some spoken data we also used a corpus of White House briefings (*WHB*, c. 1,500,000 words). In addition to the White House briefings further spoken data was obtained with a previously gathered *TV news corpus* (c. 600,000 words). All of these corpora could be searched for apology take-up via search-words. This gives relative frequencies of apology lexis but also enabled us to find sites of apology take-up. Also used for the analysis was the ad-hoc search-word-generated corpus of tabloid newspapers in their online form with *apology* as part of the search terms, essentially a separate corpus consisting only of *press uptakes* of apologies (*Apologies corpus*, c. 194,000 tokens, 120 articles). One aspect of the selection of these apology-specific articles must be stated here. We did not include apologies from footballers or pop stars. They do form a large part of press coverage but it seemed that they tend to be apologizing for aspects of their personal behaviour. This behaviour may be seen as reprehensible if the protagonists are given role model status, concerning in many cases how they live their private lives: although similar circumstances of face conditions and strategic necessity apply, the public interest factor seems to be intuitively different. We decided, having to limit the research for time constraints, that this kind of apology would not form part of the research.

This corpus-assisted discourse studies approach to media evaluations of the public apology used *WordSmith Tools 5.0* (Scott 2012 [1998]) to interrogate the corpus. Patterns and phraseologies revealed the ways in which public expectations are represented, and represented as met or frustrated by public apologies. As suggested above, this study is a contribution to a number of corpus based studies dealing with aspects of pragmatics, also (im)politeness. The CADS procedures include using the software to make word lists and to compare wordlists generating keyword lists comparing the various corpora in terms of salient lexis. Keywords can then be examined under a more qualitative lens in the form of concordance lines and close text reading. A profile of how the apology scenario is treated can be built up by observing quantitative data such as collocational patterns, and by grouping key lexis according to semantic field or examining grammatical items for their role in functional units. One can also see what prosodies emerge for the key lexical items. The term *prosody*, borrowed from phonology, is used to describe a language phenomenon expressed over more than a single linguistic unit. Sinclair (2004:34, 114) defines the prosody of a lexical unit as its function in the discourse, as what it is *for*. The simplest kind of evaluative prosody is seen in collocational relations. Discussions on evaluative prosody generally revolve around items whose evaluation is not seemingly inherent in their semantics as is the case with, say, *beautiful*, *coward*, *stupid*, and so on, but whose evaluative potential is realised when interacting with other items in discourse. As we will see, although an apology is usually conceptualised as a positive act, in press uptakes the opposite appears to be true; a prosody of apology is built up by explicit evaluations and a number of terms which interact with the apology lexis.

4. Apologies and the Evaluation Nexis

Michael Reddy (1979) in his discussion of the Conduit Metaphor included the expression 'I'm sorry' as an example of semantic pathology (Ullman 1957:1229), that is, when two or more incompatible senses, capable of figuring meaningfully in the same context, develop around the same name. Reddy states that 'I'm sorry' was his favourite example of this in that it could mean 'I empathise with your suffering' or ' I admit fault and apologise', which can lead to a mismatch of intentions and expectations creating delicate and sometimes difficult situations. This problematic nature of public apologies in particular and the ways in which semantic pathology can be exploited goes some way to explain why they are a source of interest to news-workers but also to discourse-analysts. In examining the press uptakes of public apologies we are essentially looking at how they are represented and evaluated as felicitous or otherwise. Much of the interest stems from the way in which public figures sometimes seem to find it very difficult to apologise while at other times they seem unexpectedly pro-active in offering apologies, even for things for which they are not responsible. As Harris et al. (2006:721) state "The public apology is usually generated by conflict and controversy and is the response to a demand rather than a spontaneous offering." The fact that to apologise is to offer an own-face-threatening act has its dangers for public figures: issues of lack of control (Duguid 2011; Partington et al. 2013: Chapter 3) are often used as a defense which will impinge on their positive face, that is the positive, consistent, public self-image that every competent adult member of society wants to claim for him/herself (Brown & Levinson 1987:61). Evaluations are already implicit in the act of apology which could be represented as follows: 'What I did was bad. I recognise that and regret it (because I am good) and won't do it again; i.e. the past me was bad but the present me and future me is good'.

It is possible to apologise using a range of strategies and linguistic forms. As Kampf (2009:4) points out "public figures become linguistic acrobats, creatively using various pragmatic and linguistic strategies in order to reduce their responsibility for the events under public discussion." Doing acrobatics in public can be a risky business.

In the corpus data we find several examples of such acrobatics. In the field of politics there have been precedents for considering apology as an unsuccessful choice and the WHB data[3] gives several examples of the problematic nature of this particular speech-act. A concern about being seen to apologise is evident in the WHB podium utterances. Admissions of culpability have to be balanced with the need to present an identity of a competent, ethical and just individual and a struggle to avoid this is evident in the examples where apologies from the administration are under discussion. There are many examples where the spokesperson apologises freely (for lateness, for changes of programme) but any suggestion that the administration has apologised or will apologise gets a strong response:

(1) Q: The administration *apologized* to Pakistan for the NATO airstrikes that killed about two dozen soldiers.
MR. CARNEY: No, no, no. Let me say, *we expressed our condolences* to Pakistan about the *regrettable* loss of life.
Q: Will you tease out why that distinction is important? And what's the distinction?
MR CARNEY: Well, I think there's a -- it's a matter of fact that I, speaking for the White House and the President, offered condolences on behalf of him, the administration, the American people, for the tragic loss of life -- … But -- maybe I'm preempting what your

[3] Partington's detailed studies of the strategies of the participants (2003, 2006) have outlined the discourse features and the participant roles. The podium conveys the messages of the President and the administration, as they attempt to angle their presentation of their message in times of conflict, often having to deal with issues they would rather not comment on.

question was, but *there was obviously no apology* and there was an expression of condolences. (WHB)

We should notice the use of the stance adverbial *obviously*. In this example it is clear that the spokesperson wishes to make explicit the distinction between sympathy and acceptance of culpability whereas in the following example both podium and press seem to be agreeing on the fact that an apology would be worthy of interest and not in a good way.

(2) MR CARNEY: I think I made clear that if, specifically, he's saying that there's an *apology* called for because of measures that were taken that this President absolutely does not believe is the right way to go, *he's not going to apologize.*
Q: And one other question to follow up on Jessica's *mischievous inquiry about the apology*. (Laughter.) Are you *ruling out an apology*, or are you just saying it's premature because you haven't finished the investigation? (WHB)

A similar concern about not apologising is shown by David Cameron (example 3) who promises to apologise if someone else has lied to him, and the official reactions from the Metropolitan Police chief (example 4) to findings which suggest the Metropolitan Police have responsibility for a controversial death after the publication of the Cass report following an inquiry.

(3) *If it turns out I have been lied to that would be a moment for a profound apology,* and in that event I can tell you I will not fall short. Of course I regret, and I am extremely sorry about the furore it has caused. With 20:20 hindsight and all that has followed I would not have offered him the job. (Apologies corpus, Daily Mirror 2011)

(4) He unequivocally accepted the finding that a Met officer was likely to have been responsible for the death and, in an unusual move, expressed his *regret*. "I have to say, really, that *I am sorry* that in over 31 years since Blair Peach's death we have been unable to provide his family and friends with the definitive answer regarding the terrible circumstances in which he met his death," he said. Asked *if he was apologizing* for the death of Peach, he replied: *"I am sorry that officers behaved that way, according to Mr. Cass."* (SiBol Corpus, Guardian 2013)

It is indeed acrobatic to accept the findings unequivocally, saying he is sorry while at the same time using evidentiality to distance himself from the findings with *according to Mr. Cass*. The ambiguity of sorrow in this case is resolved by two different ways of not taking responsibility, declaring inability and the vague description of the original offence: *behaved in that way*. These two examples show potential public apologisers faced with the press asking questions and revealing a great concern about the performative.

5. Evaluation

When an apology is performed or described the thing being apologised for, the person apologising, the quality of the apology and the reception of the apology can all be evaluated as good or bad[4] and these evaluations can be mitigated by hedging, or up-scaled with intensification or saturation, along a set of parameters. Evaluation here is considered as being the indication that something is good or bad (Hunston & Thompson 2000; for corpus-based studies of evaluation, see Bednarek 2006; Morley & Partington 2009; Hunston 2010; Partington et al. 2013: Chapter 2) and, as Labov (1972) reminds us, it is often the main aim of the discourse.

> Every act of evaluation expresses a communal value system and every act of evaluation goes towards building up that value system. This value system is in turn a component of the ideology of the society that has produced the text. (Hunston & Thompson 2000:6)

Evaluation can also be implicit or "conceptual", with no obvious linguistic clues, exploiting systems of shared values. Humorous opinion pieces can often show a certain amount of creativity in their evaluations:

(5) In an age when *mealy-mouthed apologies* are the norm, usually couched in passive tense terms that deny agency, *Monbiot's was the real deal, a hands-around-the-ankle, whipping-at-Canterbury-Cathedral-followed-by-walking-barefoot-to-Jerusalem job*. (SiBol corpus, Telegraph 2013)

Hunston and Thompson argue, for instance, that what is good or bad is frequently construed in terms of goal achievement; things which are deemed to be good help someone to achieve their objective, whereas those evaluated as bad are whatever hampers or thwarts the achievement of their goal (2000:14). Signalling one's evaluations has two major functions. First of all, it expresses group belonging by (seemingly) offering a potential service to the group by warning of bad things and advertising good ones.

[4] The Sorry Watch website has as its slogan "Sorry Watch: Analyzing apologies in the news, media, history and literature. We condemn the bad and exalt the good" (http://sorrywatch.com).

Moreover, it can assure an audience that the speaker/writer shares its same value system. In this way it helps "to construct and maintain relations between the speaker or writer and hearer or reader" (Hunston & Thompson 2000:6). Signalling evaluations both explicitly and implicitly, can be used to direct, control and even manipulate the behaviour of others, generally to the advantage of the individual performing the evaluation (and this is where the social and individual functions of evaluation combine). Evaluation is the engine of argumentation. Journalists can employ it to convince an audience of what should be seen as right and proper and what not. Thus, as well as reflect, it can impose, overtly or covertly, a value system. In our corpora, which represent a number of discourse types over an extended period of two decades, we found evaluation patterns on a number of parameters: of timeliness, sincerity, spontaneity and, tellingly, what might be called the humiliation factor.

6. Findings

In order to see what the salient lexis is in articles which deal specifically with apologies we can compare the wordlists from a general newspaper corpus and the specific apologies corpus to obtain the keywords. When the ad-hoc apology corpus is compared with the SiBol corpora there is obviously a set of items relating directly to the speech act (*apology*, *apologies*, *apologise*, *apologising*, *regret*, *regrets*, *sorry*) as can be seen in Figure 1, since the articles themselves are all examples of press uptakes of public apologies; and more unsurprisingly because the performative formed the search word. We find other related lexical items such as *contrition*, *contrite*, *culpable*, *remorse*, *repentance* and a set of negative lexical items related to the reasons for an apology (*mistakes*, *errors*, *error*, *mistake*, *culpable*, *blame*, *wrong*, *inappropriate*, *failings*, *wrongdoing*, *serious*, *unacceptable*, *appalling*, *false*, *furious*, *reckless*). We find also a set of the keywords which are adjective or adverbial intensifiers such as *unreserved, unreservedly*, *deeply*, *profoundly*, *absolutely*, and an interesting set which might be called the humiliation factor, comprising *humiliating*, *grovelling*, *abject*, *shamed*, *damning*, *shameful* (see Figure 2 which also shows how the intensifiers have been used with similar ratios over the period of at least a decade). These lists can give us an idea of the flavor of press uptakes of apologies.

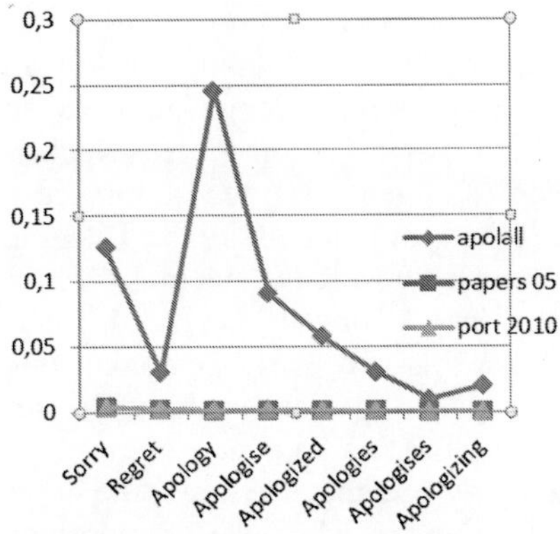

Key. Apolall: ad hoc apologies corpus; papers 05: SiBol corpus 2005 partition; port 2010: SiBol corpus 2010 partition

Fig. 1: Relative frequency of apology lexis in the keyword lists comparing SiBol and the ad hoc corpus

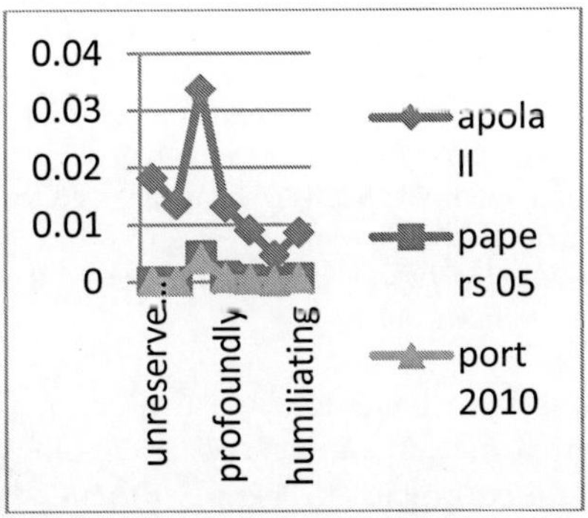

Key. Apolall: ad hoc apologies corpus; papers 05: SiBol corpus 2005 partition; port 2010: SiBol corpus 2010 partition

Fig. 2: Relative frequency of intensifying lexis in the keyword lists comparing SiBol and the ad hoc corpus

6.1 Evaluation and Attribution

As in much press discussion of performatives (see also Duguid 2009) we find a large number of text-related nouns (*words*, *wording*, *statement*, *tweet*, *comments*, *rant*, *allegation*, *questions*, and *response*). We also find reporting verbs (*admitted*, *insisted*, *claimed*, *said*, *told*, *tweeted*, *retweeted*, *published*, *disclosed*, *expressed*, *lied*, *refused*, *accepted*, *revealed*, *concluded*, *misrepresented*, *defamed*) among the keywords suggesting that there is a great deal of reflexive language used around the topic of apology. Indeed we find many opinion-pieces which choose to hold forth on the topic of apologies in general, often quoting research; the Hargie et al. paper for instance is quoted at length by the Telegraph. After a less than successful apology has been covered in the press (for instance the bankers, Maria Miller, Nick Clegg, Tony Blair, Lord Rennard) we find this strategy, suggesting that this is a hardy perennial topic which journalists feel they can resort to again and again, using a Google search, or perhaps even a Google-scholar search to aid them.

When a public apology becomes the news, the news reports tend to use the evaluations of other voices while the opinion-piece writers use their literary skills or box of rhetorical tricks to evaluate the apology. Here is an example from BBC television news where members of the public (labeled VOX in the corpus) are shown giving their evaluations before the news-presenter (NP) calls on the opinion of a specialist editor.

(6) <VOX><unnamed1> So these people may shed *crocodile tears* but the blame for a lot of people being put out of work and lot of industries closing.
<VOX><unnamed3> anybody who thinks that that's a *genuine apology* I would advise them maybe to go and see a psychiatrist.
<NP><Alagiah_George> Well, our business editor Robert Peston is here with me now.
Well *the public clearly weren't very impressed* Robert, what do you think? (BBC TV news corpus)

The news-workers here have selected evaluations which concern the parameter of sincerity or authenticity of an apology (in this case the bankers') but use other voices to express them. Hunston (2000:178) identifies subtle forms of attribution, such as those embedded within averrals, and discriminates between sourced and non-sourced averrals. This distinction provides options available to the writer or speaker to mark his/her attitude towards the attribution.

6.2 Parameters of Evaluation

If we look at the item *apology* across all the corpora, not just the small ad-hoc corpus, we can discern a number of evaluative parameters from the L1 collocates (appearing immediately to the left of *apology*) (Table 3).

Tab. 3: Collocates of *apology* arranged according to parameters of evaluation

PARAMETER	EXAMPLES OF L1 COLLOCATES
Openness	*private, public*
Status	*general, personal, private, royal*
Form	*brief, court, direct, formal, n-page, n-second, 32-second, official, on/off-air, printed, published, telephone, televised, written*
Timing and timeliness	*belated, earlier, immediate, late, old, prompt, swift, quick*
Quality and quantity	*big, clear, feeble, full, full and humble, fulsome, half, mealy-mouthed, n-worded, non-, part, partial, profound, profuse, proper, real, simple, traditional, unconditional, unequivocal, unqualified, unreserved*
Expectation	*much-needed, only now, rare, unprecedented*
Delivery features	*brusque, mumbled, tearful*
Authenticity	*genuine, heart-felt, sincere*

The parameter of authenticity is an interesting one. In reality, of course, sincerity and true penitence are something only a first-person account or an omniscient author can reliably tell us about, although they can be speculated upon, as witnessed in the newspaper data considered so far. So although theoretically only the apologizer can *know* private feelings of penitence, the corpus shows that evaluations about these are used regularly in press uptakes which invoke the qualities of an apology and judgments are made as if from privileged access to the private feelings of the apologiser, using evaluative items such as *genuine*, *heartfelt*, *sincere.* The uptake suggests that the journalists, or those whose evaluations they choose to include, consider themselves judges of authenticity, and usually feel it is lacking. Of the examples of the positive adjectives *genuine* and *sincere*, half of them are in fact questioning sincerity or denying sincerity and the others are quotations from the spokesman or lawyer of someone who has apologized. This is yet another example of newspaper predilection for negativity (Bell 1991):

(7) But Mr. Panton, a government adviser, told a press conference: "I know the difference between a *genuine* apology and an apology which is based as a consequence of legal and political expediency. This apology is perhaps in the latter category." (SiBol Corpus, Guardian 2013)

(8) No word of real regret. No hint of *genuine* contrition. The chilling conclusion to be drawn from Tony Blair's *half 'apology'* in the Commons is that having led Britain to war on a false prospectus, he would be quite prepared to do it again. (Apologies corpus, Daily Mail 2004)

(9) The words 'I of course unreservedly apologise' passed her lips. Seldom has a sentence sounded so *insincere*. (Apologies corpus, Daily Mail 2014)

The expressions used in a public apology are thus not always a guide to how it will be perceived and judged by the public and media. Intensification will not always be rewarded as a genuine element of sufficiency.

6.3 Apology as Performance

On many occasions an apology will be treated almost as if it were a stage performance and evaluated in terms of verisimilitude via body language and appearance as if the apologizer is both actor and scriptwriter; we find terms relating to appearance, seeming and outward signs, to histrionics, donning as if of a costume, delivery, reading as if of a script (and e.g. *show* and *act*, or *an act of*):

(10) Had she *shown* humility on Thursday she might have pulled things round, but she *seemed to lack remorse* and in politics, if you have done wrong, you can't afford to behave like that. (Apologies corpus, Observer 2014)

(11) A *Prime Ministerial apology*, replete with that *familiar, histrionic* sympathy which on Wednesday he took out of the I Share Your Pain drawer? He *donned it after dusting it down*, and proceeded to deplore the injustice done to the Guildford Four and their families. (SiBol corpus, Telegraph 2005)

(12) How strikingly suspect, then, were the precise words with which he *couched* his apology: "We are profoundly, and, I think I would say, unreservedly, sorry at the turn of events." After the words "we are" and during the word "profoundly", his body experienced an extraordinary swerve from the shoulders, like a rugby player trying to dummy a pass. *It was as if he was not at all comfortable delivering the words, was, indeed, making a feint. His lack of authenticity was exposed* by his use of the words "I think I would probably say" before "unreservedly apologise". Think? Probably? Good grief man, how could you possibly only "think" that "probably" you are sorry about a balls-up of such a catastrophic scale, one that may even have ruined your business career? One does not make qualifications about something one feels unreservedly. (Apologies corpus, Guardian 2009)

(13) And only a lawyer would say this when fighting for his job: 'I have expressed a degree of regret that can be equated with an apology.' But that was the Defence Secretary's line, *coughed up without a nun's blush*, when he came to a nearly full Commons. A degree of regret. (Apologies corpus, Daily Mail 2007)

(14) Miller's statement was over so fast and *delivered so curtly, more in anger than in sorrow*, that even if the few Tory MPs who were there wanted to shout "hear, hear", they simply could not rouse themselves to do so. Young's show of support fell flat. Instead a deathly silence greeted Miller's *reading of her bitter piece*, before she slid away. (Apologies corpus, Guardian 2014)

Positive terms are often used with a considerable amount of irony to underline that spontaneity is an important value in an apology, for example *a Murdoch-style masterclass in semi-apology* (Apologies corpus, Telegraph 2012). The mix of quantity and quality needed for an apology to be considered successful is also found in an interesting aporia in the use of the evaluative *fulsome,* picked up by a letter to the Guardian.

(15) So General Sir Michael Jackson described the prime minister's response to the Saville report as a *"fulsome apology"*. The dictionary defines fulsome as "cloying, excessive, and disgusting by excess of flattery, servility, exaggerated affection". (SiBol corpus, Guardian 2010)

There are many examples of *fulsome apology* in the press corpora and it is not always possible to discern whether this is irony in the text or insincerity in the writer (Louw 1993).

(16) Eventually, after intervention from my MP, I received not a *grovelling and fulsome apology* from a senior civil servant, but a letter full of jargon from a clerk. (SiBol corpus, Telegraph 2010)

Here the suggestion is that *fulsome* would be the kind of apology the writer would have wanted. It is also an example of how humiliation is seen as a positive factor in apologies.

6.4 The Humiliation Factor

Media interpretations show a preference for this factor in their evaluations, *grovelling* and *humiliating* are keywords in the comparison of the apologies corpus and the SiBol corpora and both are high among the

L1 collocates for *apology* along with *abject*, *embarrassing*, *sorry.*[5] The sense is that of pleasure in the pain of the public figure having to apologise. We can get further evidence of what this means if we then look to see what else collocates in R1 position with the lexical items *grovelling* and *humiliating* in the corpora: we find a lexical set of items *climb-down*, *defeat*, *failure*, *U-turn*, which show a semantic preference for negative evaluation, failure to achieve goals; important in a political context is the fact that this involves a lack of control over events and outcomes. Apologies are thus represented and recontextualised, not as a praiseworthy attempt to redress a wrong, but as a sign of failure and lack of firm purpose, a failure of goal achievement. The concordance lines show how the apologiser's status is often highlighted by being given in full and an examination of the contexts through concordance lines reveals that many elements in the clusters have the semantic feature of lack of control, of the control being in someone else's hands (Partington et al. 2013), for example *forced into*, *forced to*, *had to*, *once again* (17iia-17iif):

(17) ia. after *the Prime Minister* issued a *grovelling apology* to Brits (Apologies corpus, Daily Mail 2011)
ib. *Scotland Yard chief Sir Ian Blair* made a *grovelling apology* (Apologies corpus, Daily Mail 2007)
ic. *MP George Galloway* last night made a *grovelling apology* for (Apologies corpus, Sun 2012)
id. *Met chief's grovelling apology* on Dizaei inquiry (Apologies corpus, Daily Mail 2011)
ie. Spat comes as *Cameron* issues *grovelling apology* (Apologies corpus, Daily Mail 2011)
iia. The BBC *owes it* to McAlpine *to grovel and keep groveling* (Apologies corpus, Daily Mail 2011)
iib. BBC Breakfast presenters *forced to* make *grovelling apology* (Apologies corpus, Sun 2012)
iic. Millionaires blamed over Britain's banking meltdown were *forced to make grovelling apologies* (Apologies corpus, Sun 2009)
iid. was last night *forced into a humiliating apology* (Apologies corpus, Daily Mirror 2007)
iie. (IPCC), which *had to* issue *a humiliating apology* (SiBol corpus Telegraph 2010)

[5] They should perhaps have paid attention to the strictures of Debretts: "If you are offered a genuine apology, acknowledge it graciously and accept it. An urge to elicit grovelling self-abasement is both childish and offensive" (http://www.debretts.com/british-etiquette/.../apologising).

iif. *Once again* the BBC has issued *a humiliating apology* for its output (SiBol corpus Guardian 2010)

Being forced in to an apology tends to pose the question of sincerity, and spontaneity as opposed to being *grudging.* As Harris et al. (2006:715) put it: "The public apology is usually generated by conflict and controversy and is the response to a demand rather than a spontaneous offering."

6.5 The Apology as Strategy

The evaluators of public apologies can also, when questioning the authenticity, represent the act to be a strategy of self-deprecation and deliberate self-positioning, as *self-serving*, *status-enhancing*.

(18) DAVID Cameron made *a self-serving apology* for his sexist remarks *to try to woo women voters* yesterday. The Tory leader said he was "hugely sorry" for any offence and admitted his Government had to do more to win female support. (Apologies corpus, Daily Mirror 2011)

They evaluate negatively this use of control rather than a lack of it, which involves less face loss. Such a strategic use of apology is also linked to the important factor of time, as other researchers have found: "An apology following a prolonged delay is more likely to be perceived as insincere, viewed as 'too little, too late' and seen as strategic rather than genuine" (MacLeod, 2008). Furthermore, as we find in our data, a failure to issue a timely apology can be regarded as further compounding the original harm and the longer an apology is delayed the less genuine it is likely to be perceived (example 19), although being quick to apologise is not always evaluated positively (examples 20 and 21) and sometimes it is suggested that even the length of contrition should not be left to the apologiser (example 22):

(19) Bercow had not acted "honourably" unlike other Twitter users who *quickly* agreed to settle the matter, including the Guardian columnist George Monbiot who apologized *quickly* and agreed to undertake three years of charity work in recompense. (Apologies corpus, Guardian 2013)

(20) *quick, brush-it-under-the-carpet* apologies, like Mitchell's (Apologies corpus, Guardian 2012)

(21) His apology was *quick and brusque.* (He) looked like a businessman processing a complaint against his company (Apologies corpus, Guardian 2012)

(22) But when you're being contrite, *it's not for you to decide when your contrition should end.* It's for the person, or people, you're talking to – in this case, us. (Apologies corpus, Guardian 2012)

One recent political apology in particular was taken up by all corners of the media and evaluated not only as being too late but much too little; all the media converged to comment on the length and this brevity became the main parameter for discussion in the press:

(23) To add insult to injury, Mrs. Miller's 'apology' in parliament was churlish, unrepentant and *lasted a pitiful 32 seconds.* (Apologies corpus, Daily Mail 2014)

(24) Culture Secretary Maria Miller today delivered a blunt, *30-second apology* after being ordered to repay £5,800 in expenses. (Apologies corpus, Daily Mail 2014)

(25) Mrs. Miller's *32-second* Commons apology left voters deeply unimpressed – nearly three-quarters say her statement was inadequate. (Apologies corpus, Daily Mail 2014)

(26) she has been required only to deliver a *perfunctory, half-minute apology.* And what an insult to Parliament that dismissive, *71-word statement* was. (Apologies corpus, Daily Mail 2014)

(27) Her apology to parliament *was 32 seconds long*, prompting criticism from Tory backbencher Mark Field that it was "unacceptably perfunctory". (Apologies corpus, Guardian 2014)

(28) An apology which has been *widely criticised for its tone and brevity.* (Apologies corpus, Daily Mirror 2014)

The suggestion is that an apology is an ordeal which the press do not like to see got over too quickly.

7. Conclusions

In the corpus we find, as did Ancarno (2011:14), many explicitly evaluative, meta-pragmatic comments, where news-writers explicitly attempt "to influence/negotiate how an utterance is or should be understood, utterances where news-writers indicate to the reader how public apologies should be interpreted based, for example, on their wording or the performance of the public figure." The discourse of public apologies can be a site for ideological battles, where a re-contextualization and re-conceptualisation of public discourse can take place and evaluation is a key factor. Such explicitly evaluative meta-pragmatic comments shed light on how the media foreground their ideas about what makes for a successful public apology.

These press uptakes can be seen as indicators of the way the media is dominant in public apology processes, being the main source of our access to them, although the appearance of Twitter-related items in the keywords list might suggest that this is changing and investigations of new media would merit further research. Like Bell and Garrett (1998), Philo (2007) and Cotter (2010), this paper is interested in the discursive processes that shape the news where media texts are considered to reflect existing ideologies, while also contributing to construct new ones or to transform existing ones, affecting apologies and more broadly the '*discourse of accountability*' (see Buttny 1993). First and foremost in the press discourse of accountability, apologies are evaluated negatively so it would corroborate a tendency for the 'news value' (Bell 1991) of negativity to be explicitly preferred by news-writers in apology press uptakes.

Ancarno suggests that future work could turn to the examination of other kinds of apology uptakes in the print and broadcast media, and that opinion-led apology press uptakes would be of interest; our data does indeed provide evidence of opinion-led uptakes and our mixed corpus provides another finding related to attribution and averral. It would appear that opinion writers differ in the way they represent what makes a successful public apology, by expressing explicitly personal opinions; the news reports, on the other hand, do use explicit evaluations but through the quotation of other peoples' opinions. As Jullian points out:

> [t]he skilled exploitation of the interplay between averral and attribution allows the writer to construct a stance by transferring the role of the averrer. Thus, authors can make convenient use of attribution by quoting heavily evaluative materials while delegating their accountability to someone else. (Jullian 2008:120)

In conclusion, we see then that the press likes a public apology as a performative. It is considered newsworthy and has been represented in similar ways over time. When we look for apology-related lexis in the SiBol corpora, we find the same patterns with very little change over time, and little difference between tabloid and broadsheet, when comparing the SiBol corpus with an ad-hoc corpus containing only apology uptakes. Apologies are mediated, labelled and evaluated with negative evaluations prevailing over positive, which are few and tend to be lower in intensity. A frequent conceptualization of the public apology is as a strategic move in self-representation on the part of politicians and other prominent figures and as part of a repertoire of political choices. The issue of trust and the public perception of politicians and press alike is an integral part of the evaluations. Politicians and their spokespersons and journalists, all create versions of reality, construct narratives and frame them in their utterances. For the politicians the question is how far reception might be affected by the receiver's awareness of any simulation of the interpersonal function through meanings and forms involving a strategic calculation of effectiveness. We react differently when we scent strategy. When an apparently spontaneous gesture, phrasing, emphasis or hesitation is perceived as being consciously manufactured it loses its original effect in much the same way as an original metaphor or figure of speech becomes a cliché or a dead metaphor.When public figures use apologies for their own benefit, the felicity conditions for apologies are seriously undermined and the sincerity is called into question. An increased awareness of process which reflects strategic purposes makes both press and public resistant to the perlocutionary intent. The relationship between politics and media has made us aware of how much narratorial interference and selective framing takes place in mediated political discourse. Most importantly, we see that apologies are overwhelmingly treated as loss of face. Among the parameters of evaluation, the humiliation factor is a preferred trope in both broadsheets and tabloids. This in turn explains why public figures are reluctant to apologise, only to find when they do that their apology is evaluated negatively for lack of timeliness or for being grudging. Thus press uptakes of public apologies can be seen as an example of the way the media significantly re-contextualises and re-conceptualises expert or elite figures in political and public discourse by questioning sincerity, criticizing timeliness or quality and by turning a praiseworthy act of corrective face-work into a blameworthy failure and evidence of loss of control. When reporting public apologies the press sets itself up as a judge, acting as omniscient narrator with privileged access to private feelings in the case of this public act, explicitly attempting to negotiate the way in which an utterance should be understood indicating to the reader how public apologies should be interpreted.

References

Aijmer, Karin. 1996. *Conversational Routines in English: Convention and Creativity*. London: Addison Wesley.

Ancarno, Clyde. 2011. Press representations of successful public apologies in Britain and France. *University of Reading Language Working Papers* 3. 3-15.

Archer, Dawn & Jonathon Culpeper. 2009. Identifying key socio-pragmatic usage in plays and trial proceedings (1640-1760): An empirical approach via corpus annotation. *Journal of Historical Pragmatics* 10. 2. 286-309.

Baker, Paul. 2005. *Using Corpora in Discourse Analysis*. London: Continuum.

Bednarek, Monica. 2006. *Evaluation in Media Discourse.* London: Continuum.

Bell, Alan. 1991. *The Language of News Media.* Oxford: Blackwell.

Bell, Alan & Peter Garrett. 1998. Conversation analysis: Neutralism in British news interviews. In Alan Bell & Peter Garrett (eds.), *Approaches to Media Discourse*. Oxford: Blackwell. 252-267.

Blum-Kulka, Shoshana & Elite Olshtain. 1984. Requests and apologies: A cross-cultural study of speech act realization patterns (CCSARP). *Applied Linguistics* 5. 196-213.

Brown, Penelope & Stephen C. Levinson. 1987. *Politeness.* Cambridge: Cambridge University Press.

Buttny, Richard. 1993. *Social Accountability in Communication.* London: Sage Publications.

Cotter, Colleen. 2010. *News Talk: Investigating the Language of Journalism.* Cambridge: Cambridge University Press.

Culpeper, Jonathan. 2008. Reflections on impoliteness, relational work and power. In Derek Bousfield & Miriam Locher (eds.), *Impoliteness in Language*. Berlin: Mouton de Gruyter.17-44.

Duguid, Alison. 2009. Insistent voices: Government messages. In John Morley & Paul Bayley (eds.), *Corpus-Assisted Discourse Studies on the Iraq Conflict* Oxford/New York: Routledge. 234-260.

—. 2011. Control: A semantic feature in evaluative prosody. Paper presented at the *Corpus Linguistics Conference 2011*. Birmingham, UK, 20-22 July 2011.

Fishman, Joshua. 1980. Minority language maintenance and the ethnic mother tongue school. *Modern Language Journal* 64. 2. 167-172.

Fraser, Bruce. 1981. On apologizing. In Florian Coulmas (ed.), *Conversational Routine*. The Hague: Mouton de Gruyter. 259-271.

Goffman, Ervin. 1971. *Relations in Public*. New York, NY: Basic Books.

Hargie, Owen, Karyn Stapleton & Dennis Tourish. 2010. Interpretations of CEO public apologies for the banking crisis: Attributions of blame and avoidance of responsibility. *Organization* 17. 6. 721-742.

Harris, Sandra, Karen Grainger & Louise Mullany. 2006. The pragmatics of political apologies. *Discourse & Society* 17. 715-737.

Hoey, Michael. 1991. *Patterns of Lexis in Text.* London/New York: Routledge.

Hunston, Susan. 2000. Evaluation and the planes of discourse. Status and value in persuasive texts. In Susan Hunston & Geoff Thompson (eds.), *Evaluation in Text*. Oxford: Oxford University Press. 176-206.

—. 2010. *Corpus Approaches to Evaluation: Phraseology and Evaluative Language.* London/New York: Taylor & Francis.

Hunston, Susan & Geoff Thompson (eds.). 2000. *Evaluation in Text*. Oxford: Oxford University Press.

Jeffries, Lesley. 2006. Journalistic constructions of Blair's 'apology' for the intelligence leading to the Iraq War. In Sally Johnson & Astrid Ensslin (eds.),

Language in the Media: Representations, Identities, Ideologies. Advances in Sociolinguistics. London: Continuum. 48-69

Jucker, Andreas H., Daniel Schreier & Marianne Hundt. 2009. Corpus linguistics, pragmatics and discourse. In Andreas H. Jucker, Daniel Schreier & Marianne Hundt (eds.), *Corpora: Pragmatics and Discourse.Papers from the 29th International Conference on English Language Research on Computerized Corpora*. Amsterdam: Rodopi. 3-9.

Jullian, Paula M. 2008. *An Exploration of Strategies to Convey Evaluation in the Notebook Texts*. Unpublished PhD thesis. University of Birmingham.

Kampf, Zohar. 2009. Public (non-)apologies: The discourse of minimizing responsibility. *Journal of Pragmatics*. 41. 11. 2257-2270.

—. Journalists as actors in social dramas of apology. *Journalism* 12. 1 71-87

Labov, William. 1972. *Language in the Inner City*. Philadelphia: University of Pennsylvania Press.

Lakoff, Robin. 2001. Nine ways of looking at apologies: The necessity for interdisciplinary theory and method in discourse analysis. In Deborah Schiffrin, Deborah Tannen & Heidi E. Hamilton (eds.), *The Handbook of Discourse Analysis*. Oxford: Blackwell. 199-214.

Louw, Bill. 1993. Irony in the text or insincerity in the writer? The diagnostic potential of semantic prosodies. In Mona Baker, Gill Francis & Elena Tognini-Bonelli (eds.), *Text and Technology. In Honour of John Sinclair*. Amsterdam/Philadelphia: John Benjamins. 157-176.

Macleod, L. H. 2008. A Time for Apologies: The Legal and Ethical Implications of Apologies in Civil Cases. *Cornwall Public Inquiry: Phase 2 Research and Policy Paper.* http//www.enquetecornwall.ca/en/healing/research/.

Martin, James. R. & Peter. R. R. White. 2005. *The Language of Evaluation: Appraisal in English*. Basingstoke: Palgrave.

McEnery, Tony, Paul Baker & Christine Cheepen. 2002. Lexis, indirectness and politeness in operator calls. *Language and Computers* 36. 1.53-69.

Meier, Ardith. 1998. Apologies: What do we know? *International Journal of Applied Linguistics* 8. 215-231.

Morley, John & Alan Partington. 2009. A few frequently asked questions about semantic – or evaluative – prosody. *International Journal of Corpus Linguistics* 14. 2. 139-158.

Owen, Marion. 1983. *Apologies and Remedial Interchanges: A Study of Language Use in Social Interaction.* New York: Mouton.

Partington, Alan. 1998. *Patterns and Meanings.* Amsterdam/Philadelphia: John Benjamins.

—. 2003. *The Linguistics of Political Argument: The Spin-doctor and the Wolf-pack at the White House*. London/New York: Routledge.

—. 2004. Utterly content in each other's company: Semantic prosody and semantic preference. *International Journal of Corpus Linguistics* 9. 1: 131-156.

—. 2006. *The Linguistics of Laughter: A Corpus-Assisted Study of Laughter-talk.* London/New York: Routledge.

Partington, Alan, Alison Duguid & Charlotte Taylor. 2013. *Patterns and Meanings in Discourse: Theory and Practice in Corpus-Assisted Discourse Studies*. Amsterdam/Philadelphia: John Benjamins.

Philo, Greg. 2007. Can discourse analysis successfully explain the content of media and journalistic practice? *Journalism Studies* 8. 175-196.

Reddy, Michael. 1979. The Conduit Metaphor. In Andrew Ortney (ed.), *Metaphor and Thought*. Cambridge: Cambridge University Press. 284-324.

Scott, Mike. 2012 [1998]. *WordSmith Tools 5.0*. Liverpool: Lexical Analysis Software.

Scott, Mike & Christopher Tribble. 2006. *Textual Patterns: Key Words and Corpus Analysis in Language Education*. Amsterdam/Philadelphia: John Benjamins.

Sinclair, John. 2004. *Trust the Text: Language, Corpus and Discourse*. London/New York: Routledge.

Stubbs, Michael. 1996. *Text and Corpus Analysis: Computer-assisted Studies of Language and Culture*. Oxford: Blackwell.

Taylor, Charlotte. 2009. Interacting with conflicting goals: Impoliteness in hostile cross-examination. In John Morley & Paul Bayley (eds.), *Corpus Assisted Discourse Studies on the Iraq Conflict: Wording the War*. London/New York: Routledge. 208-233.

—. 2011. Negative politeness features and impoliteness functions: A corpus-assisted approach. In Bethan Davies B., Andrew J. Merrison & Michael Haugh (eds.), *Situated Politeness*. London: Continuum. 209-231.

Tognini Bonelli, Elena. 2001. *Corpus Linguistics at Work*. Amsterdam/Philadelphia: John Benjamins.

Ullman, Stephen. 1963. *The Principles of Semantics*. 2nd ed. Oxford: Blackwell.

FACEBOOK.COM/WHITEHOUSE: A MULTIMODAL ANALYSIS OF THE SOCIAL-MEDIA RECONTEXTUALIZATION OF THE INSTITUTIONAL ENCODER

ILARIA MOSCHINI
UNIVERSITY OF FLORENCE, ITALY

Abstract: In May 2009, the White House blog announced the creation of the official pages of the US government on platforms like Facebook, MySpace and Twitter in order to expand the ways in which the Administration communicated to the public. Such digital remediation of the White House's voice leads to a reconceptualization of institutional discourse since it recontextualizes a formal, impersonal, top-down kind of discourse on informal, multisemiotic and peer-to-peer semiotic platforms. It also originates a form of hybridized textuality that merges different modes and codes of communication into a liminal public/private narration. The present chapter takes the preliminary steps in mapping the transformations undergone by US institutional language when 'translating' official messages using Facebook, the world's largest social networking site. More in detail, it starts from the analysis of the main generic features of Facebook as a semiotic platform to focus on the meaning-making strategies chosen to linguistically and semiotically encode the image of the sender in the *About* section of the White House Facebook's profile. The methodological framework adopted to decode this complex social, cultural and textual phenomenon encompasses a combination of Multimodal Analysis, Critical Discourse Analysis, Functional Linguistics, Conceptual Metaphor Theory and Web Genres Theory.

1. "Fans, Friends and Followers"

In May 2009, Macon Phillips, the then-director of the digital strategy of the White House, posted a message on the official blog (http://www.whitehouse.gov/blog/2009/05/01/whitehouse-20; accessed May 1, 2014) declaring that, following President Obama's latest weekly address, the government was "taking steps to expand how the Administration is communicating to the public" and that it was possible to monitor the flow of institutional messages in the official pages on social media platforms like Facebook, MySpace and Twitter.

The message clarifies the aim of such institutional 'social shift' – to "reach beyond the halls of government to engage the public" – and features a call to participation, with the invitation to "hearing from […] fans, friends and followers". Emphatic accent and alliteration in end-focus position bring to the fore and map the kind of role-relationships between the White House and the public that the new social media are intended to shape. The interpersonal roles of the recipients are labeled within the jargon of the social media: *friends* describes the peer-to-peer tenor relationship which is distinctive of Facebook; *followers* refers to the unbalanced role-relationship that is established between senders and receivers on Twitter; and *fans* reflects unequal status and can be seen as the textual marker of a precise worldview, that of "fanatics" (Jenkins 1992), whose decoding and encoding practices have been affecting the creation of both social media platforms and user generated contents (Moschini 2014).

This tenor construction offers a substantial glimpse into the process of *hybridization* between American institutional language and the language of the web, which I observed in my analysis of the 2008 Presidential elections (Moschini 2010). Indeed, the technological revolution – and the growth of the so-called *new media* in particular – has led to the emergence of new forms of textuality that have progressively hybridized more traditional textual artifacts (Fairclough 2006, 2011).

Regarding American political discourse, its web contextualization has given rise to a public/private narration where official codes get massively mashed up with items of popular culture: a narration that is intrinsically multimodal since it merges different modes and codes of communication and it is natively postmodern because it re-adapts verbal, visual and musical pieces integrating them with original productions (Moschini 2010, 2012). Additionally, the contextual configuration of contemporary American political language (e.g. presidential speeches or campaign messages) appears to be highly influenced by digital media in terms of tenor construction and lexical selection while its connotation seems to be affected by the constituent libertarian promise of the digital mediational means, which is deeply imbued with American liberal values (Moschini 2013).

As part of the previously mentioned research on the *webridization* of American political discourse, the present chapter takes the first steps in mapping the transformations undergone by US institutional language when 'translating' official messages using Facebook, the world's largest social networking site. This type of 'translation' originates a reconceptualization of institutional discourse since it recontextualizes a formal, impersonal, top-down discourse on an informal, multi-semiotic and peer-to-peer structured social network.

More in detail, this chapter starts from the analysis of the main generic features of the digital platform to focus on the meaning-making strategies chosen to linguistically and semiotically encode the image of the sender in the *About* section of the White House Facebook's profile. The methodological framework adopted encompasses a combination of Multimodal Analysis, Critical Discourse Analysis, Functional Linguistics and Web Genres Theory.

2. The Conceptual Background of *Webridized* Discourse Analysis

As I said above, to decode this example of *webridized* textuality– a complex social, cultural and textual phenomenon – I will integrate Multimodal Analysis with insights from Critical Discourse Analysis, Functional Linguistics and Web Genres Theory. Working definitions of the terms adopted throughout are given below.

Discourse is a broad term that comprises "a whole palette of meanings" (Titscher et al. 2000:25) ranging from linguistics, through sociology, philosophy and other disciplines. Following Hodge and Kress (1993 [1979]), I use *discourse* in its Foucaldian sense, as closely linked to ideology through a sort of hyponymic relationship where discourses systematically and hierarchically articulate the beliefs and values of a given society into discursive practices and instantiate them into specific texts. In line with both Functional Linguistics (Halliday 1978; Halliday & Matthiessen 2004 [1985]) and Critical Discourse Analysis (Fairclough 1995), I take a *text* to be both the concrete representation of discourse(s) and the result of social processes, since texts or "discursive units" have the potential to store complex social and cultural meanings produced in a particular historical situation. Consequently, our role as analysts is to decode the process of textual meaning-making in order to shed light on the connections between discourse, reality and culture. In addition to that, since texts are "encoded in and determined by discourse and genre" (Wodak 2008:298), discourse practices can be analyzed in terms of how actors exploit different genres to express their ideas, opinions and messages, legitimize their own actions, and delegitimize their opponents in different situations and contexts (Chilton & Schäffner 2002).

The kind of discursive units I will be dealing with are mainly political and institutional texts. Following Martin Reisigl's (2008:248) categorization of sub-genres of political speeches, they would associate to the following *fields of political action*: the formation of public attitudes, opinions and will; political advertising; and political-executive administration. According to Reisigl (2008:247), a field of action is a "functional concept" that can be conceived as a "framework of social interaction". He associates to these different fields a list of sub-genres such as presidential speeches, opening and commemorative speeches, and State of the Union addresses.

Turning to *recontextualization*, the term identifies the transformative trajectories of discourse across times and places in an intertextual chaining (Fairclough 1992) or genre chaining (Swales 2004) that may also involve changes in genre and even in mode. The concept was originally developed as a tool for analyzing pedagogic texts (Bernstein 1990, 1996) and has been extended to examine discourse as it unfolds across a number of interrelated social contexts (Linell 1998). It offers analysts a potent tool for understanding how and why the same meaning has been reified and materialized through different discourses and mediational means, but also for tracing the possible shifts in meaning and in communicative purposes, since the ultimate meaning of texts depends on their context. This is true especially in the contemporary communicative scenario, where the above-mentioned transformative processes are amplified and further reshaped by the affordances provided by digital media, and where meaning not only travels across different platforms, but is natively and structurally created out of dispersed texts connected by links. Indeed, the hypermodal dimension of digital communication implies the creation of "semiotic artifacts in which signifiers on different scales of syntagmatic organization are linked in complex networks or webs" (Lemke 2002:300). In hypertexts,

> it is not simply that we juxtapose image, text, and sound; we design multiple interconnections among them, both potential and explicit […]. The links might be invisible, discoverable by exploring the technology that actuates them. They might be partially explicit (e.g. a unit marked visually as the source of a linking vector), but the target of the link, the nature of the meaning relation between source and target, and whether the link is reversible might not be explicit. (Lemke 2002:300)

As pointed out by Askenhave and Nielsen (2005), non-linear, multi-semiotic, digitally-mediated texts challenge the traditional functional genre model since they add (at least) a two-dimensional perspective to genre analysis in order to account for the fact that web documents not only act as texts but also as *media*. Also, such web-mediated texts often combine (written) language with other modes that make meaning (images, music, videos) and all modes are reshaping their functions in these 'new' texts (Adami & Kress 2014). This challenges the notion of what might be considered as texts and how we should analyze the meaning-making processes of different modes that constitute them. The natural corollary stemming out of this new conceptualization of texts is

> [a shift of] the center of gravity from linguistic to semiotic concerns, [in that] when all the resources which matter in meaning are at issue, then the tools of one discipline – linguistics and its satellite (sub-)disciplines – can no longer be sufficient to provide satisfactory accounts of the materials to hand and the questions they pose. (Adami & Kress 2014:231)

On these grounds, I will integrate linguistic analysis with a hypermodal and multimodal approach that takes into consideration the socio-semiotic resources for meaning making available to the "discourse community" (Swales 1990). This shall provide us with a better understanding of the complex semantic negotiations brought about by the digital recontextualization of US political discourse.

3. Facebook as a Semiotic Platform

Facebook (*Fb*), the world's largest social networking site (Eisenlauer 2013), was founded in 2004 by a Harvard sophomore as an exclusive community service for Harvard students; it was later expanded to Stanford, Columbia and Yale and, shortly after, opened to everyone (http://newsroom.fb.com/company-info; last accessed in May2014).

The social network was originally mapped on yearbooks, a type of books that is published annually by many American high schools and colleges to celebrate the past school year. Indeed, the first version of the social network was created as a sort of substitute for the official electronic version of the yearbook or *facebook*, that is the colloquial term used by students of some American universities to define the electronic directory with their photos and basic data (Carlson 2010). In these books, students are identified by means of their pictures and information and each of them is usually given the same textual space: such semiotic structure encodes the representation of a group of peers which, in the case of American Ivy League college students, constitutes a very elitist group.

The *Fb* social media platform rhetorically reproduces a similar tenor structure, as signaled by the word *friends*, the term chosen to identify registered users (see Section 1). In addition to that, people who decide to become members of the platform can create their own personal page (profile), where they can upload personal information and are also enabled to write comments and share messages with people who belong to their circle of friends. From this basic description of the main features of the social media (which will be amplified when analyzing the different sections of the platform), it is possible to grasp how the design of the digital tool combines the yearbook model with another textual model, the web genre of diary blogs that started circulating in the late Nineties in the U.S. Indeed,

> the online diary – whether called a diary or a blog, [...] began to appear on the Internet in 1995, typically developing out of the personal home pages of individuals already involved with Internet technologies [...]. In 1997 people started creating pages that became known as weblogs (or "blogs") – these were daily lists of annotated links to other sites, without extended commentary or personal narratives [...]. In 1999 free software became available that allowed users who did not know HTML to make and post a blog or diary. As a result, blogging became an accessible activity for significantly more people, and the numbers of both diaries and blogs mushroomed [...]. Collapsing these related forms into one, the latest generation of writers marry personal narratives (like a diary) with critical commentary about the Web and its content (like a blog). (McNeil 2005)

Structurally, a *weblog*, or *blog*, can be defined as a "frequently modified webpage containing individual entries displayed in reverse chronological sequence" (Herring et al. 2004:1) where, as a consequence, the most recent post appears to be the first. Bloggers usually upload their blogs with comments and criticism that range from the most private to the most public topic (Rosenberg 2010) and their style is personal and informal (Herring et al. 2007). As argued by Puschmann (2013), even if blogs have aged and have been merging with newer forms of Computer-Mediated Communication, such as status updates on social networking sites, "some linguistic properties of blogs are highly stable" and, precisely, "what remains unchanged is that blogs structure digital content sequentially and that they are more frequently maintained by individuals than institutions or companies" (p. 84). More in detail, "the core cohesive element of a blog is time [since] blog entries are paradigmatically linked by chronology [that] acts as the governing organizational principle for information in blogs" (p. 91). As regards personal encoding, Puschmann underlines that "with relatively few exceptions, a blog is a controlled discourse environment belonging to an individual and shaped largely by his or her personal tastes and needs; therefore, the needs a blog fulfills are more individually shaped than in most other genres of public expression" (p. 98).

The diary or personal journal blog is a widespread sub-genre of blogs and can be considered as the digital evolution of the paper diary (Crowston & Williams 2000). As we know, paper diaries and journals are a non-fictional literary genre that began to flourish in the late Renaissance with the rise of Humanism. Indeed, the diary is essentially a type of autobiographical writing, a regularly kept record of the diarist's reflections and activities, and personal journal blogs enhance the self-narrative features of diaries interlacing them with the hypertextual characteristics of the web and with its multimodal affordances.

The semiotic signs that are used on the *Fb* social platform to recall a blog are a "timeline" marking the inverted chronological order of posts and the "speech balloons" that map the encoder as a 'SAYER', thus emphasizing the conversional aspect of blog self-narrations. Like diaries, where people usually keep a record of personal and to some extent intimate events and thoughts, many users' posts on *Fb* are characterized by a form of self-writing where self-labeling data characterize the encoder.

As regards the textual structure of the digital platform, Eisenlauer (2013) defines *Fb* as a "closed hypertext", in which template-based text generation techniques interlace personal data into the more or less static and pre-set design of the platform. The layout, the structure and the communicative properties of the software service affect the form and content of media messages since *Fb* relies on subject-based templates that result in a more or less fixed hierarchical structure. More in detail, the latter enables and restricts the *Fb* participants' semiotic choices (sign- and structure-related) when presenting themselves and/or connecting to other members.

Turning to the multimodal digital 'translation' of institutional messages, I lie the main emphasis on the semantic short circuits that may arise from the recontextualization of a formal, impersonal, top-down institutional discourse into a personal, leisure-centered, peer-to-peer structured social network, which appears to be semiotically mapped on a combination of the yearbook textual model with the web genre of diary blogs.

4. The White House *Fb* Profile: The Analysis of the *About* Section

The White House staff created a public profile where the uploaded messages are open to all *Fb* registered users. As regards the interpersonal metafunction, such public profiles actually shape a tenor construction where the sender features a higher role than those who receive the messages. Indeed, people can only *like* the profile and then follow the messages that, whenever posted, start being framed in their own pages thanks to a digital process of automatic recontextualization of the users' data. Such role-relationship reproduces the un-balanced tenor typical of institutional discourse, despite the peer-to-peer connotation of the social media platform.

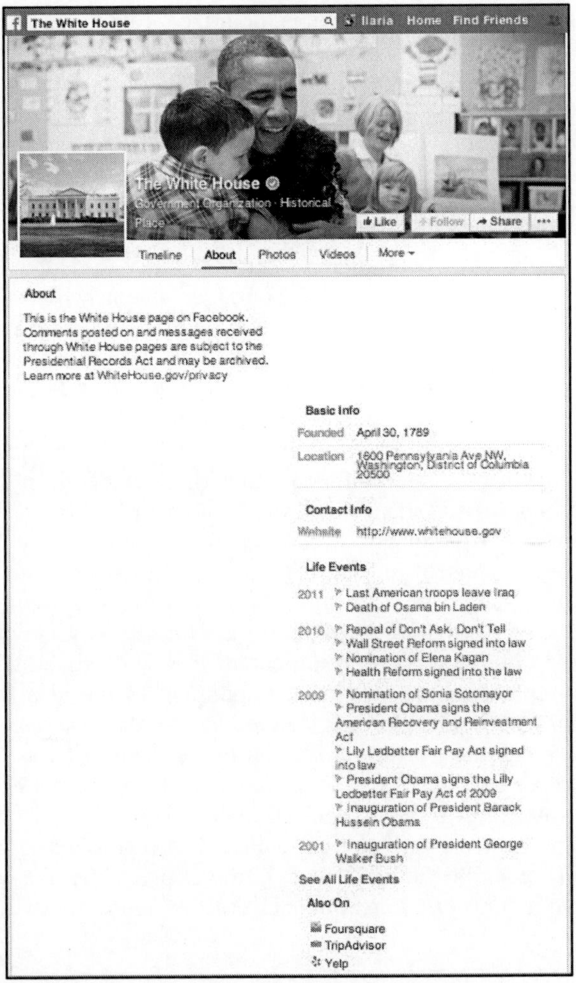

Fig. 1: The White House Facebook profile: the *About* section

As anticipated, in this paper I concentrate on the analysis of the *About* section of the profile, reproduced in Figure 1 (https://www.facebook.com/WhiteHouse/info; accessed May 1, 2014) where main presentational information about the sender is given in line with the yearbook model. The textual organization of this page is shaped by the template of the social media platform and features three main blocks: one visual horizontal block situated at the top of the page and two mainly verbal parallel blocks that run vertically through the rest of the space.

The composition of the page is polarized following an Ideal-Real structure according to which the informational values associated to the sections of the page itself are different: the Ideal one – situated at the top of the page – conveys "the idealized or generalized essence of the information [and also its] most salient part" (Kress & van Leeuwen 1996:193), while the Real one, that is the rest of the page, "presents more specific information [...], more practical information" (Kress & van Leeuwen 1996:194). Such a pre-set polarized layout confers salience to the horizontal block, a *multimodal cluster* (Baldry & Thibault 2006:31) situated within the first scroll of the computer screen, where we find two images (the profile picture and the cover photo)[1] and a set of structural links that, in the *reading mode*, are illocutionary speech acts which invite people to perform an action, and in the *navigational mode* become buttons that activate *Fb* functions (Askenhave & Nielsen 2005).

As regards the representation of the sender, the highest level of modality of the profile is instantiated into a blue rounded icon that appears on the right side of the name: it is the symbol of a verified page and a semiotic marker of trustiness, which certifies the identity of the sender. The two labels chosen to verbally define the White House in this hypertextual self-narrative (Thibault 2012) – *government organization* and *historical palace* – are the 'CARRIERS' of a semantic polysemy that can be decoded only with reference to American history. Indeed, the White House as a palace represents the physical embodiment of the idea (Seale 2001 [1992]), engraved in the founding 'sacred scriptures' (*The Declaration of Independence* and the *Constitution*), that the government was founded on the protection of God-given freedoms, an idea which lies at the heart of the so-called "American Civil Religion" (Bellah 1967).

The White House as a historical palace thus represents a "multimodal metaphor" (Forceville 2006:381) and, more precisely, the multimodal realization of a *conceptual metaphor* (Lakoff & Johnson 1980) according

[1] Notice that pictures change periodically. All the *Fb* contents analyzed in my paper were last accessed in May 2014.

to which "the architectural plan is a metaphor of the [American] socio-political project" (Moschini 2007:253). This conceptual *architectonic metaphor* (Moschini 2007:258) is deeply rooted in US culture and can be traced back to Hector St. John de Crevecoeur and to the third epistle of his famous *Letters from an American Farmer* (1782).

As a matter of fact, the third letter is a reflection on the nature of the American people, where the author uses the fair view admired by the enlightened Englishman, arriving on the new continent, as a metaphor for the new society that offers itself to his "contemplation". As we can read in the fragment quoted below, the "pleasing uniformity" of the habitations reflects the "pleasing equality" of the American society, defined as "the most perfect society now existing in the world", whose perfection stems from the protection of God-given inalienable natural rights among which there is freedom:

> I wish I could be acquainted with the feelings and thoughts which must agitate the heart and present themselves to the mind of an enlightened Englishman, when he first lands on this continent. […] [A] modern society offers itself to his contemplation […]. A pleasing uniformity of decent competence appears throughout our habitations […]. We are the most perfect society now existing in the world. Here man is free, as he ought to be; nor is this pleasing equality so transitory as many others are [...]. (de Crevecoeur 1782)

In America, the link between city, society and God dates back to the colonial period. Indeed, the Puritans, in their cities, aimed to reproduce the perfection of the divine architecture since they believed that architectural structures were a microcosm of God's exact structure of the Universe and a constant reminder of the way He wanted them to live (Wright 1993). As a consequence, the delightfulness perceived by the human eye – or the "pleasing uniformity" described by Crevecoeur – derives directly from the contemplation of God's creation (Moschini 2007:259).

The profile picture of the White House offers a "naturalistic representation" (Kress & van Leeuwen 1996:170) of the historical palace and, together with the two labels (*government organization* and *historical palace*), also constitutes a *multimodal cluster* (Baldry & Thibault 2006:31), which conveys the idea that the urban project stands for the American social project. Indeed, the *intersemiotic polysemy* that emerges from the co-contextualization of the verbal and the visual components (Liu & O'Halloran 2009:375) leads to the encoding of the above-mentioned conceptual "architectonic metaphor".

As regards the cover photo (Figure 1), it features President Barack Obama in the act of embracing children in a schoolroom. The image provides a visual representation of what Lakoff would define as *Nurturant Parent Morality* (2002 [1996]:108), a moral system built around the model of an emphatic idea of family that constitutes the basic worldview of the Democratic party and one of the main pillars of Barack Obama's rhetoric (Lakoff 2009). According to the cognitive linguist, "there are two varieties of moral nurturance, one about individuals and the other about social relations" (Lakoff 2002 [1996]:120), and the connection between nurturance and social ties can be articulated as follows: Moral Agents Are Nurturing Parents; Social Ties Are Children Needing Care; Moral Action Is the Nurturance of Social Ties (Lakoff 2002 [1996]:120). In this context, the cover photo of the White House *Fb* profile represents the President as a Moral Agent who is taking care of Social Ties, here personified by children, and it also offers a social media recontextualization of Lakoff's (2002 [1996]:121) *Social Nurturance* metaphor.

Returning to the composition of the page, the two vertical parallel panes feature a blank setting that confers salience to the written text (see Figure 1) and is framed by the black titles of the *Fb* template (*About/ Basic Info/ Contact Info/ Life Events*), which is semiotically mapped on the model of blogs and yearbooks. The personal stance encoded in the template gives rise to a semantic short-circuit with the kind of language used by the White House staff. Indeed, the message in the left block (which I quote below) presents a very formal register with a certain degree of epistemic modality:

> This is the White House page on Facebook. Comments posted on and messages received through White House pages are subject to the Presidential Records Act and may be archived. Learn more at WhiteHouse.gov/privacy.

This portion of text offers an example of the *marketization* of institutional language (Fairclough 2011:15): the imperative form *learn* is a typical marker of promotional discourse that implies the second person form of address, 'you', without a direct textual reference. Users are invited to deepen their knowledge by activating the hypermodal link to the *Online Privacy Policy Informational* page of the White House website.

The semantic short circuit between the high degree of personalization of the digital platform and the formality of institutional language is evident also in the right vertical block, where the "Life Events" of the White House are narrated. It is present especially in the first entry dated 1789 (Figure 2), where the term selected to identify the 'birth' of the encoder is *founded*, a verb that pertains to the semantic sphere of objects rather than to that of people. Indeed, it can mean either "to establish or originate an institution" or "to plan and begin the building of a settlement" (OED). Such semantic ambiguity is caused by the ellipsis of the subject both in the timeline entry and in the post that the timeline link activates.

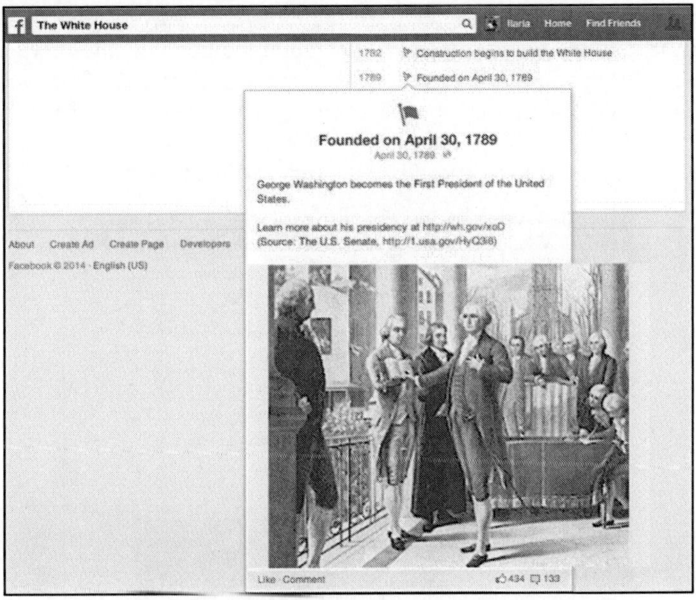

Fig. 2: The 'Founding' Entry

Additionally, the speech balloon opened by the "transversal" reading reproduces the previously analyzed "architectonic conceptual metaphor" because the date refers to the day when George Washington took his oath of office as the first President of the United States.

The post celebrates the "government" – metonymically represented by the President – not the "historical palace", since the place to build the Capital City would not be established until the signing of the *Residence Act* of 1790. As a matter of fact, George Washington's inaugural ceremony took place on the balcony of Federal Hall on Wall Street in New York. Such "conceptual metaphor" is further strengthened by the hypertextual structure of the digital platform because – from the users' perspective – the image of the first President, the link to the White House website and the timeline entry can be "interpreted as cohesive and coherent profile components, […] contextualized as illocutions serving self-presentation" (Eisenlauer 2013).

The third voice of the "Life Events" of the White House (Figure 3) sets the model of all the entries until the one describing the Inauguration of President Barack Obama in 2009. The message presents an *intersemiotic parallel structure* (Liu & O'Halloran 2009:373) that amplifies the multimodal discourse and features the image as the hypernym of the verbal text. As regards the visual representation of the participant, President Adams is portrayed as if he were "on offer", as if he were "an object of contemplation" (Kress & van Leeuwen 1996:124). Crucially, this rhetorical strategy is frequently exploited by the pictorial genre of portraits historically devoted to memorialize the rich and the powerful.

Fig. 3: The Inauguration of President John Adams

5. Final Remarks and Future Developments

The above-mentioned textual construction is also used for all the posts on the White House *Timeline* page from the first one (dated 1789) until the Inauguration of President Theodore Roosevelt in 1901, since they faithfully reproduce the entries of the "Life Events" of the *About* section; while the posts from the beginning of the twentieth century to nowadays present different communicative strategies. More particularly, they feature a progressive hybridization with postmodern, libertarian and play-oriented participatory discourse, the origin of which can be traced back to the hacker culture (Coleman 2013).

It is self-evident that, in this process – what I define '*geekization*' – the knowledge of the hacker culture is central to understanding the actual realization of meaning in the social media platform. Indeed, as Manovich (2001) affirms, participatory discourse lies at the heart of the software architecture because since the 1980s the software has shaped not only the set of semiotic patterns that new media users may exploit to create meaning, but has also materialized postmodernism, the "new cultural logic of modern society".

The cultural component is central also in this first part of my analysis, where reference to the founding ideas of American socio-political culture allows the decoding of the conceptual metaphors that frame the hypermodal image of the sender. Therefore, I would like to conclude by saying that in my future analysis the combination of the different theoretical strands adopted here will be more structurally integrated with the study of the socio-cultural components of the texts and of their metaphorical realizations, which appears to be especially useful in understanding the strategies used in the social-media recontextualization of the image of the institutional encoder.

References

Adami, Elisabetta & Gunther Kress. 2014. Introduction: Multimodality, meaning making, and the issue of 'text'. In Gunther Kress, Roberta Facchinetti & Elisabetta Adami (eds.), *Multimodality, Meaning Making and the Issue of 'Text'*. Special Issue. *Text & Talk* 34. 3. 231-237.

Askehave, Inger & Anne E. Nielsen. 2005. Digital genres: A challenge to traditional genre theory. *Information Technology and People* 3. 120-141.

Baldry, Anthony & Paul J. Thibault. 2005. *Multimodal Transcription and Text Analysis. A Multimedia Toolkit with Associated On-line Course*. London: Equinox.

Bellah, Robert. 1967. Civil religion in America. *Dædalus, Journal of the American Academy of Arts and Sciences* 96. 1. 1-21.

Bernstein, Basil. 1990. *The Structuring of Pedagogic Discourse: Class, Codes and Control. Vol. 6.* London/New York: Routledge.

—. 1996. *Pedagogy, Symbolic Control and Identity: Theory, Research, Critique.* London: Taylor and Francis.

Carlson, Nicholas. 2010. At Last – The full story of how Facebook was founded. *Business Insider*. March 5. http://www.businessinsider.com/how-facebook-was-founded-2010-3#we-can-talk-about-that-after-i-get-all-the-basic-functionality-up-tomorrow-night-1. Accessed 01-05-2014.

Chilton, Paul & Christina Schäffner. 2002. *Politics as Text and Talk. Analytic Approaches to Political Discourse*. Amsterdam/Philadelphia: John Benjamins.

Coleman, Gabriella E. 2013. *Coding Freedom. The Ethics and Aesthetics of Hacking*. Princeton/Oxford: Princeton University Press.

Crowston, Kevin & Michelle Williams. 2000. Reproduced and emergent genres of communication on the World-Wide Web. *The Information Society* 16. 3. 201-216.

de Crevecoeur, Hector St. John J. 1792. *Letter from an American Farmer, Letter III "What is an American"*. http://xroads.virginia.edu/~HYPER/CREV/letter03.html. Accessed 01-05-2014.

Eisenlauer, Volker. 2013. *A Critical Hypertext Analysis of Social Media: The True Colours of Facebook*. London/New York: Continuum.

Fairclough, Norman. 1992. *Discourse and Social Change*. Cambridge: Polity Press.

—. 1995. *Critical Discourse Analysis: The Critical Study of Language*. London/New York: Longman.

—. 2006. *Language and Globalization*. London/New York: Routledge.

—. 2011. Discourse hybridity and social change in Critical Discourse Analysis. In Srikant Sarangi, Vanda Polese & Giuditta Caliendo (eds.), *Genre(s) on the Move: Hybridisation and Discourse Change in Specialised Communication*. Napoli: Edizioni Scientifiche Italiane. 11-26.

Forceville, Charles. 2006. Non-verbal and multimodal metaphor in a cognitivist framework: Agendas for research. In Gitte Kristiansen, Michel Achard, René Dirven & Francisco J. Ruiz de Mendoza Ibañez (eds.), *Cognitive Linguistics: Current Applications and Future Perspectives*. Berlin/New York: Mouton de Gruyter. 379-402.

Halliday, Michael A. K. 1978. *Language as Social Semiotics*. London: Edward Arnold.

Halliday, Michael A. K. & Christian Matthiessen. 2004 [1985]. *An Introduction to Functional Grammar*. London: Edward Arnold.

Herring, Susan, Inna Kouper, Lois A. Scheidt & Elijah L. Wright. 2004. Women and children last: The discursive construction of weblogs. In Laura J. Gurak, Smiljana Antonijevic, Laurie Johnson, Clancy Ratliff & Jessica Reyman (eds.), *Into the Blogosphere: Rhetoric, Community, and Culture of Web-logs*. http://blog.lib.umn.edu/blogosphere/women_and_children.html. Accessed 01-11-2014.

Herring, Susan, Lois A. Scheidt, Inna Kouper & Elijah L. Wright. 2007. A longitudinal content analysis of weblogs: 2003-2004. In Mark Tremayne (ed.), *Blogging, Citizenship, and the Future of Media*. London/New York: Routledge. 3-20.

Hodge, Robert & Gunther Kress. 1993 [1979]. *Language as Ideology*. London/New York: Routledge.

Jenkins, Henry. 1992. *Textual Poachers: Television Fans and Participatory Culture. Studies in Culture and Communication*. London/New York: Routledge.

Kress, Gunther & Theo van Leeuwen. 1996. *Reading Images: The Grammar of Visual Design*. London/New York: Routledge.

Lakoff, George. 2002 [1996]. *Moral Politics. How Liberals and Conservatives Think*. Chicago/London: The University of Chicago Press.

—. 2009. The Obama Code. *The HuffingtonPost*, Feb 24. http://www.huffingtonpost.com/george-lakoff/the-obama-code_b_169580.html. Accessed 01-05-2014.

Lakoff, George & Mark Johnson. 1980. *Metaphors We Live By*. Chicago/London: The University of Chicago Press.

Lemke, Jay. 2002. Travels in Hypermodality. *Visual Communication* 1. 3. 299-325.

Linell, Per. 1998. Discourse across boundaries: On recontextualizations and the blending of voices in professional discourse. *Text* 18. 2. 143-157.

Liu Yu & Kay L. O'Halloran. 2009. Intersemiotictexture: Analyzing cohesive devices between language and images. *Social Semiotics* 19. 4. 367-388.

Manovich, Lev. 2001. *The Language of New Media*. Cambridge, MA: The MIT Press.

McNeill, Laurie. 2005. Genre under construction: The diary on the internet. *Language@Internet* 2. Article 1. http://www.languageatinternet.org/articles/2005/120. Accessed 01-11-2014.

Moschini, Ilaria. 2007. Brave new edens. In Gabriella Del Lungo, Laura Jottini & John Douthwaite (eds.), *Cityscapes: Islands of the Self, Vol. 2. Language Studies*. Cagliari: CUEC. 253-267.

—. 2010. Race 2.0 or the 'Webridization' of electoral discourse. *Il Politico* 75. 2. 133-161.

—.2012. Evoluzione del concetto di testo. In Francesca Ditifeci (ed.), *Il testo al centro. Atti del Convegno in onore di Gigliola Sacerdoti Mariani*. Firenze: Consiglio Regionale della Toscana. Edizioni dell'Assemblea. 163-183.

—. 2013. Liberty icons: Linguistic and multimodal notes on the cultural roots of digital technologies. *LEA – Lingue e Letterature d'Oriente e d'Occidente* 2. 537-552. http://www.fupress.net/index.php/bsfm-lea/article/view/13844/13604.

—. 2014. 'You should've seen Luke!' or the multimodal encoding/decoding of the language of postmodern 'webridized' TV series. In Gunther Kress, Roberta Facchinetti & Elisabetta Adami (eds.), *Multimodality, Meaning Making and the Issue of 'Text'*. Special Issue. *Text & Talk* 34. 3: 283-305.

OED: *Oxford English Dictionary*. 2nd ed. and later additions. http://www.oed.com.

Puschmann, Cornelius. 2013. Blogging. In Susan Herring, Dieter Stein & Tuija Virtanen (eds.), *Pragmatics of Computer-Mediated Communication*. Berlin/New York: De Gruyter. 83-108.

Reisigl, Martin. 2008. Rhetoric of political speeches. In Ruth Wodak & Veronika Koller (eds.), *Handbook of Communication in the Public Sphere.* Berlin/New York: Mouton de Gruyter. 243-269.

Rosenberg, Scott (ed.). 2010. *Say Everything: How Blogging Began, What It's Becoming and Why It Matters*. New York, NY: Three Rivers Press.

Seale, William. 2001 [1992]. *The White House: The History of an American Idea.* Washington, DC: The White House Historical Association.

Swales, John M. 1990. *Genre Analysis. English in Academic and Research Settings*. Cambridge: Cambridge University Press.

—. 2004. *Research Genres. Explorations and Applications*. Cambridge: Cambridge University Press.

Thibault, Paul J. 2012. Hypermedia selves and hypermodal stories: Narrativity, writing and normativity in personal blogs. In Mariavita Cambria, Cristina Arizzi & Francesca Coccetta (eds.), *Web Genres and Web Tools*. Como/Pavia: Ibis. 5-49.

Titscher, Stefan, Michael Meyer, Ruth Wodak & Eva Vetter (eds.). 2000. *Methods of Text and Discourse Analysis*. London: Sage Publications.

Wodak, Ruth. 2008. The contribution of critical linguistics to the analysis of discriminatory prejudices and stereotypes in the language of politics. In Ruth Wodak & Veronika Koller (eds.), *Handbook of Communication in the Public Sphere.* Berlin/New York: Mouton de Gruyter. 291-316.

Wright, Gwendolyn. 1993. *Building the Dream. A Social History of Housing in America*. Cambridge, MA: The MIT Press.

DIGITAL VIVIDNESS: REPORTING AVIATION DISASTERS ONLINE

CARMEN SANCHO GUINDA
UNIVERSIDAD POLITÉCNICA DE MADRID, SPAIN

Abstract: In this chapter I explore the features and resources of the online aviation-catastrophe reporting issued yearly by the U.S. National TransportationSafety Board (NTSB) and its current and characteristic tendency towards 'journalistic vividness' thanks to computer-mediated communication. In particular, I focus on the structure, format, content and textual network of its dockets, nowadays subsumed within a constellation of narrative genres with multiple affordances and subjected to a number of socio-pragmatic and socio-political constraints. To that end I study markers of vividness from both a qualitative and quantitative approach, scrutinizing an electronic corpus of over 1,500 samples of fatal probable-causea ccident dockets between 2005 and 2012. The theoretical framework I draw on is eclectic and fuses Corpus Linguistics, Pragmatics, and Genre, (Critical) Discourse, and Multimodal Analysis. My claim is that NTSB dockets are evolving into a popularised blend of technical report, entertainment storytelling and informative journalism.

1. Storytelling in a Multimodal Era: What Counts?

Computer-Mediated Communication (henceforth CMC) often makes narratives adopt the form of *multimodal composites* (Hoffman 2010:11) that appropriate generic conventions already established in older media, mix them up with visual and aural perception, and add variables such as interactivity or hypertextuality (Bazzanella 2010). More specifically, and attending to the continuum of possible narratives proposed by Ochs and Capps (2001), thanks to CMC the *classical* or *default* narratives, sociologically approached, turn into *hypernarratives*, approached conversationally due to their greater participatory nature. While default narratives are featured as highly tellable, linearly composed, relatively detached from their context, and reported by a single active teller who expresses a constant moral stance, the *tellability* (Norrick 2000) of hypernarratives is moderate, their composition multilinear, and they tend to be embedded in their contexts and reported by multiple co-tellers who transmit a vague, fluid moral stance.

In this chapter I will study a singular point of intersection between these two narrative modes: the aircraft-accident dockets issued yearly online by the *U.S. National Transportation Safety Board* (*NTSB* for short), whose computer-mediated dissemination[1] seems to have notably increased the degree of *vividness* (Sancho Guinda 2014) with which they are told. In what follows I will begin by trying to delimit what is understood by vividness, then go on to describe the aviation-accident docket genre according to the four parameters for genre description put forth in Genre Analysis (purpose, participants, process and product), and, finally, look at how, at which levels and under what constraints, vividness manifests itself in NTSB aviation-accident synopses. My major claim will be that these texts are evolving into what could be termed *catastropops*, a blend of informative journalism, technical report and entertainment storytelling.

As a dictionary entry, the definition of *vividness* has much to do with *detail*, and, therefore, with *distance*. The *Merriam Webster Dictionary* online, for example, equates the concept with the quality of "seeming like real life because it is very clear, bright, or detailed", and the printed version of the *Collins Dictionary and Thesaurus* (2000) with *intensity*, *striking realism*, *freshness* and *trueness to life*. Certainly, we may want to add, realism depends on detail, and detail can only be perceived from a closer perspective, by means of a *zoom-in* that may enhance either *content* or *form*. The former involves engaging in disclosure regarding *intimacy* (that is, information open or vetoed to certain circles) and *accuracy* (more fine-grained descriptions or graphic accounts), whereas the latter involves increasing the sense of *immediacy* (spatiotemporal) and *subjectivity* (i.e. in the sequencing of information, its fore- or backgrounding, and the choice of reporting structures). CMC, however, poses a paradox concerning distance, and, importantly, the related notion of vividness: its audience and participants are physically distant, even more than the ones reached by any publisher, but its affordances permit the shortening of such distance (e.g. through magnifying devices that augment visual detail, a certain freedom in the choice of reading paths through different buttons and hyperlinks, and even synchronous communication). But, on the other hand, is vividness all that counts? No other world transportation agency divulging its investigations online is as vividness-committed as the NTSB. For one,

[1] *CM dissemination* involves proactively divulging information online instead of merely 'releasing it' (that is, declassifying it to prevent it from being confidential). The NTSB (http://www.ntsb.gov/) has been disseminating its accident reports online since July 1, 2009 (Sancho Guinda 2013).

the *Air Accident Investigation Branch* (*AAIB*) in the United Kingdom issues its dockets in a structured abstract or executive summary format, with headers, numbered and bulleted points for identified factors and actors within each section, and a brief synopsis of the history of flight (see example 1) formed by minimal narratives (Labov & Waleztky 1967), consisting of two narrative clauses that interrelate kernel events or actions, or one event/action and a state/condition:

(1) […] The aircraft departed Biggin Hill for a private flight to Pau, France, but shortly after takeoff initiated a return to Biggin Hill after reporting engine vibration. During the downwind leg for Runway 21, the aircraft descended. The flight crew reported a major power problem just before it struck the side of a house. An intense fire developed. None of the two flight crew and three passengers survived. (AAIB, Aircraft Accident Report No. 3/2010 (EW/C2008/03/03))

AAIB reports, it seems, prime rigour, clarity and concision over vividness. By contrast, MacPherson's (1998) commented compilation of NTSB cockpit/cabin voice recordings (CVRs) previous to accidents, a source of a very different kind, emphasizes the drama inherent in CVR transcripts and closes every final comment with the formula *All souls aboard were lost* when there are no survivors, or substitutes the determiner *all* by a numeral if there are some. Notice, however, that MacPherson is a bestseller-minded novelist and a magazine and newspaper journalist, more concerned with audience impact than with technical aspects, unlike NTSB docket writers. Considering the Board's expertise and official status, nobody would expect any trace of emotion in its texts, although this expectation is not always met (example 2):

(2) […] While on the mission a radio distress call "Mayday, Mayday, Mayday, we are going down", was heard on the mission operating frequency. […] (NTSB DFW05FA086)

The important question, therefore, is: What may lead NTSB writers to write such extremely vivid texts, then? If, as pointed out above, their dockets are a middle ground between default- and hyper-narratives, then the reason for this lies, in the first place, in their highly tellable nature. They are permanently newsworthy as they comply with several of the key *reportability* or *tellability* conditions set by Harcup and O'Neill (2001): *low frequency* (aircraft disasters are statistically infrequent and sometimes one-off events), *unexpectedness* (they can hardly be predicted), *high intensity* (they are tragic), *negativity* (they catch attention more than positive events), *meaningfulness* (they happen to individuals but have a communal repercussion), *time interruption* (they are a breach in the everyday), *spatial transcendence* (especially with the global audiences addressed by CMC), and *otherness* (they bring to the fore ethical issues that may unite or divide social groups).

Secondly, there are *co-narrators*, which implies more democratisation and contributes to vividness in the service of the NTSB's verdicts. We could say, in fact, that those licensed narrating voices metaphorize that of the NTSB, and that the apparently fluid moral stance they convey endorses the Board's viewpoint, authority and control. Thus, whereas the aviation community (present in technical intertexts and phraseologies) and the story actors and witnesses (embodied in direct speech insertions) dilute narrative agency through their multivocality, their goal is to achieve monovocal credibility to brand the Board as a coherent and compact organism.

Thirdly, NTSB docket narratives are deeply embedded in the context of the Board's reporting network (Figure 1), thus informing some genres and banking on others. For instance, dockets inform abstracts and executive summaries, and full reports draw on specialists' slideshows and in turn influence animations. It is important to note that, together with abstracts, press releases and executive summaries, dockets are *lay genres*. That is, they require no expertise to be understood, or if they do, technical contents are glossed. This reader-considerateness, or friendliness, is not found either in expert genres – which have experts as their intended readers –, such as the full report or the legal documents that originate from the full report, or in the animation and the presentation slideshow, which could be seen as taking an *intermediate* position between lay and expert genres.

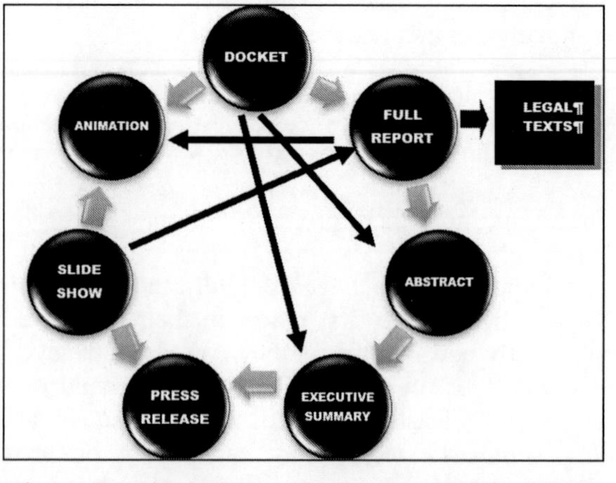

Fig. 1: Narrative genres in the networked context of the NTSB

Lastly, NTSB writers combine linearity with non-linearity and hypertextuality at will, without following a strict protocol, as if the many hands involved in the collaborative docket-writing enterprise of the NTSB had generated two distinctive styles: some dockets start with the history of flight in strict chronological sequence (example 3), present the findings obtained from expert analyses, and interpret them in the Board's final verdict (example 4). Others start *in medias res*, without a proper framing of the accident, and insert witnesses and actors' sound bites in direct speech before tackling the findings and offering a judgment. It may even be the case that the docket begins with a *lumped summary*; that is, with an anti-climactic anticipation of the accident causes stated later in the findings section (example 4).

(3) **NTSB Identification:** DCA12MA020
Nonscheduled 14 CFR Part 135: Air Taxi & Commuter
Accident occurred Wednesday, December 07, 2011 in Las Vegas, NV
Probable Cause Approval Date: 02/20/2013
Aircraft: EUROCOPTER FRANCE AS350B2, registration: N37SH
Injuries: 5 Fatal.

NTSB investigators traveled in support of this investigation and used data obtained from various sources to prepare this aircraft accident report.

The Safety Board's full report is available at http://www.ntsb.gov/investigations/reports_aviation.html. The Aircraft Accident Report number is NTSB/AAR-13/01.

On December 7, 2011, about 1630 Pacific standard time, a Sundance Helicopters, Inc., Eurocopter AS350-B2 helicopter, N37SH, operating as a "Twilight tour" sightseeing trip, crashed in mountainous terrain about 14 miles east of Las Vegas, Nevada. The pilot and four passengers were killed, and the helicopter was destroyed by impact forces and postimpact fire. The helicopter was registered to and operated by Sundance as a scheduled air tour flight under the provisions of 14 Code of Federal Regulations (CFR) Part 135. Visual meteorological conditions with good visibility and dusk light prevailed at the time of the accident, and the flight operated under visual flight rules.

[…]

(4) **NTSB Identification:** WPR09LA378
14 CFR Part 91: General Aviation
Accident occurred Saturday, August 01, 2009 in Caldwell, ID
Probable Cause Approval Date: 3/3/2010
Aircraft: Gray RV-6, registration: N69KG
Injuries: 1 Fatal.

<u>According to a family member of the pilot</u>, the airplane had sat on the airport's ramp for about a year without having been flown. About a week

> before the accident, the pilot flew the airplane once around the traffic pattern. On the day of the accident, the pilot had removed and sandblasted the spark plugs, checked the cylinders for compression, and removed and cleaned the air filter; the filter was reported to have had "some goop" on it. A witness reported observing the airplane take off, and, as it went by him at 100 to 200 feet above ground level, he heard a "popping noise." He subsequently observed the airplane make a quick left turn to a left downwind leg, and as the airplane continued on the downwind he observed the nose increase in pitch, but it was not climbing. As the airplane came abeam the numbers, it made a steep left turn, followed by the nose dropping before it dove into the ground and erupted in flames. The airplane was consumed by a post impact fire. A post accident examination of the engine revealed no anomalies with the cylinders and valve train. All spark plugs were found to have excessive gaps, and all but one failed a bench check when exposed to pressure greater than 80 psi. A post accident examination of the airframe revealed no anomalies. No aircraft or engine logbooks were located during the investigation.
>
> The National Transportation Safety Board determines the probable cause(s) of this accident as follows:
>
> The pilot's failure to maintain adequate airspeed that led to a stall/spin while maneuvering in the traffic pattern.
>
> Full narrative available

All dockets contain the clickable legend *Full narrative available*, which guides readers to the full report, illustrated with still photographs and diagrams. In addition to this generalized hypertextuality, less than 1.5% of the over two thousand docket samples online have very recently been complemented with animations and hyperlinks that take the readers/viewers to the related networked genres, allowing them to choose their own reading paths and the level of expertise with which to get informed.

1.1. What NTSB Dockets are Like: Purpose, Participants, Process and Product

The NTSB's accident investigations and reporting *are aimed at prevention*, not at blaming or assigning legal responsibilities. They intend to detect causes, spot deficiencies in the system, and recommend safety measures for future actions. The *participants* or *genre users* are many and diverse: aviation authorities, investigative boards and organisations worldwide (e.g. the *ICAO – International Civil Aviation Organisation*), aircraft and engine manufacturers, insurance companies, legal staff (judges, prosecutors, lawyers), victims and their families, scholars, universities, aeronautical schools, and the press.

The *process* NTSB dockets involve, is a collaborative writing endeavour with several rounds of editing and proofreading. A first draft is written by field researchers and revised by colleagues, authorities, and occasionally by manufacturers. If passed by the Board, the document may then be just released (i.e. de-classified) or made public (i.e. actively disseminated in the media). Proactive digital dissemination has been the Board's option since July 1, 2009.

As a *product* (see Example 4, all emphases mine), NTSB dockets have a variable extension that ranges from 100 words to two pages, being the average length that of a conventional research article abstract (i.e. from 200 to 400 words). They may appear online independently, under the name of *accident dockets* or *accident synopses*, or be part of *the full report*, in which case they are recast as two pieces: the *abstract*, preceding the table of contents, and the *executive summary*, after the table of contents and before the factual information of the accident.

Abstracts tend to be highly meta-referential (they use expressions of the type *this report describes*... or *Safety issues discussed in this report include*...) and are normally composed of two paragraphs, with the opening one informing concisely about the circumstances and outcome of the accident, and the second enumerating the safety issues dealt with in the document (e.g. in-flight engine diagnostics, forensic analyses and recommendations). As for the executive summary, it may be a facsimile of the independent docket/synopsis if this has been written in a matter-of-fact fashion. In other words, dockets and executive summaries are virtually identical if the docket does not introduce direct testimonies from witnesses and strictly confined to the chronology of the history of flight, the accident aftermath (injuries to people and other damage), to relevant meteorological, medical and pathological data, and aircraft and airport conditions.

According to content, independent dockets/synopses are classified into six types by the NTSB, depending on the severity of the accident outcome and the investigation stage they report. They may summarize *fatal* accidents (i.e. causing deaths and equipment destruction), *non-fatal* accidents (i.e. involving injuries, material damage and a reduction in safety margins because of an excessive workload, physical distress, or incomplete or inaccurate operations), and *incidents* (i.e. nuisances, operating limitations, or the need to use emergency procedures). Simultaneously, they may be *factual* (i.e. merely informing about accident circumstances because some other government is in charge of the investigation), *of probable cause* (i.e. providing an evidence-based speculation about accident causes), or *preliminary* (i.e. written at an early investigation stage and therefore giving a provisional account).

Formally, every docket is divided into two distinct parts (examples 3 and 4): one formed by the *headings*, which resemble those of a structured abstract, and the other by the *body* of text, where attribution, and particularly reporting verbs, play a crucial structural role by ascribing information either to the testimonies of witnesses and actors, the wreckage evidence, or to expert action behind data interpretation and the final verdict. The underlined parts (author's emphasis) in example (4) signal an attributive progression from the pilot's most intimate circle through witnesses, expert analysts, and finally to the highest hierarchy within his community of practice – the NTSB as governmental agency.

Unquestionably, the most salient formal feature of dockets is their *hybridization* (Fairclough 2006; Gotti, Berkenkotter & Bhatia 2012) as they are at the same time retrospective and prospective (they analyze past events and make recommendations for the future), objective and subjective (they join data and their interpretation, sometimes emotionally tinged), informative, performative (with formulae such as *the NTSB determines...*) and prescriptive (when explicit recommendations are given). They are also literate and oral (as they employ written formulaic language and may include transcribed testimonies in direct speech), and at the same time intertextual and interdiscursive. Their intertext fuses the voices of story actors, witnesses, experts, the NTSB writer(s), and a corpus of previous NTSB texts and aeronautical literature, such as pilots' logbooks, aviation manuals or official rules and regulations. Their interdiscourse not only borrows loosely the rhetorical organization of scientific abstracts (Swales 1990) (introduction > method > result > conclusion) and the Labovian (Labov & Waletzky 1967) frame for personal narratives (abstract > orientation > complicating action > resolution > coda), but also amalgamates a series of stylistic traits from the technical report (vocabulary, syntax, institutional phraseology), the legal case (embedded witness testimonies, subordination of the narrative to the logical argument, the issuing of a verdict with formulaic expressions, the reference to normative texts), and drama and storytelling (dialogues and climactic build-ups).

We have seen that dockets are but one component of the genre *constellation* that makes up the NTSB narrative network, themselves resulting from four different kinds of narratives (Figure 2): the *statements* of the aviation staff involved in the accident, obtained through CVRs and interviews; the *supporting stories* from witnesses, colleagues and passengers (also obtained through interviews); the *interpretation* of evidence (which I have labelled *artifacts* and comprise photographs and the expert analysis of the wreckage, the terrain and the CVRs), and the *legal documents* that inform that interpretation (procedures, protocols, standards and regulations) and are generated and updated with the information contained in technical reports. Dockets, in sum, may merge three contexts – *personal (conversational)*, *technical*, and *legal* – with their respective registers.

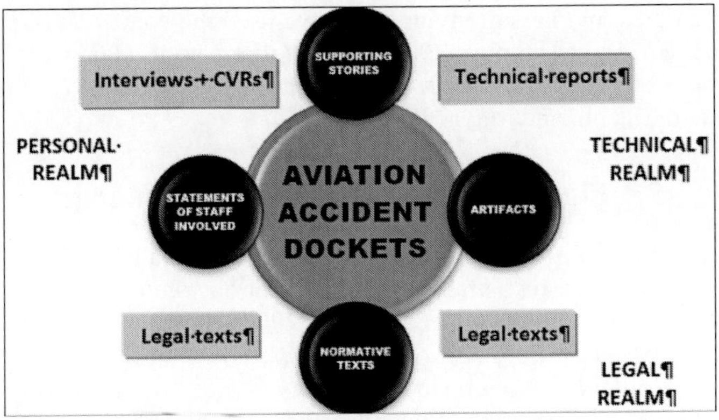

Fig. 2: Narrative network of aviation-accident dockets

As the three realms tend to blur in the course of the investigation, so do their registers intertwine in the docket, sometimes producing a sort of pastiche that gathers direct speech, technical jargon, and even legalese if excerpts of aviation rules and regulations are quoted. The private lives of crew members and maintenance employees may be made public (e.g. medical histories, marital and sentimental details) and interpreted in annotated clinical and legal terms. This *code switching*, though not present in all NTSB dockets, is highly distinctive of the institution and mirrors its policy of transparency.

2. Analytical Tools

The present study is essentially qualitative. It results from the careful manual scrutiny of an electronic corpus of 1,673 NTSB docket samples online, which encapsulate the Board's aviation-accident investigations over the time span 2005-2012 and total 540,831 tokens (words and figures).[2] The motivation to choose *fatal probable-cause* accidents has been the assumption that, being more complete, speculative and dramatic, they will be more vivid than preliminary and factual accidents and incidents. To find out about the social environment of the genre I have analysed the NTSB website and context and conducted unstructured interviews with four experts from the School of Aeronautical and Aerospace Engineering of the Technical University of Madrid, some of whom were members of the Spanair accident-investigation committee in 2008. To detect markers of vividness I have used the concordance program *AntConc 3.2.1w* (Anthony 2007) as auxiliary tool and searched for reporting verbs – drawing on the inventories provided by Thompson (1994) and Machin and Mayr (2012).

3. Findings: Vividness as NTSB Imprint

Vividness is an uncontroversially distinctive feature of the NTSB compared with the rest of world transportation agencies. It shapes its *narrative identity* (Benwell & Stokoe 2006) both institutionally and nationally, based on the *Freedom of Information Act* (*FOIA*). The FOIA, one of the pillars of American democracy, is key to the telling of the NTSB, that is, it frames (also legally) the amount of disclosure and the choice of narrative coding and, therefore, the three intertwined dimensions of linguistic, rhetorical, and pragmatic coding.

3.1 The Complex NTSB Framework: Variables and Constraints at Play in the Expression of Vividness

The narrative network of dockets and the constellation of narrative NTSB genres that subsumes it (Figures 1 and 2) are embedded in a larger social framework, dictated by the FOIA and lending itself to more vivid accident accounts than most other world transportation agencies. The FOIA was enacted in 1966 and took effect in 1967, when the NTSB started operating apart from the *Department of Transportation* (*DOT*) in the independent investigation of civil aviation accidents and incidents within the USA or involving American-registered or American-owned civil aircraft or aircraft with U.S. manufactured components in foreign airspace. The FOIA's mission is to warrant *transparency* in every

---

[2] Accident synopses are uploaded monthly to the U.S. National Transportation Safety Board Website – Accident synopses:
http://www.ntsb.gov/_layouts/ntsb.aviation/month.aspx.

administrative account, which is achieved in two main fronts: *accessibility* and *informativeness* (Figure 3). Accessibility requires *wide dissemination* as much as minimal *intelligibility* of texts, which in turn requires that the message be both *explicit* and *memorable.* For these reasons the NTSB has opted for an online hypertextual divulgation of its activity, for glossing specialized contents and using metadiscourse instead of a telegraphic style, and for adopting a storytelling format in many dockets (which includes the aforementioned code switching, also impinging on explicitness and memorability). Informativeness covers two key aspects: *level of disclosure* and *democratic reporting.* The first refers to the sphere (private or public) where the events being recounted take place, as well as to the amount of detail with which they are presented. The second brings multivocality to the account so as to ensure that the reporting is plural and from different angles to avoid bias. Interestingly, the combination of verbal, visual and aural modes of communication contributes to greater explicitness and memorability, discloses more and gives more detail because it may show what very few people can see or hear (e.g. the cockpit and CVRs and the flight trajectories recreated in animations, invisible to crew and passengers).

Fig. 3: Mission of the FOIA

Aside from the socio-legal variable of the FOIA, there are three discursive factors encouraging or limiting vividness in NTSB narratives: the relation of *goal* to *efficacy*, the *Cooperative Principles*, and the *Politeness Maxims.* Let us examine each one in turn. Crucially, the objective of NTSB reports is *prevention*, but it must be added that it cannot be successfully achieved without some retention of the accident circumstances and actors' behaviours. This retention may occur at three successive levels of memory (Connerton 1989): *personal*, *cognitive*,and *habit-based.* Personal memory is activated through testimony – victims and witnesses recollect what happened, and in doing so try to fit events and perceptions into known schemata (e.g. usually by means of onomatopoeias, similes, analogies and metaphors) (example 5). Cognitive memory is this accommodation of new experiences into old mental categories. The final step towards prevention, habit memory, consists in the acquisition of desirable motor mechanisms to automate reactions and procedures for the future, and it is frequently fostered by rules and recommendations stemming from the study of testimonies and the expert analysis of evidence. Striking as it may seem, NTSB recommendations are always implicit, to be inferred from the negative criticisms in the verdict. Evaluative words such as 'inadequate', 'improper', or 'failure' are common to appraise crew behaviour (see the verdicts in examples 3, 4 and 6).

(5) The friend heard a "thud" and the engine sounds stopped. (NTSB LAX06FA06)

(6) The National Transportation Safety Board determines the probable cause(s) of this accident as follows:
The pilot's improper decision to hover out-of-ground-effect in a tailwind, and his failure to maintain aircraft control. A factor in the accident was the tailwind.

Storytelling (or the existence of characters, a plot and an evolution over time) is decisive in the acquisition of habit memory because it acts as a mnemonic and engagement device, two functions tribal societies have for centuries been aware of. Stories optimize such acquisition process as their advantages are indeed many: they allow for climaxes and dialogues, which sustain the addressee's interest, are more engaging (i.e. favour involvement), and provide more information and detail (Tadros 1993; Bloor & Bloor 2007). According to Tannen (1989), embedded dialogues highlight the social nature of interactions and are more dramatic – liminal between repetition and image. If we depicted the incidence of storytelling in the NTSB genre constellation (Figure 4), we would see that it roughly unfolds along a cline of high vividness in the lay genres (press release, docket and animation), with a point of inflection in slideshow presentations and a stretch of minimum vividness in expert genres (the full report) or in lay genres within them (the abstract and the executive summary), with a slight growth in the legal documents derived from the investigation, given that some may contain statements in direct speech. Let us not forget that, although abstracts and executive summaries may be very similar to dockets (executive summaries do in fact compound the docket and the end of the abstract), they are invariably factual and do not tend to gloss over technolects.

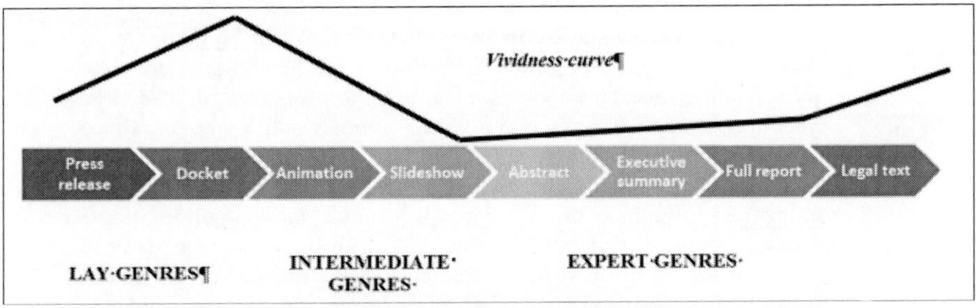

Fig. 4: Vividness cline in the NTSB genre constellation

Curiously, genres that are bimodal (e.g. full reports, which are verbal and visual) or multimodal (e.g. animations and slideshows) are not necessarily the most vivid ones: vividness reaches its peak in dockets, which are strictly verbal but introduce the most dialogue and explicit detail and, at times, a filmic or cinematic style that could be conceived of as *proto-multimodal* because of its visual and dynamic nature, due chiefly to sentence structure, its averred tone, the active voice, and tense shifts. A good case in point is the history-of-flight excerpt in example (7), framed by the conventional attribution structures in the past simple (to bring in the testimonies of witnesses or evidential proof, as in the first line) and by the Board's performative *determines*, in the present tense and announcing the verdict. In between there is an alternation of present and past tenses, with a clear predominance of present ones. Here present tenses are of two different kinds: one conferring to the account the aforesaid verbal proto-multimodality, and another one generalizing in relation to norms, habits and procedures. I use bold, single underlining for the former, and bold italics for the latter. As can be seen, the NTSB writer transmits a sense of immediacy by means of an agile syntax – brief averred (Tadros 1993) sentences in the active voice –, which is iconic of short-duration actions. The excerpt describes a camera's performance and the language is itself cinematographic.

(7) […] **The video equipment** that **was carried** by the cinematographer **captured** the collision. **The cinematographer** **<u>jumps</u>** with the last tandem jumpers**. The tandem chute** **<u>deploys</u>** at 3 minutes and 7 seconds into the video, 13 seconds later **the chute** **<u>deploys</u>.** During his descent, **he** **<u>removes</u>** the helmet-mounted camera and **<u>looks into</u>** the view making a few remarks about the jump. **He** **<u>places</u>** the

> cinematographer's camera back to its original position and continues to capture; **the sky is** overcast and visibility is good. **The view pans** to the right and **captures** three skydivers with chutes deployed at an altitude above him. At approximately 4 minutes and 54 seconds into the video, **a sound** similar to an airplane engine **can be heard** at an increasing level for 5 seconds. At 4 minutes and 59 seconds, **the view pans** slightly left and a sound similar to an impact is heard. **The view becomes** blurry and **pans** rapidly. At 5 minutes and 2 seconds, **three frames capture** what **appears to be** an aircraft in close proximity banking away and to the right of the camera's view. **The view continues** to pan rapidly for about 6 seconds showing shots of the ground, sky, and parachute. **The camera stabilizes** and **records** until impact with the ground at 5 minutes and 46 seconds. **One of the master tandem jumpers** on that jump **stated that** the pilot **did not give** a briefing on which runway or approach he was going to use. **The norm *is*** for the jumpers to avoid crossing runways below 1,000 feet and to stay away about 300 feet from the runways, and the pilot to avoid jumpers at all time. Due to **the amount of jumps** that ***are*** performed per day **there is** no briefing before each flight. **Approaches and runway selection *depends*** on the individual pilot. **A representative of the operator stated that** only **verbal guidance *is given*** to the pilots to follow the FAA rules and **it *is*** up to their discretion for approaches and runway selection. **The acting airport manager stated that *there is*** no agreement for airport operations between the skydive operator and the city, only the lease agreement. **The city did develop** a voluntary noise abatement procedure outlining areas to avoid. **The several pilots at the airport stated that** for several years **they communicated** with the city regarding safety concerns with approaches and runway selection by the skydive operator. **They stated the city did not correct** the situation.
> **The National Transportation Safety Board *determines*** the probable cause(s) of this accident as follows: The pilot's inadequate visual lookout.(NTSB MIA05LA096)

Having looked at the important functions of storytelling, we may now wonder how it has changed in CMC contexts. Without a doubt, CMC narratives are, as said at the outset of this chapter, *timeless* (they are not conditioned by time restrictions), *multi-sensorial* (with simultaneous visual and aural stimuli), more *global* or *expansive* (they reach wider audiences and are inserted in a network matrix), more *cooperative,* and less *linear* – to the extent that for some narratologists (Ryan 2004) the hypertext is to be considered a 'virtual storyteller'. They have also become *multidisciplinary* and in consequence more complete, *reactive* to changes in the environment and *interactive* (i.e. responsive to deliberate user actions), and according to Ryan (2004), *modular* (as they are composed of many interdependent objects), and *volatile* (their signs and semiotic repertoires are updated, improved and rewritten). They have also increased the narratee's *autonomy* by enabling him/her to choose his/her own reading/listening/watching itineraries, and have gained much *flexibility* in adapting to his/her knowledge background by providing themyriad of constellated genres of Figures 1 and 4 – expert, intermediate and lay – to inform about the same subject matter. However, besides all this, NTSB stories have become more *subjective*, moving from a pole of factual, emotionally detached reporting (typical of the AAIB and other boards) to one of drama and self-involvement, even though the ultimate responsibility for the selection of information, emphasis and textual structure remains unknown. Which individuals within the Board decide to divulge certain non-technical details or resort to tense and code shifts? Who organizes a given text climactically or opts for attaching an animation of the accident to complement dockets, and why? How many Board members endorse such decisions? Does any polemic arise in that respect? These questions will stay unanswered for us outsiders, but we may try to answer (or perhaps just content ourselves with launching) others, such as what frame in the constellation marks *textual closure* – is it the mere exhaustion of the topic, or the limited number of hyperlinks and buttons? Or do both factors play a role, in combination with the genre user's informative need, which tells him/her when to quit? –; which elements are to be taken as *paratext* – Are animations subservient to dockets and full reports? –; or how vivid aviation-accident reporting can be – Are there any limits?

The answer to the last question is better addressed in terms of the Gricean (Grice 1975) and Politeness (Leech 1983) Maxims. The provision of detail, which suggests credibility, is triggered by the *Maxim of Quality*, whereby we are supposed to tell the truth and thus to be accurate ("Do not say what you believe to be false"; "Do not say that for which you lack adequate evidence"). This very effect is exerted by the politeness *Maxim of Sympathy* ("Maximize empathy and solidarity with others"), as we will shortly see. Yet detail may as well lead to over-accuracy and digression, contradicting the *Maxim of Quantity* ("Make your contribution as informative as is required – for the current purposes of the exchange"; "Do not make your contribution more informative than is required"), *Relation* ("Be relevant"), and the *Maxim of Manner* ("Be brief – avoid unnecessary prolixity"), and incurring a *face-threatening act* (*FTA*) that may cause damage to the reader/hearer's image, whose freedom may be obstructed (*negative FTA*) and his/her feelings and wants ignored (*positive FTA*). Put differently: for the sake of accuracy, excessive emotions, socially-sensitive topics or inappropriate details (in general or in a particular context) may be brought up, transgressing the principle of positive politeness. And likewise, addressees may be deprived of chances and tools for interpretation if they are imposed a single version of reality, which may be additionally subjective, as happens when the private undisclosed intentions of story actors are indirectly reported through highly assumptive verbs such as *feared* or *suspected*. Then it is the negative politeness principle that is transgressed, because only one unproven view is being imposed on the interlocutor. Further, an excess of detail may clutter the account and obscure it, going against two other aspects contemplated by the *Maxim of Manner*, namely clarity and order ("Avoid obscurity of expression"; "Avoid ambiguity", "Be orderly") and the politeness *Maxim of Generosity* ("Minimize effort from others"), as it may hinder comprehension.

Conversely, detail is curbed by the Gricean maxims of Quantity, Relation and Manner, and by the politeness maxims of *Tact* ("Minimize imposition to others") and *Approbation* ("Minimize negative criticism of others"). Through the latter, criticism of unacceptable behaviours (the pilot's, for example) is mitigated, out of solidarity, by means of nominalization and passivization, which weaken agency and with it responsibility. All in all, NTSB dockets exhibit a tension between opposing communicative forces (Figure 5) that engender a peculiar *'pragmatics of catastrophe'*, characteristic of the NTSB.

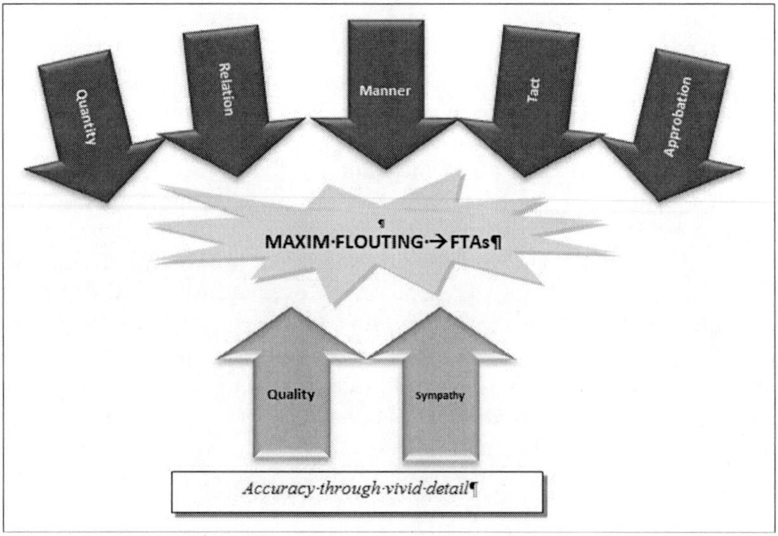

Fig. 5: Opposing pragmatic forces in NTSB dockets

Surprisingly, though, such pragmatic tension is not found in press releases, which should compete with dockets and animations as lay genre for a first contact with the accident information and enhance vividness more than any other NTSB text because their focus is not technical but purely journalistic, and vividness is the banner of contemporary journalism practice (Kennamer 1988). Moreover, press releases are as conspicuous and accessible as dockets and animations in the NTSB website, and their extension is as variable as that of dockets, so visibility and size can be discarded as vividness factors. The slight traces of vividness detectable in press releases are confined to mingling (quasi-) minimal narratives with the connotative load of certain keywords and phrases such as *(multiple) fatalities*, *fatally injured*, *was/were killed*, *deadly*, or *died* (examples 8-11, bolds added) and sporadically interspersed direct speech quotations.

(8) **NTSB LAUNCHES TEAM TO INVESTIGATE AIRCRAFT ACCIDENT IN ALASKA**
AUGUST 10, 2010
The National Transportation Safety Board has launched a Go Team to investigate last night's airplane crash near Dillingham, Alaska.
At about 8:00 p.m. Alaska Daylight Time, a DeHavilland DHC-3T (N455A) crashed 10 miles northwest of Aleknagik, Alaska. Reports are that 5 of the 9 persons on board **died** in the accident. […]

(9) **NTSB LAUNCHING TEAM TO INVESTIGATE TOUR HELICOPTER ACCIDENT IN NEVADA**
DECEMBER 8, 2011
The National Transportation Safety Board has launched a 12-member Go-Team to investigate the crash of a helicopter on a sight-seeing tour that occurred near Las Vegas at about 5:00 p.m. PT on Wednesday. Preliminary reports indicate that all five persons on board the helicopter **were fatally injured.** […]

(10) **NTSB GO TEAM HEADING TO MONTANA TO INVESTIGATE PLANE CRASH**
MARCH 22, 2009
The National Transportation Safety Board has dispatched a Go Team to investigate an airplane crash in Butte, Montana.
At approximately 3:00 pm MDT a Pilatus PC-12/45 (N128CM) crashed into Holy Cross Cemetery on approach to Bert Mooney Airport in Butte, Montana. **Multiple fatalities** have been reported.

(11) **SERIES OF OPERATIONAL ERRORS LED TO 2009 AIRPLANE CRASH IN MONTANA**
JULY 12, 2011
WASHINGTON - The National Transportation Safety Board determined **today** that the cause of the March 2009 **deadly** crash of a Pilatus airplane was a series of operational errors made by the pilot.

> The pilot failed to ensure that a fuel system icing inhibitor (FSII), commonly referenced by the brand name "Prist", was added to the fuel prior to the accident flight. The pilot also failed to take appropriate remedial actions, including diverting to a suitable airport, after the airplane warning systems indicated a low fuel pressure state that ultimately resulted in a significant lateral fuel imbalance. And, the pilot lost control while maneuvering the left-wing-heavy airplane near the approach end of the runway.
> **"The pilot's pattern of poor decision making set in motion a series of events that culminated in the deadly crash,"** said NTSB Chairman Deborah A. P. Hersman. **"Humans will make mistakes, but that is why following procedures, using checklists and always ensuring that a safety margin exists are so essential - aviation is not forgiving when it comes to errors."**

A plausible explanation for this feeble vividness of press releases could well be their inherent transiency: they are deictically anchored to the moment of reporting through the present perfect tense and adverbials such as *today* (example 11), which turn them quickly into dated archival narratives. Referring to the same past events, this rapid transformation stands in stark contrast to the timelessness of docket accounts and may contribute to spare the need for detail. The genre's concision is apparently a less strong argument, as press releases, like dockets, should theoretically be concise but in practice their prolixity varies across transportation agencies and their associated cultural and legal contexts.

The pragmatic tension over vividness, as this section will show, is not only verbal but also visual and aural. The vividness strategies of NTSB accident animations, which truly compete with dockets for a lay audience, have complementary communicative repercussions and give addressees a more prominent role as decoders, since detail is more subtle and not as overtly marked as in verbal narratives. In their pursuit of precision, expert animation artists, in collaboration with field researchers, expert analysts and Board members may incur over-accuracy, counterbalanced by both pragmatic maxims and the *Principle of cognitive overload* (Chandler & Sweller 1991). Very succinctly, its tenet is that for multimodal instructional messages to be effective, they must avoid saturating the learner's working memory with animations and competing written language (i.e. on-screen text). On the contrary, detail is stimulated by the *Principle of multiple representation* (Mayer & Moreno 2002), which holds that the combination of words and images is more mnemonic than only words.

3.2 Types of Vividness: Communicative Implications

The over-accuracies provoked by the urge to communicate reliability may flout the Gricean Cooperative Principle (i.e. with an anti-economic, apparently irrelevant and non-linear reporting) and cause interferences between politeness maxims (e.g. between those of Sympathy, Generosity and Tact). The next subsections illustrate and comment on some of these flouts, paying heed to the type of information they emphasize or sacrifice.

3.2.1 Verbal Vividness

NTSB writers reproduce testimonies verbatim to sound credible in two senses: one, to provide first-hand information, nota paraphrase or an imposed interpretation, and the other to demonstrate that such information comes from thorough research and documented sources (i.e. field interviews, CVRs, aeronautical and legal literature). This fidelity, however, may transgress the maxims of Quality (example 12), Quantity and Manner (example 13), and Quantity and Relation (example 14). Vague choral testimonies in free indirect speech (example 12), for example, become inaccurate as to the number of individuals who really and exactly uttered the words between inverted commas. Other direct speech embeddings, such as the one in example (13), respect the Quality Maxim but make it difficult for readers to follow the course of events and discriminate who said what. This increases reading effort and contradicts the Generosity Maxim. And whereas the meticulous detail indirectly reported in examples (14) and (15) may simply suggest superfluous disclosure with a greater or lesser degree of privacy violation, the sympathetic tinge of condolence of example (16) conflicts with the maxims of Tact and Relation, adds outrageous drama and involuntarily ends up in an FTA towards possible survivors and their families. Bolds are mine in all cases.

(12) […] Family members **reported that** the pilot was **"sick of flying"** and they were concerned about his **"lack of time to sleep".** (NTSB DEN05FA087)

(13) […] A witness stated, **"I looked out of my window right in front of my desk** after a co-worker said **'Oh my God'."** (NTSB CHI07FA140B)

(14) […] Around the time of the accident the owner and his spouse were **in their front yard with their coffee and newspaper** walking towards the back of the house when they saw the accident airplane. (NTSB LAX05FA062)

(15) […] The **pilot's girlfriend** alerted local authorities that the pilot had called her at 0400, as **he was depressed** over their **recent breakup.** (NTSB ATL07LA119)

(16) […] **The airplane sank almost immediately,** and the pilot said he had to cut his seatbelt to get out. He said he was **unable to rescue** any of his 3 passengers, **his juvenile daughters,** before the airplane **sank in about 800 feet of water.** (NTSB ANC05LA027)

Two powerful detail deterrents are the politeness maxims of Tact and Approbation. Tact prevents over-interpreted reportings, and in effect the most abundant type of quotative in NTSB dockets is the *neutral structuring* verb (e.g. *ask*, *say*, *state*, *tell*), which introduces a saying without evaluating it explicitly. Its percentage, well over those of other reporting structures (Figure 6), reaches 87%. Subjectivity is heavily restrained in reporting, since *meta-propositional* verbs interpreting the speaker's intentions (e.g. *encourage*, *persuade*, *urge*, *warn*) present a negligible occurrence of 1%. Also minor (4%) is the prevalence of *transcript* verbs (e.g. *add*, *deny*, *repeat*, *reply*), which marks the development of discourse by indicating how the proposition relates to the previous message. With a slightly higher incidence (8%), *metalinguistic* and *descriptive* verbs respectively specify the language function (e.g. *describe*, *explain*, *instruct*, *narrate*) and the manner and attitude of speakers (e.g. *mutter*, *shout*, *whisper*).

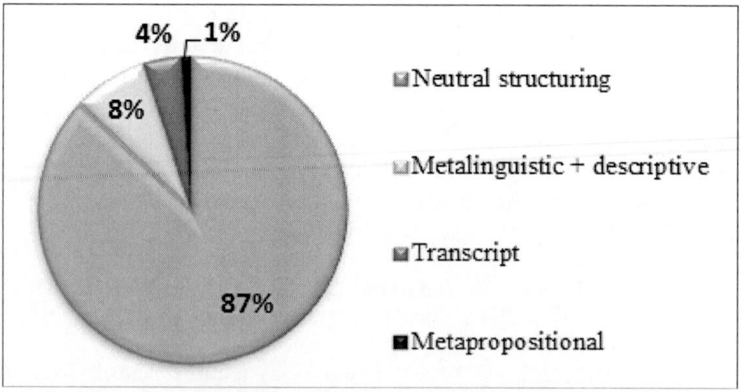

Fig. 6: Distribution of reporting verbs in NTSB dockets

Approbation shuns FTAs of harsh criticism and direct blaming, and, through passivization (example 17) and nominalization (example 18) the variables of causality, responsibility, temporality, and any kind of specificity (such as who is the agent or the patient affected) become of secondary concern. Guilty pilots are depicted as affected entities instead of agents, the message is vague and under-informative, and thus the maxims of Quality and Quantity are flouted (emphasis added).

(17) […] Toxicological testing revealed that **the pilot was impaired** due to **alcohol ingestion.** (NTSB ERA11F232)

(18) […] Contributing to the accident was the **pilot's impairment** from multiple drugs. (NTSB CEN11FA666)

A face-saving way for the NTSB to counterbalance the vagueness produced by the Approbation Maxim is to criticize covertly with direct speech in the mouth of story actors and witnesses (example 19). In this way, the Board highlights foolhardy demeanours without much involvement:

(19) […] The witness said that the passenger told them that he and other pilot **were "going to show you guys what flying is about".** (NTSB LAX06LA110)

This strategy coexists with the overt evaluative terms referred to in subsection 3.1, whose relative weight is shown in Table 1: expectedly, overt terms are much more numerous because they are applied to technical faults, while passives and nominalizations fulfill a different function—the censorship of misbehaviour based on the non-compliance of ethical basics.

Tab. 1: Occurrences of criticism collocations

COLLOCATION	HITS	FUNCTION
Pilot's failure + Infinitive (e.g. control, maintain, land)	625	Technical Criticism
Pilot's improper + Noun (e.g. calculation, planning, inspection)	105	
Pilot's inadequate + Noun (e.g. supervision, installation, performance)	91	
Pilot's impairment	27	Moral Criticism
The pilot was impaired	20	

3.2.2 Audiovisual Vividness

Animations were incorporated to the NTSB genre constellation in 2013. Currently they total 25 samples online, accessible through a separate button at the bottom of the Board's website and interconnected with dockets and other genres with clickable indications on the right-hand side, once the animation is running. In principle, animations should be subordinate to dockets, as most of the information they convey is redundant, although from different standpoints: either *internal* (framed within the cockpit and playing CVRs) or *external*, in which the aircraft's trajectory is shown by vectors (lines and arrows) on aerial maps or realistically simulated scenarios. The full animation typology is shown below: external animations may be *flight paths* (Figure 7) and *weather animations* (Figure 8), while *3D reconstructions* (Figure 9) join the internal and external perspectives. Occasionally, animations may shift to still photographs and video-clips from surveillance cameras to show the instant of the crash or its aftermath.

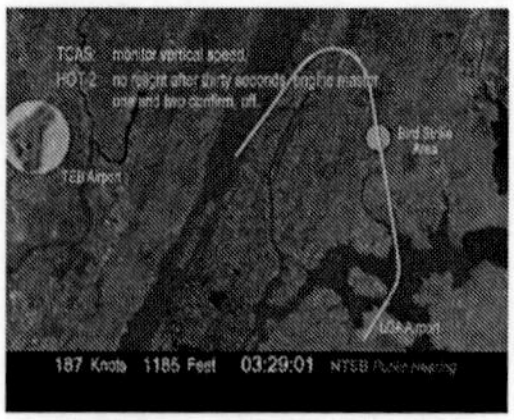

Fig. 7: Flight path

Fig. 8: Weather animation

Fig. 9: 3D reconstruction

Consequently, animations perform an 'optical' or 'zoom-in/out' function that could be taken as paratextual or ancillary, but, as suggested above, they do compete with dockets as a first approach to an accident. Images are not a second way to the tale but a *means of evocation*– recollections from memory (Kibédi Varga 1988) – and *emotional mediators*, because they arouse emotion before risk or danger can be consciously judged. Experiments on risk perception (Xie et al. 2009) have proved that the presence of images increases the perceived risk, and probably this finding is being exploited by the NTSB. It is also significant that 56% of the animations uploaded recreate fatal mishaps and that several of them include CVRs and 3D reconstructions, two affordances that may turn them into an FTA to the victim's families, as they can listen to the late crew's voices in their last moments and may find the recreation trivialized by the 'videogame air' of the 3D scenery. But above this predicament, the NTSB's goal for efficiency impels it to meet the principle of multiple representation by attaching auditory narratives from black boxes, and to pre-empt cognitive overload by taking the following measures, which abort detail:

- Provide just few animation samples of short duration and representative of common and uncommon accidents and incidents.
- Trace flight paths at a very slow pace and on the same scale for all samples.
- Provide 'realistically schematic', not full-detail graphics.
- Select only relevant CVR conversation snippets or radio exchanges and their on-screen transcripts.
- Simplify the number of cockpit flight instruments to avoid distractions.

Animated vividness does not act so much on subjectivity but on immediacy and intimacy. It is true that representations in animations are more 'scientific' or 'subjective' than naturalistic icons, but issues such as narrative focalization, moral judgment (non-existent because the speakers in CVRs tell the story as it progresses in a fake real-time frame), the revelation of veiled information inside or outside the cockpit, or the recovery of the crew's agency (a similarity to press releases) through CVRs acquire a paramount importance. Inevitably, some features are lost in the *transduction* (Kress 2010) or translation between modes: there is no longer any reporting from external narrators and thus little framing of the accident, only a complicating action that frequently starts *in medias res,* and the illusion that events are happening in real time, being measured by cabin instruments and the ideal displacement of vectors over aerial maps and photographs. Information is less filtered and watchers become *voyeurs* left to their own devices to sort out detail from core narratives, appraise performances, and imagine real actions and settings out of the symbolic.

4. A Final Thought: Is Vividness a Political Tool?

In these 'webridized' (Moschini 2014) times, where genre contamination is ubiquitous and the distinction between news and entertainment is not always clear-cut (Cotter 2013), can we speak of vividness as a political tool? Digital media, undeniably, have broadened discourse communities both geographically and socio-culturally, and if, as claimed by Mauranen (2013), "communities make the genres", popularization[3] is supposed to be the dominant trend in CMC from now on. Here we have seen how *vividness* may be selectively turned into a marker of popularization and into an instructional tool to reach lay audiences: through the vivid detail of

[3] *Popularisations* (Hyland 2009:152-153) are disseminations of specialized content to non-expert audiences with a diverse array of formats and assortment of topics.

dockets and animations non-experts are addressed outside arcane professional genres, albeit at the cost of some pragmatic risks.

Vividness can then be a tool for control, but also for branding. The NTSB's institutional branding is a *narrative self* (Polkinghorne 1991) consisting in a sense of connectedness that unifies local asynchronous stories and polyphonic identities into a corporate cultural plotline and a voice of authority. To do so following the FOIA spirit, which regulates public administrative communications, NTSB writers 'capture' lay audiences with hybridized genres – dockets and animations – that complement and at the same time compete against each other. Vividness takes active part in such hybridization, grounded in an unusual storytelling format alien to the rest of transportation agencies all over the world. If vividness serves to fight expertise-based exclusion and democratize communication, it might be considered a political tool for spreading the U.S. Government's ideology. But is the NTSB's genres fabric therefore a 'metaphor of a national metaphor' – the *melting pot*? Will NTSB intermediate and expert genres also evolve into *catastropops* and acquire features of dockets and animations sometime in the future? Will NTSB writers find a way to report catastrophe without incurring FTAs or flouting the Cooperative Principle and the Politeness Maxims? This chapter definitely raises more questions than it answers.

References

Anthony, Laurence. 2007. *AntConc 3.2.1w.* http://www.antlab.sci.waseda.ac.jp/software.html.

Bazzanella, Carla. 2010. Contextual constraints in CMC narrative.In Christian R. Hoffmann (ed.), *Narrative Revisited. Telling a Story in the Age of New Media.* Amsterdam/Philadelphia: John Benjamins. 19-37.

Benwell, Bethan & Elizabeth Stokoe. 2006. *Discourse and Identity.* Edinburgh: Edinburgh University Press.

Bloor, Thomas & Meriel Bloor. 2007.*The Practice of Critical Discourse Analysis.* London: Hodder Arnold.

Chandler, Paul & John Sweller. 1991. Cognitive load and the format of instruction. *Cognition and Instruction* 8. 4. 293-332.

Collins English Dictionary & Thesaurus. 2000. London: HarperCollins.

Connerton, Paul. 1989. *How Societies Remember.* Cambridge: Cambridge University Press.

Cotter, Colleen. 2013. Re-contextualizing the reporter: Linking news discourse to professional practice. Paper presented at the conference *Discourse in and through the Media. Recontextualizing and Reconceptualizing Expert Discourse.* Modena, Italy, 6-8 November 2013.

Fairclough, Norman. 2006. *Language and Globalization.* London/New York: Routledge.

Gotti, Maurizio, Carol Berkenkotter & Vijay K. Bhatia, 2012. Introduction. In Carol Berkenkotter, Vijay K. Bhatia & Maurizio Gotti (eds.), *Insights into Academic Genres*. Bern: Peter Lang. 9-28.

Grice, Paul. 1975. Logic and conversation. In Peter Cole & Jerry L. Morgan (eds.), *Syntax and Semantics, 3: Speech Acts*. New York: Academic Press. 41-58.

Harcup, Tony & Deirdre O'Neill. 2001. What is news? Galtung and Ruge revisited. *Journalism Studies* 2. 2. 261-280.

Hoffmann, Christian R. 2010. Introduction. Narrative revisited. Telling a story in the age of new media. In Christian R. Hoffmann (ed.), *Narrative Revisited. Telling a Story in the Age of New Media.* Amsterdam/Philadelphia: John Benjamins. 1-18.

Hyland, Ken. 2009. *Academic Discourse. English in a Global Context.* London/New York: Continuum.

Kennamer, J. David. 1988. New values and the vividness of information. *Written Communication* 5. 1. 108-123.

Kibédi Varga, Áron. 1988. Stories told by pictures. *Style* 22. 2. 194-208.

Kress, Gunther. 2010. *Multimodality. A Social Semiotic Approach to Contemporary Communication.* London/New York: Routledge.

Labov, William & Joshua Waletzky. 1967. Narrative analysis: Oral versions of personal experience. In June Helm (ed.), *Essays on the Verbal and Visual Arts*. Seattle, WA: University of Washington Press. 12-44.

Leech, Geoffrey. 1983. *Principles of Pragmatics.* London/New York: Longman.

MacPherson, Malcolm. 1998. *The Black Box. Cockpit Voice recorder Accounts of In-Flight Accidents.* London: HarperCollins.

Machin, David & Andrea Mayr. 2012. *How to Do Critical Discourse Analysis. A Multimodal Introduction.* London: Sage.

Mauranen, Anna. 2013. The research blog genre – New or ancient?. Paper presented at the conference *Discourse in and through the Media. Recontextualizing and Reconceptualizing Expert Discourse*. Modena, Italy, 6-8 November 2013.

Mayer, Richard E. & Roxana Moreno. 2002. Aids to computer-based multimedia learning. *Learning and Instruction* 12. 107-119.

Merriam Webster: http://www.merriam-webster.com/dictionary/. Accessed 10-06-2014.

Moschini, Ilaria. 2014. "You should've seen Luke!" or the multimodal encoding/decoding of the language of postmodern 'webridized' TV series. *Text & Talk* 34. 3. 283-305.

Norrick, Neal R. 2000. *Conversational Narrative*. Amsterdam/New York: John Benjamins.

Ochs, Elinor & Lisa Capps. 2001.*Living Narrative*: *Creating Lives in Everyday Storytelling.* Cambridge, MA: Harvard University Press.

Polkinghorne, Donald E. 1991. Narrative and self-concept. *Journal of Narration and Life History* 1. 2-3. 135-153.

Ryan, Marie-Laure. 2004. Will new media produce new narratives? In Marie-Laure Ryan (ed.), *Narrative across Media. The Languages of Storytelling.* Lincoln, NE: University of Nebraska Press. 337-359.

Sancho Guinda, Carmen. 2013. The tell and show of aviation-catastrophe synopses. In Maurizio Gotti & Carmen Sancho Guinda (eds.), *Narratives in Academic and Professional Genres*. Bern: Peter Lang. 385-412.

—. 2014. Multimodality in aviation-accident reporting. Paper presented at the *5th international conference* in the *360° series Encompassing the Multimodality of Knowledge*. Aarhus, Denmark, 8-10 May 2014.

Swales, John M. 1990. *Genre Analysis. English in Academic and Research Settings.* Cambridge: Cambridge University Press.

Tadros, Angele. 1993. The pragmatics of text averral and attribution in academic texts. In Michael Hoey (ed.), *Data, Description,Discourse*. London: Harper Collins. 98-114.

Tannen, Deborah. 1989. *Talking Voices, Repetition, Dialogue, and Imagery in Conversational Discourse.* Cambridge: Cambridge University Press.

Thompson, Geoff. 1994. *Reporting.* London: HarperCollins.

Xie, Xiao-Fei, Mei Wang, Ruo Guzhang, Jie Li & Yu Qing-Yuan. 2011. The role of emotions in risk communication. *Risk Analysis* 31. 3. 450-465.

SECTION IV:

NEW MEDIA IN CORPORATE COMMUNICATION

SOCIAL MEDIA IN CORPORATE COMMUNICATION: FOCUS ON TEXT AND DISCOURSE

GIULIANA ELENA GARZONE
UNIVERSITÀ DEGLI STUDI DI MILANO

Abstract: This study investigates the impact of increasing recourse to web-mediated affordances, and in particular Web 2.0 platforms, on business communication. The discursive and textual peculiarities of the social network sites taken into consideration (blogs, Facebook and Twitter) are analysed in order to identify the differences in text and discourse construction in comparison with traditional printed genres and with less innovative computer mediated environments. The textual and discursive approaches characterising the three applications under investigation are also examined comparatively in light of the distinctive characteristics of each of them. The results obtained are evaluated in the context of the evolution of the genre repertoires now available to companies for their communication effort, with a focus on the changes brought about by recourse to social network sites in corporate marketing policy, public communications, and relations with customers and stakeholders. In order to illustrate these notions, for exemplification, a case study is presented, PepsiCo, using a corpus extracted from PepsiCo's blogs, and from its Facebook and Twitter corporate profiles. The tendencies identified have important implications both for the conceptualisation of communication in the web-mediated environment and for linguistic and discourse analytical research in this domain. They also have important implications for training, as they require not only new skills, but also new literacies, and new ways of managing language and discourse.

1. Introduction

In the last few decades business communication has been revolutionized by the rise and spread of new media and new communication environments, mostly associated with Computer- and Web-Mediated Communication, but also with other communication technologies, e.g. mobile phones, whose affordances are increasingly converging (Twitter is a case in point). Technological innovations have opened up new, unexpected and virtually boundless discursive and social spaces, which host a variety of genres either derived from pre-existing ones, or native to the technological environment.

In particular, newly emerging web genres, and especially Web 2.0 applications, are characterised by an increasingly participatory character, favouring the user's involvement and active role and the emergence of novel, less constrained, communicative practices. This participatory agenda is evident in popular social media like Facebook, YouTube, MySpace, Pinterest, Flickr, Twitter, Tmblr, as well as in environments such as blogs, discussion forums or online debates, which have been harnessed to different degrees for use in corporate communication (Fernando 2007).

Recourse to innovative technologies has also had systemic consequences, resulting in a re-organization of the genre repertoires relied on by companies and organizations, often with an effect of "generification" (Swales 2004:4-6), i.e. an ever greater diversification and proliferation of genres within each single domain, as is apparent in business communication.

1.1 Aim, Scope and Method

This study focuses on business communication and looks at the impact on it of increasing recourse to web-mediated affordances, and in particular Web 2.0 platforms, i.e. a set of tools that make it easy for people to create and publish content on the web, share ideas, express opinions and make recommendations (Evans & McKee 2010:4). It identifies their distinctive features, and considers the consequences of their use in terms of marketing policy, public communications, and relations with customers and stakeholders. Against this background, it aims at ascertaining how language, textuality and discourse are used in the new communicative environments, highlighting changes with respect to more traditional computer-mediated environments.

With these objectives in mind, the discursive and textual peculiarities of computer-mediated genres, especially those based on Web 2.0 applications, are examined in order to identify the differences in text construction in comparison with traditional printed genres and with more traditional computer mediated genres.

These aspects will be evaluated in the context of the genre repertoires now available to companies for their communication effort, within the more general framework of the communication mix selected in each case. As social media feature both contents posted by companies, and contents posted by users, mainly in response to companies – comments, likes and shares – the main focus will lie in companies' contributions, seen as manifestations of corporate strategic decisions about how to exploit social media.

The basic methodological framework of this study lies in discourse analysis as well as in genre analysis (cf. e.g. Brown & Yule 1983; Bhatia 1993, 2004; Schiffrin et al. 2001; Swales 2004; Blommaert 2005). Reference will also be made to studies of linguistic communication in web-mediated environments (e.g. Herring 1996; 2004; Garzone et al. 2007; Baron 2008) with special attention to Web 2.0 (cf., among others, Thurlow & Mroczek 2011; Campagna et al. 2012; Tannen & Trester 2013) and, in particular, to studies focusing on corporate communication (e.g. Puschmann 2010). A small ethnographic component is also featured, as findings were discussed with Community Managers of one of the most important Italian social media communication agencies.

In the next sections the peculiarities of web-mediated communication will be briefly reviewed, before going on to analyse the distinctive characteristics of selected Web 2.0 applications on which this study focuses. For exemplification, the analysis relies on a case study, PepsiCo, "one of the world's leading food and beverage companies", holding "a complementary food and beverage portfolio that includes 22 brands", amongst them Pepsi (cf. the corporate website <http://www.pepsico.com/Company> , "Who we are"). The corpus was extracted from PepsiCo's blogs, and from its Facebook and Twitter corporate profiles, and comprises texts posted from September 2013 to July 2014, divided into three sub-corpora. Details of the corpus are as follows:

Tab. 1: The corpus

	PepsiCo Corpus	Blogs	Facebook	Twitter
Tokens	73,204	27,522	28,858	16,824
STTR	41.85	45.26	39.67	36.70

The analytical approach was mainly qualitative, and confirmation of findings was sought by means of computer queries using the Wordsmith 5.0 software suite (Scott 2008).

2. Analysis: Text and Discourse in Web-Mediated Genres

The web-mediated environment is characterised by a cluster of inherent properties that strongly impact on the linguistic, textual and discursive features of communicative events and strategies (Garzone 2007:20-26):

- extension in participation framework with respect to traditional media, i.e. potentially global reach;
- multimodality resulting from "the articulation in one or more semiotic modes of a discourse" (Kress & Leeuwen 2001:40);
- interactivity and co-articulation, two strictly related properties that are essential in Web 2.0 applications as they favour dynamic user participation (cf. O'Reilly 2005; Harrison & Barthel 2009), with different degrees of freedom in allowable contributions (e.g. only comments in blogs, but self-standing posts and comments on Facebook and Twitter);
- hypertextuality, i.e. the fact of being part of a system consisting of "a series of text chunks connected by links which offer the reader different pathways" (Nelson 2008:2). Unlike the early pre-set hypertexts published on CD-ROMs, which were closed systems, each hypertextual system on the web is now open to global interconnexity and provides access to an immense number of other hypertextual systems, thus realizing realizing Roland Barthes' description of ideal textuality (Barthes 1970/1974; cf. also Landow 1992:3-4).

Hypertextuality brings with it various fundamental features, among them the need for the user to activate multiple reading modes, i.e. the *reading-as-such* mode and the *navigating mode* (Askehave & Ellerup Nielsen 2004, 2005), and *granularity* (cf. Garzone 2007:23-25). The latter property, which is especially relevant for the analysis of how text and discourse are handled in the web-mediated environment, results from the fact that in most cases when documents are longer than a screenshot, they are broken down into sections, published on different pages and connected by means of hyperlinks; so they become "nodes" for internal navigation paths, and are also connected intertextually with other external documents (texts, pictures, photos, videos, etc.). This propensity to use text in separate blocks provides the 'grain' of a hypertext. Furthermore, on each single page written texts tend to be arranged in columns or in short graphically separated blocks, usually called *lexias* (Landow 1992/1997:34, following Barthes 1970/1974 who introduced the French word *lexie*), in conformity with Web-writing handbooks' recommendations to surmount the difficulty users may experience reading across the computer screen.

Overall it can be stated that in web communication there is a tendency, at different levels, to break text down into sections, either corresponding to a screenshot or smaller, and use hyperlinks to connect them, so that the user is put in a position to recompose it as s/he thinks fit.

The properties discussed so far also apply to social media applications, which however also exhibit other peculiarities of their own.

2.1 The New Media in Business Communication

While in the past companies' most popular form of presence on the web was the corporate website, today there is growing awareness of the visible impact of web 2.0 applications in the global marketplace. Business enterprises ever more frequently make recourse to social technologies that are capable of producing a long-term organizational impact and offer unprecedented business opportunities. In this respect, there is a wide choice of applications, which share some common characteristics, qualifying as "social network sites", i.e. in Boyd and Ellison's (2008) definition, "web-based services that allow individuals [as well as companies] to (1) construct a public or semi-public profile within a bounded system, (2) articulate a list of other users with whom they share a connection, and (3) view and traverse their list of connections and those made by others within the system" (Boyd & Ellison 2008:211). The main social network sites are blogging, Facebook, Twitter, MySpace, YouTube, Pinterest, Instagram, Tumblr, LinkedIn, Google plus, etc.

Figure 1 shows the relevant extent of use of different kinds of computer applications, with Facebook being the most popular, followed by Twitter, LinkedIn and Blogging.

In addition to the characteristics discussed so far, shared by all forms of web-mediated communication, for their possible use in corporate communication Web 2.0 applications offer the advantage of having a "larger footprint" than traditional genres (Evans & McKee 2010:9), as they reach out for potential customers and stakeholders, and involve them in a shared experience. Thus we are far beyond the traditional role of media advertising, which has traditionally been that of creating and maintaining awareness (J. Myers 2010): in Social Media, technology and human interaction intersect, favouring customers' engagement, i.e. enhancing their active participation. This means moving out of the Information Age and into what Jack Myers terms the *Relationship Age*™ (J. Myers 1998, 2010).

Of course, each different application has its peculiar characteristics, advantages and limits, offering options but at the same time imposing certain constraints.

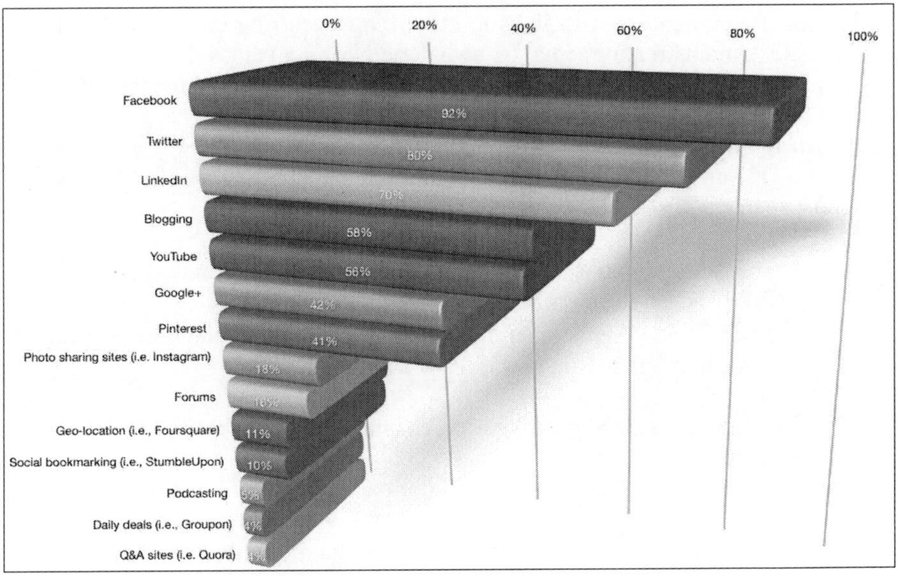

Fig. 1: Commonly used media platforms (Seelzner 2013)

Here, three different social media will be discussed – blogs, Facebook and Twitter –, which have been on stage for differing periods of time, having been launched respectively in 1997, 2004 and 2006. The analysis will focus on discursive and textual aspects, with the aim of understanding the communicative and linguistic strategies peculiar to each of them.

2.2 Blogs

Originally diary-like textual productions, blogs have developed into a whole range of different sub-genres, which are usually divided into two broad categories, personal blogs and thematic blogs, as proposed by Krishnamurthy (2002), and confirmed by Grieve et al. (2010) who, through a factor analysis of functional linguistic variation in blogs, have identified thematic and personal blogs as the major blog text-types.

The recognised formal features of blogs as a genre[1] are: reverse chronology of entries, constant and frequent updating; a combination of

[1] Notice that here blogs are considered to be a genre. For a different view, see e.g. Miller and Shepherd (2009), who have cast doubts on the generic integrity of this communicative format, arguing that "the blog [...] is a technology, a medium, a

personal commentary with links to other blogs (Herring et al. 2005) or to websites, mainstream media or social networks such as Facebook (G. Myers 2009:28-37; cf. also Miller & Shepherd 2004:4; Herring et al. 2005:1).

In textual terms, blogs are made up of two different types of entries, which in all cases include the author's picture or icon. The two components are:

- posts, including a date, a time stamp, and a permalink, usually followed by a repertoire of links;
- optional comments reacting to or discussing the content of relevant posts (Riboni 2014a:44-45).

In this analysis only posts will be considered, as the main focus is on companies' contributions.

Of the social media under discussion here, blogs were the first to be tapped for corporate communication purposes. Their use has now become well established, although it does not fulfil the hyperbolic expectations of their early days on account of various factors, e.g. problems of control, legal risks involved for companies that use them inadequately and doubts about the actual Return of Investment of maintaining a blog (Puschmann 2010:82-83). In spite of the increasing popularity of newer social media for use in marketing, blogs are still a powerful tool in internal as well as external corporate communication from public relations to marketing. Though not "a magic formula" (Puschmann 2010:83), they can be used for customer fidelization, customer service, product promotion, business related news, as they enable the company to keep an individualized dialogue going with stakeholders, and in particular with actual and potential customers, in complex textual form (being in this respect different from social media like Facebook and Twitter, as shall be seen shortly). In this respect, a crucial factor is the 'conceptualized audience' for whom the posts are written, as it has an impact on text construction and linguistic choices. As Puschmann (2009a) points out the conceptualized audience is a construct of the blogger (in this specific case of the Company maintaining the blog), and includes those whom the blogger seeks to affect (the *targeted audience*, or TA: stakeholders, traders, retailers, consumers, policy-makers, etc.), as well as those whom s/he acknowledges as

---

constellation of affordances – and not a genre" (Miller & Shepherd 2009:283). For arguments against Miller and Shepherd's conceptualization, see Garzone (2012:236).

potential readers but does not target ('overhearers') (cf. also Puschmann 2013:93-94).

A critical factor for corporate blogs to be viable as marketing tools is that they need to have explicit and stable communicative goals, a problematic requisite if one considers the inherent instability of the genre. Therefore, careful planning and vetting is necessary involving a refocalization of the genre in terms of topic and knowledge management (Puschmann 2010:90) and a shift to a more reader-focused approach.

On account of their versatility, companies often maintain more than one blog, using each of them for a different purpose. For instance, in a study of the three blogs maintained by Kodak (Garzone 2012), it was found that, although some distinctive features of the genre are present in all of them, the three blogs diverge in some aspects: *A 1000 Words* is characterised by an openly personal focus, being presented as a conversation place where personal stories and thoughts are shared; *Plugged In* focuses on technology; *Grow your Biz* aims at corporate customers' assistance. Nevertheless, in all three the individualistic, existential component that is distinctive of blogs is maintained, albeit to a different degree, and is exploited mainly to promote the sale of Kodak products.

Recourse to blogs offers the opportunity to talk diffusely about various aspects of a company's life, in a way that traditionally would not have been possible in communication aimed at the public at large (i.e. advertising) but only in press releases, which were – and still are, although to a lesser degree – addressed to a particular audience (the industry, journalists, banks, financial operators, etc.). Such aspects include the illustration of results in corporate policy, the company's R&D efforts, technological achievements, organization or participation in events, and a whole range of activities that fall under the scope of corporate social responsibility, e.g. sustainability, environmental concerns, efforts in humanitarian aid, development programmes, ethical choices. In the latter areas, blogs offer an effective tool for leveraging philanthropic and sponsorship investments that otherwise are difficult to exploit in terms of company image (Parker 1991; Garzone 2010:52-56).

In order to discuss the peculiarities of corporate blogs PepsiCo will be used as a case study. This company has a blog hub which provides access to three main blogs, all of them of the topic-centric type (Puschman 2013:90-94):

- *Performance Notes* (http://performancenotes.pepsico blogs.com). Defined on its homepage as "The leadership blog", it is allegedly maintained by its top managers, focuses on events and initiatives organized or sponsored by PepsiCo;

- *Living the Promise* (http://livingthepromise.pepsicoblogs.com) "Pepsico's Employee Blog", declared to be maintained by middle managers, focuses on the company's activities mainly on a geographical basis;
- *Food Frontiers* (http://foodfrontiers.pepsicoblogs.com) is a blog in which the company intends "to engage on dialogue and technical policy topics involving the food industry and in broad science".

Posts on these blogs are mostly signed by individual bloggers that are presented as members of the "blogging team", which on *Living the Promise* and *Performance Notes* also includes the corporate subject "PepsiCo" presented by means of its icon (Figure 2).

Fig. 2: The PepsiCo corporate icon

Even a superficial look at the posts published on these sites shows that in discursive terms the original diary-like nature of blogs is hardly maintained as often posts are more similar to press releases (Jacobs 1999; Catenaccio 2008) or journalistic texts (van Dijk 1988; Conley 2002). Although a promotional component is also present, all three blogs qualify as *image blogs* as they openly aim to create a positive public perception of the company and shape the public debate on it and its products (Puschman 2009b:57). This is done by occasionally presenting the company's initiatives and giving information on its actions, products, policies, etc., laying emphasis on topics that have a positive connotation in themselves (e.g. innovation, success, delivery, achievement, health, etc.) or have become positively connoted in contemporary culture (sustainability, conservation, environment, partnership, community, etc.).

The main focus is usually on Pepsi's policies, and in particular on commitments in favour of health, environmental sustainability, development and aid, on the one hand, and on initiatives aimed at innovation and, occasionally, at cultural promotion (e.g. Pepsi music academies) on the other. This emerges clearly from the following representative examples:

(1) It turns out that PepsiCo is leading the way in environment-friendly measures to reduce waste, such as reusing wasted cellulose fiber. PepsiCo is working on ways to reuse waste like oat husks and orange peels, reports Reuters. (Daniel Pellegrom, "An R&D effort for enviro-friendly packaging", *Food Frontiers*, 8 March 2014)

(2) PepsiCo respects the human right to water and has committed, through its "Performance with Purpose" vision, to help protect and conserve global water supplies especially in water-stressed areas, as well as provide access to safe water. (Pedro Padierna, "More Countries, More Water: AquaFund achieves larger Impact in México", *Perfomance Notes*, 11 February 2014)

(3) At PepsiCo, diversity and inclusion is about creating a culture of respect and trust that makes our company stronger and allows us to win together. In honor of Lesbian, Gay, Bisexual and Transgender (LGBT) Pride Month, celebrated each June in the United States, the Chicago chapter of EQUAL, PepsiCo's LGBT employee resource group, organized an event asking heterosexual PepsiCo associates to become LGBT allies. (PepsiCo, "Ally Pledge Week," *Living the Promise*, 25 June 2014)

These examples provide a clear illustration of Pepsi's communicative strategies in depicting itself as a company that in its operations chooses environment-friendly policies (example 1), is active in water access campaigns (a recurrent theme in Pepsi's communication, example 2) and in the promotion of diversity and other civil rights (example 3). This strategy is obviously aimed at constructing an image of the company as caring for all the issues discussed and actively working to solve them, be they geared to corporate success or committed to social responsibility. For this purpose, also presuppositions (Levinson 1983:181-184) are often exploited, a device which is also often relied on in other promotional corporate genres, and in particular in advertising (cf. Ge 2011). Some examples can be found in the following text from the *Notes on Progress* blog:

(4) World Water Week is underway in Stockholm and this year's theme is water cooperation, following on the United Nation's call for 2013 as the International Year for Water Cooperation. For PepsiCo this is a perfect opportunity to highlight *its comprehensive approach to water stewardship*, including *the key partnerships that help the PepsiCo Foundation provide access to safe water* as well as *the company's operational successes to increase water use efficiency.*

(Tom Schueneman, "Water Cooperation: Progress through Partnership", *Notes on Progress Blog*, 5 September 2013)

In this excerpt the ideational function formally prevails, and the use of evaluative language is combined with recourse to presuppositions in order to bring home the following statements:

- "its comprehensive approach to water stewardship!" → *PepsiCo has a comprehensive approach to water stewardship,*
- "the key partnerships that help the PepsiCo Foundation provide access to safe water" → *PepsiCo Foundation provides access to safe water,*
- "the company's operational successes to increase water use efficiency" → *PepsiCo Foundation has been successful in increasing water use efficiency.*

As regards agentivity, in some cases, the approach is more ideational: the company is referred to in the third person by its brand name (examples 1, 2 and 3) or, in other cases, the text is organized more interpersonally and the first person plural is used, as in example 5:

(5) Like many organizations, we have been on a sustainability journey, […] (R. Delaney, "Progress on the Environmental Sustainability Journey", *Performance Notes Blog*, 2 July 2014)

In actual fact, the use of first-person plural statements, either purporting the company's actions or commissively talking about future interventions, is more prominent on the blogs analysed than on the other two social media considered, with a frequency of 1.12%, against 0.62% on Facebook and 0.46% on Twitter. This indicates that the blogs are aimed at conveying a sense of collective identity, which is all the more plausible as two of them are presented as maintained by staff members.

Overall, blogs qualify as a versatile form of communication, suitable for different uses, which makes up for certain shortcomings traditionally felt in corporate communication, above all in terms of desire to reach the mass public.

In textual terms, one important factor is that blogs have no formal limits in terms of text length. In most cases, the blog's homepage shows a short stretch of text (in PepsiCo's case, from about 40 to 150 words), but deeper inside documents can be as long as the writer desires them to be. The maximum length actually found in posts on the PepsiCo blogs is around 400 or 500 words, although of course there are other corporate blogs featuring texts that are much longer and have to be scrolled or are divided into several pages. Thus, the text is subject to the granularity typical of websites, but imposes no limits on text length.

Therefore it is not surprising that blog posts host a variety of different text types, the prevalent one being expository (Werlich 1976/1983:38-39), as is obvious in a genre that in its corporate use has a declaredly informative focus:

(6) Chickpeas are a major pulse crop in Ethiopia, and are important for both the domestic and export market. With an average of 22 percent protein, chickpeas can serve as a more sustainable alternative to meat. They are also rich in fiber, complex carbohydrates, vitamins, and minerals such as iron, and low in endocrine-disrupting phytoestrogens. ("Chickpea Growing Tehcniques", *Food Frontier*, 3 February 2014)

The scientific tone of this paragraph befits a blog whose aim is to highlight the company's commitment to promote sustainability and adequate nutrition, and disseminate relevant knowledge, as is made explicit in many statements on the Company's websites and social media profiles. Take, for instance, the vision statement published on the PepsiCo global page:

> Our vision is put into action through programs and a focus on environmental stewardship, activities to benefit society, and a commitment to build shareholder value by making PepsiCo a truly sustainable company (http://www.pepsico.com/Purpose/Our-Mission-and-Values)

or the mission statement on the PepsiCo facebook profile:

(7) At PepsiCo, 'Performance with Purpose' means delivering sustainable growth by investing in a healthier future for people and our planet (<https://www.facebook.com/PepsiCo>).

Here PepsiCo's slogan, in use since 2010, is expanded in highly evaluative language in terms of commitment to sustainable growth and people's health, conceptualizing Pepsi's mission in terms of social responsibility.

The narrative text type (Werlich 1976:55ff.) is also often present, with a reporting function, and in most cases provides the frame for the whole text:

(8) Derek Yach was recently one of the plenary speakers at the recent Grantmakers In Health Annual Meeting in Baltimore. Grantmakers In Health (GIH) is an organization dedicated to helping foundations and

corporate giving programs improve the health of all people. ("Derek Yach at the Grantmakers in Health Annual Meeting", *Food Frontier*, 4 April 2013)

The directive (or 'instructive') text type (Werlich 1976:72ff.) can also be found, although less frequently, for example in "how to" or "advice" posts:

(9) *1. Be Curious. Hunt the world for insights and information, for the new and different, and for the exciting and unusual. 2. Love Diversity. Nurture yourself with diversity. Never be afraid of it. 3. Listen with Humility.* ("Ten Qualities of a Creative and Innovative Culture", *Notes on Progress*, 1 July 2013)

It is important to note that these blogs do not command a high number of comments, which – as is well known – are a potential component of this genre, but in some cases are absent or are only a few. This seems to indicate that in the case of PepsiCo the overall discursive strategies characterising the company's posts are not effective in starting a dialogic relationship with users, probably on account of their orientation that is more informative than interpersonal.

In light of this brief analysis it can be stated that blogs are far reaching tools of communication for business, with a high potential for interactivity, which however is not always fully tapped (Massarotto 2007). They provide the opportunity for a company to get some information and ideas through to the Web audience, and obtain some feedback when posts do trigger comments. As regards length, choice of topics covered, and linguistic and textual makeup, blog posts are to some extent similar to press releases (although with different peripheral features), but they are contextualised in an environment that is geared to fostering a sense of community, being obviously addressed at a virtually unlimited group of Internet visitors and offering the user an option to interact with the blogger.

2.3 Facebook

Facebook offers companies a communicative space that they can use, but do not own. The main advantage is that of building a community around the company's brand name and products. For a company the main purpose of being on Facebook, and on other social networks, is *engagement* – today a keyword in marketing, above all on social media – which among other things means making the customer feel part of an in-group ("community building"). If traditional advertising and PR aimed at exposure and impression, in the case of Facebook the technology pushes towards collaboration: customers or stakeholders become real participants rather than viewers (Evans & McKee 2010:11-12). In this context, leaving behind the "read only" approach of traditional media also means that not only can companies listen to consumers through the new media, but there is also the opportunity for consumers to participate actively so that "marketplace information comes directly from the consumers and heads toward the business" (Evans & McKee 2010:10). Thus clues to improvements in business management may come directly from the customer, providing a basis for a company to gain competitive advantage. And this is an invaluable asset.

PepsiCo's corporate page on Facebook presents an overall image-building orientation that is similar to that of its blogs. While Pepsi's Facebook consumer page, dedicated to the cola beverage, is aimed at a core audience of 18- to 35-year-olds, being part of the "Live for Now" marketing campaign, and achieves millions of likes, in competition with Coca Cola (Lightfoot 2013), the corporate page is aimed at an audience of stakeholders or occasional visitors and concentrates on corporate values, although it is also occasionally used for marketing and product promotion, especially for those products that do not have their own dedicated profile, as well as for consumer monitoring.

In terms of textual characteristics, in the overwhelming majority of cases, corporate posts on Facebook, whatever their length, are accompanied by a photograph as can be seen in Figure 3 below, which features a section of the PepsiCo corporate page on Facebook, launching a new product – bottled flavoured water in various tastes:

Fig. 3: Posts on PepsiCo's profile on Facebook

The text reads as follows:

(10) PepsiCo
October 1
The newest member of the PepsiCo family makes a splash today! Welcome, Aquafina FlavorSplash!
[photo]
Learn more: http://bit.ly/1dU0xJH

This post commanded 2,337 likes, 49 shares, and 17 comments. Amongst the comments, some are very favourable, e.g. *genial*, *very good*, *nice to see a variety*, in some cases reinforced by PepsiCo.

(11a) M Umar Amin Awan very good
October 1 at 9:08pm · Like
(11b) PepsiCo Glad you like it, M! :)
October 1 at 9:12pm · Like

(12a) Arturo Marin Need some huge media behind this brand so we can have a successful launch, great tasting flavors!
October 2 at 3:12am via mobile · **Like**
(12b) PepsiCo We're very excited about it, Arturo! Glad you like it!
October 2 at 2:53pm · **Like**

As can be seen in the sequences above, in many cases PepsiCo replies to comments for the obvious purpose of starting a dialogue, as in the following example:

(13a) Krista Senese They're a pretty bunch! [referring to the new Aquafina products]
October 1 at 8:50pm · Likc
(13b) PepsiCo You've got that right, Krista! Which one is your favorite?
October 1 at 8:51pm ·

In the way of product promotion and feedback, Facebook is also used to probe customers' feelings, asking them short questions, probably more for the purpose of drawing their attention to a certain product than for actually conducting market research, which would require large scale in-depth investigations. In the following case a question is asked about a dip (14a) and the next day the results are given (14b):

(14a) PepsiCo October 3
Do you like your salsa mild, medium, or hot? Comment to move our salsa meter!

(14b) PepsiCo October 4
Thanks for all the replies! 9 votes for mild, 8 votes for hot and 2 votes for medium!

In the utilization of Facebook for corporate image building, sometimes the focus is more on public relations and posts feature announcements of, or comments upon, important initiatives or events in the company's life which would otherwise be unknown to the public at large:

(15) PepsiCo October 1
We're honored to be included on Interbrand's list of Best Global Brands for another year in a row.
Read all about it. http://bit.ly/19RHNI4

(16) PepsiCo September 13
As a company doing business in more than 200 countries and territories, diversity and inclusion are essential.
We're honored to be recognized again this year in HispanicBusiness Media Inc.'s Best Companies for Diversity Report: http://bit.ly/18ZdIVd

Noteworthy is that in both examples the announcement of the recognition to the company is coloured with a personal emotional note (*we're honoured....*).

In other cases, it is addressee participation that is foregrounded by formulating the announcement in an imperative form:

(17) September 30, 2013
DISCOVER Essential New Young Artists on our final Pepsi Chart this week and tune in over at http://pepsi.beatport.com/. Who is your favourite new discovery?

Another category of announcements given on Facebook includes events in which the Company is not directly involved, but which are considered in some respect to be relevant to its activities or its image. Consider example (18), where relevance is obviously in terms of values supported:

(18) PepsiCo August 28
Today, thousands are at the site of the March on Washington on the 50th anniversary of MLK's 'I Have a Dream' speech.
Marching for equality, 50 years later, read the story of our own Westley Dickerson, who was there in 1963 and 2013: http://bit.ly/15ksDXT

In terms of linguistic makeup, although there are no real length limits, Facebook posts tend to be short. This is presumably due the communicative characteristics of the medium which enables "conversations" rather than presentations; thus for the sake of effectiveness short texts are preferred, with an average of 35 to 50 words, although in some cases there can be longer posts. So the scope for linguistic variation is relatively small.

The most frequent structure for a Facebook post is a sentence containing a statement (in speech act terms, mostly a constative, e.g. "as a company doing business in more than 200 countries and territories, diversity and inclusion are essential"), to which a second sentence is usually added that is more evidently interpersonal. As confirmed by insiders, this is the recommended prototypical form for the Facebook post. Often the subject, and Theme, of the main statement is PepsiCo referred to by name, or by a first person singular pronoun or possessive, or the name of a product. In some cases, as in (16) above, the company is not the subject but is thematised anyway (*as a company doing business in 200 countries....*). A possible alternative form for the opening sentence is the imperative, as in example (17) (*DISCOVER Essential New Young Artists...*) enhancing the interpersonal tone. The imperative is also a favourite for the second sentence, which is often in the form of an exhortation (*read more*, *read all about it*, *download*, etc.) – as in examples 10 (*welcome*) and 15 (*read all about it*) above – often ending with an exclamation mark (e.g. *Comment to move our salsa meter!*, from example 14a) to confer a strongly conative tone. In other cases, the second sentence is in the form of a question, sometimes with a personal focus (e.g. *Who is your favourite new discovery?*, example 17) or focuses on PepsiCo products and is obviously aimed at starting a dialogic sequence, as in (13b) (*Which one is your favourite?*).

Like PepsiCo here, companies turn the sequence of replies into a dialogue, responding to some of the comments, often in an emotional tone realized by means of an exclamation mark, as in examples 11b and 12b (*Glad you like it!*), thus presenting the company as a 'human' participant in the conversation. In some cases, PepsiCo's intervention also contains a question thus turning the relevant reply into the first part of a new adjacency pair, as in (13a) and (13b).

In Facebook texts, discourse connectors are less frequent than in the blog posts analysed in the previous section. Table 2 shows the frequency of some of the main discourse connectors in the three sub-corpora (actually all those appearing in the corpus). It indicates that on Facebook paratactic conjunctions *but* and *so* are several times less frequent than in blogs, as are hypotactic conjunctions *because*, *when* and *while*.

Tab. 2: Connectors in the three sub-corpora

CONNECTOR	BLOGS	FACEBOOK	TWITTER
But	0.14	0.06	0.01
So	0.15	0.02	0.01
Because	0.06	0.03	0
If	0.07	0.07	0.06
since	0.03	0.03	0
That	0.31	0.33	0.08
When	0.11	0.09	0.05
While	0.09	0.01	0
Total	0.96	0.65	0.22

In a context of lower discourse connector frequency, cohesion also relies on relevance (Grice 1989:27; Sperber & Wilson 1995:2-9) or, occasionally, on lexical repetition, as with the reiteration of *diversity* in (16) above and of the verb *march* in example (18).

In light of this short discussion it can be concluded that compared to blogs, Facebook posts are more fragmented textual artefacts, which tend to be centred around a single announcement, piece of information or question, with relatively less frequent recourse to grammatical cohesive devices.

2.4 Twitter

Twitter will be taken here as representative of the type of social network site that is generically referred to as a *microblog* (e.g., in addition to Twitter, also Tumblr, Flickr). As is well known, microblogs are characterised by the extreme shortness of the contributions allowable, in the case of Twitter max 140 characters. Emerging from the convergence of the concept of blogs and social media applications with the needs of mobile communication (i.e. phone apps), Twitter is a most readily interpersonal, dialogic environment. It lends itself to host all sorts of short observations, pieces of information and conversations. Companies exploit it for community building and engagement, as well as a quickest means to convey information flows (Paganoni 2012; Riboni 2014b). Its informative function is realized through rapid spot-like communiqués, which often simply signal the topicality of a given fact, event or notion and invite the user to get more information. In order to make this task easier they mostly feature a hyperlink, which in some cases is the only content of a tweet, thus using intertextuality to make up for its brevity. In a company's editorial plan, there are some topics that are covered on all the social media deployed, with texts that are similar but in each case adapted to the medium, and others that are covered only on one, which is identified as more suitable to convey that kind of content.

The difference between the use of text and discourse on Facebook and on Twitter respectively can easily be appreciated if one compares the way the same piece of information is treated on each of the two applications. See the case of example (15) above, which for the sake of convenience is repeated below:

(15) PepsiCo October 1
We're honored to be included on Interbrand's list of Best Global Brands for another year in a row.
Read all about it. http://bit.ly/19RHNI4. (*Facebook*)

This Facebook post would be nearly short enough as to be simply transferred to Twitter as is (140 characters). Instead, on Twitter it is further shortened to 87 characters eliminating the emotional bit (*we're honored...),* and the statement is turned into a non-finite sentence. Most importantly, this very short text is preceded by a hashtag:

(19) #PepsiCoProud to be included again on @Interbrand's Best Global Brands list: http://bit.ly/19RHNI4 (*Twitter*)

In this case the #PepsiCoProud hashtag makes it possible to retrieve all the messages that illustrate facts or initiatives of which the PepsiCo company may be proud, while the *@character* refers to, and provides a direct connection with, the brand management consultancy Interbrand.

This illustrates an aspect of communication on Twitter that according to Zappavigna (2011; 2012) is one of its most salient peculiarities, i.e. the crucial role played by punctuation that, thanks to electronic affordances, makes texts published on this social media *aggregatable* and *searchable*.

The @ character followed by a username in a medial or final position provides reference to a user, as in example 19. In initial position, it can indicate either the subject (*@WalmartGreen is doing great sustainability work and we are glad to be a partner: http://pepsi.co/yIQxF*) or encode vocatively the user to whom a tweet is addressed (*@PepsiCo team good luck going into ur final week on #PepsiCorps 2014*), while in combination with RT (*RT@username*) it indicates that what follows is to be attributed to the user specified, being a retweet, i.e. the total or partial reporting of another tweet *RT @diplomasnow: Thank you* @PepsiCo *Fdn for your continued commitment to our work and the students we serve!*).

The other recurrent form of punctuation, *hashtags*, are words or phrases prefixed with the symbol # that are used in this environment to identify all the messages where such words appear as related to a given topic, thus making it possible to retrieve the whole set of posts dealing with such topic. Thus Zappavigna sees them as crucial in that they confer searchability upon Twitter discourse. Furthermore, by means of hashtags users can "increase the 'loudness' of their discourse by increasing the likelihood that their words will be found." They function as "both a label for the potential discourse community that they establish and render searchable the coupling that occurs in the tweet" and are inherently dynamic, shifting to respond to changes in the users' social world (Zappavigna 2012:87). In this way they also make it more probable that users may be followed by others. He calls this effect *ambient affiliation* (Zappavigna 2011:800; 2012:83), a sense of community and engagement fostered by the Twitter environment. As hashtags enable users to search topics of their interest and share associated values (Zappavigna 2013:91), in the corporate context they are exploited to enhance brand loyalty and stimulate positive feelings towards a company.

Under a textual perspective, this same function of hashtags can provide a powerful tool of cohesion in an environment where text is by definition fragmentary. It makes it possible for users to reconstruct how a certain topic is dealt with in messages that are not adjacent; symmetrically, by making recourse to a hashtag users can contextualize their tweets placing them within the context of an ongoing conversation whose pieces – however dispersed – can be identified and recomposed into a textual complex.

On a corporate Twitter profile, tweets can deal with all sorts of themes – some evidently relevant to corporate image and product promotion, others less obviously so.

In particular, product promotion is effected either directly from the corporate account or by retweeting from the relevant product's profile. For instance in the following tweets there is a question about a product, as is only natural given the importance of the "listening" component in corporate participation in social media:

(20) **PepsiCo**@PepsiCo23 Set
Have you ever sprinkled Life Cereal on top of @MullerQuaker yogurt? pic.twitter.com/tl85V8e5BP

(21) **PepsiCo**@PepsiCo20 Set
It's nearly Autumn! Are you drinking your @Lipton tea hot or iced these days?

In the following examples, the tweet is aimed at engaging the user, by inviting him/her to retweet, and thus using him/her as an active agent in product promotion, in a "conversational marketing" (Kelley 2009; De Felice 2010; cf. also Riboni 2012) or "viral marketing" style (Rayport 1996).

(22) **PepsiCo**@PepsiCo 4Oct
Retweet if you'd try these Soy Sauce and Onion chips from Brazil! pic.twitter.com/jL2ZZlE0sc (4 October 2013)

In many other cases the promotional component is less evident, as reference is made to events in which the company is involved or to facts or events that foreground the company's areas of commitment or values, covering more or less the same topics that are dealt with on Facebook, e.g. environment conservation:

(23) **PepsiCo**@PepsiCo24 Set
Our Eco-Challenge program, sponsored w/ @YABTs & @OAS_official, helps eco-entrepreneurs solve environmental problems: http://pepsi.co/zgXLg (17 July 2014)

In the following examples, the company praises "our associates" and "our family members" among the volunteers participating in the fighthunger campaign:

(24) **PepsiCo**@PepsiCo24 Set
Proud of @luv2bmissyb & our associates volunteering @FeedingAmerica food banks for the 4th straight year #FightHunger pic.twitter.com/PLTf2lpbyN.

(25) **PepsiCo**@PepsiCo24 Set
Great day for service! Big thanks to @rachaelhowell & all our family members volunteering across America #fighthunger pic.twitter.com/XKYdAaUyl8

In linguistic terms, tweets are obviously conditioned by their shortness. In a context of minimal syntactic complexity, the prevailing structures are:

- verbless sentences (example 25)
- sentences with a non-finite verb form (examples 19 and 24)
- directives (example 22)
- short statements, often with the verb *to be* (example 21)
- short questions, by far the most frequent form, sometimes combined with a short statement, or a directive.

This means that overall texts tend to be absolutely fragmented. As can be seen in Table 2 above, connectors are used much more rarely than on blogs and on Facebook, with much lower frequencies of hypotactic conjunctions (*that*, *when*). Some are totally absent (*because*, *since*, *while*), and paratactic conjunctions show much lower frequencies. For instance, *but* and *so*, have a frequency of only 0.01% as against respectively 0.06% and 0.02% on Facebook, and 0.14% and 0.15% on the blogs.

It is also interesting to note that there are hardly any other forms of cohesion among the tweets posted by the company, although there is certainly a form of conditional relevance between a tweet and the relative comments by users: actually every tweet and the relevant comment could be interpreted as an adjacency pair. As pointed out above, across more than two or three tweets the only real form of textual cohesion is given by hashtags, which means that a paralinguistic element activated by new technological affordances takes over an important textual function from the linguistic elements that have traditionally performed it.

It can thus be concluded that verbal communication through the new media is not only subject to constraints that have an impact on sociolinguistic, textual and discursive variables, with ample consequences in terms of language choices and genre characterisation, but it also changes the functions of resources that so far had been seen only as marginal and having an exclusively local scope, and in particular punctuation.

3. Conclusions

What emerges from the discussion is that overall companies tend to take a holistic approach to the choice of contents for the Web 2.0 applications they deploy in their communication effort, with some contributions that are definitely promotional, and others that are aimed at building a sense of community with users on the basis of their preference for the firm's brands and products, but, first and foremost, they are aimed at leveraging on values, interests and activities. As Jack Myers (2010) points out, today "advertising and media are shifting from "reach and frequency" as primary objectives to "building brands and profits"." The basic idea in corporate investment in the social media is that of fostering rapport and loyalty with customers, who will then develop a positive attitude to the company and its products, and informally act as agents conveying that kind of attitude to other consumers. Figure 4 below shows the changes brought to the traditional "purchase funnel" by recourse to social media marketing.

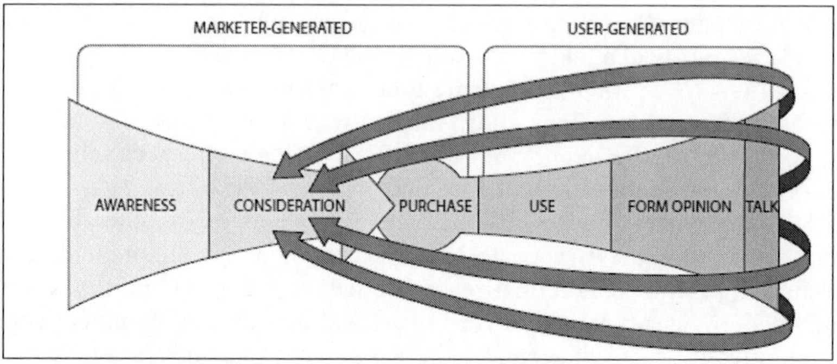

Fig. 4: The Social Feedback Cycle (Evans & McKee 2010: 5)

The funnel is expanded to include the post-purchase experiences of the customer. Social Media connect these experiences back to the purchase process through a social feedback cycle, denoted by the arrows, essentially based on advocacy (cf. among others Jansen et al. 2009; Evans & McKee 2010). It is interesting that in the case of Twitter the positive feedback/advocacy cycle can be realized simply by means of retweets.

But to be effective, a company's communication effort on social networks has to be managed in the best possible way, with frequent updates and continuous attention to users' reactions and comments. In the case of PepsiCo updates are less frequent than one would expect for a highly connected multinational corporation, and this accounts for the limited interaction it achieves, with disappointingly few comments, a problem that has been identified also on Pepsi's consumer Facebook page (Moth 2013). Incidentally, this drawback seems to affect less small- and medium-sized firms, which can assess the results of their social media investments more easily than the big corporations for whom it is more difficult to evaluate the real impact that the enterprise's presence on social media may actually have on performance.

From the point of view of enterprise organization, this means that communication on social networks is problematic to manage unless it is approached anew in terms of general communication policy, selection of contents, discursive strategies, linguistic choices, use of visual and other semiotics resources, and, last but not least, timing, given that an effective social media management requires continuous and timely updating, several times a day. This is why many companies prefer to outsource this activity to specialised agencies that command adequate expertise to use these potentially precious resources in a way that is as efficient and as effective as possible.

As regards the specifically linguistic research question asked at the beginning, the comparison between blogs, Facebook and Twitter posts clearly shows that the tendency is towards increasing fragmentation and shortening of texts. In blogs, textuality as we know it survives, in Facebook posts texts tend to be short, but to some extent still cohesive, while on Twitter units of conceptual meaning or speech acts are presented in isolation, with the smallest possible deployment of linguistic resources, and the virtual disappearance of cohesive devices. Cohesion is realized, instead, through hyperlinks and hashtags, thus providing evidence that technology is supplanting (meta)discursive resources in text and discourse construction.

The progress of this process of deconstruction and fragmentation of text and discourse has accompanied the history of web-mediated communication, starting with the parcelization of text into lexias on webpages, gathering momentum as it went along with the introduction of new platforms and applications. This has been parallel to a process of increasing dialogicisation and users' participation or "engagement".

These tendencies have important implications both for our conceptualisation of communication in the web-mediated environment and for linguistic and discourse analytical research in this domain.

The inherent characteristics of the new media have also important implications for training, as they require not only new skills, but also new literacies, and new ways of managing language and discourse.

References

Askehave, Inger & Anne Ellerup Nielsen. 2004. *Webmediated Genres. A Challenge to Traditional Genre Theory. Working Paper nr. 6*. Aarhus: Center for Virksomhedskommunication.

—. 2005. What are the characteristics of digital genres? – Genre theory from a multi-modal perspective. *Information Technology & People* 18. 2. 120-141.

Baron, Naomi. 2008. *Always On: Language in an Online and Mobile World*. Oxford/New York: Oxford University Press.

Barthes, Roland. 1970/1974. *S/Z*. Transl. by Richard Miller. New York: Hill and Wang (*S/Z*. Paris: Éditions du Seuil).

Bhatia, Vijay K. 1993. *Analysing Genre: Language in Professional Settings*. London: Longman.

—. 2004. *Worlds of Written Discourse*. London: Continuum.

Blommaert, Jan. 2005. *Discourse*. Cambridge: Cambridge University Press.

Brown, Gillian & George Yule. 1983. *Discourse Analysis*. Cambridge: Cambridge University Press.

Boyd, Dana M. & Nicole B. Ellison 2008. Social network sites: Definition, history, and scholarship. *Journal of Computer-mediated Communication* 13. 1. 210-230.

Campagna, Sandra, Giuliana Garzone, Cornelia Ilie & Elizabeth Rowley-Jolivet (eds). 2012. *Evolving Genres in Web-mediated Communication.* Bern: Peter Lang.

Catenaccio, Paola. 2008. *Corporate Press Releases. An Overview.* Milano: CUEM.

Conley, David. 2002. *The Daily Miracle: An Introduction to Journalism.* 2nd ed. Melbourne: Oxford University Press.

De Felice, Luca. 2010. *Marketing Conversazionale. Dialogare con i clienti attraverso i social media e il Real-Time Web di Twitter, FriendFeed e Facebook.* Milano: Il Sole 24 Ore.

Evans, Dade and Jake McKee 2010. *Social Media Marketing. The Next Generation of Business Engagement.* Indianapolis, IN: Wiley Publishing.

Fernando, Angelo. 2007. Social media change the rules. *Communication World* 24. 1. 9-10.

Garzone, Giuliana. 2002. Describing e-commerce communication. Which models and categories for text analysis?. *TEXTUS* 14. 2. 279-296.

—. 2007. Genres, Multimodality and the World Wide Web: Theoretical issues. In Giuliana Garzone, Gina Poncini & Paola Catenaccio (eds.), *Multimodality in Corporate Communication. Web Genres and Discursive Identity*. Milan: Franco Angeli, 15-30.

—. 2010. Multiple sponsorships and advertising in the discursive construction of corporate identity. In Paola Evangelisti Allori & Giuliana Garzone (eds.), *Discourse, Identities and Genres in Corporate Communication: Sponsorship, Advertising and Organizational Communication*. Bern: Peter Lang, 52-77.

—. 2012. Where do web genres come from? The case of blogs. In Sandra Campagna, Giuliana Garzone, Cornelia Ilie & Elizabeth Rowley-Jolivet (eds.), *Evolving Genres in Web-mediated Communication*. Bern: Peter Lang. 217-242.

Garzone, Giuliana, Gina Poncini & Paola Catenaccio (eds). 2007. *Multimodality in Corporate Communication. Web Genres and Discursive Identity*. Milan: Franco Angeli.

Grice, Paul. 1989. Logic and Conversation. In Paul Grice, *Studies in the Ways of Words*. Cambridge, Mass./London: Harvard University Press. 22-40.

Grieve, Jack, Douglas Biber, Eric Friginal & Tatiana Nekrasova. 2010. "Variations among blogs: A multi-dimensional analysis". In Alexander Mehler, Serge Sharoff & Marina Santini (eds.), *Genres on the Web: Computational Models and Empirical Studies*. Dordrecht: Springer. 303-322.

Harrison, Teresa M. & Brea Barthel. 2009. Wielding new media in Web 2.0: Exploring the history of engagement with the collaborative construction of media products. *New Media & Society*. 11. 1-2. 155-178.

Herring, Susan C. 1996. *Computer-Mediated Communication. Linguistic, Social and Cross-Cultural Perspectives*. Amsterdam/Philadelphia: John Benjamins.

Herring, Susan C., Inna Kouper, John C. Paolillo, Lois Ann Scheidt, Michael Tyworth, Peter Welsch, Elijah Wright and Ning Yu. 2005. Conversations in the blogosphere: An analysis 'from the bottom up'. *Proceedings of the 38th*

Hawaii International Conference on System Sciences. Proceedings of the 38th Hawaii International Conference on System Sciences. Los Alamos: IEEE Press. 1-11.

Jacobs, Geert. 1999. *Preformulating the News. An Analysis of the Metapragmatics of Press Releases*. Amsterdam/Philadelphia: John Benjamins.

Jansen, Bernard J., Mimi Zhang, Kate Sobel & Abdur Chowdury. 2009. Twitter power: Tweets as electronic word of mouth. *Journal Of The American Society For Information Science And Technology* 60. 11. 2169-2188.

Kelley, Braden. 2009. Conversational marketing white paper. *Blogging Innovation.* http://www.business-strategy-innovation.com/Conversational-Marketing-White-Paper.pdf.

Kress, Gunther & Teo van Leeuwen. 2001. *Multimodal Discourse*. London: Arnold.

Krishnamurthy, Srikant. 2002. The multidimensionality of blog conversations: The virtual enactment of September 11. Paper presented at *Internet Research 3.0*, Maastricht, The Netherlands.

Landow, George P. 1992/1997. *Hypertext: The Convergence of Contemporary Critical Theory and Technology*. Baltimore, MD: Johns Hopkins University Press.

Levinson, Stephen C. 1983. *Pragmatics.* Cambridge: Cambridge University Press.

Lightfoot, Paul. 2013. Pepsi Losing 'Cola Wars' to Coca Cola on Facebook. http://socialmediachimps.com/analysis/pepsi-losing-cola-wars-to-coca-cola-on-facebook/.

Ge, Liping. 2011. Pragmatic functions of presupposition in advertising English. *Asian Culture and History* 3. 1. http://www.ccsenet.org/journal/index.php/ach/article/view/8920/6565.

Massarotto, Marco 2007. *Social network: costruire e comunicare identità in rete.* Milano: Apogeo.

Mehler, Alexander, Serge Sharoff & Marina Santini. 2010. *Genres on the Web: Computational Models and Empirical Studies*. Dordrecht: Springer.

Miller, Carolyn R. & Dawn Shepherd 2004. Blogging as social action: A genre analysis of the weblog. In Laura Gurak et al. (eds.), *Into the Blogosphere: Rhetoric, Community, and Culture of Weblogs.* http://blog.lib.umn.edu/blogosphere/blogs_as_virtual.html.

—. 2009. Questions for genre theory from the blogosphere. In Janet Giltrow & Dieter Stein (eds.), *Genres in the Internet: Issues on the Theory of Genres.* Amsterdam/Philadelphia: John Benjamins, 263-290.

Moth, David. 2013 How Pepsi uses Facebook, Twitter, Pinterest and Google+. https://econsultancy.com/blog/63062-how-pepsi-uses-facebook-twitter-pinterest-and-google.

Myers, Greg 2009. *The Discourse of Blogs and Wikis*. London: Continuum.

Myers, Jack. 1998. *Reconnecting with Customers: Building Brands and Profits in The Relationship Age*. Encino, CA: Spurge Ink!.

—. 2010. Five rules for success in The Relationship Age^{TM}. MyersBizNet 21.12.2010. www.mediabiz bloggers.com/jackmyers.

Nelson, Theodore. 1981/2008 *Literary Machines*. Watertown, MA: Eastgare Systems.
O'Reilly, Tom. 2005. What is Web 2.0. Design patterns and business models for the next generation of software. http://oreilly.com/ web2/archive/what-is-web-20.html.
Paganoni, Maria Cristina. 2012. Online branding from hybrid ads to corporate twittering. In Sandra Campagna, Giuliana Garzone, Cornelia Ilie & Elizabeth Rowley-Jolivet (eds.), *Evolving Genres in Web-mediated Communication*. Bern: Peter Lang. 311-330.
Parker, Ken 1991. Sponsorship. The research contribution. *European Journal of Marketing* 25. 11. 22-30.
Puschmann, Cornelius. 2009a. Diary or megaphone? The pragmatic mode of weblogs. Paper presented at the conference *Language in the (New) Media: Technologies and Ideologies* 39, 1-7. September 3-6 2009, Seattle, WA, USA. http://www.mendeley.com/research/diary-megaphone-pragmatic-mode-weblogs/.
—. 2009b. Lies at Wal-Mart. Style and the subversion of genre in the *Life at Wal-Mart* blog. In Janet Giltrow & Dieter Stein (eds.), *Genres in the Internet: Issues on the Theory of Genres*. Amsterdam/Philadelphia: John Benjamins. 49-84.
—. 2010. *The Corporate Blog as an Emerging Genre of Computer-Mediated Communication: Features, Constraints, Discourse Situation,* Göttingen: Universitätsverlag Göttingen.
—. 2013. Blogging. In Susan C. Herring, Dieter Stein & Tuija Virtanen (eds.), *Pragmatics of Computer-Mediated Communication*. Berlin/New York: De Gruyter. 83-108.
Rayport, Jeffrey. 1996. The Virus of Marketing. *Fast Company.* http://www.fastcompany.com/magazine/06/virus.html.
Riboni, Giorgia. 2012. Twittering Away: *Whole Foods Market* and Conversational Marketing in 140 Characters. In Sandra Campagna, Giuliana Garzone Cornelia Ilie & Elizabeth Rowley-Jolivet (eds.), *Evolving Genres in Web-mediated* Communication. Bern: Peter Lang, 289-310.
—. 2014a. *Nuovi media e discorso politico. I blog nelle elezioni presidenziali americane*. Saarbrücken: Edizioni Accademiche Italiane.
—. 2014b. From blogging to microblogging: The case of whole foods market. In Giuliana Garzone & Cornelia Ilie (eds.), *Genres and Genre Theory in Transition. Specialized Discourses across Media and Modes*. Boca Raton, FL: Brown Walker Press. 149-170.
Schiffrin, Deborah, Deborah Tannen, & Heidi E. Hamilton (eds.). 2001. *Handbook of Discourse Analysis*. Oxford: Blackwell.
Scott, Mike. 2008. *Wordsmith Tools 5.0*. Liverpool: Lexical Analysis Software.
Sperber, Dan & Deirdre Wilson. 1995. *Relevance: Communication and Cognition*, 2nd ed. Oxford/Cambridge: Blackwell Publishers.
Stelzner, Michael. 2013. *2013 Social Media Marketing Industry Report.* Social Media Examiner. http://www.socialmediaexaminer.com/SocialMediaMarketingIndustryReport2013.pdf.

Swales, John. 2004. *Research Genres: Explorations and Applications*. Cambridge: Cambridge University Press.

Tannen, Deborah & Anna Marie Trester (eds). 2013. *Discourse 2.0. Language and New Media.* Washington DC: Georgetown University Press.

Thurlow, Crispin & Kristine Mroczek. *Digital Discourse. Language in the New Media*. Oxford: Oxford University Press.

van Dijk, Teun A. 1988. *News as Discourse*. Hillsdale, NJ: Lawrence Erlbaum Ass. Publishers.

Werlich, Egon. 1976/1983. *A Text Grammar of English.* Heidelberg: Quelle & Meyer.

Zappavigna, Michele. 2011. Ambient affiliation: A linguistic perspective on Twitter. *New Media & Society* 13. 5. 788–80.

—. 2012. *Discourse of Twitter and Social Media*. London/New York: Continuum.

From Corporate Websites to Consumer Blogs: Analyzing Recontextualization of Brand Identity in Fashion Discourse

Belinda Crawford Camiciottoli

University of Pisa, Italy

Abstract: This study focuses on the linguistic expression of brand identity and how it is recontextualized from the producer's to the consumer's perspective across two digital genres: corporate websites and consumer blogs. The analysis is situated in the discourse of the fashion community, where brands are often identified with iconic personalities and the world of luxury, and thus offer richly articulated descriptions. The methodological approach integrates quantitative text-mining and qualitative textual analysis. Small specialized corpora were compiled from the websites of three fashion brands. Three parallel corpora were then compiled from fashion blog posts that discussed the same brands. The software *WMatrix* was used to extract all adjectives from the six corpora, which were then manually analyzed to identify those that encoded various attributes of brand identity (e.g., *modern*, *elegant*, *light*). The results showed that brand identity as communicated on corporate websites is often recontextualized within the social community of fashion bloggers, who add new and creative meanings that expand on those originally defined by companies. The findings can be useful in the context of brand management to determine which attributes are perceived most favourably by consumers and should thus be reinforced.

1. Introduction

In language studies, *recontextualization* broadly refers to a process by which some part of discourse is extracted from one communicative context and fitted into another one. With respect to the concept of *contextualization* that focuses on dynamic interactions involved in situated language use (Gumperz 1992), recontextualization instead emphasizes changes in meaning as parts of discourses or genres are relocated from one context to another. Linell (1998:155) notes that recontextualization "involves transformations of meanings or meaning potentials in ways that are usually quite complex". More specifically, during a process of recontextualization, elements of discourse may be transformed through simplification or condensation, but also by refocusing, expansion, and elaboration (Bernstein 2003). A case in point is the corporate annual report that typically makes its way through an intertextual genre chain: from the original financial statement produced by the accounting department, to the financial press release issued to media sources, to the final product published on the Internet. Throughout the genre chain, meaning is alternately condensed (in the numerical data contained in the financial statement), elaborated (in the integrated verbal message of the press release) and expanded (in the management narrative and images incorporated into the complete report).

According to Linell (1998), recontextualization can be manifested at different levels of discourse. It is *intratextual* when it occurs in the same text (e.g., anaphoric reference), *intertextual* when it refers to different texts in specific contexts, or *interdiscursive* when it involves different genres, discourses or activity types.[1] In addition, various aspects of discourse can be recontextualized to take on new meanings, including not only linguistic expressions, but also knowledge and values in a broader sense (Linell 1998).

The media play an important role in the process of recontextualization, as highlighted in research carried out by Calsamiglia and van Dijk (2004) that focused on semantic devices (e.g., definition, description and metaphor) used in the Spanish daily press to report scientific findings. Interestingly, the press emphasized the social dimension of knowledge, e.g., the scientists involved, conflicts, and real-world applications of the findings, rather than the specific scientific content. In fact, the authors of this study affirm that:

> the mass media are not passive mediators of scientific knowledge, but actively contribute in the production of new, common knowledge and opinions about science and scientists – including information and views that do not derive from scientific sources. (Calsamiglia & van Dijk 2004:351)

---

[1] Although conceptually related, Linell (2009:199) distinguishes between *genre* and *activity type*, with the former described as "more discourse-focused" and the latter as "more related to actions, situations and social encounters". In the context of this research, corporate websites and consumer blogs appear to integrate elements of both.

Recontextualization has been fruitfully applied as an analytical framework to study discourse processes in different domains of specialized communication. With reference to political discourse, Wodak (2011:185) showed how authentic discourse from the "daily politics" of a member of the European Parliament collected by means of ethnographic research was recontextualized in a radically different communicative context, i.e., the "fictionalized politics" of a popular television series set in the US political world. In particular, the complex and multi-faceted realities of politics that emerged from the discourse of the member of the parliament underwent an interesting process of simplification for lay viewers. Closer to the discourse domain of the present study, Thomas (2003) applied the construct of recontextualization to show how management discourse is transformed as it moves through three different spheres of activity: academia, consultancy and practice. In the context of corporate communication, Catenaccio (2006) compared the information in press releases issued by the Enron company during the accounting scandal of 2001 with the subsequent coverage of the issue in the financial press. Through a process of recontexualization, information contained in the press releases was selectively reproduced in financial news sources, transforming original meanings into alternative and more distinctly evaluative ones.

An interesting perspective on the notion of recontextualization has been offered by Sarangi (1998). He suggests that recontextualization is actually a somewhat fuzzy concept; it involves not only the transfer and transformation of meanings between different contexts of usage, but also plays an important role in the construction of (self)identity in a given interactional context. With particular reference to professional settings, recontextualization has been used to acquire a better understanding of how identities are negotiated during interaction. The nexus between recontextualization and identity constitutes an important issue in the present study which focuses specifically on brand identity as defined by companies on the one hand, and as perceived by consumers on the other. The following subsection will provide an overview of brand identity as a fundamental aspect of corporate communication.

1.1. Brand Identity

Two important concepts in corporate communication are *identity* and *image*. The former refers to the defining attributes (e.g., vision, values, people, products and services) that a company seeks to communicate externally, while the latter refers to how a company is perceived among its stakeholders, including employees, customers and the public at large (Argenti 2009). Successful companies are able to communicate strong corporate identities that are in alignment with the externally perceived corporate image (Belasen 2008). Closely linked to corporate identity is the concept of *brand identity* which refers to a unique set of meanings that a company defines for its brand, and then aims to establish in the mind of consumers, also known as *brand associations*. These are encoded through the descriptive and evaluative lexis (e.g., *elegant*, *modern*, *traditional*) used by both producers and consumers to characterize brands (Keller 2003). Linguistic expressions are also used to communicate aspects of *brand personality*, a notion which further articulates brand identity as "the set of human characteristics associated with a brand" (Aaker 1997:347). In a study based on 37 well-known brands representing various types of products, Aaker (1997) identified five major dimensions of brand personality: *sincerity*, *excitement*, *sophistication*, *competence* and *ruggedness*. These were then further articulated into various facets. For example, the dimension *sophistication* contains the facets *upper class*, *charming*, *glamorous*, *smooth*, and *good-looking*, while *excitement* contains *daring*, *trendy*, *spirited*, *cool*, *unique* and *imaginative*. Like brand associations, brand personality is also a component of brand identity. As noted by Temporal (2002:1), "the brand can be viewed as a product, a personality, a set of values, and a position it occupies in people's minds." As we have seen, *brand associations*, *brand personality* and *brand identity* are similar and to some extent overlapping concepts. However, for the sake of clarity, hereinafter I will primarily use the term *brand identity*.

When companies are able to establish and consolidate a distinctive brand identity, they can better steer consumer perceptions in the desired direction and differentiate themselves from competitors. In an ideal situation, the brand identity that a company defines for itself and communicates to its consumers should align with what consumers actually perceive. As a consequence, companies invest a great deal of effort to promote brand identity. Today more and more companies are using digital forms of communication for this purpose. In particular, the corporate website has become an important resource used by companies to effectively position themselves in the market, and thus have an impact on consumer choices (Salvi, Turnbull & Pontesilli 2007). Web-based communications are designed by professional marketing experts for both informative and promotional purposes, i.e., "to convey attitudes, evaluation and opinions towards the products they sell and towards their customers" (Alejo González 2005:42). For this reason, web-based communications can play a key role in shaping the desired brand identity.

In this subsection, I have provided an overview of the concept of brand identity from the perspective of the producers. I now shift the focus to the consumers of brands, with particular reference to online communities and fashion discourse as the communicative setting of the present study.

1.2. Fashion Blogs as Online Communities of Consumers

In marketing research, digital platforms provide an interactional space for consumers to engage in 'virtual' conversations about brands and products (Muniz & O'Guinn 2001; Szmigin, Canning & Reppel 2005). Online interactions have the potential to provide extensive amounts of authentic and spontaneous data produced by the discourse participants in the role of consumers (current or potential),or simply enthusiasts of a particular brand or product (Cova 1997).

From a generic perspective, blogs are produced largely by laypeople who utilize them for a variety of reasons. In the case of consumer blogs, users typically aim to retrieve and exchange information and opinions about a particular brand, product or service. Following Puschmann (2013:90), these types of blogs can be described as "topic-centric" rather than "author-centric". The former focus the external world, aiming to provide information and express opinions, while the latter focus on the internal world of the author in the context of self-reflection. A good example of a topic-centric consumer blog is the highly popular TripAdvisor used by millions of people around the world to obtain and share information about travel destinations and related services. Alongside such practical uses, bloggers also communicate with each other for social purposes. According to Miller and Shepherd (2004), many people engage in this activity to develop and manage relationships with other bloggers, thus positioning themselves within a desirable social community. Moreover, blogs allow users to express their unique voices and attitudes, thereby constructing self-identity through their commentary on the mediated reality of the Internet which they, in turn, become a part of (Miller & Shepherd 2004).

Today consumers of fashion are among the most ardent participants in the blogosphere (cf. Thomas, Peters & Tolson 2007; Rickman & Cosenza 2007), and therefore represent a particularly interesting and fertile research context. In fact, at the time of writing, there were 16,486 fashion blogs, according to Technorati, an Internet search engine that tracks and provides statistics on blog activity. Due to their very nature, fashion brands have a highly elaborated visual dimension and are often closely linked to the charismatic personalities of their designers and namesakes (e.g., Valentino,

Calvin Klein, Giorgio Armani, Karl Lagerfeld). Fashion discourse, i.e., "ways of talking about fashion" (Thompson & Haytko 1997:15) is often peppered with evaluative adjectives used to encode opinions and attitudes in relation to fashion brands and products, for example *elegant, sophisticated* and *charming*, as mentioned in the previous section. In addition, fashion brands have been described as having an emotional component, in terms of the positive or negative feelings that they may evoke (Xun & Reynolds 2010). Thus, the discourse of fashion consumers typically contains richly articulated and emotionally-loaded linguistic expressions, which also encode personal meanings and identity, i.e., how fashion consumers perceive themselves and others in relation to a particular brand (Thompson & Haytko 1997). In this sense, fashion blogs could perhaps be seen as a combination of author-centric and topic-centric blog types (Puschmann 2013).

Drawing on all the notions discussed thus far, the aim of this study was to explore the phenomenon of recontextualization across two digital genres of fashion discourse used to convey brand identity: corporate websites of fashion houses and consumer blogs dedicated to fashion brands. More specifically, I sought to determine whether brand identity in the fashion industry may be recontextualized from the producer's to consumer's perspective through an analysis of descriptive and evaluative adjectives. To do so, I addressed the following research questions:

- Which adjectives are used to encode company-defined brand identity?
- Is there alignment between the adjectives used by companies and their consumers?
- Is there evidence of the recontextualization of brand identity from the producer to the consumer?

2. Methodology

2.1. Data Sources and Dataset Compilation

To investigate the recontextualization of brand identity from producers to consumers of fashion, it was necessary to identify sources of data that were representative of both types of discourse participants. For producers, textual data were collected from the corporate websites of three fashion brands. The texts contain brand and product descriptions, brand-related press releases and interviews with in-house designers, all of which are used to promote the brand, while defining desirable facets of brand identity. In an effort to ensure adequate comparability of the data, the three brands were selected on the basis of key similarities.[2] They are all globally recognized high-fashion brands that are headquartered in Italy. They all compete in the luxury fashion market, and thus have the potential to offer particularly rich textual descriptions of their products. In addition, the founders of the three fashion houses are widely considered to be iconic figures in the fashion industry whose professional and personal lives generate intense interest among fashion consumers and enthusiasts. This was a particularly important feature in the choice of the three brands. More specifically, the more popular the designers, the more likely consumers are to engage in 'conversations' about them and their related brands, also by means of ICT-mediated forms of communication. For this reason, a top-ranking fashion blog was identified as the source of textual data that encodes consumer perceptions of brand identity. The blog contains multi-authored posts that describe and evaluate fashion brands/products, after which an unlimited number of users may insert follow-up comments. Posts and comments are archived on the blog website for a period of approximately three years, thus enabling a sufficient amount of textual data to be collected. In addition, the blog incorporates a tagging tool based on fashion brand names which greatly facilitated the identification and collection of posts/comments that contained discourse about the brands in question. The textual data from the three fashion brands' corporate websites and the corresponding posts/comments from the fashion blog were compiled into three comparable datasets, one for each brand (A1/A2, B1/B2, C1/C2) for a total of six datasets, as illustrated by the descriptive profiles in Table1. The figures in the table indicate some variation in terms of the word counts contained in both the corpora and the blog datasets. In addition, there is no clear trend in relation to the number of posts and relative comments across the three brands. In fact, the number of words found in each post varied considerably, with some being relatively long (>100 words) and others containing just a few short sentences. Similarly, follow-up comments could be relatively lengthy (a few sentences), while others were made up of only a few words (e.g., "Fabulous look!").

[2] For reasons of privacy, the names of the three brands have been anonymized with A, B and C, respectively.

Tab.1: The corporate datasets (A1, B1, C1) and the corresponding blog datasets (A2, B2, C2)

DATASETS	BRAND A	BRAND B	BRAND C
Corporate	A1	B1	C1
N. words	10,778	6,212	7,561
Blog	A2	B2	C2
N. words	6,548	7,497	10,556
N. posts / comments	25 posts/ 26 comments	26 posts/ 56 comments	39 posts/ 32 comments
Blog timeframe	Sept 08- March 13	Aug 08- March 13	Aug 08- March 13
DATASETS	BRAND A	BRAND B	BRAND C

2.2. Data Analysis

The six datasets were analyzed in various phases that combined quantitative corpus methods and qualitative textual analysis (research question 1). The first step was to determine which adjectives were used by the three fashion brands to encode brand identity. This was accomplished by processing the three corporate datasets with *CLAWS4* part-of-speech (POS) tagger, a software program that automatically tags each token according to its word class (cf. Garside & Smith 1997).[3] To illustrate this procedure, a screenshot from the tagging software is reproduced in Figure 1 with a sample sentence from the corporate dataset A1.

The tagged files were then analyzed with the concordance tool of *WordSmith Tools5.0* (Scott 2010), using the general adjective tag JJ to retrieve all adjectives in the three datasets. The concordance lines were re-sorted to group items together, thus facilitating follow-up qualitative analysis to distinguish adjectives that could be linked to various attributes of brand identity. This entailed a filtering process to include only adjectives that were used to describe or evaluate the brand and its products (e.g., *red*, *modern*, *elegant)*, while excluding adjectives that had neutral meanings in this context (e.g., *other*, *certain*, *only*).[4] For the purposes of this study, *descriptive* adjectives are those that refer to visual and structural attributes, e.g., *black*, *chunky*, *double-layered*, *embroidered*. *Evaluative* adjectives are instead those used to encode attitudes, e.g.,

[3] *CLAWS4* (*Constituent Likelihood Automatic Word Tagging System*) was developed by the University Centre for Computer Corpus Research on Language of Lancaster University (UK). The developers indicate that the software has an accuracy rate of 96-97%.

[4] Although other parts-of-speech can also encode descriptive and evaluative meanings, to render the analysis manageable only adjectives were considered.

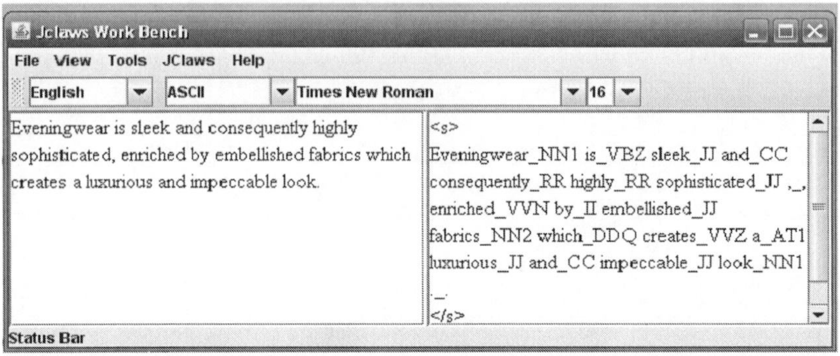

Conventions: NN1=singular common noun, VBZ=is, JJ=general adjective, CC=coordinating conjunctions, RR=general adverb, VVN=past participle of lexical verb, II=general preposition, NN2=plural common noun, DDQ=*wh*-determiner, VVZ=s-form of lexical verb, AT1=singular article.

Fig.1: Screenshot of JClaws GUI for the CLAWS4 POS tagger

confident, *beautiful*, *charming*, *discreet*. The identification of evaluation adjectives was broadly inspired by Martin and White's (2005) *appraisal* framework which articulates attitude into: affect (expression of feeling), appreciation (evaluation of entities) and judgment (evaluation of behaviors).[5] It must be recognized that almost any adjective has the potential to take on a descriptive or evaluative meaning, depending on its context of usage. However, this analysis will be limited only to adjectives that were explicitly descriptive or evaluative of the brand and associated products or entities. For illustrative purposes, a software screenshot of a sample of re-sorted concordances from one of the corporate datasets (C1) is shown in Figure 2. Here all the adjectives were interpreted as descriptive and/or evaluative of the fashion brand except for *possible* (407), *professional* (412) and *projected* (413), which were subsequently removed. At times, the co-text in the concordance lines was not sufficient to accurately identify the referent of the adjective, so it was necessary to return to the original text file for expanded context. The filtered concordance lines were further edited to eliminate multiple occurrences of the same adjective. This reduced output was then used to produce final lists of adjective types for the three corporate datasets.

---

[5] A systematic categorization of the adjectives that emerged from the dataset using the appraisal framework (Martin & White 2005) is beyond the scope of this study. However, this would be an interesting aspect to explore in further research to understand how nuances of attitude may be encoded in fashion discourse.

N	Concordance
399	are_VBR more_RGR personal_JJ and_CC precise_JJ ,_, for_IF a_AT1
400	woman_NN1 's_GE unique_JJ personal_JJ allure_NN1 "_" ._. The_AT 3_MC
401	confections_NN2 heavy_JJ on_II pink_JJ and_CC ruffles_NN2 figure_VV0
402	bustled_VVD a_AT1 sensual_JJ pink_JJ gown_NN1 ._. If_CS there_EX
403	has_VHZ a_AT1 pale_JJ ,_, blush-pink_JJ hue_NN1 ._. The_AT fragrance_NN1
404	such_II21 as_II22 a_AT1 hand-pleated_JJ leather_NN1 tote_NN1 with_IW
405	-_- were_VBDR all_DB pleated_JJ ._. Of_RR21 course_RR22 ,_,
406	,_, as_CSA the_AT positive_JJ critical_JJ response_NN1 to_II
407	make_VV0 it_PPH1 possible_JJ to_TO cover_VVI an_AT1
408	personal_JJ and_CC precise_JJ ,_, for_IF a_AT1 young_JJ
409	hems_NN2 ,_, utterly_RR precise_JJ and_CC controlled_VVD -_- and_CC
410	in_II the_AT prestigious_JJ atelier_NN1 situated_VVN in_II
411	of_IO beads_NN2 on_II a_AT1 pretty_JJ ballerina_NN1 dress_NN1 ;_; a_AT1
412	as_II33 her_APPGE professional_JJ endeavours_NN2 ._. The_AT
413	,_, the_AT designers_NN2 projected_JJ video_NN1 animations_NN2 of_IO

Fig. 2: Screenshot of a sample of re-sorted adjectives (Source: *WordSmith Tools*)

To determine possible alignments between company-defined and consumer-perceived brand identity (research question 2), each adjective in the lists described above was queried in the corresponding blog datasets (i.e., A2, B2, C2). During this process it was necessary to verify within the context usage that the retrieved items displayed in the concordances actually referred to the brand question. As multi-authored texts, blog posts and comments often contain adjectives used to qualify other entities that are not related to the particular brand (e.g., *blue sky*, *new way*, *young actor*). Adjectives may even be used to qualify other brands within the same post/comment. These cases were removed from the data, leaving only the adjectives that bloggers had clearly used to qualify the brand in question. A percentage of alignment for each brand was calculated from the ratio between the number of common items found in the blog datasets and the total number of adjective types present in the corporate datasets.

To look for evidence of recontextualization of brand identity from the producer's to the consumer's perspective (research question 3), the three blog datasets were further elaborated to facilitate additional qualitative analysis of adjective usage. Again using the concordancer, all the adjectives in the blog datasets were retrieved using the general tag JJ and frequency lists were compiled. The lists were then scrutinized to identify items that could be semantically linked to the common items that had emerged from the previous analysis. These items were then analyzed qualitatively in the blog datasets within their context of usage to gain insights into possible new facets of brand identity as recontextualized by the bloggers.

3. Results and Discussion

3.1. Quantitative Analysis

For the three corporate datasets (A1, B1 C1), Table 2 reports the results of the preliminary filtering phases of the concordance output. The table reports raw frequency counts (N) and normalized parameter of occurrences per thousand words (ptw) for: (i) the total number of adjectives retrieved from the initial JJ tag query, (ii) the number of descriptive/evaluative adjectives after filtering, and (iii) the number of different descriptive/evaluative adjective types.

As can be seen, even if the datasets are relatively small in terms of their word counts, the number of adjectives contained in each (both pre- and post-filtering) is high enough so that the use of automated POS tagging is the only feasible way to achieve a comprehensive and exhaustive analysis. From a comparative perspective, there are no particularly strong differences across the three brands. At the final level of adjective type, any differences are largely evened out, although Brand A presents slightly higher frequencies, with 19.6 ptw vs. 14.5 ptw and 15.2 ptw, for Brands B and C, respectively. This relative uniformity may be explained by the similar product types and target market of the three brands, as well as the same promotional nature of the texts collected from the websites that aim to highlight the qualities of the brands.

Tab. 2: Frequencies of adjectives in the corporate datasets

CORPORATE DATASET	ADJECTIVES (PRE-FILTERING) N (PTW)	DESCRIPTIVE/ EVALUATIVE ADJECTIVES (POST-FILTERING) N (PTW)	DESCRIPTIVE/ EVALUATIVE ADJECTIVE TYPES N (PTW)
A1	1067 (98.9)	689 (63.9)	211 (19.6)
B1	706 (113.6)	456 (73.4)	90 (14.5)
C1	599 (79.2)	403 (53.3)	115(15.2)

Table 3 provides examples of the range of descriptive/evaluative adjective types found in the three corporate datasets. For reasons of space, only the initial part of the alphabetically ordered lists are shown. A quick comparison of the three lists reveals numerous overlapping items (e.g., *aristocratic*, *avant-garde*, *beautiful*, *contemporary*, *creative*, *easy*, *elegant*), as well as several common items between two brands (e.g., *airy*, *cool*, *edgy*, *eclectic*). Across the three brands, many of the adjectives can be semantically linked to the dimensions of brand personality delineated by Aaker (1997). In particular, *aristocratic*, *chic*, *classic*, *cosmopolitan*, *couture-quality*, *debonair* and *elegant* can all be grouped under the dimension of *sophistication*, while *casual*, *comfortable*, *compatible*, *double-layered*, *essential* and *everyday* reflect the dimension of *ruggedness*. *Adventurous*, *avant-garde*, *dashing*, *eccentric*, *edgy*, and *extreme*, correspond to the dimension of *excitement*. Interestingly, all three brands communicate dimensions of identity that seem to be polar opposites, particularly in the context of the fashion world, i.e., *sophistication* vs. *ruggedness*. This is likely to reflect an effort to appeal to different types of consumers and expand their market share.

Tab. 3: Examples of descriptive/evaluative adjective types in the corporate datasets

BRAND A	BRAND B	BRAND C
adventurous, aesthetic, *airy*, *aristocratic*, astonishing, athletic, authentic, *avant-garde*, bare, *beautiful*, beguiling, beige, black, blue, brogue-style, bronzed, brown, casual, celebrated, chic, chromatic, chunky, classic, clean, cloud-colored, comfortable, compatible, confident, *contemporary*, *cool*, cosmopolitan, *creative*, dashing, debonair, decorative, defined, delicate, delightful, detailed, different, distinctive, dramatic, *easy*, eccentric, *eclectic*, eco-friendly, *edgy*, effervescent, *elegant*, enriched […]	*aristocratic*, artistic, authentic, *avant-garde*, *beautiful*, beige, black, blue, brocade-detailed, brown, burgundy, butterfly-shaped, calf-length, charming, chunky, classic, collegiate, comfortable, cone-shaped, *contemporary*, cosmopolitan, *creative*, cropped, curved, dandy-esque, delicate, different, double-layered, *easy*, eccentric, *eclectic*, *elegant*, embossed, embroidered, envelope-shaped, eternal, extreme, fascinating, feminine, fitted, flared, floral, […]	accessorized, *airy*, ambitious, appealing, *aristocratic*, artistic, authentic, *avant-garde*, *beautiful*, black, blue, blush-colored, blush-pink, bold, brown, buoyant, candid, casual, charming, classic, clean, colorful, *contemporary*, *cool*, courtly, couture-quality, coveted, *creative*, crisp, decisive, defining, delicate, desired, detailed, different, discreet, discriminating, distinctive, dusky, dusty, *easy*, *edgy*, elaborate, *elegant*, embellished, embroidered, enchanting, essential, everyday, […]

As luxury brands that compete with each other within the same high-fashion market, it is not surprising that they may use identical adjectives to describe and qualify their products. However, a closer look at the sample lists reveals some adjectives that express distinctive facets of identity. For example, Brand A uses *athletic*, *cloud-colored*, and *eco-friendly* associated with sports and nature. Among the adjectives of Brand B, we find *butterfly-shaped*, *cone-shaped*, *cropped*, *curved*, and *envelope-shaped* that encode a sense of architectural precision in design. Brand C emphasizes an identity linked to softness and femininity with adjectives such as *blush-*

colored, *blush-pink*, *charming*, *delicate* and *enchanting*. Thus, the three brands appear to balance an identity that conveys traditional dimensions of brand personality (Aaker 1997), but also unique facets of identity that distinguish them from each other.

With reference to potential alignments between company-defined and consumer-perceived brand identity, Table 4 lists adjectives that were found to overlap between the corporate datasets and their corresponding blog datasets. The numbers in parentheses after some adjectives indicate multiple occurrences in the blog datasets. As can be seen, the lists also include nouns that functioned as adjectives, as tagged by CLAWS4 (e.g., *luxury*, *top*). The table also reports the total number of common adjectives for each brand (N) and the percentage of alignment, i.e., the ratio between N and the total number of adjective types present in the corporate datasets as shown in Table 3.

Tab. 4: Common adjectives between corporate and blog datasets

BRAND	COMMON ADJECTIVES	N	% ALIGNMENT
A	beautiful (2), black, chic, classic (2), compatible, cool, different, elegant (2), embellished, exclusive (3), favorite, feminine, fluid, glossy, great, high-end, high-quality, high-tech, Italian, luxury, metallic, neat, new (6), pink, plush, retro, sculpted, seductive, soft, striking, tailored, theatrical, top, traditional, undulating, unstructured, urban, white, young	49	23.2
B	beautiful (3), bright, chic, classic, comfortable, different, elegant (3), feminine, irresistible, Italian, massive, modern, new (2), perfect, pink, quilted, seductive, sexy (2), simple, strong, sweet, timeless (2), traditional, white	31	33.3
C	airy, beautiful, creative, elegant, enchanting, detailed, feminine, gorgeous (2), iconic, important, lovely, Italian, light, luxury, natural, new (7), red, stylish, unique, white	27	23.5

As can be surmised from Table 4, the percentage of alignment between the adjectives used in the corporate datasets to define the identity of the three brands and those used by consumers in the corresponding blog datasets did not show strong differences. For Brands A and C, the percentage of alignment was essentially the same, while for Brand B it was somewhat higher. However, the key point here is what degree of alignment these figures actually represent – high or low? To answer this question, we need to consider that the adjectives found in the corporate websites were produced by the companies as a single entity to communicate a decisively promotional message. The fact that roughly 20 to 30% of these converged precisely with those produced by multiple individuals in a widespread and non-homogenous online community that interacts for social purposes suggests an interpretation that leans more towards a high degree of alignment rather than a low one. Evidently, the three brands have succeeded in establishing some key facets of brand personality in the minds of their consumers, since the latter reproduce them exactly when expressing their perceptions of the brands. On a descriptive level, it is interesting to note that all three brands communicate their cultural identity with the adjective *Italian*, which is also perceived by their consumers. In addition, colors also appear to play an important role in brand identity. The adjective *white* is present in all the common lists, while *pink* occurs in two (Brand A and B). On the other hand, *black* and *red* are found only in Brands A and C, and therefore constitute unique attributes. It should be noted that all three brands are all well-established firms in the luxury fashion industry with founders who are often described as 'legendary' in the fashion press and media channels. As undisputed market leaders, it stands to reason that they have been able to convey a desired brand identity clearly and effectively.

3.2. Qualitative Analysis

The qualitative analysis of the adjectives used to express brand identity was undertaken in two steps. First, the common adjectives listed for each brand in Table 4 were carefully studied to identify clusters of semantically-related adjectives that encode distinctive and particularly strong 'themes' of brand identity, beyond the single matching adjectives. For Brand A, a theme of *softness* emerges in a cluster formed by *fluid*, *soft*, *undulating* and *unstructured*. For Brand B, the cluster *irresistible*, *sexy*, and *seductive* reflects a theme of *seduction*, while for Brand C the cluster formed by *enchanting*, *feminine* and *lovely* transmits a theme of *femininity*. The presence of distinctive thematic clusters for each brand seems to reinforce aspects of company-defined brand identity that were clearly perceived by consumers. Other thematic clusters appear in a transversal way across the three brands. The theme of *exclusivity* can be interpreted from the adjectives *different*, *exclusive* and *unique*, while the theme of *modernity* surfaces from *young*, *modern* and *new*. The fact that the three brands also promote similar themes of identity which are also perceived by their consumers tends to reinforce their status as market competitors.

As a second step, the common adjectives in Table 4 were used as a basis for identifying other adjectives in the blog datasets that could signal recontextualized meanings. More specifically, the lists of all the adjectives found in the blog datasets were perused to identify additional items that were semantically related to the common adjectives, but transformed their meanings in some way. This process brought to light an interesting trend. In several cases, the fashion bloggers extended the company-defined brand identity, often demonstrating a high level of creativity and adding new facets of meaning. For instance, the common adjectives *metallic* and *glossy* for Brand A were extended in meaning by bloggers with *shining*, *glittering*, *bejeweled* and *starry* (examples 1 and 2), which seem to integrate an idea of luxury and glamor. For Brand B, the common adjective *simple* was extended with *crisp* and *razor-sharp* (examples 3 and 4), adding a sense of precise modern tailoring. For Brand C, the common adjectives *airy* and *light* were extended with *paper-thin*, *gossamer-light*, *see-through*, *lacy*, and *peep-toe* (examples 5 and 6), which incorporate nuances of seduction.

(1) The night sky over the Sahara gave <Brand name> the inspiration for their Spring 2011 collection. That meant molto navy and plenty of *glittering*, *starry* sparkles.[6] (A2)

(2) <Brand name's> dress and *bejeweled* bodysuit from this year's Grammys was so tiny that it took two devoted <Brand name> staffers to fit on the mannequin. (A2)

(3) We like the idea of a woman in a suit in front of the flashbulbs - in a *razor-sharp* white tux by <Brand name> (B2).

(4) <Brand name> looks elegant, *crisp* and chic every time. (B2)

(5) For their Spring 2011 ad campaign, <Brand name> tapped three of the hottest models of the moment to showcase their *gossamer-light* collection. (C2)

(6) Last season, sheers ruled the runways. And this season? They're still here. *See-through* styles showed up at <Brand name>, among others. (C2)

A further illustration of how brand identity may be recontextualized from the producer to the consumer can be seen in a comparison of the common adjectives as found on the corporate websites with their enhanced representations in the corresponding blog datasets. In this case, we have an instance of *interdiscursive* recontextualization (Linell 1998) as it occurs across two completely different genres and activity types. Example 7 illustrates how the adjectives *seductive* and *elegant* are used on the

[6] Fashion bloggers sometimes insert words in languages other than English in blog posts (e.g., *molto*, *jolie*, *bella figura*), perhaps to emphasize certain opinions and attitudes, or to draw attention to specific features of the brand, while implying a certain level of cultural sophistication at the same time.

corporate website of Brand A to promote important facets of brand identity. Example 8 shows how *seductive* is recontextualized in the corresponding blog dataset with the colloquial form *super-hot* used to positively evaluate the appearance of person wearing the brand.[7] Example 9 shows how *elegant* is 'modernized' by a blogger with *ultra-chic*. For Brand B, on the corporate website we find the adjective *sexy* (example 10), which the bloggers glamorize and even personify by attributing human behaviors to the brand with the items *femme fatale* and *naughty* (example 11). In example 12, Brand C uses the adjective *plush* on its website to convey an identity associated with luxury and richness. Examples 13 and 14 illustrate its recontextualization by bloggers in terms of physical sensations (taste and touch) with the adjectives *chocolaty* and *textured* (referring to a hotel with interiors designed by the brand) and *plush-piled*.

(7) <Brand name> combines *seductive* charm with modern elegance, interpreting the contemporary woman's lifestyle in an *elegant* Prêt-à-Porter collection. (A1)

(8) She looks *super-hot*! The dress suits her perfectly. (A2)

(9) This denim trench is truly *ultra-chic*. (A2)

(10) The <Brand name> woman is strong. [...] She wears very high heels which, in any case, give her both an extremely feminine and *sexy* way of walking and unmistakable posture. (B1)

(11) <Brand name's> *femme fatale* heels inset with fishnet leather look like *naughty* ankle socks. (B2)

(12) Even the padded jackets appear light, as though deconstructed, with neat *plush* linings. (C1)

(13) The whole place had a *chocolaty, textured* luxury. (C2)

(14) <Brand name> offered the trusted house style: soft, fluid and *plush piled* jackets and pants. (C2)

The above examples illustrate a process of recontextualization of brand identity as it moves from the discourse of an expert community of professional practice to the 'virtual' conversations of a lay public of consumers. Compared to the fairly conventional linguistic representations found on corporate websites (e.g., *elegant*, *seductive*, *plush*), in the blog datasets we find a number of creative and innovative alternatives (e.g., *super-hot, femme-fatale*, *chocolaty*) that integrate new shades of meaning. Interestingly, these findings contrast with Wodak's study (2011) in which the recontextualization of meanings from the authentic communications of a politician underwent a process of simplification in the fictionalized

[7] The *Oxford English Dictionary* (http://www.oed.com/) defines *hot* as *sexually attractive* (of a person).

political drama television series. In this case, however, the recontextualization of fashion discourse from corporate websites to consumer blogs suggests a process of expansion and elaboration (Bernstein 2003), in which bloggers added new and differently nuanced meanings. This could be influenced by the 'real-world' setting of corporate websites and blogs, as opposed to the 'simulated' setting of a television series.

The linguistic choices used by the fashion bloggers to encode their perceptions of brand identity reflect a much broader range of meanings than those found on the corresponding corporate websites, which seems to capture their unique social and interactional experience in the blogosphere. Following Sarangi (1998), the distinctive adjectives used by the bloggers to express their perceptions of brand identity also seem to have a parallel function, i.e., the construction of a self-identity as highly informed and opinionated commentators within the fashion discourse community.

4. Concluding Remarks

This analysis has offered some insights into how brand identity emerges in fashion discourse, and how it is recontextualized as it shifts from the expert professional communications of fashion houses to the social interactions of lay fashion bloggers. The study was confined to only three cases and should therefore be seen as exploratory in nature. However, the exhaustive analysis of adjectives as expressions of brand identity performed on a relatively limited amount of data nonetheless succeeded in providing some answers to the three research questions posed at the outset. With reference to the first, the analysis of texts collected from the corporate websites of the three brands revealed a wide range of descriptive and evaluative adjectives used to encode and promote the desired brand identity. Across the three corporate datasets, the type of adjectives that emerged were very much in line with previous work by Aaker (1997) that identified key facets of brand identity. In addition to many common adjectives, each brand also presented some distinctive items that communicate unique facets of identity with respect to their competitors. Concerning the second research question, a comparative analysis of the adjectives in the corporate datasets vs. the corresponding blog datasets indicated a relatively high degree of alignment between company-defined and consumer-perceived brand identity. This result suggests that all three brands have been successful in communicating brand identity to their consumers and reinforces their status as competitors within the same market.

The recontextualization of brand identity from the expert producer to the lay consumer was addressed by the third research question. Comparative qualitative analysis of common adjectives between the corporate and the blog datasets provided some evidence of this phenomenon. More specifically, in comparison with the professional writers of the corporate website texts, the fashion bloggers used adjectives that added new and innovative meanings that went well beyond the company-defined attributes. Moreover, the bloggers use of adjectives to express their perceptions of brand identity seemed to reflect a self-ascribed role as knowledgeable and highly articulate commentators in the fashion world. In other words, they exploited the blogs to construct a self-identity and position themselves within the 'virtual' interactional setting (Sarangi 1998). The important role of ICT in the recontextualization of meanings must also not be overlooked. As noted by Calsamiglia and van Dijk (2004), the media can have a strong impact on the transformation of knowledge from one context to another. Blogs represent a new form of media that can be accessed by vast numbers of people around the world, thus greatly enhancing possibilities for recontextualization.

The type of research undertaken in this study could be expanded by focusing on other types of attributes that may play an important role in the definition and perception of brand identity. As briefly mentioned in the discussion of the findings, the adjective *Italian* was used by companies to define their brands and was also perceived by consumers. This transversal presence suggests that cultural perceptions play an important role in brand identity. It would be interesting to analyze brand identity from a cross-cultural perspective, using textual data collected for brands of various national origins. This could shed light on the relative importance of cultural aspects of brand identity in an increasingly globalized world of consumers. An analysis of brands that target different types of fashion brands beyond the well-established luxury sector (e.g., retail or emerging brands) would also be worthwhile to show how conventional facets of brand identity may be recontextualized in diverse markets.

On a practical level, the findings of this study can be useful in the context of marketing and brand management. Traditionally, marketing professionals have relied on instruments such as focus groups, questionnaires and interviews to procure brand-related information. However, analyzing linguistic data from authentic online sources with relatively user-friendly corpus techniques offers advantages to better monitor and understand fast-changing consumer attitudes and opinions. As an initial step, they could first analyze their own marketing communications to ensure that the desired brand identity is actually emerging and then make any necessary adjustments. They could also analyze consumer-produced online texts to determine which facets of brand identity are perceived most favorably in order to reinforce or reshape the company-defined brand identity. Professionals may also be interested in analyzing the brand-related communications of their competitors which can be easily collected from freely available digital platforms. All of these sources of business intelligence can be extremely useful when making strategic choices about brand management, and thus help companies to become more successful.

References

Aaker, Jennifer L. 1997. Dimensions of brand personality. *Journal of Marketing Research* XXXIV. 347-356.

Alejo González, Rafael. 2005. Textual metadiscourse in commercial websites. *Ibérica* 9. 33-52.

Argenti, Paul A. 2009. *Corporate Communication. Fifth Edition*. New York, NY: McGraw-Hill.

Belasen, Alan T. 2008. *The Theory and Practice of Corporate Communication: A Competing Values Perspective.* Thousand Oaks, CA: Sage Publications.

Bernstein, Basil B. 2003. *The Structuring of Pedagogic Discourse. Vol. IV. Class, Codes and Control*. London/New York: Routledge.

Calsamiglia, Helena & Teun A. van Dijk. 2004. Popularization discourse and knowledge about the genome. *Discourse & Society* 15. 4. 369-389.

Catenaccio, Paola. 2006. 'Looking beyond today's headlines': The Enron crisis from press release to media coverage. In Marina Bondi & Julia Bamford (eds.), *Managing Interaction in Professional Discourse. Intercultural and Interdiscoursal Perspectives*. Rome: Officina Edizioni. 159-172.

Cova, Bernard. 1997. Community and consumption: Towards a definition of the linking value of product or services. *European Journal of Marketing* 31. 3/4. 297-316.

Garside, Roger & Nicholas Smith. 1997. A hybrid grammatical tagger: CLAWS4. In Roger Garside, Geoffrey N. Leech & Tony McEnery (eds.), *Corpus Annotation: Linguistic Information from Computer Text Corpora*. London: Longman. 102-121.

Gumperz, John J. 1992. Contextualization and understanding. In Alessandro Duranti & Charles Goodwin (eds.), *Rethinking Context: Language as An interactive Phenomenon*. Cambridge: Cambridge University Press. 229-252.

Keller, Kevin L. 2003. Brand Synthesis: The Multidimensionality of Brand Knowledge. *The Journal of Consumer Research* 29. 4. 595-600.

Linell, Per. 1998. *Approaching Dialogue: Talk, Interaction and Contexts in Dialogical Perspectives*. Amsterdam/Philadelphia: John Benjamins.

—. 2009. *Rethinking Language, Mind, and World Dialogically: Interactional and Contextual Theories of Human Sense-Making*. Charlotte, NC: Information Age Publishing.

Martin, James R. & Peter R. R. White, 2005. *The Language of Evaluation. Appraisal in English*. Houndsmills, Basingstoke: Palgrave MacMillan.

Miller, Carol R.& Dawn Shepherd. 2004. Blogging as social action: A genre analysis of the weblog. *Into The Blogosphere: Rhetoric, Community, and Culture of Weblogs*. http://Blog.Lib.Umn.Edu/Blogosphere/Blogging_as_Social_Action_Pf.Html.

Muniz, Albert M., Jr. & Thomas C. O'Guinn. 2001. Brand community. *Journal of Consumer Research* 27. 4. 412-432.

Puschmann, Cornelius. 2013. Blogging. In Susan C. Herring, Dieter Stein & Tuija Virtanen (eds.), *Pragmatics of Computer-Mediated Communication*. Berlin/New York: De Gruyter. 83-108.

Rickman, Tracy Anna & Robert M. Cosenza. 2007. The changing digital dynamics of multichannel marketing. The feasibility for the weblog: Text mining approach for fast fashion trending. *Journal of Fashion Marketing and Management* 11. 4. 606-621.

Salvi, Rita, Judith Turnbull & Alessandra Pontesilli. 2007. The English of companies online: National identity and global culture. In Julia Bamford & Rita Salvi (eds.), *Business Discourse: Language at Work*. Rome: Aracne. 9-45.

Sarangi, Srikant. 1998. Rethinking recontextualization in professional discourse: An epilogue. *Text* 18. 2. 301-318.

Scott, Mike. 2010. *WordSmith Tools Version 5.0*. Liverpool: Lexical Analysis Software.

Szmigin, Isabelle, Louise Canning & Alexander E. Reppel. 2005. Online community: Enhancing the relationship marketing concept through customer bonding. *International Journal of Service Industry Management* 16. 5. 480-496.

Temporal, Paul. 2002. Corporate identity, brand identity and brand image. http://www.brandingasia.com/columns/Temporal10.Htm.

Thomas, Jane B., Cara Okleshen Peters & Holly Tolson. 2007. An exploratory investigation of the virtual community Myspace.Com. What are consumers saying about fashion? *Journal of Fashion Marketing and Management* 11. 4. 587-603.

Thomas, Pete. 2003. The recontextualization of management: Adiscourse-based approach to Analysing the development of management thinking. *Journal of Management Studies* 40. 4. 775-801.

Thompson Craig J. & Diana L. Haytko. 1997. Speaking of fashion: Consumers' uses of fashion discourses and the appropriation of countervailing cultural meanings. *Journal of Consumer Research* 24. 1. 15-42.

Wodak, Ruth. 2011. *The Discourse of Politics in Action. Politics as Usual*. Houndmills, Basingstoke: Palgrave Macmillan.

Xun, Jiyao & Jonathan Reynolds. 2010. Applying netnography to market research: The case of the online Forum. *Journal of Targeting, Measurement and Analysis for Marketing* 18. 1. 17-31.

SECTION V:

EMPOWERING THE AUDIENCE

"I'M NOT AN EXPERT": LAY KNOWLEDGE, ITS CONSTRUCTION AND DISSEMINATION IN PERSONAL WEBLOGS

PETER SCHILDHAUER
UNIVERSITY OF HALLE-WITTENBERG
BIELEFELD UNIVERSITY, GERMANY

Abstract: While many knowledge dissemination studies focus on expert-lay people constellations, this paper emphasises the lay people sphere. It draws on the concept of lay theories as a framework to analyse the textual construction of lay knowledge. The paper argues that the construction and dissemination of lay knowledge plays a central role for the online genre *personal weblog* and presents results of the mainly qualitative analysis of a diachronic blog corpus. From a macro-perspective on blog postings, the paper shows that a dual structure of narrating and reflecting on personal experiences is a key pattern in this respect; the analysis of underlying and explicit IF-THEN relations as well as evidentiality markers complements these results on a micro-level. Furthermore, the paper argues that the textually constructed lay knowledge is disseminated intentionally and serves both explanatory and instructive purposes. A case study of a personal weblog which in its entirety constructs a complex lay theory and competes explicitly with expert theories rounds up the paper and shows how far the genre personal weblog can be carried in terms of lay knowledge construction and dissemination.

1. Introduction[1]

"What if *everyone* wrote about their *issues*. We could all *learn* from each other. […] We could grow more quickly, accomplish more in our lives, live more richly, have more fun." (Dave Winer 1995, in Rosenberg 2009:53; emphasis added, P.S.). When Dave Winer, a key figure of the earliest years of blogging, wrote these lines in 1995, he could not know that only a few years later, countless bloggers would do exactly that: they

[1] I would like to thank my colleagues Jana Pflaeging and Alexander Brock, the two anonymous reviewers and Davide Mazzi (CLAVIER 13) for their valuable comments on earlier drafts of this paper.

would write about their issues not only to grow themselves but also to let others profit from their so-called *issues*.

A keyword Winer uses is *learn*, which situates blogging in the context of knowledge dissemination. Not surprisingly, blogs have been investigated under this particular perspective, currently with a focus on research- and science blogs. However, Winer's *everyone* includes many more than just (professional) experts disseminating knowledge about *their [academic] issues* to the lay public. Winer's *everyone* also comprises those bloggers who write about *(everyday) issues* and non-professionally share their experiences, views and insights. Can this also be termed *Knowledge Dissemination* (*KD*)? In this paper, I will argue that these practices can indeed be described as knowledge dissemination practices. I will draw on the theoretical framework of lay theories and investigate the blog-genre *personal weblog* through this lens.

This paper is arranged as follows: Section 2 will review research on blogs and KD, thus defining and underlining the relevance of investigating (i) lay knowledge dissemination with respect to (ii) the personal weblog genre, and stating my research questions. Section 3introduces the diachronic blog corpus this study is based on and gives an outline of my methodology. Sections 4 and 5 will present qualitative analyses of rather simple lay theories which are put to explanatory and instructive use, respectively. Section 6 analyses *Compassionate Council* (http://tinyurl.com/council-pb) – a personal weblog which not only constructs a complex lay theory of the human psyche but also explicitly competes with expert theories.[2] Section 7 draws conclusions regarding the research questions.

2. Blogs and Knowledge Dissemination

2.1. Knowledge- and Science Blogs

Blogs have been the subject of intensive research for over 10 years now. As far as their role in the dissemination of knowledge is concerned, research so far has focused mainly on two aspects. Firstly, some studies pursue questions of how blogs can be used for knowledge production, organization and management in professional contexts. Blogs which are used in this respect have been labelled termed *k-logs* (for knowledge log) by Herring and associates (Herring et al. 2004, 2005, 2006). Röll (2004)

---

[2] In the author's words, he is not an expert nor does he "hide behind childish stories of superiority, spiritual, or otherwise" (compassionatecouncil.blogspot.co.uk/2007_09_01_archive.html).

and, more recently, Efimova (2009) follow this line of research. Both focus on the uses and possible benefits of blogs for knowledge workers. Efimova(2009, Chapter 3), for instance, reports on "blogging PhD ideas" and "the weblog as a personal knowledge base" but also investigates "employee blogging at Microsoft" (Efimova 2009, Chapter 6). In like manner, Röll's work is primarily located in a professional rather than a private sphere.

Secondly, we can perceive a growing interest in the role blogs play as a medium of knowledge-mediation at the intersection of two social systems: the *Academia* on the one hand and the *lay* public on the other. The interest in those science blogs, in the motives of both their authors and readers as well as discursive strategies of disseminating (academic) expert knowledge out of the ivory tower, is probably particularly fuelled by the growing pressure on members of the academic world to make their knowledge publicly accessible.[3]

2.2. The Paradigm of KD Studies

The scholarly interest in science blogs is in line with the general paradigm of KD studies. Works in this field investigate how "expert" knowledge, which is produced in one social sphere of our "post-modern knowledge society" (Kastberg 2007:9), is disseminated to the public sphere of lay people. They investigate how specific genres and/or discursive strategies are employed to achieve this aim (see, e.g., Gülich 2003; Wichter & Antos 2001). Others decidedly address questions of how this transfer can be optimized (for one, Antos et al. 2005). Traditionally, the roles of experts and laypeople are evoked and connected to a knowledge asymmetry between the knowing expert and the layperson. The term knowledge, central to these works, shows many facets.[4] The definition of knowledge "in pragmatic terms, [...] as beliefs that are shared by epistemic communities" (Calsamigilia & van Dijk 2004:373) seems to be the preferred one in discourse studies. Knowledge is thus defined as being bound to a particular social sphere, which in turn is characterized by its focus on knowledge.

Even though this focus is highly relevant in a "hyper-complex" (Kastberg 2007:11) society, I would like to point out some problematic

---

[3] For a review of current research, see Puschmann & Mahrt (2012: 171-179); cf. also Fritz & Bader (2010), Fritz (2011, 2013), Kjellberg (2009), Luzón (2013), Mauranen (2013).

[4] For an overview of several perspectives on knowledge as a concept, see Antos (2005:346-359).

aspects: to begin with, the roles of experts and laypeople are problematic concepts in themselves (Puschmann & Mahrt 2012:171-172; Baderschneider & Kessel 2010:13). Secondly, exclusively focusing research on the expert-lay people divide overlooks the fact that knowledge can be and doubtlessly is also communicated among the laypeople themselves (Baderschneider & Kessel 2010:13; see also Antos 1996, 2005:346).

2.3. Lay Knowledge and Lay Theories

This becomes especially obvious when knowledge is not defined in the rather narrow terms mentioned above but, rather, as the sum of an individual's subjectively important mental representations (Antos 2005:343-345; Ballod 2007:159). As soon as knowledge is understood in these broad terms, two major questions arise:

(1) Where does this knowledge come from and how can it be better understood and characterized?
(2) If this knowledge is communicated, how does this happen?

As far as Q1 is concerned, I cannot go into much detail here but refer the interested reader to Kruglanski (1990) and Kruglanski et al. (2010) on lay epistemics. However, some part of the knowledge lay people possess can be captured in social sciences and applied linguistics via recourse to the notion of *lay theories* (or *subjective theories*; see Groeben 1988). In essence, lay theories are supposed to arise directly from everyday experience. They do not merely accumulate concepts (in the sense of knowing that A exists) but are rather characterised by relating different concepts to one another, often by establishing *IF-THEN*-relations (e.g. *IF I have A, I can do B*). This underlying conditional can be characterised as *inferential conditional* according to Declerck and Reed (2001:284): It takes the form *IF +p THEN +q*, where *p* "is, or forms part of, the epistemological basis for inferring the truth of Q" (Declerck & Reed 2001:291). For instance, the concepts KNIFE and CUTTING VEGETABLES can be related by *IF I have a knife THEN I can cut vegetables*, where the premise *p* includes the knowledge about knives as sharp kitchen tools. Lay theories are aimed at explanation and prediction (as are scientific theories) but they are also particularly relevant for guiding actions in specific situations.

Lay theories show striking analogies to scientific (expert) theories (Antos 1996:28-32; Kruglanski 1990:192). However, they differ fundamentally from expert theories in that they lack a formalised methodology and tend to be resistant to falsification (Antos 1996:32-34).

2.4. Texts, Knowledge Construction and Dissemination

With regard to the communication of knowledge in general and lay knowledge in particular (Q2), texts play a decisive role. On the one hand, they are a means of representing knowledge in the form of semiotic representations (Antos 1997:47-49). On the other hand, these semiotic representations are a result of the transformation of mental structures into the particular structures of the chosen semiotic system – e.g. the linear structure of language. This is what *text production* is about. These transformation processes can lead to combining concepts in innovative ways, changing perspectives on established knowledge structures and even to the emergence of new ideas. Producing texts is therefore tightly linked to knowledge *evolution* (Antos 1997:52; see also Hayes 1996; Kohanyi 2009). This seems to be particularly true for texts produced with a focus on the writing process – e.g. in *creative writing* settings or when texts are produced as a relaxing free-time activity (Perry 2009; Runco 2009).

2.5. *Personal Weblogs* and Lay Knowledge

The *personal weblog* as a blog-genre is (among others) defined by being situated in a private sphere of leisure time and hobby writing (Lomborg 2009, 2014:74-75; Schildhauer 2014:197-198). Taking into consideration what was said in Sections 2.3 and 2.4, this genre is therefore of special interest to the present study.

Furthermore, sharing personal experiences has been identified as one of the most prominent functions of this genre in the diachronic study outlined in Schildhauer (2013). Accordingly, the genre personal weblog has been assumed to partly continue traditions connected to diary- and journal writing (Balakina 2011:29-33; Herring & Paolillo 2006:454; Karlsson 2006:8-9; Kitzmann 2003; Kitzmann 2004:58-59; McNeill 2009:147; Schildhauer 2014:397-399; van Dijck 2004; Yus 2011:97) and thus to be connected with genres which are stereotypically associated with chronicling and reflecting on personal experiences.

Considering (i) the importance of personal experiences both for lay theories and personal weblogs and (ii) the decisive role of (on-going) text production for the construction of lay theories (Section 2.4), it seems plausible to examine the role played by the construction and dissemination of lay knowledge with regard to this genre. To my knowledge, personal weblogs have not been researched under this specific perspective yet. Myers's (2010) discourse study of blogs is an exception: His remarks on evidentiality markers in blogs are highly relevant to the analysis of knowledge construction and dissemination in personal weblogs. Markers of induction (Myers 2010:116) such as the verbs *find* and *realize* have proved to be an important linguistic marker of processes of lay knowledge construction (see also Chafe 1986).

2.6. Research Questions

The aim of the present study is to examine the role that both the construction and the dissemination of lay knowledge play with regard to the genre *personal weblog*. This general aim is based on the hypothesis that personal weblogs as an everyday genre – partly continuing traditions of the diary and the journal – naturally lend themselves to activities such as making sense of the world around us and sharing these insights with others. A primarily qualitative approach is taken to answer the following research questions, which are entailed by the general aim of the study:

Q1. How is the construction of lay theories reflected in the macro-linguistic structure of personal weblog postings, for instance regarding functional stages and topic treatment?
Q2. What linguistic markers occur on a micro-structural level?
Q3. Can we assume that this knowledge is also intentionally disseminated to an audience rather than merely recorded for the author's own sake? If yes, what strategies are employed in order to stress the relevance of the constructed lay knowledge beyond the individual level?
Q4. How can the communicative purpose of presenting lay knowledge in personal weblogs be characterised (e.g. instructing the reader)?
Q5. How central is the construction and dissemination of lay knowledge to personal weblogs as a genre?

3. Study Design

3.1. Corpus

The present study is based on the DIAchronic BLOg Corpus (*DIABLOC*), which was compiled using the *Internet Archive* (www.archive.org) and applying an ethno-category based approach. Table 1 provides an outline of corpus structure and size.

Tab. 1: The *DIABLOC* (available at http://www.pschildhauer.com)

			BLOG-PAGES	POSTINGS
Period I: *Weblogs*		1997-2000	30	775
PERIOD II: *PERSONAL WEBLOGS*	**II.A**	2002-2005	100	1091
	II.B	2006-2008	100	786
	II.C	2009-2012	100	901
		Total:	330	3553

Part I contains 30 of the earliest *weblogs* (1997-2000), which form the root of the subsequent differentiation of several more specific weblog genres. In this group, we find "celebrities" of the first blogging community such as Dave Winer's *Scripting News* and Jessie James Garrett's *Infoshift*. In order to compile these texts, I used Garret's listing of *ye olde school*-weblogs as well as Cameron Barrett's blog roll on his weblog *Camworld,* which the author used to collect "other sites like his" (Blood 2000). Both sources taken together provide a useful gateway to the weblogs of the first-generation community.

Part II assembles 300 specimens of the genre *personal weblog*. These texts were compiled by using the oldest blog directory available – the *Globe of Blogs* (http://www.globeofblogs.com). This directory was founded in 2002 and contains a system of categories that authors can use in order to classify their blogs. One meta-category is termed *Personal Weblog*. I entered the list pages contained in this category via the Internet Archive. The prospective corpus texts were put to several tests in order to ensure the validity of each text for the respective period. The corpus contains the homepage of each blog with the respective postings.[5]

3.2. Method

In the current paper I availed myself of the results of a previous study on the textual functions of personal weblog postings (Schildhauer 2013) as a starting point. This study resulted in categories which are primarily defined by functional but also by structural characteristics. They are prototypically organised and exhibit overlaps with neighbouring categories. Labelled according to the terminology prevalent in the blogging community, central categories include *Filter*, *Update*, and *Sharing Experience*

[5] See Schildhauer (2014:97-114) for more on DIABLOC's compilation.

(Schildhauer 2013:123-126). I think of these categories as types of entries rather than types of blogs as we can often find two or three of them on one blog. In order to examine their degree of typicality of the personal weblog, the percentage of blogs in my corpus which exhibit a particular category was calculated. The number of postings of a particular category in each blog was not relevant to this analysis: A category was counted as "exhibited" when the respective blog contained one or more instances. In case of postings which had to be assigned to two (overlapping) categories, both were coded.

For the present study, I re-examined two categories which can be assumed to be (i) highly typical of the genre personal weblog and (ii) of special relevance with respect to the construction and dissemination of lay knowledge: *Sharing Experience* and *Giving Advice*. The Filter-category, i.e. the presentation of annotated lists of web sources, has been excluded from the present study not because it was irrelevant for the study of knowledge dissemination but because it focuses on accumulating and managing *expert* knowledge rather than lay knowledge as defined above. I paid special attention to both the rhetorical macro-structure of the postings in question and their linguistic micro-structure. I also focused on a single personal weblog which turned out to be exceptional in my corpus and which illustrates how far the personal weblog can be carried in terms of lay knowledge construction and dissemination.

4. Simple Lay Theories and their Dissemination in Personal Weblogs

4.1. Making Sense of the World

A considerable number of postings in my corpus is dedicated to the recording and reflection of personal experiences. Postings of the category *Sharing Experience* spread rapidly in the course of the transition from period I to period II. Throughout period II, the category can be found in more than 60% of the personal weblogs in my corpus. It can therefore be considered particularly typical of the genre.

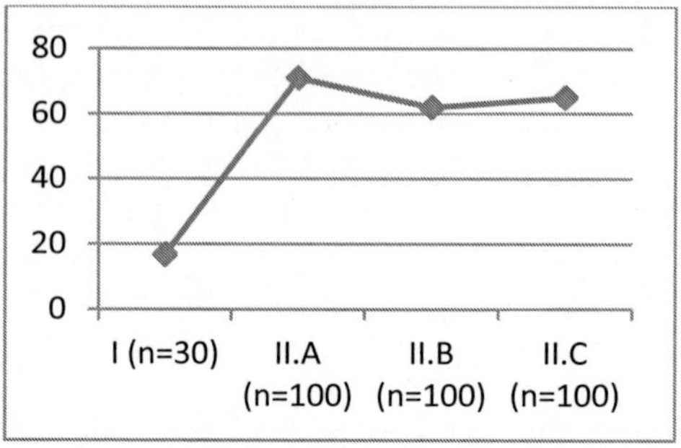

Fig. 1: Blogs exhibiting *Sharing Experience*

The classical weblog of the first period typically collected and commented on web-based sources. In other words, a classical weblog accumulated and shared expert knowledge and won their authors an expert reputation in a certain field (Blood 2002:12-14). Juxtapositions such as "These are diaries, not Weblogs; Weblogs are about links" (Blood 2004:54) illustrate that some first-community bloggers looked down on blogs predominantly sharing personal experiences.

However, it is already among the lists of links in some *classical* period I-weblogs where we find scattered postings (or sections of postings) reflecting on the daily, as in the following example from Brigitte Eaton's *EatonWeb* (period I):[6]

(1) 2.28.00
some more musing about living online. i was in the salon on saturday waiting for my sister to get done with a client (so she could dye my hair purple), and sat talking to my step-mom, who was also waiting for my sister to get done with the paying client. anyway, she mentioned that it was surprising that it hadn't rained that much today, i responded with "oh, is there supposed be a storm coming in?". when she said yes, it hit me that other people tune in to the weather and get a forecast of what the weather will be like for the next couple days. i just walk out my door and see what it's like. the weather doesn't matter online. 22:14 (*EatonWeb*, period I: http://tinyurl.com/eatonweb)

[6] This and the following examples have not been edited in any way beyond adapting font type, size and colour as well as layout features to the conventions of this paper.

The passage is introduced by *Some more musing about living online*, which sets a topical focus beyond the narration of a subjectively important event. The noun *musing* also signals an intention beyond the mere narrative action. In the first section, the event is narrated – an everyday conversation at the hairdresser's about the weather. Apparently we deal with a posting of the kind which are the reason why "[f]rom their earliest days, blogs were dismissed as a mundane form in which people told us, pointlessly, what they had for lunch" (Rosenberg 2010).

There is more to this posting, however: the second section serves as a reflection of this every-day experience on two levels. Firstly, the experience is evaluated on a personal level, indicated by the use of first-person pronouns: *it hit me that other people tune in*; *I just walk out my door*. Secondly, there is a more general level: *The weather doesn't matter online*. The partial recurrence of the key word *living online* in the last sentence forms a cohesive frame which connects introduction and conclusion of the posting. The posting thus exhibits a dual structure, moving from a narrative part to a reflection passage. The caesura between both parts is marked by a shift from past to present tense: *it hit me* [past tense] *that other people tune in to the weather* [present tense].

A chain of implicit IF-THEN deductions underlies the reflection part: IF the author's step mom can answer with *Yes* to the question about the storm, THEN she must be convinced to possess adequate evidence for saying so (cf. Grice 1975:46); IF her step-mom can be sure about what the weather will be like, THEN she will probably know the weather forecast; IF the author does not know about the weather, THEN it is because of her leading a life centred on online-events and guided by other priorities. This insight in the difference between two ways of life can be considered a simple lay theory: it stems directly from personal experience, is therefore subjectively important, and apparently based on implicit IF-THEN relations.[7]

[7] Notice that I have tried to adapt Declerck & Reed (2001) to my purposes and then model the deduction process in rather small steps, i.e. I tried to limit the number of premises additional to the one expressed by the *p* clause. However, I would like to point out that this model serves illustrative purposes only and abstracts away from a number of implicit premises for matters of convenience. For instance, the first two IF-THEN relations are rich in premises as they presuppose Grice's (1975) Cooperative Principle and the Quality Maxim in particular, which in turn entail complex sets of assumptions about human communicative behaviour. The inferential conditionals presented here can therefore be characterised as "involving an inferential bridge" (Declerck & Reed 2001:290) and extrapolating both "from a

The author did not keep her lay theory to herself but published it online. Efimova (2009:81) states plausibly: "It is reasonable to assume that those who do not want their words to be read by a broad audience would use another medium [and not the blog, P.S.]." The topical announcement at the beginning of the passage "Some more musing about living online" can also be understood as an instance of recipient design: following Grice's (1975:46) Maxim of Relevance, Brigitte Eaton sets the topical frame for the post. Those who are interested in reflections on living online may read it; others will probably not. A network of cohesive ties such as recurrences (*client*, *sister*) and junctions (*when*) render the passage coherent. It is therefore possible to view this passage not only as an instance of recording experiences and constructing lay knowledge, but also one of disseminating this knowledge to readers interested in similar topics (Myers 2010:93; Puschmann 2013:86; Schildhauer 2014:239).

In the context of the history of the genre *personal weblog*, the posting from *EatonWeb* provides an early example, actually pre-dating the emergence of the personal weblog as a distinct genre. As shown in diagram 1 above, the category *Sharing Experience* constitutes an integral part of the personal weblog from period II.A onwards. Most interestingly, the dual pattern of narration and reflection observed in the *EatonWeb*-example stabilises, as the following example from period II.A illustrates:[8]

(2) Tuesday, August 16, 2005
Looking for a place to live shouldn't be difficult. I've found that to be sheer myth.
I've recently been looking for a house or townhouse to rent. [...] My husband's favorite is when they ask for no pets or smoking. It's a really good rule except when you take a tour they have a cat or dog and smoke!! I guess that rule doesn't apply to them. If it's money they want, they ask for a lot of it!!
I've realized there is no easy way to look for a place to live. You will waste time and money. I think the real truth is that you need divine intervention or lot's of luck!! (*Mysteries of M*, period II.A: http://tinyurl.com/mysteries-pb)

---

general pattern" (ibid.:292) and "via inferential bridges" (ibid.:292-294). In like manner, this appears to hold true for the IF-THEN relations in examples (2) to (5).

[8] As every pattern leaves room for variation, not all *Sharing Experience* postings show an elaborated reflection section. Some only hint at a reflection of the experiences narrated, others only exhibit reflections on an individual and not on a more general level.

Example (2) from the personal weblog *Mysteries of M* also begins with a topical introduction (*Looking for a place to live*) similar to the opening of example (1). The next sentence, however, already provides a first conclusion drawn from the personal experiences still to be narrated, which is indicated by the verb *find* as a marker of inductive evidentiality (Myers 2010:115-116). In what follows, the author provides a summary of several house viewings, which already involves generalisations of reoccurring incidents (*My husband's favorite is when they[...]*) and thus provides evidence of some reflection on the narrated events. Additionally, example (2) provides a 'pure' reflection passage such as the one in example (1). Interestingly, it is also marked by the (grammatically altered) recurrence of the topical key phrase *Looking for a place to live*, which connects introduction and conclusion. The reflection is introduced by the lexical verb *realize*, which is also an indicator of inductive evidentiality. The announcement of *the real truth* supports the assumption that the reflection is carried out on a general level, not an individual one, stressing the relevance of the knowledge beyond the individual author-centred level. The dual structure from example (1) is thus also underlying example (2). At the same time, example (2) also illustrates the potential for variation within the dual-structure-pattern. Underlying IF-THEN relations can also be detected in this example. For instance, they also form the basis for the final reflection: IF looking for a place to live is that hard, THEN you need divine intervention or lots of luck.

The second-person pronoun used in the final passage can be interpreted in two different ways: In its general reading, it supports the impression of a reflection carried out on a more general rather than an individual level. It could, however, also be read as directly addressing the audience. In both cases, I think it is reasonable to assume that (i) lay knowledge in form of a simple lay theory is constructed and (ii) this knowledge is intentionally disseminated to an interested readership (possibly addressed directly in the last paragraph).

As both (1) and (2) use assertive speech acts exclusively, we can assume that the lay theories presented in these postings are primarily aimed at making sense of personal experiences and at offering explanations and predictions. In the next section, I will turn to postings aimed at providing guidance for future actions.

4.2. Guiding Future Actions

While the postings in (1) and (2) are aimed at making sense of personal experiences, other postings and even entire blogs in the corpus are dedicated to giving advice on a variety of topics. The percentage of personal weblogs containing posts of this function in general increases continuously over the periods of the corpus:

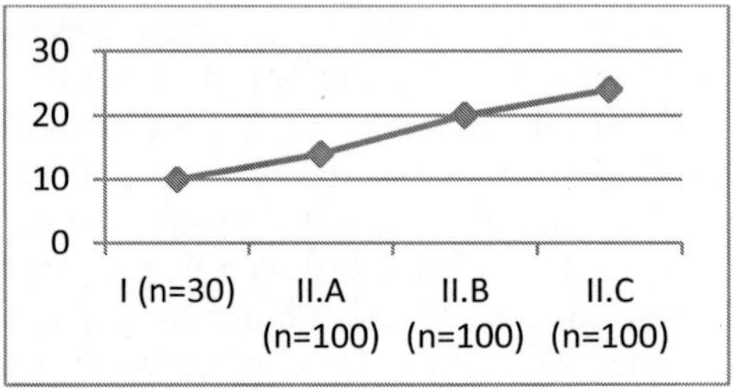

Fig. 2: Blogs exhibiting *Giving Advice*

In the context of my paper's focus on the communication of knowledge among lay people, postings of the category *Giving Advice* such as the following are interesting:

(3) I decided that if I went into high school the same way I did last year, I was going to be more fucked then my computer. I realized I needed a plan...and a list. Oh how I love making lists. Anyway, I started to look around me and realize some things. Like, I never say, "Hi" first and never offer hugs...and I never call my friends just to talk...that I never make plans. Things of that nature...as the govenator would say. So I made a list. Well, I actually made commandments. Sorry to all you easily offended Catholics there. I suppose that I could keep this list to myself, but where's the fun in that...so here goes nothing.
THE TEN COMMANDMENTS
...of social behavior in high school
1. Walk with absolute confidence
2. Smile and look people in the eyes
3. Initiate conversation
4. Know your friends, know your enemies
5. Hug and be hugged
6. Do things you sometimes don't want to do
7. Flirt
8. Make your own luck
9. Don't let what other people say get to you
10. Never give up, never! (*Life of L*, period II.A: http://tinyurl.com/life-l-pb)

The blog posting in (3) is also based on personal experiences as examples (1) and (2),but puts the reflection section at the beginning, which can be inferred by the use of verbs like *decide* and *realize* – the latter has already been described as evidentiality marker in example (2). The author's problematic life at high school has been the subject of numerous blog postings before. The author can therefore build on shared knowledge accumulated via several blog posts. Obviously, the post presented here relates the results of an extended reflection phase taking into account all the experiences narrated in previous posts and beyond. The dual structure of narration and reflection is thus extended beyond the individual post in this example, with cohesive devices such as the NP *last year* underlining the connection with previous postings.

Other than (1) and (2), for which only *underlying* IF-THEN relations could be detected, (3) opens with an explicit conditional. The conditional is part of a *that*-clause introduced by the verb *decide*. The past tense in the *if*-clause is therefore most likely not to be interpreted as a hypothetical past (Quirk et al. 1985:1010) but as the result of a backshift of tenses typical of reported speech (ibid.:1026).[9] The conditional has the logic structure *+p* then *+q* and can therefore be described as *direct inferential* (Declerck & Reed 2001:285-287), with the verb *decide* lexicalising "the inferential speech act" (ibid.:287).

Other than the reconstructed underlying IF-THEN relations in (1) and (2), however, the opening conditional of (3) refers to a specific *upcoming* situation. Therefore, it also carries the reading of *actualization-triggering P-clauses* with a "'cause and effect' connotation: the actualization of the P-situation [*if*-clause, P.S.] triggers the actualization of the Q-situation [matrix clause, P.S.]" (Declerck & Reed 2001:278).[10] In the specific case, actually *going into high school the same way I did last year* will lead to (i.e. actualize) the state of being *fucked up*. From a pragmatic point of view, then, the opening conditional in (3) becomes part of an argumentative strategy, which we can label *pragmatic argumentation* following van Eemeren et al. (2007:166): the contents that follow are

[9] This interpretation is supported by the fact that the matrix clause does not contain a past modal (Quirk et al. 1985: 1010).

[10] Declerck and Reed (2001: 284) point out the different shades of meaning of actualizing and inferential conditionals: "Inferential conditionals differ from actualization-conditioning P-clauses in that they are concerned with the validity of an inferential reasoning process involving both P and Q rather than with the relation between the actualization of the P-situation and that of the Q-situation." On the basis of this differentiation, I would like to argue for the inferential reading of the underlying conditionals in (1) and (2) and favour the actualization reading of the opening sentence in (3) (which does not exclude that an inference based on experience underlies this conditional).

argued for on the basis of non-recommendable consequences – both in relation to the author *and* to a reader sharing similar experiences of failure in such a social context.

The list of *commandments* is obviously based on further IF-THEN relations of the kind 'IF you do not do X THEN you will not be socially successful at high school'. As is typical of commandments, the author's guidelines all contain a verb in the imperative mood – both in the positive (*Make your own luck*) and in the negative (*Never give up*). The tenth commandment is marked by an exclamation mark and seemingly contains both the most important guideline and the essence of the author's high school experiences.

Example (3) thus exhibits a special property that lay theories may have, namely their relevance as guidelines for (individual) action. The *commandments* certainly are of relevance to the author's own future actions.[11] As far as their relevance to others is concerned, however, the author seems to be unsure: she plays down the role her guidelines might play for others by referring to a merely entertaining function (*where's the fun in that*) and announcing her list as *here goes nothing*.

Other authors seem to be more confident concerning the relevance of their conclusions:

(4) Thursday, March 8, 2012
A warning
Okay, I admit it. I made a boo boo. I posted on the U.K. Amazon readers site by mistake. […] I got so many vicious replies, people accusing me of trying to sneak in self promotion (as if that's punishable by death), people reading the book samples and then saying how much they sucked, people posting on the forum calling me all kinds of horrible things. […]
My warning to all authors out there is to stay away from the Amazon forums altogether. It's not worth the little promotion you get with all the jerks surfing them who have nothing better to do than rip apart your self-esteem. […] (*Always Writing*, period II.C: http://tinyurl.com/writing-pb)

At first sight, the posting resembles those presented in examples (1) and (2) in that it follows the dual structure of narration and reflection in a rather prototypical way. First, the author confesses that he posted promotional links by accident on an Amazon readers' forum, receiving

[11] See Schildhauer (2014:43-44) for the analysis of another posting from this blog reporting the author's failure to follow the guidelines.

vicious replies in return. Second, the author draws conclusions, with the caesura being marked by a shift from past tense to present tense.

In the reflection passage, the author explicitly warns *all authors*. The use of directives instead of assertives has already been shown for example (3). In this case, however, the directive is not aimed at the author's self and is not presented as of doubtful relevance to the audience. Rather, the directive illocution is marked explicitly and decidedly addressed at a conceptualized audience of (fellow) authors. The warning constitutes the essence of a lay theory: It is grounded in personal experience, arises by via implicit IF-THEN relations of the kind *IF you get replies that vicious, it is better to stay away from these forums*, and – most importantly – is meant to guide future actions while showing concerns for fellow authors.

4.3. Interim Conclusion

In sum, the discussion so far has shown that postings in personal weblogs provide clear evidence of the construction and dissemination of lay theories: *personal experiences* are used to draw conclusions not only on an individual but also on a more general level by drawing on implicit IF-THEN relations. A dual structure of narration and reflection has been shown to be the typical pattern, with room for variation as illustrated by some of the examples. The dual structure probably also reflects the construction of lay knowledge in the writing process. In some cases, this mode of reasoning is made explicit by using markers of inductive evidentiality. The resulting lay theories either serve as explanations, making sense of personal experience, or as guidelines for future actions.

Their publication on the internet is an indicator of the fact that they are intentionally disseminated (Efimova 2009:81). There are, however, other signals such as providing a topical orientation, constructing a cohesive frame, addressing the audience explicitly as well as the use of illocutionary force-indicating devices which support the assumption of intentional dissemination of lay knowledge.

While the examples presented constitute rather simple lay theories which are focused on a quite limited set of experiences and IF-THEN relations, the next chapter will provide a case study of a rather complex lay theory aimed at explaining human nature in general.

5. Case Study: A Complex Lay Theory in *Compassionate Council*

The personal weblog *Compassionate Council* was most likely launched in July 2007 (http://tinyurl.com/council-pb).[12]As Table 2 shows, the blog-page contained in my corpus features postings from the second half of 2009. *Compassionate Council* was consequently grouped into period II.B.

Tab. 2: Postings on the Homepage of *Compassionate Council*

POSTING TITLE	DATE (2009)	TOKENS
Is There Any Such Thing As Total Freedom?	Fri, Oct 16	128
Accumulation is the Movement of Becoming: Part 11	Sat, Oct 10	788
Accumulation is the Movement of Becoming: A Prequel	Thu, Oct 8	723
The Individual is a Complex Movement of Mind.	Tue, Oct 6	787
Freedom and Responsibility.	Sun, Oct 4	657
Accumulation is the Movement of Becoming: Part 10.	Fri, Oct 2	644
The Inflexibility of Mind.	Mon, Aug 17	535
Accumulation is the Movement of Becoming: Part 9.	Fri, Aug 14	646

The blog-page presents only blurbs of the respective postings. However, all postings but the most recent one (Oct 16) could be accessed in their full version via the Internet Archive. The mean length of the postings fully archived is 682.86 tokens, which is considerably higher than the mean of all period II.B blogs in the corpus (269.51).

Posting titles are either formulated as hypotheses or as questions clearly delimiting a particular problem. Some postings on the homepage are obviously part of a series: *Accumulation is the Movement of Becoming*. Indeed, the personal weblog contains some other series, for instance *Thought Creates Time* and *The Root of all Suffering*. Series are frequently interrupted by independent posts such as *The Individual is a Complex Movement of Mind*. Assuming that the postings were published in the sequence of their production, this reflects a complex thinking process on several issues almost simultaneously.

A general topical focus can be detected: all of the postings deal with aspects of the human psyche including some philosophical asides. This observation is also supported by the label cloud (Cole 2010:11) in Figure

[12] The first posting contained in the archives of the blog and particularly a posting entitled *About* date from July 2007.

3, which contains words such as *consciousness*, *conditioning*, *awareness*, *thought*, *mind* and others:

Fig. 3: Label cloud of *Compassionate Council*

Similarly, a *WordSmith* analysis of the full versions of the postings listed above returns the following keywords: *movement*, *mind*, *memory*, *continuity*, *word*, *content*, *reality*, *accumulation*, *image* and *knowledge*.

Example (5), a blurb, provides an illustration:

(5) Accumulation is the Movement of Becoming: Part 9
We have been taking a brief look at the nature of time and now let us turn our attention to language, another aspect of thought. Language is an extraordinary ability of mind and one that gives the accumulating movement a powerful sense of permanence. For in the very nature of language lies duality, or the necessary existence of both a subject and an object. A sense of duality also arises with memory and perception, but as we have been saying, none function without all the others as well; it is one indivisible movement. (*Compassionate Council*, period II.B)

The beginning of the posting *We have been taking a brief look at* obviously serves as a connector to earlier postings of the series. The use of the pronoun *we* and expressions such as *we have been taking a brief look, now let us turn our attention to [...]* establishes stylistic similarity to academic discourse.[13] In contrast to the examples analysed so far, (5) does

[13] See Young (1994) on macro- and micro-features of university lectures. These include, among others, the use of inclusive *we* (Quirk et al. 1985:341) and

not contain any first-person singular pronoun. Indeed, a *WordSmith* frequency analysis revealed that *I* is only ranked 42nd with a frequency of 0.33%. In this, *Compassionate Council* sharply contrasts both with the *British National Corpus* (BNC, http://corpora.lancs.ac.uk/BNCweb/), where *I* ranks 12th, and every period of my corpus, where *I* ranks 7th (period I), 3rd (period II.C) and 2nd (periods II.A and II.B). Obviously, the narration of events with the author as subject is not as important as in the examples analysed in the previous section. Resemblance to academic genres is also found in a mean word length of 4.74, which, while clearly differing from the overall corpus values of period II.B (4.2), comes close to the 4.8 value that Biber (1988:255) gives for academic prose.

The recurrence of the key terms *language*, *accumulating movement* and *duality* in (5) creates a dense network of cohesive ties. The sentence-initial causal junction *for* suggests both an argumentative way of treating the topic and the fact that relations and dependencies between several concepts as parts of *one indivisible movement* are elaborated on. The label cloud (Figure 3), the overview of postings in Table 2, as well as the keyword- and frequency analyses, suggest that the entire personal weblog serves the purpose of creating a coherent theoretical construct which incorporates these scientific key concepts.

It is, however, rather unlikely that these terms are used with the meanings established in their scientific disciplines: *accumulation*, or *accumulating movement*, for instance, are defined in the context of the series as an activity of the mind aiming at gathering knowledge. Other terms receive their meaning in relation to this central concept. In (5), *Language*, for instance, is partly defined by its function to give a "sense of permanence" to the accumulating movement of the mind. This suggests that we can observe the formation of a theory defining its *own* axioms and central concepts as part of its own self-referential linguistic sub-system. Even though the author of *Compassionate Council* uses established scientific terms, he only adopts their signifiers and creates a competing signified for each of them.

The contents of a disclaimer posting published in September 2007 can be interpreted in the light of these observations:

---

directives/exhortatives such as *let us turn to* in (5), by which "the lecturer is alerting students about what is to come" (Young 1994:169). Hyland and Tse (2004:169) also mention endophoric markers such as *as we have been saying* in (5) as an important feature of metadiscourse in academic texts.

(6) Disclaimer: I Have No More, Or Less, Authority Than You.
I am blogging today to let you all know that I never speak or write with any more or less authority than you, the reader, have. I am not an expert, nor do I hide behind childish stories of superiority, spiritual, or otherwise. […] I am not here to distinguish myself from those who read my posts, nor am I here to teach or persuade you in any way. […] For it isn't actually authority I speak from, it's observation, and I promise you all, I will never deny what I directly observe. […] For authority, of any kind, is not the vehicle, direct observation is and nothing stands between you and direct observation. (*Compassionate Council*, period II.B, disclaimer posting 3 September 2007)

In sum, the disclaimer posting stresses the importance of direct observations and their reflections and rejects the author's role as an expert with any kind of exclusive authority: *nothing stands between you and direct observation*.

This claim seems to contrast with the academic style of (5). It also seems to contrast with the use of established scientific terms by the author, assigning new meanings to and establishing interrelations between them. However, I would like to argue that we can observe the emergence of a complex lay theory which arises from individual experience. It is designed to explicitly compete with and stand apart from scientific theories created in the expert domain(s) of society associated with *superiority*, *authority* and *teaching*. As pointed out for lay theories in general, the theory developed in *Compassionate Council* seems to be resistant to falsification as it is firmly grounded in the author's own observations, which are – quite naturally – hard to contradict and which the author *will never deny*.

The complex lay theory constructed in *Compassionate Council* is furthermore intentionally disseminated: the author assumes a readership for his postings (*those who read my posts*) and directly addresses them with *you, the reader*. As both author and readers start off from the same basis (*direct observation*), the author explicitly rejects the notion of a knowledge asymmetry. Even though *Compassionate Council* has been shown to sharply contrast with the typical personal weblogs in my corpus, it illustrates how the genre can be and is obviously used as a means of making sense of the world and sharing individual views with others.

6. Conclusions

This paper examined the role played by both the production and the dissemination of lay knowledge in personal weblogs. Lay knowledge has been defined as largely consisting of lay theories. In this final section, I would like to sum up my argument by returning to the research questions posed in Section 2.6:

Q1 *Macro-linguistic structure*: On a macro-structural level, the analysis revealed that a dual structure is a typical means of constructing lay theories in personal weblogs. More particularly, a narrative of a subjectively important event is followed by a reflection passage used to draw conclusions on an individual and often also on a more general level.

Q2 *Micro-linguistic structure*: The caesura between both parts is often mirrored in the linguistic micro-structure, e.g. in a shift of tenses from past to present. Both parts are linked by underlying IF-THEN relations. Markers of inductive evidentiality such as the verbs *find* and *realize* point to this type of reasoning.

Q3 *Intentionality and relevance*: Lay theories in personal weblog postings are intentionally disseminated, published online and directly addressed to an intended readership, as suggested by the following features: (i) meta-comments on the relevance of the contents for the readership, e.g. announcing *the real truth* in (2); (ii) cohesive devices, which are particularly apparent in (1); (iii) topical signals, e.g. *living online* in (1), *looking for a place to live* in (2), and the announcement of *A warning* in (4).

Q4 *Purpose*: Lay theories are used for both an explanatory and an instructive purpose.

Q5 *Genre perspective*: It seems plausible to assume that the construction and dissemination of lay knowledge in general plays a decisive role for the genre personal weblog. The case study on *Compassionate Council* has additionally shown that the personal weblog is not only used to construct simple lay theories based on daily experiences but also to build complex theoretical buildings which are explicitly contrasted with expert theories and their air of 'authority' and 'superiority'.

To conclude, personal weblogs as a genre serve the basic human need for understanding the world around us and sharing this knowledge with others – lay people like us.

References

Antos, Gerd. 1996. *Laien-Linguistik: Studien zu Sprach- und Kommunikationsproblemen im Alltag : am Beispiel von Sprachratgebern und Kommunikationstrainings*. Tübingen: Niemeyer.

—. 1997. Texte als Konstitutionsform von Wissen: Thesen zu einer evolutionstheoretischen Begründung der Textlinguistik. In Gerd Antos, Heike Tietz & Wolfgang Heinemann (eds.), *Die Zukunft der Textlinguistik: Traditionen, Transformationen, Trends*. Tübingen: Niemeyer. 43-63.

—. 2005. Die Rolle der Kommunikation bei der Konzeptualisierung von Wissensbegriffen. In Gerd Antos, Sigurd Wichter & Jörg Palm (eds.), *Wissenstransfer durch Sprache als gesellschaftliches Problem*. Frankfurt am Main: Peter Lang. 339-364.

Antos, Gerd, Sigurd Wichter & Jörg Palm (eds.). 2005. *Wissenstransfer durch Sprache als gesellschaftliches Problem*. Frankfurt am Main: Peter Lang.

Baderschneider, Nina & Katja Kessel. 2010. Laienlinguistik – Profilinguistik: Kommunikationsmodelle und Definitionen. In Albrecht Greule & Katja Kessel (eds.), *Linguistik zwischen Profis und Laien: Beiträge von Studierenden der Germanistik*. München: Meidenbauer. 9-23.

Balakina, Julia. 2011. *Anglicisms in Russian and German Blogs: A Comparative Analysis*. Frankfurt am Main: Peter Lang.

Ballod, Matthias. 2007. *Informationsökonomie – Informationsdidaktik: Strategien zur gesellschaftlichen, organisationalen und individuellen Informationsbewältigung und Wissensvermittlung*. Bielefeld: Bertelsmann.

Biber, Douglas. 1988. *Variation Across Speech and Writing*. Cambridge: Cambridge University Press.

Blood, Rebecca. 2000. *Weblogs: A History and Perspective*. http://www.rebeccablood.net/essays/weblog_history.html.

—. 2002. *The Weblog Handbook: Practical Advice on Creating and Maintaining your Blog*. Cambridge, MA: Perseus.

—. 2004. How blogging software reshapes the online community. *Communications of the ACM* 47. 12. 53-55.

Calsamigilia, Helena & Teun van Dijk. 2004. Popularization Discourse and Knowledge about the Genome. *Discourse & Society* 15. 4. 369-389.

Chafe, Wallace L.. 1986. Evidentiality in English conversation and academic writing. In Wallace L. Chafe & Johanna Nichols (eds.), *Evidentiality: The Linguistic Coding of Epistemology*. Norwood, NJ: Ablex Pub. Corp. 261-272.

Cole, Allan. 2010. *Build Your Own Wicked WordPress Themes*. Collingwood: SitePoint.

Declerck, Renaat & Susan Reed. 2001. *Conditionals: A Comprehensive Empirical Analysis*. Berlin/New York: Mouton de Gruyter.

Efimova, Lilia. 2009. *Passion at Work: Blogging Practices of Knowledge Workers*. Unpublished dissertation. Universiteit Utrecht, Enschede.

Fritz, Gerd. 2011. Texttypen in wissenschaftlichen Blogs: Eine exemplarische Analyse am Beispiel des Language Log. In Gerd Fritz & Thomas Gloning (eds.), *Digitale Wissenschaftskommunikation – Formate und ihre Nutzung*. Gießen: Gießener Elektronische Bibliothek. 205-287.

—. 2013. *Dynamische Texttheorie*. Gießen: Gießener Elektronische Bibliothek.

Fritz, Gerd & Anita Bader. 2010. Digitale Formate in der Wissenschaftskommunikation: Konstellationen und Konvergenzen. In Hans-Jürgen Bucher (ed.), *Neue Medien – neue Formate: Ausdifferenzierung und Konvergenz in der Medienkommunikation.* Frankfurt am Main: Campus Verlag. 337-355.

Grice, Herbert P. 1975. Logic and conversation. In Peter Cole & Jerry L. Morgan (eds.), *Speech Acts.* New York: Academic Press. 41-58.

Groeben, Norbert. 1988. *Das Forschungsprogramm Subjektive Theorien: Eine Einführung in die Psychologie des reflexiven Subjekts*. Tübingen: Francke.

Gülich, Elisabeth. 2003. Conversational techniques used in transferring knowledge between medical experts and non-experts. *Discourse Studies* 5. 2. 235-263.

Hayes, John R. 1996. A new framework for understanding cognition and affect in writing. In C. Michael Levy & Sarah E. Ransdell (eds.), *The Science of Writing: Theories, Methods, Individual Differences, and Applications*. Mahwah, NJ: Lawrence Erlbaum. 1-27.

Herring, Susan & John C. Paolillo. 2006. Gender and genre variation in weblogs. *Journal of Sociolinguistics* 10. 4. 439-459.

Herring, Susan, Lois Ann Scheidt, Sabrina Bonus & Elijah Wright. 2004. *Bridging the Gap: A Genre Analysis of Weblogs.* http://tinyurl.com/herrscheidt04. (retrieved 25-07-2014).

Herring, Susan, Lois Ann Scheidt, Inna Kouper & Elijah Wright. 2006. *A Longitudinal Content Analysis of Weblogs: 2003-2004.* http://tinyurl.com/herring2006.

Herring, Susan C., Lois Ann Scheidt, Elijah Wright & Sabrina Bonus. 2005. *Weblogs as a Bridging Genre. Information Technology & People* 18. 2. 142-171. doi: 10.1108/09593840510601513.

Hyland, Ken & Polly Tse. 2004. Metadiscourse in academic writing: A reappraisal. *Applied Linguistics* 25. 2. 156-177.

Karlsson, Lena. 2006. Acts of reading diary weblogs. *Human IT* 8. 2. 1-59.

Kastberg, Peter. 2007. Knowledge Communication: The emergence of a third order discipline. In Claudia Villinger & Heidrun Arbogast-Gerzymisch (eds.), *Kommunikation in Bewegung: Multimedialer und multilingualer Wissenstransfer in der Experten-Laien-Kommunikation.* Frankfurt am Main: Lang. 7-24.

Kitzmann, Andreas. 2003. That different place: Documenting the self within online environments. *Biography* 26. 1. 48-65.

Kitzmann, Andreas. 2004. *Saved from Oblivion: Documenting the Daily from Diaries to Web Cams*. New York: Peter Lang.

Kjellberg, Sara. 2009. Scholarly blogging practice as situated genre: An analytical framework based on genre theory. *Information Research* 14. 3. Paper n° 413.

Kohanyi, Adèle. 2009. 'The more I write, the better I write, and the better I feel about myself': Mood variability and mood regulation in student journalists and creative writers. In Scott Barry Kaufman & James C. Kaufman (eds.), *The Psychology of Creative Writing.* New York: Cambridge University Press. 41-56.

Kruglanski, Arie W. 1990. Lay epistemic theory in social-cognitive psychology. *Psychological Inquiry* 1. 3. 181-197.

Kruglanski, Arie W., Edward Orehek, Mark Dechense & Antonio Pierro. 2010. Lay epistemic theory: The motivational, cognitive, and social aspects of knowledge formation. *Social and Personality Psychology Compass* 10. 4. 939-950.

Lomborg, Stine. 2009. Navigating the blogosphere: Towards a genre-based typology of weblogs. *First Monday* 14. 5. doi: doi.org/10.5210/fm.v14i5.2329

—. 2014. *Social Media, Social Genres: Making Sense of the Ordinary.* London/New York: Routledge.

Luzón, María José. 2013. Public communication of science in blogs: Recontextualizing scientific discourse for a diversified audience. *Written Communication* 30. 4. 428-457.

Mauranen, Anna. 2013. Hybridism, edutainment, and doubt: Science blogging finding its feet. *Nordic Journal of English Studies* 13. 1. 7-36.

McNeill, Laurie. 2009. Brave new genre, or generic colonialism? Debates over ancestry in internet diaries. In Janet Giltrow & Dieter Stein (eds.), *Genres in the Internet: Issues in the Theory of Genre.* Amsterdam/Philadelphia: Benjamins. 143-161.

Myers, Greg. 2010. *The Discourse of Blogs and Wikis*. London: Continuum.

Perry, Susan K.. 2009. Writing in flow. In Scott B. Kaufman, and & James C. Kaufman (eds.), *The Psychology of Creative Writing.* New York: Cambridge University Press. 213-224.

Puschmann, Cornelius. 2013. Blogging. In Susan Herring, Dieter Stein & Tuija Virtanen (eds.), *Pragmatics of Computer-mediated Communication*. Berlin: De Gruyter Mouton. 75-100.

Puschmann, Cornelius & Merja Mahrt. 2012. Scholarly blogging: A new form of publishing online or science journalism 2.0? In Alexander Tokar, Michael Beurskens, Susanne Keuneke, Merja Mahrt, Isabella Peters, Cornelius Puschmann, Timo van Treek, K. Weller (eds.), *Science and the Internet*. Düsseldorf: Düsseldorf University Press. 171-181.

Röll, Martin. 2004. Distributed KM: Improving knowledge workers' productivity and organisational knowledge sharing with weblog-based personal publishing. http://blogoehlert.typepad.com/eclippings/files/distributedkm.pdf.

Rosenberg, Scott. 2009. *Say Everything: How Blogging Began, What it's Becoming, and Why it Matters*. New York: Three Rivers Press.

Rosenberg, Scott. 2010. Postscript: Four cases for the persistence of blogging. http://tinyurl.com/23ccksb.

Runco, Mark A. 2009. Writing as an interaction with Ideas. In Scott Barry Kaufman & James C. Kaufman (eds.), *The Psychology of Creative Writing.* New York: Cambridge University Press. 180-209.

Schildhauer, Peter. 2013. The textual functions of personal weblogs: Stability, diversity, and change. In Anne Ammermann, Alexander Brock, Petra Bucher, Peter Schildhauer & Jana Pflaeging (eds.), *Facets of Linguistics: Proceedings of the 14th Norddeutsches Linguistisches Kolloquium 2013 in Halle an der Saale*. Frankfurt am Main: Peter Lang. 117-130.

—. 2014. *Textsorten im Internet zwischen Wandel und Konstanz: Eine diachrone Untersuchung der Textsorte Personal Weblog*. Martin-Luther-Universität, Halle-Wittenberg.

van Dijck, José. 2004. Composing the self: Of diaries and lifelogs. In *fibreculture* 3.

van Eemeren, Frans H., Peter Houtlosser & A. Francisca Snoeck Henkemans (eds.). 2007. *Argumentative Indicators in Discourse: A Pragma-Dialectal Study*. Dordrecht: Springer.

Wichter, Sigurdand & Gerd Antos (eds.). 2001. *Wissenstransfer zwischen Experten und Laien: Umriss einer Transferwissenschaft*. Frankfurt am Main: Peter Lang.

Young, Lynne. 1994. University lectures: Macro-structure and Micro-features. In John Flowerdew (ed.), *Academic Listening: Research Perspectives.* Cambridge: Cambridge University Press. 159-176.

Yus, Francisco. 2011. *Cyberpragmatics: Internet-mediated Communication in Context*. Amsterdam/Philadelphia: Benjamins.

KNOWLEDGE DISSEMINATION ONLINE: THE CASE OF HEALTH INFORMATION

JUDITH TURNBULL
SAPIENZA UNIVERSITY OF ROME, ITALY

Abstract: One of the most frequently searched topics on the Internet is healthcare information, which should enable a patient to understand more fully his illness. It is therefore fundamental for managing chronic illnesses, where the newly acquired knowledge not only has to be understood, but also acted upon in order to live with the condition. Much of the content of healthcare information on the Internet is produced and distributed one-way; the message is created and controlled in a top-down fashion from expert to layperson. However, this conventional concept of knowledge dissemination is undergoing a transformation. Patients can now take an active role not only in the management of their own illness, but also in knowledge dissemination through Web 2.0, which allows user-generated content to be uploaded in a virtual community, a blog or on social networks. Lay knowledge, as the expression of personal experience and understanding of illness, is in fact playing an increasingly important role within the patient-centred approach. The study analyses three websites about diabetes and identifies the strategies adopted to recontextualise specialised knowledge as appropriate to the lay audience. It also shows how lay knowledge is incorporated and exploited to overcome the gap between expert and layman.

1. Introduction

Knowledge Dissemination takes place in a number of contexts and with different levels of participant experience; it may involve expert-to-expert communication, communication from expert to semi-layman (e.g. a science journalist), from expert to novice, who is still at some stage in his/her training in the specialized field, or from expert to the public at large, with a supposed total lack of knowledge. Consequently, knowledge dissemination can fulfil different purposes, whether it be in a professional context, pedagogical settings at various levels (school or university), or simply for information, edification and personal cultural development, as in popularizations.

The *knowledge transfer* involved in this type of expert-layman communication is referred to by a variety of terms, popularization, translation, transposition and re-contextualization. Whatever the label attached to it, it involves a simplification that remodels both the content and the language to suit the new target audience, so that it is close to general discourse and everyday experiences and is cognitively accessible to lay people. It aims to bridge the knowledge gap between expert and layperson.

This paper, however, investigates knowledge dissemination in the context of the communication of health information on the Internet, which fulfils a very different function and in very specific circumstances. *Health information* aims to provide knowledge and advice about medical conditions for the empowerment of patients, to promote health literacy, improve chronic disease self-management and help people gain control, solve problems and make decisions about their health. *Empowerment* is also about respecting patients' rights and voice.

This reflects a shift in the role of the patient from passive recipient to active consumer of health. The traditional, paternalistic approach to patient care tends to ignore personal preferences. In fact, the medical profession has been calling for a *patient-centred approach* to medical care for nearly fifty years (Balint 1969) and it is considered crucial for *high quality care* (Mead & Bower 2000). It views the patient not just in terms of his illness or a set of symptoms, but rather as a person with emotions, feelings, needs and preferences. An essential element of this approach is *empathy*, which involves the ability to understand another person's experiences and feelings and view them from their perspective (Hojat et al. 2002:1563).

Much of the content of healthcare information on the Internet is produced and distributed one-way; the message is created and controlled in a top-down fashion. However, the conventional concept of knowledge dissemination as a top-down process, from expert to layperson, is undergoing a transformation that is actually being driven by the Internet. On the one hand, patients are much more informed because they have access to so much information. On the other, they can now take an active role not only in the management of their own illness, but also in knowledge dissemination through Web 2.0, which allows user-generated content to be uploaded in a virtual community, a blog, or on social networks. *Lay knowledge*, as the expression of personal experience and understanding of illness (Williams & Popay 2006:122), may contest the objectivity of expert knowledge, but within the patient-centred approach lay knowledge plays an important role.

Although the Internet brings great benefits by stretching out to large numbers of people, one-to-many communication is not easy. 'The many' are an unknown and undefined public, which comes from a wide range of social, economic and cultural backgrounds, covering all ages and bringing a variety of life experiences and levels of education. They are not a discourse community with a common level of shared knowledge and interests, making it more difficult to calibrate the information at a level that is sufficiently simple, without going to an extreme, and overstepping the mark by dumbing down.

This difficulty is compounded by the fact that health information is not only aiming to improve the factual knowledge of the patient, but also convince him of the necessity and the advantages of adopting a particular treatment or lifestyle. Medical information, therefore, has to adopt a form of argumentation that has been described as *info-suasive*, in which information and persuasion are blended inextricably (Schulz & Rubinelli 2008). Another feature that needs to be taken into consideration is *trust*. Information and advice will be accepted only if trust is established between writer and reader. The source of the information needs to be credible (Neubaum & Krämer 2014:1) and trust is greatest between people who share group identities and have similar values (Earle 2010:543).

Health information is one of the most frequently sought topics on the web. Studies show that people use the Internet mostly to search for information about a specific condition, rather than about healthy lifestyles or healthcare services (McMullan 2002:26). The topic of this study is diabetes, a life-long health condition whose clinical profile needs to be thoroughly understood by the patient and probably by his or her family too. He not only needs to be persuaded to adopt a healthy lifestyle to avoid serious, at times life-threatening, complications, but he also has to understand how the body processes food to produce energy for body cells and how insulin plays a vital role in the process. He has to be able to balance diet, insulin or other medication and physical activity to avoid too high or too low blood sugar levels on a day-to-day basis. In other words, knowledge about his condition will help him achieve a better quality of life, with less anxiety and more control.

Much research has been done in recent years on health communication (Michiulette et al. 1992; Delp & Jones 1996; Wyatt 2000; Houts et al. 2006; Jordan et al. 2010; Sechrest 2010), and many governments have been trying to promote health literacy to enable people to become more responsible for their well-being and management of their health. This study aims to investigate how medical information can be recontextualised into effective communication and knowledge dissemination online for such a wide audience. More specifically, it will investigate the strategies and rhetorical devices used to make the information cognitively accessible and engage the reader to make it persuasive.

2. Knowledge Transfer

Knowledge transfer has to work on two equally important levels – the *cognitive dimension* and the *communicative dimension* (Moirand 2003). The cognitive dimension is involved in the transmission of information, through explanations and reformulations of states and objects of knowledge, whilst the communicative dimension refers to the way writers use language to negotiate the social relationship with their readers.

It will also be useful to consider the knowledge transfer process in health communication as composed of four fundamental phases (Michiulette et al. 1992; Delp & Jones 1996; Parrish 2001; Houts et al. 2006), in which the different strategies may be used: (i) attracting the attention of the reader; (ii) enhancing comprehension; (iii) aiding retention and recall; (iv) encouraging adherence to the advice.

2.1 The Cognitive Dimension

A number of studies about popularizations and medical discourse between doctors and patients have broadly classified the strategies used to transfer knowledge from expert to layman as *Illustration* (also *Formulation* or *Explanation*) and *Reformulation*, each of which has, in turn, a number of subcategories. Illustration strategies are the procedures chosen to present knowledge, that is, the verbalization of complex or abstract knowledge to facilitate comprehension, which allows lay users to relate new knowledge to old knowledge. These include description to explain unknown things, definition to explain unknown words or terms, exemplification that allows speakers to express complex concepts in terms of everyday experience, scenarios to draw up possible situations, events or reactions, various forms of metaphorical language, including analogy and comparisons (Gülich 2003:241) and lastly, concretization, the rewording of abstract information in a non-abstract manner.

Table 1 provides an outline of the strategies and the terminology adopted in Ciapuscio (2003), Gülich (2003) and Calsamiglia & van Dijk (2004).

Tab.1: Knowledge transfer strategies

CIAPUSCIO (2003)	GÜLICH (2003)	CALSAMIGLIA & VAN DIJK (2004)
Formulation Metaphorical language Exemplification Scenarios Concretization	*Illustration* Metaphorical language Exemplification Scenarios Concretization	*Explanation* Denomination Definition/Description Exemplification Generalization Analogies
Reformulation Referential expression + Treatment expression	*Reformulation* 3-part structure: Reference expression, Marker, Treating expression	*Reformulation* Paraphrase

Reformulation strategies are procedures to change or modify what has already been said, to clarify the meaning and make it more comprehensible. In conversation reformulation is part of an ongoing process between interlocutors to construct and negotiate meaning. In written text its purpose is to foresee and forestall possible misunderstandings. These strategies may be subdivided into Repetition and Paraphrasing. Sometimes the new notion or technical term is introduced first and then followed by an explanatory reformulation or paraphrase, or, vice versa, the technical term is given as the reformulation.

Both Illustration and Reformulation strategies may be used separately or combined to complement each other (Gülich 2003:242) and are concerned with the concretization of abstract information.

2.2 The Communicative Dimension

Equally important is the communicative dimension involved in knowledge dissemination. As expert-layman communication "must always adapt to the appropriateness conditions and other constraints of the media and communicative events" (Calsamiglia & van Dijk 2004:371), particular attention needs to be given to the context of the communication, its participants, their roles and positions, register, genre, its communicative function and the channel of communication. In the knowledge asymmetry inherent in expert-layman communication interpersonal relations are fundamental.

This is especially true of health communication, where friendliness and sensitivity play an important role in chronic disease management. Indeed, communication that is more patient-centred is associated with greater patient satisfaction, better adherence, and improved disease outcomes (Moscovitz et al. 2013:392). Credibility needs to be established to inspire trust.

A useful framework for studying the communicative dimension of online medical communication between expert and layman can be found in Giannoni (2008) and Hyland (2010). Although these papers are concerned with academic discourse, the popularizing features they discuss act as a good starting point. In fact, as Giannoni suggests (2008:213), popularization is "a matter of degree and operates along a continuum", from researchers to practitioners to the educated public as readers of popularizing articles in the fields of science and medicine. If we stretch this continuum further beyond the educated public, we can include the public at large as representative of the heterogeneous audience on the Internet.

In his paper Hyland uses the term *proximity* to refer to:

> a writer's control of rhetorical features which display both authority as an expert and a personal position towards issues in an unfolding text. It involves responding to the context of the text, textually constructing both the writer and reader as people with similar understandings and goals […]. It is concerned with how writers represent not only themselves and their readers, but also their material, in ways which are most likely to meet their readers' expectations (2010:117).

Among the devices that can help engage with the reader are questions, marked lexis, personalization, humour and metaphors (Giannoni 2008; Hyland 2010).

Adolphs et al. (2004) also provides a useful guide for the analysis, because it is specifically concerned with healthcare encounters and focuses in part on "enlisting the participation or involvement of the recipients of health advice [which is] by no means automatic or straightforward" (2004:16). They identify the use of personal pronouns, modals and the logical operators *if* and *or* as important devices for focussing attention on the caller, in our case the reader, and consequently involving him/her in the discourse, as well as info-suasively presenting advice as possible solutions.

3. Online Communication

In spite of the apparent ease with which information can be accessed on the Internet, searching and gathering information is not as simple as it would appear. The sheer amount of information available on the Internet can be overwhelming, which means that complex metacognitive skills are required, such as planning, search strategies and evaluation of information (Tarpley 2001; Johnson 2007). Arguably, "[i]nternet literacy is not the ability to use a set of technical tools: rather it is the ability to use a set of cognitive tools" (Johnson 2007:433). It involves reading text, interpreting images, listening to music or watching a video, so it is in no way a passive experience. As a consequence, the ordinary man-in-the-street has to be multi-literate (Caballero 2008:15), and therefore the transposition and simplification needs to be made carefully.

However, the channel itself assists in this transposition. Firstly, information is presented through hypertext, which organizes information into small, independent, self-contained pages in a similar way to a narrative structure which divides a 'story' into chunks and orders events in time in a logical and predictable sequence, what Chafe (1980) refers to as sub-chunking (quoted in Stewart 2004:125). The division first into pages and then into sections or paragraphs filters and streamlines information, making the acquisition of the information gradual and accumulative.

Secondly, the Internet offers numerous opportunities through multimodality. Communication entails obviously much more than just language; it draws on a multiplicity of modes, which include visual, spoken, gestural, written and other resources, all of which contribute to meaning. Modes are the sets of semiotic resources for making meaning and realizing communication; they work in distinct ways, making the choice of mode a central aspect of interaction and meaning. Research in health communication has shown how important an integrated approach of text and images is in the successful transfer of knowledge (Michiulette et al. 1992; Delp & Jones 1996; Parrish 2001; Houts et al. 2006).

Multi-modal features are certainly not new, as they have long been present in printed text genres, with a combination of words and images, but what is peculiar to web-mediated communication is the possibility of combining these with other media, as for example sound and moving images (Askehave & Nielsen 2005:139). The use of visuals can enhance understanding of information and the learning process; videos and animation may be particularly helpful in the transfer of knowledge, as they can be used to explain a complex object, structure or process through a demonstration. They can also give a physical, albeit virtual, presence either to a professional/expert to replicate more closely a consultation or to people who have had first-hand experience of a situation and want to share their story, thus creating empathy and solidarity. All these modes will make the information more direct and engaging.

However, there still remains the difficulty of a heterogeneous audience, making it hard to define the level of shared cultural, institutional and world knowledge and adjust the rewriting accordingly (van Dijk 2005). This virtual situation may lead to a tendency towards generalizations in order to accommodate as many situations as possible and hence give less personal and specific information. Another consequence could be a completely depersonalised text, using neutral language so as not to alienate readers, but, at the same time, this will make it more difficult to engage with the reader. For example, the use of humour or evaluative language, very effective devices for aligning writer and reader by creating empathy and a common ground between the two, may be limited. Both humour and evaluation are culture-specific, and people's sense of humour may vary extensively even within the same culture.

Empowerment also requires the reader to act upon the information acquired and therefore we can suppose that a persuasive argument could be an important component of the discourse of empowerment: "[a]rgumentation aims at a higher level of commitment from the audience: it not only seeks to persuade, but also to convince, or to bring about a change in the audience" (Carter 2000:85). Harvey et al. (2013) and Adolphs et al. (2004) suggest that giving advice is a delicate task, because it is generally considered face-threatening in Anglo-Western contexts. Certainly the addresser is giving recommendations of what s/he thinks is best, which leaves an option open to the patient to adhere to the advice or not. The reader, nevertheless, may not be very receptive to advice and view it as indirect criticism. This means that the argument presented to persuade the reader needs to be not only 'reasonable' in the sense of logical, but also 'acceptable' to his/her point of view (Grasso et al. 2000:1078).

Although hypertext lends itself well to knowledge transfer because the information is broken up into manageable chunks, there is still the need to make it convincing and compelling. However, the lack of a predefined sequence in hypertext is in direct conflict with the sequential logic and structures of argumentation. Indeed, the non-linearity of hypertext sets up a number of challenges for argumentation, which traditionally relies on sequential structures, such as *if*-conditionals or cause-effect sentences. Unlike textual units such as paragraphs and chapters that depend on neighbouring text units for coherence, self-contained web pages are like islands of meaning, free floating and independent (Carter 2000:86). This fragmentation is what makes argumentation difficult in hypertext and therefore more dependent on the strategies used to create empathy with the addressee to be convincing.

4. Corpus Construction

Three British websites, which were accessed in July 2013, have been analysed in order to explore the different ways medical information about diabetes may be transferred online.

Patient.co.uk is managed directly by doctors and contains information on a wide variety of medical and health topics, including many pages on diabetes. The second website is *diabetes.org.uk*, which is run as a registered charity and works to raise awareness about the condition, collect funds, as well as provide support to sufferers. Its membership includes healthcare professionals, volunteers and diabetics. The third and last website under investigation is *diabetes.co.uk*, a community website whose information is provided by diabetes experts, but, above all, by diabetics themselves who share their knowledge and first-hand experiences.

A selection of the webpages was made to include only those parts of the websites dealing with strictly medical questions that explain blood sugar levels, treatment and possible complications. These are common to all three websites. The numerous pages on legal, social and economic issues of diabetes, such as driving, insurance, employment, travel, have been omitted because they were not covered in one of the three websites (patient.co.uk).

Tab. 2: Webpages included in the corpus

patient.co.uk (42,810 tokens)	***diabetes.org.uk*** (28,934 tokens)	***diabetes.co.uk*** (49,874 tokens)
Diabetes Type 1 Diabetes Type 2 Treatment for Type 2 diabetes Diabetes and high blood pressure Diabetes, foot care and foot ulcers Diabetic retinopathy Diabetic kidney disease Peripheral neuropathy Weight reduction Healthy eating Impaired glucose tolerance Glucose tolerance test Tests for glucose and HbA1c Atheroma	Guide to diabetes What is diabetes? Type 1 diabetes Type 2 diabetes Newly diagnosed? Managing your diabetes Monitoring your diabetes Diabetes complications	Type 1: Symptoms; Newly diagnosed; Controlling type 1 diabetes Type 2: Symptoms; Newly diagnosed; Controlling type 2 diabetes; Diet for type 2; Lifestyle changes; Risk factors Living with diabetes Treatment Complications

The texts in the webpages are expository, accompanied at times by diagrams and videos, which usually show clinical advisors giving information or fellow diabetics narrating their knowledge and personal experiences of the condition. The videos analysed in this study were *What happens when you have diabetes?* (8.45 mins.), *How to recognise and treat a hypo* (4.49 mins.) and *Rebel, rebel* (4.36 mins.). Each website also hosts an online discussion forum in which readers can post their queries and suggestions. It is a way of sharing and exchanging ideas, experience and knowledge. For the purpose of this study only one of the many threads was examined to investigate how the participants interact. The analysis has followed a qualitative approach.

5. Analysis of Linguistic Features in Interactions

In this section four different aspects of health communication will be analysed to show how knowledge transfer strategies are adopted and combined with the affordances offered by a website. It opens with an analysis of the knowledge transfer strategies adopted by the professional experts (metaphorical language and concretization) to illustrate how the cognitive elements of the information are communicated. This is followed by an analysis of a discussion in a forum, which is not moderated by an expert and therefore shows the value of lay knowledge. Lastly, the info-suasive aspect of health communication will be analysed.

5.1 Metaphorical Language

Metaphorical language is an important feature of both cognitive and communicative strategies. It includes analogies, similes, metaphors and comparisons. Metaphors are one of the main semantic means of establishing links between two domains of experience, meaning or knowledge and therefore are very frequent in knowledge dissemination texts or popularizations to bridge the gap between expert knowledge and the layman. According to Lakoff and Johnson (1980:5), "the essence of a metaphor is understanding and experiencing one kind in terms of another". The source domain may not always be more 'concrete', but it should be more familiar to the reader. However, it has been observed in face-to-face communication that methods other than metaphors are often preferred, namely exemplification, scenarios and simple concretization (Gülich 2003:245), because metaphors, even the most effective, require elaboration whereas the other strategies will probably be more immediate and real. In the case of online communication, where negotiation of meaning and feedback is missing, more direct and simple strategies are preferable.

In fact, there are only a few conceptual metaphors in the three websites, but there is one analogy that can be found in all three and is used either in a simile or a metaphor. Glucose or sugar is referred to as 'fuel for the body's cells' (SUGAR/GLUCOSE AS FUEL; BODY'S CELLS AS AN ENGINE). It is clearly a dead metaphor that requires no elaboration, so it does not complicate comprehension, but simply makes the meaning more explicit.

(1) Glucose is like a fuel which is used by the cells in the body for energy. (patient.co.uk - webpage)
(2) Insulin is the hormone produced by the pancreas that allows glucose to enter the body's cells, where it is used as fuel for energy so we can work, play and generally live our lives. It is vital for life. (diabetes.org.uk - webpage)
(3) Ketoacidosis can occur if the body spends a significant amount of time with too little insulin to refuel the cells of the body. (diabetes.co.uk - webpage)

However, the *diabetes.org.uk* website, whose composition of contributors is very heterogeneous as it is made up of health professionals, volunteers and patients, then goes on to use another metaphor to explain the function of insulin and what happens when it fails to work.

(4) Diabetes develops when glucose can't enter the body's cells to be used as fuel. This happens when either:
- There is no insulin to unlock the cells (Type 1)
- There is not enough insulin or the insulin is there but not working properly (Type 2). (diabetes.org.uk - webpage)

Insulin is compared to a key which opens the lock on the door of cells to allow glucose to enter. The text is so short and succinct, that it is quite difficult to understand and appreciate fully the meaning of the metaphor. However, the metaphor is represented graphically with an image of a door with two padlocks to help elucidate the meaning (Hyland 2010:119). The first padlock has no key (insulin) to unlock the door as in Type 1 diabetes, whilst the second padlock has a key but there is no keyhole so the insulin cannot work properly, as in Type 2 diabetes.

Already the metaphor is becoming clearer. But further down the same webpage the metaphor is used once again in a video called *What Happens When You Have Diabetes?* An off-screen voice explains what diabetes is about, whilst the animation illustrates the relationship between food, glucose and insulin in a healthy person, a person with Type 1 diabetes and a person with Type 2 diabetes.

The image this time is of a wall of cells with two possible scenarios. The first is where access for the glucose to enter the cells is denied, because there is no key (insulin) and it builds up in the blood stream. In the other, access is limited, because the cells are furred up or insulin is not working properly and therefore some glucose, represented by the letter *g*, passes into the cells, but a lot remains outside and therefore does not have any effect.

Although the video lasts over 8 minutes and gives a detailed description of what happens in the body and the symptoms of diabetes, the tone is very relaxed and conversational:

(5) It's a bit like- insulin is a key unlocking the door … (diabetes.org.uk - video)

(6) Somebody who's got undiagnosed Type 1 diabetes is going to start feeling very tired, lethargic and unable to sort of go about their normal daily routine. (diabetes.org.uk - video)

Each time the metaphor is presented it delves a little deeper and becomes more complex in its explanation, giving a slightly different representation, so that the reader/viewer can gradually grasp its full meaning and significance. This example shows the usefulness of visuals, whether images or animation, when combined with text to enhance understanding and how the multimodal potential of the Internet can be exploited.

5.2 Concretization

For knowledge transfer to be successful, it requires a process of transformation from the abstract to the concrete. To illustrate how this can be done, the following example is taken from a video on the *diabetes.org.uk* website, in which information and advice are given by a clinical advisor. She explains what hypoglycemia is, its symptoms and how to deal with it using various strategies mentioned above.

She starts with a definition in technical terms, followed by a reformulation and an explanation in very plain English to convey the significance of a low blood glucose level (*hypo*).

(7) Hypoglycemia, we'll refer to it as hypo, describes when the blood glucose level falls below 4 mmol/l per litre. This isn't high enough to provide energy for the body's needs. (advisor, diabetes.org.uk - video)

She then suggests a number of scenarios to illustrate the possible causes of a hypo:

(8) A hypo happens because of a variety of reasons.
It could be there's a mismatch between your diabetes medication and your food.
It could be unplanned or strenuous activity.
It could be due to drinking too much alcohol, especially without eating. (advisor, diabetes.org.uk - video)

And lastly, she gives examples of warning signs that a hypo is on its way:

(9) There are a variety of warning signs and it's important to know what yours is.
Here are some examples:
feeling hot and sweaty […]
getting anxious
losing concentration. (advisor, diabetes.org.uk - video)

After she has finished her explanation, she leaves the floor to three young diabetic women who tell their own stories about hypos and how they cope with them. The information given by the clinical advisor was presented in short, simply constructed statements, which is in sharp contrast with the very natural, spontaneous speech of the women, who use expressions to downscale the intensity of their statements, such as *quite*, *slightly*, *a bit*. This makes the discourse very conversational with the effect of reassuring the reader that hypos, though frightening, are actually manageable.

(10) I can usually tell the signs because I get quite shaky legs. I feel tired, I sometimes feel quite confused, a little bit panicky sometimes. (woman 2, diabetes.org.uk - video)

(11) The signs I am about to have a hypo are that I start to feel slightly irritated, just little things that start to niggle me and I'll notice my irritation. I'll begin to feel a bit weak and shaky and often I'll be quite hungry and wonder why. (woman 3, diabetes.org.uk - video)

The second part of the video discusses what to do in case of a hypo. Once again, the advisor uses short, direct statements and lists to describe what to do.

(12) Once you recognize your hypo warning sign, it's important to take action to prevent it becoming more severe.

You will find out what is the best treatment for you. But again here are some examples:
It could be a non-diet drink
Glucose sweets
Or soft-centred sweets.
The amount depends on your age and the size you are. Remember to avoid foods containing fat,
such as chocolate or milk, because they will act too slowly. […] (advisor, diabetes.org.uk - video)

The women's individual stories repeat and reformulate the information given by the advisor, but in a completely different register. The speech is totally spontaneous and unscripted, with very colloquial language, hesitations and corrections.

(13) I'll have some glucose tablets. I'll have maybe some fruit juice and I'll …, and sometimes it takes a bit of discipline to wait 10 minutes because I feel yuck, … to wait 10 minutes and then test my blood again and then have some more glucose tablets or more fruit juice. (woman 1, diabetes.org.uk - video)

This juxtapositioning of the expert healthcare professional's advice and the personal anecdotes and experiences that confirm and reinforce what has been said by the expert gives rise to a concretization of the abstract information and knowledge. The fact that it is presented in a video, giving a face to the information, makes it more real, immediate and engaging.

5.3 Who is the Expert?

So far, the discussion has focused on knowledge dissemination in the sense of expert-layman communication. In her 2003 article Gülich raises the question of who is actually an expert in a discussion about a medical condition. Certainly the healthcare professional, whether s/he is a doctor, nurse or clinical advisor, will be an expert, trained and qualified in the subject. But what about the patient?

> In medical communication, the so-called non-expert is an expert in at least one respect – his or her own illness. This is so not only because he or she acquires illness related knowledge and becomes a 'specialist' in dealing with his or her own chronic illness. The subjective side of this illness, experience with its development or, for example, how and to what degree pain is felt – these are things inaccessible to the medical expert – only the person affected can transmit these things. (Gülich 2003:247-8)

In a chronic condition like diabetes, in time the patient will gain great knowledge and experience, which may be useful for fellow sufferers. Asking a peer may also be easier than asking a professional for advice for fear the question may sound stupid. In fact, all three websites have a forum that is not moderated by an expert and therefore allows a spontaneous exchange of ideas between peers who form a kind of community of practice.

patient.co.uk had very few queries about diabetes and even fewer responses so that there were no long discussions. Maybe the virtual presence of the doctors 'inhibits' the forum. The other two websites have very active forums in which extended exchanges take place. The thread or discussion analysed here comes from the *diabetes.co.uk* website and is once again about hypos.

The exchanges took place over a two-month period. It starts by Switch presenting his problem, namely that he has a hypo every Wednesday about the same time. This is followed by a barrage of questions from fellow diabetics, brainstorming the situation. Switch picks up on a suggestion about stress causing blood sugar levels to fall, and a debate arises. Contrasting opinions by different forum members are also expressed on whether he should reduce his insulin intake or try simpler solutions such as a glass of pop or boiled sweets.

At this point Gezzathorpe tries to make a witty comment about the situation,

(14) I'm quite enjoying all this. Are you? (Gezzathorpe, diabetes.co.uk - forum)

but he is immediately jumped upon by the other members for his unsympathetic comments.

(15) Gezzathorpe what is your problem? Are you on something? Or are you just very bored? If you don't have anything to contribute to a topic, can't you just ignore it? (equipoise, diabetes.co.uk - forum)
(16) Shame on you! 😈 (paul-1976, diabetes.co.uk - forum)

In the next four postings there is a return to the 'conversation' in which Switch reports back after about six weeks on how things are going and receives warm and encouraging replies from hale710 and erinkirby.

(17) Glad to see things moving in the right direction! Next step is to eliminate the low completely😀 (hale710, diabetes.co.uk - forum)

(18) Thanks for the update, it's good to know you've managed to stop the hypos while you're at work, but as hale710 says it would be good to eliminate them totally. (erinkirby, diabetes.co.uk - forum)

The exchanges work out as if they were a conversation between all forum members and not just with Switch, especially as each one picks up on a previous posting, as for example *Good point Erin* (martwolves, diabetes.co.uk). As expected, the language is extremely colloquial.

(19) Maybe chuck a few more carbs into the mix at brekkie, but do something to counter the sugar crash on Wednesday. (martwolves, diabetes.co.uk - forum)

As the conversation develops, some particular features emerge. Firstly, group members take on multiple roles. Sometimes, as experienced diabetics, they act as if they were healthcare professionals, asking Switch numerous questions in order to draw information that can help solve the problem.

(20) Is there anything you do differently on a Wednesday that you don't normally do during the rest of the week? Anything that involves more exercise? Anything stressful, or less stressful than normal? Anything that involves something that is mentally challenging? (switch, diabetes.co.uk - forum)

They also act as big brothers or sisters, reprimanding him and 'ticking him off', but always expressing their concern and giving their support and encouragement:

(21) If you have it every week at the same time hasn't something like this occurred to you before? Hypos shouldn't be a regular occurrence and should be the exception rather than the rule. Look after yourself, mate. (martwolves, diabetes.co.uk - forum)

But at the same time, they remain firmly one of the group (*I'm a fine one to talk*), as peers, not superior in any way even if they are older or more experienced (*I average about 7-10 hypos per week*). As Erin says:

(22) But I'm a fine one to talk as I average about 7-10 hypos per week! (erin, diabetes.co.uk - forum)

As a community, they have a strong sense of belonging, expressing encouragement and good will:

(23) Hope you get it sorted soon. (angieG, diabetes.co.uk - forum)

They often close their postings with a saying, sometimes humorous (24) or reassuring (25).

(24) Prevent complications - shut the gate before the cows get out or the bull gets in. (itts, diabetes.co.uk - forum)
(25) If you see someone without a smile give them one of yours. (angieG, diabetes.co.uk - forum)

The other interesting feature is the sense of identity that emerges from the forum. They all use nicknames or abbreviated names, perhaps to maintain their anonymity and feel freer to respond. Sometimes their location is given, but, most importantly, they identify themselves by their diabetic status. For example, Angie was given a diagnosis originally as Type 2, but this was then corrected to Type 1. She gives her blood glucose levels to show how and when the diagnosis was changed, all of which gives an indication of their insider knowledge. This background information builds up their identity and may even be considered to represent their 'credentials' for taking an active part in the forum.

Throughout the discussion, with the exception of Gezzathorpe, there is a clear sense of solidarity, comradeship and sincere interest in Switch's problem; all are collaborating and working together to find a satisfactory solution.

5.4 Persuasion to Promote Adherence

The first two parts of this analysis showed how websites can attract the attention of readers and facilitate their comprehension of the information by drawing on both cognitive and communicative devices. In this section we will consider how the websites try to convince the reader to follow and apply the advice and information given, which is, after all, their main purpose and objective.

Personalization is a key factor for engaging with a reader. Citing Storey (1997), Adolphs et al. (2004:17) state that the frequent use of *you* is believed to be a feature of persuasive discourse.

All three websites have a frequent use of personal pronouns with quite similar results. They all appear in the top 12 words in the frequency lists produced with ConcApp (1993-2003).

Tab.3: Personal pronouns

	patient.co.uk	*diabetes.org.uk*	*diabetes.co.uk*
you	2.2705%	2.3363%	1.2251%
your	1.8827%	2.1532%	1.1750%
we	0.0374%	0.1002%	0.1363%
us	0.0023%	0.0380%	0.0602%
our	0.0304%	0.0622%	0.1664%

It may be a little surprising that the online community website, *diabetes.co.uk*, has a lower frequency of *you* and *your*, but this is compensated by a greater frequency in *we* forms. The reason for this is that *we* is inclusive here and refers to 'we diabetics' as fellow sufferers (26: *us*, *our*). Elsewhere, *we* refers to the organization itself (27) and to human beings in general (28: *we*, *our*).

(26) This is useful as it means that our pancreas is still able to give us a bit of a hand in helping to control our sugar levels. (diabetes.co.uk - webpage)
(27) We offer an advocacy service to people with diabetes on issues in connection with their condition. (diabetes.org.uk - webpage)
(28) Insulin is the hormone produced by the pancreas that allows glucose to enter the body's cells, where it is used as fuel for energy so we can work, play and generally live our lives. (patient.co.uk - webpage)

Adolphs et al. also suggests that the modals *can* and *may* (29) and, in a sense, the connectors *if* and *or* (30) act as politeness markers to introduce optionality and soften the imposition of giving advice.

(29) Diabetes can be a lot to take and you may wish to request to join a diabetes education course in your area. (diabetes.co.uk - webpage)

However, often these personalizing features are interspersed with depersonalised and factual discourse, which presents a logical explanation of why the patient should act. It does so by using third-person verbs or passive constructions with non-human subjects (e.g. *a very high blood glucose can develop*; *this causes … and serious illness which can be life threatening*; and *If left untreated*):

(30) If you are not treated, or use too little insulin, a very high blood glucose level can develop quite quickly - over several days. If left untreated this causes lack of fluid in the body (dehydration), drowsiness, and serious illness which can be life-threatening. (patient.co.uk - webpage)

It seems that general descriptions of this kind are given in an impersonal form, especially when the consequences appear to be quite serious, perhaps to be less alarming. However, in the community and charity websites advice given as a warning seems to be expressed in an indirect and factual way (*Anyone suffering from diabetes faces the risk .... The longer a person has diabetes, ...*), even in response to a personalised question (*Am I at risk from diabetic retinopathy?*).

(31) Am I at risk from diabetic retinopathy?
[...] Anyone suffering from diabetes faces the risk of developing diabetic retinopathy and other diabetes complications.
The longer a person has diabetes, the greater the risk of developing diabetic retinopathy becomes. (diabetes.co.uk - webpage)

Whereas *patient.co.uk* and *diabetes.org.uk* use neutral lexis, the online community website, *diabetes.co.uk*, in keeping with its more direct and involved approach, uses marked evaluative lexis, general (32: *particularly dangerous*) and/or colloquial (33: *It's ... scary*), to engage directly with the reader.

(32) Retinopathy can affect all diabetics and becomes particularly dangerous when it is left untreated. (diabetes.co.uk - webpage)
(33) It's a scary prospect but we can help to prevent the onset of complications. (diabetes.co.uk - video)

Certainly *dangerous* and *scary* would not usually be considered as markedly evaluative lexis, but in the context of health communication they take on an emotive and forceful meaning. However, whilst emphasising the dangers of complications, the website is also reassuring and encouraging by introducing the idea of possibility to do something about prevention. Possibility (*It is possible for people to …*) means opportunity and ability, if the patient is willing:

(34) With good diabetes control and living a healthy, active lifestyle, it is possible for people to go a number of decades complication free. (diabetes.co.uk - webpage)

In a video on *diabetes.co.uk* called *Becca's Story A Rebel*, we can find a different approach to persuading people to follow advice. Becca is a young diabetic, sitting in front of a mirror putting her make-up on, with the camera behind her so we see her face in the mirror.

(35) Oh, I was a rebel me. My Mum used to say to me, the only way she could get me to do something was to tell me not to do it. And then, I

found out I had diabetes. All those rules. Take your blood, take your insulin, have you eaten, what have you eaten. Nothing could be spontaneous anymore. I hated it, everybody telling me what was best for me. I rebelled, I lied, produced perfect glucose diaries only to be found out when the nurse took the HbA1c at the clinic. (diabetes.co.uk - Becca's Story - video)

The picture she depicts of herself as a rebel is one with which many diabetics can identify, especially the young or indeed any diabetic who has difficulty in accepting the rigid regime necessary for coping with diabetes. Gradually the camera widens to show more of the room where she is.

(36) All through college I resented my diabetes. Even when I tried to pretend it wasn't there, it was always there like some niggling little voice. (diabetes.co.uk - Becca's Story - video)

She continues her story about how she got married and wanted to have a baby, so she had to change her ways.

(37) It wasn't easy. I did everything they told me to do. It wasn't easy, but for the first time in my life I prepared. I started exercising, eating properly. I did everything I could to get my HbA1c down to simple figures and then, hallelujah, I hit the target and kept it there. (diabetes.co.uk - Becca's Story - video)

Towards the end of the video it becomes obvious that she is not talking to the camera, but rather a baby in a carry cot on the bed:

(38) And you were a C section, but you were just perfect. You see, all that doing the right thing was so worth it. You see, even an old rebel has to conform, so when you look at me in 14 or 15 years' time and you think that I don't understand and I'm just a boring old fart, you'll remember I was once a rebel too. In fact, I still have my moments. (diabetes.co.uk - Becca's Story - video)

This is a story with a happy ending, narrated by a young woman in a very natural, spontaneous way. There is no attempt to 'preach' or say how you should behave, not even any explicit attempt to persuade. In Aristotelian terms, it works on the *pathos* of the audience and the ethos of Becca, insofar as she honestly and openly tells her story of success. The narration is, in fact, indirect, since the conversation with her baby is 'overheard'. This increases the *ethos* of Becca and the narrative becomes almost a parable, teaching and persuading by example.

6. Concluding Remarks

Although the comparison of the three websites was useful to support the assumptions of the study, many of the examples cited in this paper are taken from the same website, namely *diabetes.org.uk*. This was not a deliberate choice, but simply a result of the study which led to the identification of the most effective and interesting recontextualisations. The collaborators at *diabetes.org.uk* website are health professionals, volunteers and people with diabetes, their families and friends, each giving a different perspective on the condition. Not only does this lead to a wide range of styles, technical, conversational and colloquial, but we can also find a combination of strategies used together, making it very difficult to categorise language features following schemata. The intertwining of features depends on the presence of many producers and at the same time many users of the information on the websites.

However, two main characteristics of the strategies used to disseminate knowledge emerge from the analysis of this website. Firstly, the value placed on lay knowledge where the presence of experts and peers complement each other, and secondly, the use of multimodal affordances.

Expert and lay knowledge are combined, and at times integrated, as for example in the video with the clinical advisors and the three women, to blend not only the cognitive, but above all the communicative dimension of knowledge dissemination. The juxtapositioning of the knowledge of experts and fellow-sufferers helps to make the advice more appealing to readers, by sharing representations and experiences from everyday life rather than just being handed out by professionals. In this way the expert system of knowledge exploits lay knowledge to bridge the inevitable gap between expert and layman and to build up trust. It is also a way of overcoming or, at least, offsetting the inherent difficulty of following a patient-centred approach, with its focus on the individual, in a channel of mass communication. It personalises the information and relates it directly to real people.

The forums in the websites give lay knowledge even greater recognition, as they are not mediated and therefore the information and advice is uploaded in total freedom and without filters. Nevertheless, the exchanges are disciplined and regulated internally, resulting in constructive and friendly guidance and encouragement.

The other characteristic of the website was the use of the multimodal opportunities available on the web. Visuals can enhance comprehension, as in the case of the linguistic metaphor of insulin as the key to unlock the cells which was reformulated with the visual metaphors of a padlock and a keyhole. Furthermore, the dynamism of videos, in contrast with the static nature of webpages, is particularly important to attract and/or renew the attention of the reader, which will, hopefully, result in better recall of the information and therefore make it easier to put the advice into practice.

The other two websites appear to follow different strategies. *patient.co.uk*, run by doctors, seems to follow an 'illness-oriented' approach, with detailed information about the condition of diabetes and its complications, but does not call on personal accounts of how to live with diabetes. *diabetes.co.uk* also provides many technical details about diabetes, but uses only written text or videos with a formal scripted text, which does not differ much from the text on the webpage.

In spite of the simplification of the information, there is nevertheless a frequent use of technical terms and specialized terminology, with the necessary explanations, in all three websites, which serves the purpose of forming a bridge between the layman and the professional medical world that he has to enter and negotiate. In fact, Gülich (2003:240) points out how switching from colloquial to technical language and vice versa occurs frequently in expert-layman communication, but it can also be seen in the forum discussions between peers.

The results of the study reflect how the concept of authority seems to be changing, as Web 2.0 technology opens up new opportunities to all. As Sechrest (2010:2569) points out:

> Our concept of authority is evolving. There continues to be an ongoing debate on whether the 'wisdom of crowds' trumps expert opinion. The proponents of Wikipedia® and other prominent examples of 'crowd sourcing' essentially argue accuracy is an emergent property that can be expected to refine itself over time based on the large numbers of contributors it is possible to aggregate on the Internet. Others have argued we are seeing a devaluing of expertise that will eventually lead to a degradation of actual knowledge and credibility. This experiment continues to progress and the result is far from certain.

As a physician, Sechrest may feel himself threatened to some extent by patients' lay knowledge, but this study has shown how health communication would appear to endorse its value by making good use of it, especially from the communicative perspective.

References

Adolphs, Svenja, Brian Brown, Ronald Carter, Paul Crawford & Opindar Sahota. 2004. Applying corpus linguistics in a health care context. *Journal of Applied Linguistics* 1. 1. 9-28.

Askehave, Inger & Anne E. Nielsen. 2005. Digital genres: A challenge to traditional genre theory. *Information Technology and People* 18. 2. 120-141.

Balint, Enid. 1969. The possibilities of patient-centred medicine. *Journal of the Royal College of General Practitioners* 17. 269-276.

Caballero, Rosario. 2008. Theorizing about genre and cybergenre. *Computer Resources for Language Learning* 2. 14-27.

Calsamiglia, Helena & Teun A. van Dijk. 2004. Popularization discourse and knowledge about the genome. *Discourse and Society* 15. 4. 369-389.

Carter, Locke. 2000. Arguments in hypertext: A rhetorical approach. *Hypertext '00. Proceedings of the eleventh ACM on Hypertext and Hypermedia*. New York: ACM. 85-91.

Ciapuscio, Guiomar. 2003. Formulation and reformulation procedures in verbal interactions between experts and (semi-)laypersons. *Discourse Studies* 5. 2. 207-233.

Delp, Chris & Jeffrey Jones. 1996. Communicating information to patients: The use of cartoon illustrations to improve comprehension of instructions. *Academic Emergency Medicine* 3. 264-270.

Earle, Timothy. 2010. Trust in risk management: A model-based review of empirical research. *Risk Analysis* 30. 4. 541-574.

Giannoni, Davide. 2003. Popularizing features in English journal editorials. *English for Specific Purposes* 27. 212-232.

Grasso, Floriana, Alison Cawsey & Ray Jones. 2000. Dialectal argumentation to solve conflicts in advice giving: A case study in the promotion of healthy nutrition. *International Journal of Human-Computer Studies* 53. 1077-1115.

Greaves, Chris. 1993-2003. *ConcApp Concordance and Word Profiler.*

Gülich, Elisabeth. 2003. Conversational techniques used in transferring knowledge between medical experts and non-experts. *Discourse Studies* 5. 2. 235-263.

Harvey, Kevin, Miriam Locher & Louise Mullany. 2013. 'Can I be at risk of getting AIDS?' A linguistic analysis of two Internet advice columns on sexual health. *Linguistik Online* 59. 2013/2. 111-132. http://www.linguistik-online.com/59_13/harveyLocherMullany.html.

Hojat, Mohammadreza, Joseph Gonnella, Thomas Nasca, Salvatore Mangione, Michael Vergare & Michael Magee. 2002. Physician empathy: Definition, components, measurement, and relationship to gender and specialty. *American Journal of Psychiatry* 159. 9. 1563-1569.

Houts, Peter, Cecilia Doak, Leonard Doak & Matthew Loscalzo. 2006. The role of pictures in improving health communication: A review of research on attention, comprehension, recall and adherence. *Patient Education and Counseling* 61. 2. 173-190.

Hyland, Ken. 2010. Constructing proximity: Relating to readers in popular and professional science. *English for Academic Purposes* 9. 2. 116-127.

Johnson, Genevieve. 2007. Functional internet literacy: Required cognitive skills with implications for instruction. *E–Learning* 4. 4. 433-441.

http://www.wwwords.co.uk/ELEA.

Jordan, Joanne, Rachelle Buchbinder & Richard H. Osborne. 2010. Conceptualising health literacy from the patient perspective. *Patient Education and Counseling* 79. 36-42.

Lakoff, George & Mark Johnson. 1980. *Metaphors We Live By*. Chicago: University of Chicago Press.

McMullan, Miriam. 2006. Patients using the Internet to obtain health information: How this affects the patient-health professional relationship. *Patient Education and Counseling* 63. 1-2. 24-28.

Mead, Nicola & Peter Bower. 2000. Patient-centredness: A conceptual framework and review of the empirical literature. *Social Science and Medicine* 51. 1087-1110.

Michiulette, Robert, Judy Bahnson, Mark Dignan & Elissa Schroeder. 1992. The use of illustrations and narrative text style to improve readability of a health education brochure. *Journal of Cancer Education* 7. 3. 251-60.

Moirand, Sophie. 2003. Communicative and cognitive dimensions of discourse on science in the French mass media. *Discourse Studies* 5. 2. 175-206.

Moskowitz, David, Courtney Rees Lyles, Andrew J Karter, Nancy Adler, Howard Moffet & Dean Schillenger. 2013. Patient-reported interpersonal processes of care and perceived social position: The Diabetes Study of Northern California (DISTANCE). *Patient Education and Counseling* 90. 3. 392-398.

Neubaum, German & Nicole C. Krämer. 2014. Let's blog about health! Exploring the persuasiveness of a personal HIV blog compared to an institutional HIV website. *Health Communication*. doi: 10.1080/10410236.2013.856742.

Parrish, Patrick. 2001. *Instructional Illustrations*. www.comet.ucar.edu/presentations/illustra.

Schulz, Peter & Sara Rubinelli. 2008. Arguing 'for' the patient: Informed consent and strategic maneuvring in doctor-patient interaction. *Argumentation* 22. 3. 423-432.

Sechrest, Robert. C. 2010. The Internet and the physician-patient relationship. *Clinical Orthopaedics and Related Research* 468. 10. 2566-2571.

Stewart, Ann H. 2004. The role of narrative structure in the transfer of ideas. The case study and management theory. In Charles Bazerman & James Paradis J. (eds.), *Textual Dynamics of the Professions. Historical and Contemporary Studies of Writing in Professional Communities*. 120-144. http://wac.colostate.edu/books/textual_dynamics/.

Tarpley, Todd. 2001. Children, the internet, and other new technologies. In Dorothy G. Singer & Jerome L. Singer (eds.), *Handbook of Children and the Media*. Thousand Oaks, CA: Sage. 547–556.

van Dijk, Teun A. 2005. Contextual knowledge management in discourse production. A CDA perspective. In Ruth Wodak & Paul Chilton (eds.), *A New Agenda in Critical Discourse Analysis: Theory, Methodology and Interdisciplinarity*. Amsterdam/Philadelphia: John Benjamins. 71-100.

Williams, Gareth & Jennie Popay. 2005. Lay knowledge and the privilege of experience. In David Kelleher, Jonathan Gabe & Gareth Williams (eds.), *Challenging Medicine*. London/New York: Routledge. 122-145.
Wyatt, Jeremy C. 2000. Information for patients. *Journal of the Royal Society of Medicine* 23. 9. 467-471.

FROM USAGE GUIDES TO WIKIPEDIA: RE-CONTEXTUALIZING THE DISCOURSE OF LANGUAGE USE[1]

MORANA LUKAČ

LEIDEN UNIVERSITY CENTRE FOR LINGUISTICS, THE NETHERLANDS

AND ROBERT GUTOUNIG

FH JOANNEUM - UNIVERSITY OF APPLIED SCIENCES, AUSTRIA

Abstract: Since the eighteenth century the prescriptive rules for proper English language use have been documented in usage guides, a genre which traditionally provided the lists of dos and don'ts of usage for the "linguistically insecure" native speakers of English. In spite of the "descriptive turn" in the writing of dictionaries and usage guides and the influence of descriptive linguistics on language teaching, the publishing of usage guides written by the often self-appointed linguistic authorities continues to thrive until today. With the introduction of Web 2.0 the discourse on language use entered the new media enabling re-contextualisation of the previously established one-way communication between the advice-seeking lay community and the advice-giving language experts. In this paper we present the phenomenon of re-contextualisation of the discourse on language use in an online genre by analysing the Wikipedia entries and the secondary Wikipedia Talk pages on the topics related to usage and comparing them with the entries in usage guides retrieved from the Hyper Usage Guide of English database. The results show that Wikipedia entries obtain a higher level of objectivity and avoid prescriptive accounts as opposed to usage guides. We explain these findings through the principles governing the web-based collaborative processes.

[1] This paper was written in the context of the Bridging the Unbridgeable: linguists, prescriptivists and the general public project funded by the Netherlands Organisation for Scientific Research (NWO). We are grateful to the project leader Prof. Ingrid Tieken-Boon van Ostade for her comments on an earlier version of this paper.

1. Introduction: Expert Discourses on Language Use

The word *usage* in linguistic contexts has two different attitudinal connotations, one neutral and the other more judgemental and negative (Peters 2006:759-760; Busse & Schröder 2009:72). In general terms, *usage* refers to the customary or habitual way of doing something, but in the context of linguistic prescriptivism, *usage* may refer to linguistic practices that are contrasted with what is prescribed, namely the rules of the standard language (Allen 1992:1071). Such nonstandard usage is often labelled "bad usage" (Allen 1992:1071), "bad grammar" or simply "a mistake" (Bloomfield 1944:45), and it may be stigmatised in the prescriptive tradition. Linguistics as a discipline primarily aims at describing the rules of use accurately or, in the words of Charles Fries, linguists traditionally hold that "there can be no *correctness* apart from usage" (in McArthur 1992:421).

Quite contrary to these views originating from structural linguistics, the prescriptive tradition introduces evaluative judgements by prescribing certain rules for usage and proscribing others (McArthur 1992:446). The history of linguistic prescriptivism in the English language goes back to the eighteenth century (Beal 2009), when the prescriptive rules were established as a by-product of the early grammarians' attempts to codify English grammar (Peters 2006:761). In this period prescriptive rules such as the rules proscribing against double negation and split infinitives were first introduced. The history of prescriptivism in the English language is recorded and preserved in the tradition of the usage guide genre or the "paralexicographic tradition" (Peters and Young 1997:317), which continues to persist independently in spite of the "descriptive turn" in lexicography and in the writing of grammar books. The "descriptive turn" has been greatly influenced by the establishment of linguistics as a discipline and, subsequently, by using naturally-occurring data for studying language. The language advice in usage guides is still, however, for the great part the result of the topical selection, acceptability judgements and attitudes of their authors (Algeo 1991:6; Peters & Young 1997:317); in other words, usage guides are often subjective and dependent on introspection.

Usage guides, however, are not the only records of the prescriptive tradition. The history of the standard language ideology, the consciousness of the standard and of "correct" and "incorrect" language use (Milroy & Milroy 2002:25) is charted out in the "complaint tradition" (Milroy & Milroy 2002: Chapter 2), which consists of public complaints about the misuse of language and about linguistic decline, which are commonly published in letters-to-the-editor sections of newspapers and, more recently, on weblogs and Internet forums. Usage advice has also found its place in the new media genres, on specialist weblogs, wikis, and in various types of social media (Pinterest boards, Facebook groups, Twitter accounts, etc.) dedicated to usage (Schaffer 2010).

Although both the usage guide tradition and the complaint tradition serve to maintain the standard language ideology, they traditionally represent different groups of participants in the discussions on linguistic prescriptivism. On the one hand, there are the usage guide authors, the prescriptivists, and on the other the members of the general public, popularly known as language pedants or "language mavens" (Cameron 1995:vi). Since the introduction of Web 2.0, however, the two groups, the ones engaging in giving usage guide advice and the members of the general public, have no longer been clearly separated. In the medium where publishing became accessible to anyone with an Internet connection, many of the members of the general public with an interest in usage got the opportunity to create their own weblogs and contribute to discussions on language use (Schaffer 2010:23-24). One such medium where language use is discussed and described is Wikipedia, the online collaborative encyclopaedia community. In the sphere of advice on language use where linguistic authorities traditionally functioned as gate keepers, Wikipedia currently functions as a platform for translation between the groups which would otherwise not communicate. The status of grammars and usage guides as authorities is thus challenged and the questions of language use are negotiated on a more equal footing between the language experts and the general public.

In this paper we present an analysis of Wikipedia entries and the secondary Wikipedia Talk pages which editors use to discuss the respective Wikipedia entries, on usage items such as *ain't*, the split infinitive, preposition stranding, and who/whom. The reason behind choosing this particular online genre for the analysis of the discussions on and descriptions of language use is the fact that all of the content is created by the members of the general public who negotiate the content of the entries in the secondary Talk pages. On the other hand, the reason for choosing language use as a topic for demonstrating the phenomenon of re-contextualisation of expert discourse is the aforementioned established gap between the advice-giving experts and the advice-seeking laypeople.

Although Wikipedia instructs its contributors, "Wikipedians", to provide informative and descriptive accounts of usage items, the Talk pages demonstrate that many of the contributors express prescriptive attitudes towards usage. We focus here on an analysis of the prescriptive and descriptive arguments of the collaborators creating Wikipedia entries and the guiding principles of Wikipedia that provide the basis for the construction of the entries.

The second point of the analysis focuses on a comparison of the Wikipedia entries on selected usage items with their equivalent entries in usage guides, which are retrieved from the Hyper Usage Guide of English or HUGE database (developed by Robin Straaijer at Leiden University). The HUGE database (http://huge.ullet.net/) is a growing collection of usage guides covering the period from 1770 onwards. The database currently includes 77 usage guides and its aim is to combine a history of usage advice into a single library. The HUGE database has been envisioned within a research project at Leiden University Centre for Linguistics called *Bridging the Unbridgeable: linguists, prescriptivists and the general public*. In doing so, we will address in Section 5 the differences in the styles of the Wikipedia and usage guide entries, analyse the arguments provided and the language of prescription and description.

2. The Usage Guide as a Genre

The usage guide has been described as "a neglected genre" (Weiner 1988:171), although a rising number of studies have been devoted to it since the late 1980s (Busse & Tieken-Boon van Ostade 2011). The usage guide genre has been defined as "an integrative all-in-one reference work written for educated lay people that bridges the traditional divide between a grammar and a dictionary" (Busse & Schröder 2009:72). Being a usage guide author himself, Weiner (1988:173) defines the goal of usage guides as helping its users decide between alternatives which from a descriptive point both exist in language, but of which for some reason or another one is considered less good English than its alternative.

Usage guides are not intended for the language learner, but rather for the native speaker (Weiner 1988:173). Among the native speakers, the target readership of such usage guides are in Labovian terms "the linguistically insecure" (Beal 2009:42), social climbers who are not "born into" using the standard language, and who are "shamed by their English" (Beal 2009:42). As the author of the arguably most influential usage guide, *Modern English Usage*, Henry Fowler argues in his correspondence with the Oxford University Press:

> In point of fact we have our eyes not on the foreigner, but on the half-educated Englishman of literary proclivities who wants to know Can I say so-&-so?, What does this familiar phrase or word mean?, Is this use

> English? (...) the kind of Englishman who has idioms floating in his head in a jumbled state, & knows it… (In Burchfield 1991:96)

Usage guides continue to be extremely popular; a study by Busse and Schröder (2008) showed that the numbers of the usage guide publications are steadily on the rise, presumably along with the rising popularity of other guides, self-help and how-to literature.

Several linguists have provided critical accounts of the usage guide tradition. In his classification of different types of usage guides, Algeo (1991:6-13) points to the fact that the largest group of usage guides is that consisting of books that largely depend on *ipse dixit* judgements, in other words, guides that largely rely on the personal judgements of their authors (Algeo 1991:6). Usage guides on the other side of the prescriptivism-descriptivism spectrum are far and few between. An example of a more descriptive usage guide according to Algeo is *Webster's Dictionary of English Usage*, which he describes as "a book [which] does not tell people what they ought to say, but explains the options and the likely consequences of choosing one option over another" (Algeo 1991:11). Although there seems to be a chronological shift towards usage advice that is more explanatory and usage-based, some more recent publications, such as Burchfield (1996) and Garner (1998), still seem to be relying on personal, subjective judgements of their authors (Peters 2006:765). Although usage guides tend to vary considerably in the choice of their items, they usually include the traditional shibboleths of usage (Peters 2006:12) also known as "old chestnuts" (Weiner 1988:173). It can be argued that normative judgements essentially belong to usage guides. Their readers expect clear, user-friendly guidance, which is usually lacking in the more objective accounts of the more jargon-loaded grammar books and dictionaries (Busse & Schröder 2009:84).

Despite the fact that usage guides are read for their often clear-cut advice, scholars analysing the tradition of usage guides warn of their lack of lateral referencing (Peters & Young 1997:318), which serves little use to the contemporary reader who would like to be informed about current usage trends. Those works that do not include the analyses of contemporary usage do little more than replicate conservative attitudes, support "the paralexicographic tradition" and institutionalise the tradition of "tertiary responses to language", which are widely accepted regardless of their validity (Bloomfield 1944:45).

3. The History of Collaboration in Knowledge Creation: From the *OED* to *Wikis*

Collaboration in knowledge creation, as we find it today in Wikipedia, is hardly a novelty: it has been around since biblical times when scribes simultaneously edited, updated, interpreted, and reinterpreted texts as they were transcribing them (McArthur in Stvilia et al. 2008:983). One of the greatest global processes of collaboration and co-creation in the pre-computer age, which is also of special interest for linguistics, is that of the making of the *Oxford English Dictionary* (*OED*) (Simpson 2004:192-196; Stvilia et al. 2008:983; Bhalla 2011:8-9).

Besides the practice of contacting specialist consultants, the *OED* has a long history of recruiting volunteer contributors from the members of the public (Simpson 2004, 193-194; for the history of the Appeals see the *OED*'s website).[2] In 1879, the then recently appointed editor of the OED, James Murray, decided to instigate *Appeal to the English-Speaking and English-Reading Public to Read Books and Make Extracts for the Philological Society's New Dictionary* (Mugglestone 2005:15). This "crowdsourcing" process contributed significantly to the *OED*, with thousands of contributors and millions of archived physical slips which have been in use until today (see the *OED*'s website). Not unlike Wikipedia, Murray's *Appeal* encouraged democratic collaboration, which allowed everyone to take part: "This is work in which anyone can join, even the most indolent novel-reader will find it little trouble to put a pencil-mark against any word or phrase that strikes him, and he can afterwards copy out the context at his leisure" (from the *Appeal* in Mugglestone 2005:16). In order to manage the work done by the volunteers more efficiently, Murray complemented the initial *Appeal* by a pamphlet including a more targeted approach including "lists of wants" and "desiderata" which made the collaborative process more helpful for the editors (*OED*'s website). The collaboration of the *OED* with the general public has continued until today in the form of online appeals.[3]

Although quite ground-breaking, the collaborative participation on the *OED* did include organisational difficulties: the contributions were occasionally obsolete, incorrect or duplicated, and they required a substantial amount of editing and assessment from the central institution.

---

[2] "'Your dictionary needs you': a brief history of the OED's appeals to the public", http://public.oed.com/the-oed-appeals/history-of-the-appeals/. Retrieved on 20.5.2014.

[3] See "OED Appeals", www.oed.com/appeals. Retrieved on 20.5.2014.

Such issues have been largely overcome today with the development of collaborative processes which are greatly facilitated by the introduction of online content management technologies such as Wikis (Stvilia et al. 2008:984), through which thousands of contributors continue creating dictionaries (*Wiktionary*) and online grammars and usage guides (*English Grammar and Usage Wiki*).

4. Wikipedia: The Online Collaborative Encyclopaedia Community

As of April 2014, Wikipedia is the sixth most visited website in the world.[4] It has become the most widely used tool for knowledge dissemination and the largest collaborative text editing project in the history of mankind. The multilingual and freely accessible online encyclopaedia is available in 285 languages. Potentially every Internet user can edit documents on Wikipedia. To date it has approximately 31 million articles and 76,000 active contributors. Contributors are considered to be "active" with a minimum of five contributions per month. There are currently 4,518,174 articles written in English.[5] The greatest contribution of this project is the fact that through it a vast quantity of information which was previously accessible only through traditional knowledge institutions such as libraries has been greatly popularised and made available to the general public.

Wikipedia is an instantiation of the Wiki software concept, which allows users to collaborate in a web-based manner and to edit a single document. Originally it was developed by Ward Cunningham, who was looking for a tool that would enable better collaboration among developers (Ebersbach et al. 2008:14). Cunningham also introduced "wiki-philosophy", which is based on the unlimited possibility to create and edit pages, and is referred to as the "open editing concept" (Fichter 2005:47). Wiki systems are also document management systems which allow users to trace back every single change that has been made to the document and reverse it. The open editing concept was designed to enable a more democratic access to information systems to users with no advanced technological skills.

Since Wikipedia is constructed collaboratively, it can be regarded as an online community, which is defined as a group of people "who come

[4] "The top 500 sites on the web", http://www.alexa.com. Retrieved on 20.5.2014.
[5] "Wikipedia: About", http://en.wikipedia.org/wiki/Wikipedia:About. Retrieved on 25.5.2014.

together for a particular *purpose*, and who are guided by *policies* (including norms and rules) and supported by *software*" (Preece & Maloney-Krichmar 2005: Introduction, para. 3). Bruns (2008) places Wikipedia in the wider context of the social media which aim at participation by a wider audience, not just by a community of experts. Through client-based editing, the traditional linear knowledge dissemination process from the expert to the lay community has been enriched by the fact that laypeople and experts are now interacting on the same platform in a multilateral way. The representation of knowledge on Wikipedia is constructed in a self-organized way; nevertheless, Wikipedia is not an egalitarian system (Gutounig 2015:149-150). Established hierarchies and powers are, however, not attributed through external status, but through actual contribution to the system. In this way they can be defined as "meritocracies" (Bruns 2008:25).

The entries and the editing interface are just the most visible side of Wikipedia. To enable the discursive aspect of collaboration, Wikis usually have discussion functions, in the case of Wikipedia, in the form of Talk pages. These pages enable not only collective editing of the entries, but also engaging in a discussion on the topic of the entry. The Talk pages should lead to a usually temporary consensus regarding the entry in question. The basic principles of the open-editing concept combined with the traceability and discussion functions enable the self-organized editing process without central governance among people who are usually not acquainted with each other. Due to these characteristics, Wikipedia seems to establish what is considered in some aspects to be an unprecedented, emergent discourse context (Herring 2013:14).

4.1 Related Work

Due to the success of the Wikipedia project, a substantial number of scholarly publications have dealt with the phenomenon in the course of the last decade. Studies have so far focussed on the collaboration and coordination patterns in Wikipedia (Viégas et al. 2004). Researchers have devoted attention to the acts of vandalism on Wikipedia, i.e. edits that were made with bad intentions (Viégas et al. 2007:3; Potthast et al. 2008), as well as to the quality of Wikipedia entries when compared with traditional encyclopaedias (Giles 2005). These studies showed that entries in *The Encyclopaedia Britannica* and Wikipedia go head to head concerning the number of factual errors or misinterpretation of important concepts.

In linguistics, Emigh and Herring (2005) were among the first to analyse the aspect of text production on Wikipedia. By performing genre analysis on the level of formality and informality of Wikipedia entries, they found that in spite of the collaborative and open-editing approach of Wikipedia, its level of formality can be compared to that of traditional encyclopaedias. Myers (2010) devoted a book to the analysis of the discourse of blogs and Wikis. According to Myers (2010:ix), there are two main reasons to analyse Wikipedia linguistically; the first is focussing on new aspects of the language of emerging web genres, and the second is linguists' contribution to a phenomenon that has been dealt with primarily in the field of technology. In his analysis of Wikipedia, Myers primarily focussed on the interaction among "Wikipedians" on Talk pages.

4.2 The Structure of Wikipedia Entries and Talk Pages

The fact that Wikipedia entries hardly differ from the entries in traditional print encyclopaedias can be explained by the phenomenon that, since the beginnings of the project, Wikipedians "were guided by the rhetorical models of existing encyclopaedias" (Shirky 2010:116) and that they have "internalized cultural norms of encyclopaedic style" (Herring 2013:15). The formality and stylistic homogeneity of entries (Herring 2013:9) is for a large part the accomplishment of the active rank-and-file Wikipedia users, who continue changing existing text according to the stylistic norms of a traditional encyclopaedia, and who are also referred to as page "watchers" (Viégas et al. 2004:580). A relevant point of Wikipedia's departure from traditional print encyclopaedias are its secondary Talk pages, which greatly determine knowledge construction processes on Wikipedia, and which are an essential part of defining a collaborative online encyclopaedia. An example of such a Talk page can be found in Figure 1.

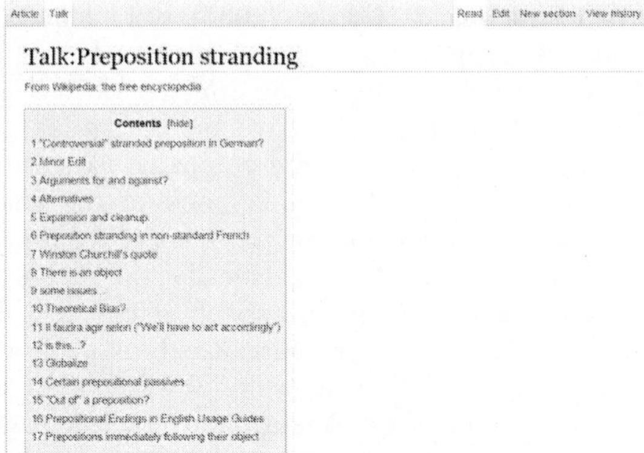

Fig.1: Talk page on Preposition stranding

Talk pages are devoted to the discussion of issues surrounding the topics on "real" pages. They provide a different forum from the Wikipedia entries, and they consist of discussions on what information should or should not be included in the main articles (Viégas et al. 2004:576). The Talk pages on Wikipedia contribute to Wikipedia being a successful system. They serve a number of functions in creating and managing articles, such as the strategic planning of edits, and the enforcement of Wikipedia policies and conducting guidelines (Viégas et al. 2007:1). Talk pages have a central role in keeping up the quality of Wikipedia entries. They are conversation places and as such are governed by different rules from the entries. For example, the entries are not deleted in the Talk pages, which is often the case with the edited content in the entries, and the participants are encouraged to sign their postings (Viégas et al. 2007:6). There are three main layout and mark-up conventions in Talk pages, (1) signatures, (2) indention and (3) discussion topics (Figure 1) (Viégas et al. 2007:6-7). The convention for the contributors to sign their postings in Talk pages is respected in 67% of the instances (Viégas et al. 2007:7). When the postings are left unsigned, only an IP address appears in the end of the posting. Users usually indent their answers to previous postings in order to visually disambiguate the relationship between the postings. Finally, contributors are instructed to put each new conversation topic at the end of the existing Talk page.

Researchers have found that the genre of Talk pages most resembles informal web discussion boards (Emigh & Herring 2005:7; Myers 2010:154-156), which is in contrast to the formal style of the entries themselves. The linguistic features identified as indicative of the informal, web-chat style are first-person pronouns, contractions, emoticons, and informal lexicon (Emigh & Herring 2005:8) as well as conversational discourse markers such as discourse particles (*well*, *umm* and *ahem*), nonwords (*ahem*, *uh huh*) and politeness markers (modals, verbs of cognition and perception, and modal adverbs) (Myers 2010: Chapter10). Politeness plays a crucial role in Talk pages, as it softens potential conflicts and contributes to the general feeling of belonging to a Community of Practice (Myers 2010:155-156).

Concerning the topics and functions of discussions on Talk pages, Viégas et al. (2007:7-8) analysed the dimensions along which contributions to Talk pages can be classified. Wikipedians most commonly use Talk pages to request for coordination of the entry edits and they also approach the participants as a community of experts and ask for information. Talk pages occasionally include off-topic remarks, which means that the participants discuss topics loosely related to the entry or rather report on their own experiences and opinions. Some of the Talk pages provide insights into "edit wars" between groups of Wikipedians, in which two people or groups of opposing opinions alternate between versions of the page. In some instances of discussions on Talk pages, participants also point to internal resources, namely, other Wikipedia pages (Viégas et al. 2007:8-9). Ferschke et al. (2012) analysed dialogue acts in Simple English Talk pages, and they found that the most common types of entries on Talk pages are information-providing comments, in which Wikipedians communicate new information, request information or suggest changes. Wikipedians tend to report on their edits in order to justify the changes made to the entries, and almost 40% of turns in Talk pages are article criticisms. It is common to start a discussion or a topic on a Talk page by referring to a particular deficiency in the accompanying article.

Myers (2010:146-154) found in the analysis of types of argumentation on Wikipedia that the rhetoric of Wikipedians is greatly influenced by Wikipedia's explicit principles: (1) Neutral Point of View, (2) No Original Research, (3) Verifiability, (4) Be bold and (5) Civility. Neutral point of view, or NPOV as Wikipedians refer to it in their discussions, implies that editors should try to include a full range of views on a topic in their accounts. No Original Research (NOR) warns editors against publishing new ideas or mentioning facts which cannot be documented instead of referring only to the available sources. Additionally, every statement needs to be verified; in case it is not, editors insert "Citation needed" tags into the entries. The "Be bold" principle of Wikipedia urges editors to rather say something roughly accurate than nothing at all, and to build up content. Finally, due to the fact that the goal behind each entry is to reach consensus, editors are urged to be polite and cooperative.

5. Analysing Wikipedia Entries on Language Use

For this study we selected seven Wikipedia entries on usage items, in alphabetical order: *Ain't*, *Double negative*, *Fewer vs. less*, *Gender neutrality in English*, *Preposition stranding*, *The Split infinitive and Whom* (Table 1). These entries were selected as they all included accounts of acceptability of usage and were described in the context of the prescriptivism-descriptivism debate.

Most of the included usage items have a longstanding place in the history of the prescriptive tradition. The prescriptive rules regarding the respective usage items could be summed up as following: Do not use *ain't* when you mean *isn't* or *aren't*. Do not use more than one negative particle to negate the same clause. Do not use *less* instead of *fewer* with plural countable nouns. Do not use gender-specific words in non-gender specific contexts. Do not place a preposition in the end of the sentence, but before the noun phrase it modifies. Do not insert anything between the infinitive *to* marker and the verb-form itself. Use *whom* as the objective form of the interrogative pronoun *who*.

In Table 1, we provide data on the selected Wikipedia entries, including their length, the number of watchers who are alerted when changes are made to each of the entries, date of page creation, total number of edits, total number of distinct authors, page views, and comparison of the data with average values for Wikipedia entries where these values are available, namely for page length, number of edits and page views. All pages on usage items are considerably more often edited when compared to an average Wikipedia entry (see column Total N of edits), which is on average edited 21.82 times. The usage entries attract more attention, contribution and updates from the editors. The entries on usage items are also considerably longer than an average entry. Although they are heavily edited, not all entries on usage items are viewed more than the average (see column Difference to avg. page views). *Preposition stranding* and *Whom* are the least popular among the selected usage entries. The *Split infinitive* and *Ain't* attract by far the most readers. Another sign of popularity are the numbers of editors of a particular entry, which are the highest for *Gender neutrality*, *Double negative* and the *Split infinitive*. In the following sections (5.1) and (5.2), we give a description of the Wikipedia contributors and we describe the entries on usage items themselves.

Title of the article	Page length in bytes	Difference to avg. page length	N of page watchers	Date of page creation	Total N of edits	Total N of distinct authors	Page views April 2014	Difference to avg. page views
Average values	2680	n/a			21.82		2095.45	n/a
Ain't	16,040	+498.5%	58	6.9.2010	199	112	18731	+793.89%
Double negative	25,007	+833.1%	68	9.3.2003	849	513	9880	+371.5%
Fewer vs. Less	6,774	152.8%	<30	17.1.2007	120	64	3710	+77.05%
Gender neutrality	33,962	+1167.24%	111	24.8.2002	1,331	551	4025	+92.08%
Preposition stranding	13,486	+403.21%	<30	27.1.2006	165	85	2033	-3.07%
Split infinitive	49,338	+1741%	118	18.11.2001	1,124	493	18761	+795.32%
Whom	21,064	+685.97%	33	4.3.2004	400	208	2095	-0.2%

*The data were retrieved from each respective article's page information (20.4.2014), Wikipedia article traffic statistics (http://stats.grok.se, 20.5.2014) and Wikimedia statistics (http://stats.wikimedia.org/, 25.5.2014).

Tab. 1: Data on selected Wikipedia entries on usage items

5.1 The Editors

Researchers usually distinguish between two general groups of Wikipedia editors (Bryant et al. 2005), i.e. novice and expert users. Novices contribute to topics they are familiar with, identifying omissions and weaknesses, and correcting them. Up to 60% of Wikipedia's registered users never make another edit after their first 24 hours.[6] The experts' goals expand as they continue contributing to Wikipedia. Although they continue to improve the quality of the content, they have an additional role in the community, as they become concerned with maintaining the quality of Wikipedia itself. Expert editors use tools such as watchlists and WikiProjects which allow them to review changes and observe instances of vandalism.

Another relevant distinction between novice and expert users is their sense of community. Whereas for novices Wikipedia seems to be a collection of articles, more experienced contributors view themselves as members of a tribe in which they establish their identity through their contributions (Bryant et al. 2005:7). Novice users usually become experts through observation and direct coaching by the more knowledgeable users (Bryant et al. 2005:8).

In this study we additionally attempted to address the question: "Who are the contributors to the entries on usage items?", and more specifically, "Are they *experts* who are dealing with language in their professional contexts?". Due to the fact that at least 30% of the editors remain anonymous (Viégas et al. 2007:7) and many do not provide biographical data on their user websites, it was impossible to present an accountable quantitative overview of the editors' professions or involvement in language-related fields. However, by observing available user websites, it is clear that a number of editors of usage entries work in language-related professions, whereas others include language and grammar among their personal interests. An author who writes under the name of Doric Loon is Professor of Translation. On his user website, he provides information about his interests and about Wikipedia edits which greatly coincide with his real-life research interests. Another frequent contributor on the usage items pages is Daniel Freeman, who in spite of not having a job which would directly qualify him as a language expert describes himself as a user of proper English (example 1):

(1) I am no great writer but I know the basics of proper English writing. I even use the word "whom" correctly! When I worked at the local

[6] "Wikipedia", http://en.wikipedia.org/wiki/Wikipedia. Retrieved on 25.5.2014.

> newspaper they called me the "comma king" because I was an expert at knowing where commas are required, and where they are optional.

Jerry Friedman is another non-expert, but, again, a contributor who qualifies as a well-informed individual teaching physics and mathematics and providing style advice for Wikipedians on his user website, an example of which is presented in (2).

(2) Have some doubt about "Note that", "Interestingly", "It is important to note that", etc. You can often just leave them out.

Gramorak is a retired language teacher who collects early grammars of English and tries to write a grammar of the English verb. SoSaysSunny double-majored in Astrophysics and Math, and says she cannot avoid noticing grammar mistakes and typos, which earned her the moniker Renegade Grammarian for contacting webmasters concerning grammar mistakes. Her "go-to" book on English usage is Fowler's *Modern English Usage*.

Although many contributions remain anonymous, and not enough biographical data on the contributors are available to draw general conclusions, it can be observed that authors with more "real-life" linguistic expertise often contribute more frequently, and assume a more relevant role in coordinating the edits than the anonymous and novice users.

5.2 Wikipedia Entries on Usage Items

Busse and Schröder (2006:71) describe usage guides as works in which the description of grammar and lexis are synthesised, contrary to the traditional division of labour between grammar books and dictionaries. The Wikipedia entries analysed here do not merely describe lexical items, as does its sister dictionary project *Wiktionary*; however, they are not usage guide entries either. Instead of instructing the readers on language use, Wikipedians are urged to create informative entries (example 3).

(3) Wikipedia is not in the business of saying how words, idioms, phrases etc., should be used (but it may be important in the context of an encyclopedia article to discuss how a word is used).[7]

---

[7] "Wikipedia: Wikipedia is not a dictionary", http://en.wikipedia.org/wiki/Wikipedia:Wikipedia_is_not_a_dictionary. Retrieved on 25.5.2014.

Nevertheless, the secondary Wikipedia pages, i.e. the Talk pages, demonstrate that prescriptive attitudes are present to a great extent among the contributors and attempts are made at the initial stages of creating the respective entries to include the correctness labels related to the particular usage items, as is evident in (4).

(4) The article reads like a style manual. The majority of the article is focused on how to use who/m, with little focus on the historical development. Look at that tiny section on its history, it doesn't even tell us what the Old English and Middle English forms were! The tone of the article has a very prescriptivist attitude, reading more like a random book on grammar than an encyclopedic article. This is unacceptable; all linguistic articles on Wikipedia are descriptivist, sensibly so. Cntrational
I agree. That is a risk with articles involving common grammatical foibles and hobbyhorses. See also Apostrophe, which needs to be guarded against amateurism of the less benign sort. So please: do more than your one edit so far, to improve the article. NoeticaTea?[8]

However, although they are often overtly expressed, prescriptive attitudes and negative value judgements of usage items rarely make it into the encyclopaedia itself, due to the interventions of Wikipedia entries such as the one in example 4. In order to explore this phenomenon, we will here first use corpus linguistics tools in order to illustrate the differences between Wikipedia entries and usage guide entries (see Section 5.3) and, secondly, illustrate the discourses situated in the prescriptivist-descriptivist discourse on the Talk pages as well as the dynamics that prevent them from becoming embedded in the respective Wikipedia entries (see Section 5.4).

5.3. Corpus-Based Comparison of Wikipedia Entries and Usage Guides

For this analysis two sub-corpora on seven usage items were created, the first being made up of Wikipedia entries, and the second from the usage guide entries available through the HUGE, in order to explore the potential differences between the two text types. The exact numbers of entries per usage item, and the number of words per each topic and per sub-corpus are available in Table 2.

---

[8] "Talk: Who (pronoun)", http://en.wikipedia.org/wiki/Talk:Who_(pronoun). Retrieved on 25.5.2014.

Usage Item	N of entries	N of usage guides containing an entry for the item	Total N of words per usage problem in HUGE (combined	Total N of words per entry in Wikipedia
Ain't	29	23	8,764	2,057
Double negative	49	40	15,440	3,394
Fewer vs. less	73	58	14,435	919
Gender neutrality	40	34	14,633	3,976
Preposition stranding	51	47	21,212	1,801
Split infinitive	71	59	34,121	6,473
Whom	87	60	38,840	2,850
			Total: 147,445	**Total: 21,470**

Tab. 2: Sub-corpora on selected usage items: HUGE and Wikipedia entries

In order of popularity among usage guides, the usage items are listed as follows: *Whom*, *Split infinitive*, *Fewer vs. less*, *Preposition stranding*, *Double negative*, *Gender neutrality* and *Ain't*. If we compare this order to the number of views of the Wikipedia entries in Table 1 (*Split infinitive*, *Ain't*, *Double negative*, *Gender neutrality*, *Fewer vs. less*, *Whom* and *Preposition stranding*), we can see that there is a considerable discrepancy between what users seem to find of most interest and what is mostly written about. For example, the most popular item in usage guides, *Whom*, is very poorly frequented on Wikipedia when compared to the other usage items. These numbers, however, cannot be compared one-to-one, since we need to take the temporal dimension into consideration, because the usage guides in HUGE date back to the late eighteenth century, and the first usage item entry in Wikipedia was created in 2001. The page view statistics on Wikipedia entries are an indicator of how interested people are in certain topics. Thus, they provide a more accurate and data-based account of the actual usage problems people are interested in, in contrast to the usage problems selected by the usage guide authors.

In comparing the two sub-corpora, the entries in HUGE and the Wikipedia entries, we used the web-based Wmatrix tool (Rayson 2009) for finding key words, and subsequently key semantic domains which would help determine significant differences between the Wikipedia-type entries and those found in usage guides. The Wmatrix tool (Rayson 2009) enables access not only to the traditional tools of corpus linguistics, such as key words, concordance lines and frequency lists, but also to both automatic part-of-speech and USAS semantic taggers (Rayson et al. 2004). In this analysis we focussed on the results obtained from comparing the key semantic domains via the USAS semantic tagger that enables the researcher to identify relevant semantic categories which are overrepresented in one corpus when compared to another. Since the two sub-corpora were small in size, especially the Wikipedia sub-corpus, instead of focussing on key words, we decided to focus on key semantic domains which facilitate the recognition of small frequency items as key if they belong to the same domain. In the analysis introduced below, we present the top key categories, which were calculated by using the log likelihood test. The minimum key value of the log likelihood statistical test was set to 15.13, which corresponds to $p < 0.0001$, and the minimum word frequency from each domain was set to 5 occurrences. The results of the analysis are shown in Tables 3 and 4. In Table 3, the lexical items overrepresented in the HUGE sub-corpus are categorised into four different semantic domains. These domains are based on the USAS tagging system, but we also slightly modified them to better fit the purposes of the analysis. The four semantic domains over-represented in usage guides when compared to Wikipedia are *Pronouns*, *Downtoners*, *Evaluation: Inaccurate*, and *In power*.

POSITIVE SEMANTIC DOMAINS IN HUGE	LEXICAL ITEMS
Pronouns	*it, one, we, they, you, what, he, which, our, these, those, your*
Downtoners: (a) Minimisers (b) Compromisers	(a) *hardly, scarcely, at least, barely, at all* (b) *quite, pretty, rather, sufficiently, reasonably*
Evaluation: Inaccurate	*incorrect, wrong, missing, error, mistake, ungrammatical, blunder*
In power	*power, rule, govern, master, hierarchy, insist, order, force, upper-class*

Tab. 3: Positive semantic domains in HUGE

The use of pronouns in register variation has been addressed in various corpus-based studies conducted, among others, by Biber (1995:30). First- and second-person pronouns have been repeatedly found to be related to interactiveness, whereas third-person pronouns tend to be related to the narrative dimension of register variation (Biber 1995:151). Usage guide authors guide the readers and provide advice. They are more narrative in their style than the factual Wikipedia entries, and they occasionally address the reader directly as in example 5.

(5) **We** do know that it had an earlier spelling an 't (or sometimes a 'n't), which you can see would not be difficult to derive phonologically from are or am; (Ward 1989, 60)

According to Quirk et al. (1985:452), downtoners are intensifying adjuncts which lower the effect on the force of the modified verbs. The difference between *minimisers* and *compromises* in Table 3 is, however, a matter of degree. Minimisers realise a greater degree of intensity and negate the full implication of the predicate. The use of downtoners and other types of hedging devices observed in example 6 can be well explained in pragmatic terms.

(6) After reading these we can perhaps conclude that the decisive influence is probably the vague impression beforehand that whom is more likely to be right; but it need **hardly** be said that slapdash procedure of that kind deserves no mercy when it fails. (Fowler 1965, 707)

The authors are attempting to emphasise an orientation to the reader by using first and second-person pronouns and hedging devices through which they attempt to gain the reader's acceptance of the proposed arguments (cf. Hyland 1998:xiii-ix).

In a study of prescriptivist language in letters to the editor (Lukač forthcoming), it will be demonstrated that the choice of lexis which indicates negative evaluation is typical of prescriptivism. In prescriptivist texts marked, non-standard forms are compared to the non-marked standard ones, and labelled *incorrect* as in example 7.

(7) A double negative does, however, sometimes survive accidentally and incorrectly in Mod.E., especially in conversation. (Treble and Vallins 1936, 65)

It should be noted though, that unlike in the usage guide *A.B.C. of English Usage* (1936) in example 7, newer usage guides do not directly refer to usage as "incorrect" *per se*. They rather refer to older sources through which such attitudes are secondarily transmitted in the form of citations, as in the following example from Webster's *Dictionary of English Usage* which cites Fowler on the usage of *ain't*.

(8) By 1926 **H. W. Fowler** could view first-person use of *ain't* quite differently from other uses: *A(i)n't* is merely colloquial, & as used for *isn't* is an **uneducated blunder & serves no useful purpose**. (Ward 1989, 60)

Finally, the lexical items from the domain *In power* are statistically overused in comparison again in Wikipedia entries due to the common reference to rules in the language of usage guides. See (9) for an example of this.

(9) The *OED* lists numerous other examples (15-20C.) of the breakdown of formal grammatical **rules governing** *who* and *whom*. (Fowler 2000, 847)

Table 4 demonstrates the domains and their respective lexical items that are over-represented in Wikipedia pages when compared to the usage guide entries. Five different domains are listed, but a number of them can be combined and ascribed to the same phenomenon. Thus, numbers and the much more common references to personal names and the media provide common evidence of one characteristic to the online encyclopaedia (see above) that is generally largely lacking in usage guides, i.e. referencing. The *Numbers* in the Wikipedia corpus most commonly refer publication dates cited and the *Personal names* are often names of authors. The domain *The Media: Newspapers* consists mostly of words that are parts of titles of journals and other types of publications.

Instead of providing *ipse dixit* judgements, such as the one common in usage guides, Wikipedia authors, guided by the Verifiability principles (see above) are obliged to support their arguments by providing external sources, which do not include only individual linguistic authorities, but also up-to-date linguistic research. External sources in Wikipedia usage item entries include usage guides, grammar books, newspaper and journal articles, encyclopaedias and academic weblogs (such as *Language Log*).

NEGATIVE SEMANTIC DOMAINS IN HUGE	LEXICAL ITEMS
Numbers (dates and page numbers)	*1925*, *p. 25*, *1998*, etc.
Languages and language varieties	*British, standard English, Cockney, Australian, Aussie, American, Scots, French, German, Greek, Latin*
Personal names	*Eric Partridge, Jonathan Swift, Dickens, George Bernard Shaw, H. W. Fowler, Shakespeare*
The Media: Newspapers	*article, press, magazine, newspaper, correspondent, headline*
Language, grammar and linguistic processes	*utterance, token, grammar, verb, plural, denote, sign, clause, imply, proverbial, speakers, usage, vowel, pronunciation, dialects, language*

Tab. 4: Negative semantic domains in HUGE

Instead of referring to grammatical rules, the Wikipedia entries focus on reporting linguistic descriptions of different types of usage in different varieties of English, and, occasionally, the editors also introduce comparisons with other languages regarding a particular usage item. For this reason, the semantic fields made up of lexical items from the field of linguistics, *Language, grammar and linguistic processes*, and *Languages and language varieties*, are over-represented when compared to the usage guides. An example of the types of accounts which rely on the specialised terminology of linguistics can be seen in the excerpt from the entry on the *Double negative* in example 10.

(10) A similar development to a **circumfix** from double **negation** can be seen in non-Indo-European **languages**, too: for example, in Maltese, *kiel* "he ate" is negated as *ma kielx* "he did not eat", where the **verb** is preceded by a negative **particle** *ma-* "not" and followed by the **particle** *-x*, which was originally a shortened form of *xejn* "nothing" – thus, "he didn't eat nothing".

To return to Biber's dimensions which were mentioned briefly in relation to the discussion of Table 3, the linguistic items which are characteristic of Wikipedia entries are more representative of informative language than of what we normally find in usage guides. Precise names (*Personal names*) and references (*Numbers*, *The Media: Newspapers*) are given, and the specialised terminology of descriptive linguistics is used, which stands in stark contrast to the rule-oriented, guiding and often prescriptive language of usage guides.

5.4 Comparing Wikipedia Talk pages and Entries on Usage

As previously mentioned, the reason why Wikipedia entries maintain a high level of quality and objectivity is that general consensus exists between Wikipedians, which is for the most part obtained by the experts, i.e. senior Wikipedians who have been around for some time. In practical terms, the quality is directly guided through the application of Wikipedia principles. In this section we will show how prescriptivist attitudes have failed to enter the articles on the described usage items, due to the application of Wikipedia principles.

As mentioned in the previous section, one of the ways in which the Wikipedia entries on usage which we analysed differ from the usage guide entries is referencing, which is due to Wikipedia's principle of Verifiability. The references and examples of proper usage in the prescriptivist tradition are the renowned literary figures, and the "one's social and intellectual betters" (Landau 1979:4). In the HUGE sub-corpus analysed here there are many instances which illustrate that the "intellectual betters" are often taken as exemplary language users, as can be seen in example 11.

(11) Than them (=than they) is used by **Adelaide Procter**; than me, occasionally in **Shakespeare**, **Swift**, **Prior**, **Pope**, **Dr. Johnson**, **Southey**, **Thackeray**, **Bulwer**, and **Clough**; than him in **Shakespeare**, **Johnson**, and **Kingsley**; than her in **Boswell** and **Prior**. It has been said in earlier paragraphs that these phrases are found in the **King James Bible**, **Caxton**, **the Genevan Bible**, **Goldsmith**, **Scott**, **Beddoes**. (Hall 1917, 293)

The discussions on Wikipedia Talk pages illustrate that entries without appropriate references are deleted from the entries (example 12), classical authors are not always seen as appropriate sources for illustrating acceptable usage (example 13), and even the traditionally reputable sources do not escape the Wikipedia editors' critical scrutiny (example 14). In example 12, the editor called Drjamesaustin is negotiating his edit with another experienced editor. The discussion is resolved when he admits to an insufficient basis for his addition to the entry, which is based on intuition and interpretation, instead of a reputable source.

(12) That's fine with me. I can cite no references to back up my interpretation – merely my Latin-influenced view of grammar – so will gladly bow to higher authority. Thanks Jerry! Drjamesaustin[9]

Some authors of usage guides uncritically list classical sources to illustrate good usage. In example 13, the editor is questioning both the sources, and the appropriateness of comparing the usage in poetry to the everyday usage.

(13) Likewise I don't see that the use in poetry is particularly important. We do need the example from Shakespeare and the one from Burns, but I don't think the Shakespeare one is necessarily "to good effect". Anyway, much though I like poetry, I'd say it's outside the mainstream of usage, so it doesn't belong in the lead. JerryFriedman

Finally, even reputable sources such as Garner's *Modern American Usage* (1998) referred to in example 14, are critically evaluated and

[9] "Talk: Split infinitive", http://en.wikipedia.org/wiki/Talk:Split_infinitive. Retrieved on 25.5.2014.

compared with other sources in order to report on insights which are most plausible or most widely accepted by the expert community. In this way, the editors avoid repeating myths that could have been presented and reported on in numerous sources but have nevertheless been disputed, such as in our example, the statement that the eighteenth-century grammarian Robert Lowth proscribed against the split infinitive (cf. Tieken 2010).

(14) The article now says that Lowth did NOT proscribe against the split infinitive. Every reference I have ever seen says that he did, and he is cited in Garner's latest usage manual. Where is the evidence he did NOT create this proscription? Manning
Manning, if you've want, you can add the cite from Garner to footnote 13 as more evidence that reputable people believe in the myth. JerryFriedman

Another Wikipedia principle which works in favour of the lack of prescriptive argumentation in the articles is the Neutral Point of View (NPOV) principle. In the words of Cameron (1995:vi), "language is, notoriously, something which engenders strong feelings". The expressions of attitudes towards language, although working against the NPOV principle, resurface in the Talk pages, while off-topic remarks on usage of the for-and-against type are common in Talk pages (example 15).

(15) Split infinitives are absolutely never acceptable as any grammarian would tell you. The idea that they are acceptable in some contexts or that this is a controversial issue among grammarians is simply a common misconception. For a reliable source, just ask any English Professor or even any K12 English teacher. The Mysterious El Willstro
You are entitled to your usage. You'll be very lucky indeed if you can find a university teacher of English who agrees with you, but K12 teacher might just be possible. Good luck with that. Doric Loon
(...)
If she'd like to contribute information with reliable published sources to the article, she's welcome to. JerryFriedman

The closed off-topic discussion in example 15 entitled "Hear me out…" is an example of an exchange of opinions about the acceptability of a particular usage item. Whereas the user introducing the topic, The Mysterious El Willstro, introduced arguments based on alleged opinions of language professionals, one of the most active editors of the article responds by requesting explicit references in print form, which The Mysterious El Willstro is not able to provide. Finally, after seven exchanges, the administrators closed the topic by citing one of Wikipedia's guidelines: "Wikipedia is not a forum".

6. Conclusion

Discussions on language use have entered the new media since the introduction of Web 2.0, one of them being the online encyclopaedia, Wikipedia. Wikipedia is primarily defined as an online collaborative community which introduced a great shift from a one-way communication pathway between expert and lay communities into a dialogue. In the language sphere, the *OED* would be an example of a forerunner of such collaboration between the two communities with its history of contributions from the general public.

The traditional sources for the "linguistically insecure" before the online usage advice came into the scene are usage guides. Although very popular among their readership, usage guides have been criticised by linguists for their authors' prescriptive attitudes and lack of referencing (Peters & Young 1997:318). In this study we compared the entries on selected usage items on Wikipedia and in the database of usage guides and usage problems developed at Leiden University Centre for Linguistics, HUGE. The Wikipedia entries on usage items have proved to be on average more visited, heavily edited and they have attracted more collaboration from Wikipedia editors than the average Wikipedia article (see Table 1). Some of the editors participating in the writing of the entries on usage items are language experts, and, usually, the more real-life expertise they have in language-related fields, the more editing and coordination they do in the entries on usage items. A corpus-based comparison of usage guide and Wikipedia entries has shown that usage guides tend to use a more narrative and personalised style, which focuses on the rules and the stigmatisation of nonstandard usage. Wikipedia entries, on the other hand, include significantly more references to other sources and lexical items that come from the specialised terminology of linguistics.

The qualitative analysis of the secondary Talk pages has shown that the main reason why Wikipedia entries manage to obtain a level of objectivity and avoid prescriptive accounts, in spite of the many editors' comments which include evaluation and negative attitudes to the nonstandard usage, is the editors' commitment to Wikipedia principles. The principle of Verifiability influences the number of references included in each entry, while the principle of the Neutral Point of View supports descriptive as opposed to the traditionally prescriptive accounts of usage guides.

Wikipedia entries on language use are a product of collaboration of many contributors as opposed to usage guides which are usually works of individual authors. Due to this fact, as well as the guidance of Wikipedia principles, balanced discussions on Talk pages and regular edits, Wikipedia entries on language use largely reflect critical, up-to-date accounts relying primarily on linguistics as a discipline and actual usage, instead of single authorities and traditional gate keepers. The actual impact of Wikipedia and other forms of social media on usage and their popularity when compared to other sources of advice on usage has yet to be explored. Widening the research scope beyond the discourse on language use, it would be worth analysing different phenomena of expert discourse re-contextualisation on Wikipedia in fields other than linguistics and looking into the effects and potential difficulties accompanying the communication between experts and laypeople facilitated by the web-based collaborative processes.

References

Algeo, John. 1991. Sweet are the uses of diversity.*Word* 42. 1-17.

Allen, R.E. 1992. Usage. In Tom McArthur (ed.), *The Oxford Companion to the English Language*. Oxford: Oxford University Press. 1071-1078.

Ayers, Phoebe, Charles Matthews & Ben Yates. 2008. *How Wikipedia Works: And How You Can Be a Part of It*. San Francisco, CA: No Starch Press.

Beal, Joan. 2009. Three hundred years of prescriptivism (and counting). In Ingrid Tieken-Boon van Ostade & William Van der Wurff (eds.), *Current Issues in Late Modern English*. Bern: Peter Lang. 35-56.

Bhalla, Gaurav. 2011. *Collaboration and Co-creation: New Platforms for Marketing and Innovation*. Dordrecht: Springer.

Biber, Douglas. 1995. *Dimensions of Register Variation: A Cross-Linguistic Comparison*. Cambridge: Cambridge University Press.

Bloomfield, Leonard. 1944. Secondary and tertiary responses to language. *Language* 20. 2. 45-44.

Bruns, Axel. 2008. *Blogs, Wikipedia, Second Life, and beyond. From Production to Produsage*. Bern: Peter Lang.

Bryant, Susan, Andrea Forte & Amy Bruckman. 2005. Becoming Wikipedian: Transformation of participation in a collaborative online encyclopedia. *Proceedings of GROUP 2005*. http://dl.acm.org/citation.cfm?id=1099205.

Burchfield, Robert W. 1991. The Fowler brothers and the tradition of usage handbooks. In Gerhard Leitner (ed.), *English Traditional Grammars: An International Perspective*. Amsterdam/Philadelphia: John Benjamins. 93-111.

Busse, Ulrich & Ingrid Tieken-Boon van Ostade. 2011. Towards a corpus of prescriptivism. Paper presented at the Helsinki Corpus Festival. Helsinki, Finland, 1 October 2011.

Busse, Ulrich & Anne Schröder. 2008. How Fowler became 'The Fowler': An anatomy of a success story. Paper presented at the workshop Normative Linguistics, ISLE-1. Freiburg, Germany, 2008.

—. 2009. Fowler's *Modern English Usage* at the interface of lexis and grammar. In Ute Römer & Rainer Schulze (eds.), *Exploring the Lexis-Grammar Interface*. Amsterdam/Philadelphia: Benjamins. 69-87.

Cameron, Deborah. 1995. *Verbal Hygiene*. London/New York: Routledge.

Ebersbach, Anja, Markus Glaser & Richard Heigl. 2008. *WikiTools. Kooperation im Web*. Dordrecht: Springer.

Emigh, William & Susan C. Herring. 2005. Collaborative authoring on the Web: A genre analysis of online encyclopedias. *HIICS '05 Proceedings of the 38th Hawaii International Conference on System Sciences*. Los Alamitos: IEEE Press. http://ella.slis.indiana.edu/~herring/wiki.pdf.

Ferschke, Oliver, Iryna Guryevich & Yevgen Chebotar. 2012. Behind the article: Recognizing dialog acts in Wikipedia Talk pages. *Proceedings of the 13th Conference of the European Chapter of the Association for Computational Linguistics*. https://www.aclweb.org/anthology/E/E12/E12-1079.pdf.

Fichter, Darlene. 2005. Intranets, Wikis, Blikis, and collaborative working. *Online* 29. 5. 47-50.

Fowler, Henry W. 1965. *A Dictionary of Modern English Usage*. New York: Oxford University Press.

—. 2000. *The New Fowler's Modern English Usage*. Oxford: Oxford University Press.

Garner, Bryan A. 1998. A *Dictionary of Modern American Usage*. Oxford: Oxford University Press.

Giles, Jim. 2005, December 15. Internet encyclopaedias go head to head. *Nature* 438. 900-901.

Gutounig, Robert. 2015. *Wissen in digitalen Netzwerken. Potenziale Neuer Medien für Wissensprozesse*. Wiesbaden: Springer VS.

Hall, John Leslie. 1917. *English Usage: Studies in the History and Uses of English Words and Phrases*. Chicago: Scott, Foresman and Company.

Herring, Susan. 2013. Discourse in Web 2.0: Familiar, reconfigured and emergent. In Deborah Tannen & Anna Marie Trester (eds.), *Discourse 2.0: Language and New Media*. Washington, DC: Georgetown University Press. 1-26.

Hyland, Ken. 1998. *Hedging in Scientific Research Articles*. Amsterdam/New York: John Benjamins.

Landau, Sidney I. 1979. The egalitarian spirit and attitudes toward usage. *American Speech* 54. 1. 3-11.

Lukač, Morana. Forthcoming. Linguistic prescriptivism in letters to the editor. Proceedings of the Workshop *Attutitudes to Prescriptivism*, Leiden University, 11 June 2013. Special issue. *Journal of Multilingual and Multicultural Development*.

McArthur, Tom. 1992. *The Oxford Companion to the English Language*. Oxford: Oxford University Press.

Milroy, James & Lesley Milroy. 2002. *Authority in Language. Investigating Language Prescription and Standardisation*. London/New York: Routledge.

Mugglestone, Lynda. 2005. *Lost for Words: The Hidden History of the Oxford English Dictionary*. New Haven, CT: Yale University Press.

Myers, Greg. 2010. *The Discourse of Blogs and Wikis*. London: Continuum.

Peters, Pam. 2006. English Usage: Prescription and Description. In Bas Aarts & April McMahon (eds.), *The Handbook of English Linguistics*. Hong Kong: Blackwell. 759-780.

Peters, Pam & Wendy Young. 1997. English grammar and the lexicography of usage. *Journal of English Linguistics* 25. 315-331.

Potthast, Martin, Benno Stein & Robert Gerling. 2008. Automatic vandalism detection in Wikipedia. *Advances in Information Retrieval. Proceedings of the 30th European Conference on IR Research*, ECIR 2008, Glasgow, UK, 30 March-3 April, 2008. 663-668.

Preece, Jenny & Diane Maloney-Krichmar. 2005. Online communities: Design, theory and practice. *Journal of Computer-Mediated Communication* 10. 4. http://onlinelibrary.wiley.com/doi/10.1111/j.1083-6101.2005.tb00264.x/full#b13.

Quirk, Randolph, Sidney Greenbaum, Geoffrey Leech & Jan Svartvik. 1985. *A Comprehensive Grammar of the English Language*. London: Longman.

Rayson, Paul. 2009. Wmatrix: A web-based corpus processing environment. Computing Department: Lancaster University. http://ucrel.lancs.ac.uk/wmatrix/.

Rayson, Paul, Dawn Archer, Scott Piao & Tony McEnery. 2004. The UCREL Semantic Analysis System. http://comp.eprints.lancs.ac.uk/922/1/usas_lrec04ws.pdf.

Schaffer, Deborah. 2010. Old whine online: prescriptive grammar blogs on the Internet. *English Today* 26. 4. 23-28.

Shirky, Clay. 2010. *Here Comes Everybody: The Power of Organizing without Organizations*. London: Allen Lane.

Simpson, John. 2004. The OED and collaborative research into the history of English. *Anglia* 122. 2. 187-208.

Stvilia, Besiki, Michael B. Twidale, Linda C. Smith & Les Gasser. 2008. Information Quality Work Organization in Wikipedia. *Journal of the American Society for Information Science and Technology* 59. 6. 983-1001.

Tieken-Boon van Ostade, Ingrid. 2010. *The Bishop's Grammar: Robert Lowth and the Rise of Prescriptivism*. Oxford: OUP.

Treble, Arthur Henry & George Henry Vallins. 1936. *A.B.C. of English Usage*. Oxford: Clarendon Press.

Viégas, Fernanda B., Martin Wattenberg, Jesse Kriss & Frank van Ham. 2007. Talk before you type: Coordination in Wikipedia. *Proceedings of the 40th Hawaii International Conference on System Sciences*.

Viégas, Fernanda B., Martin Wattenberg& Dave Kushal. 2004. Studying cooperation and conflict between Authors with history flow visualisations.*Proceedings of the SIGCHI Conference on Human Factors in Computing Systems*. Vienna: ACM Press. 575-582. http://alumni.media.mit.edu/~fviegas/papers/history_flow.pdf.

Ward, Gilman E. 1989. *Webster's Dictionary of English Usage*. Springfield, MA: Merriam-Webster.

Wardhaugh, Ronald. 1999. *Proper English: Myths and Misunderstandings about Language*. Oxford: Blackwell.

Weiner, Edmund. 1988. On editing a usage guide. In Eric G. Stanley and Terry F. Hoad (eds.), *Word. For Robert Burchfield's Sixty-Fifth Birthday*. Cambridge: D.S. Brewer. 171-183.